In praise of *Copycat Crime: How Media, Technology, and Digital Culture Inspire Criminal Behavior and Violence*

The CEOs of Google, Microsoft, Meta, and Apple need to read this book. We gamble with our future to ignore the nexus among criminality, technology, media, and the digital world. Dr. Helfgott is the first to give us a road map into this darkness—virtually unknown and often ill considered. It brings me hope for our children and grandchildren whose lives will be fully lived both online and on the ground.

—J. Reid Meloy, PhD, ABPP, forensic psychologist,
author of *The Psychopathic Mind*

We tend to think of acts of criminal violence triggered by some spectacle, scene, or narrative encountered in the media as unusual and rare events. Yet aestheticized violence has a well-documented history dating back to such popular literary tropes as the criminal as artist, murder as a fine art, and motiveless *actes gratuits*. This phenomenon has now taken on new urgency with the fast-spreading images of our media-saturated age in which performance artists are often virtually indistinguishable from performance criminals, and seemingly inexplicable acts of mimetic violence routinely erupt in fatal cycles of imitation and obsession. Drawing on data and insights compiled over the past half century in criminology, media technology, sociology, literature, and the law, Dr. Helfgott has brought much needed clarity and specificity to the broad category of copycat crime. Most significantly, she has opened promising pathways for future research and preventative action to address this increasingly pervasive, rapidly evolving, and arguably least understood manifestation of criminal behavior in our time.

—Joel Black, University of Georgia, USA

In a contemporary world of live-streamed mass shootings and televised insurrections, the mediated copycat crime has now emerged as a definitive form of social violence—and Jacqueline Helfgott's new book now emerges as the essential resource for making sense of this tragic phenomenon. Taking the reader through spirals of criminal replication and imitation, she interweaves sophisticated theory, sharp historical analysis, and useful recommendations for policy and law. All in all, *Copycat Crime* constitutes a courageous intellectual confrontation with the criminogenic dynamics of the digital age.

—Jeff Ferrell, emeritus professor of sociology, Texas Christian University,
USA, author of *Drift: Illicit Mobility and Uncertain Knowledge*

Jacqueline Helfgott has been ahead of the curve on studying the dangers of copycat effects. As her most recent book shows, hundreds of people have been murdered by people who drew inspiration from disturbing characters in movies or books, or from real life mass shooters or serial killers in the news. Helfgott's analysis of this phenomenon is thought-provoking, and the book's details on copycat attackers are a gold mine for researchers.

—Adam Lankford, professor of criminology, The University of Alabama, USA

In the 20th century, social scientists cautioned the public not to overestimate the influence of the media on violent behavior. With the explosion of digital media that relationship has changed. Jacqueline B. Helfgott's *Copycat Crime* does the vitally needed work of updating our understanding of the contagion effect of violence in the media. Linking classic theoretical perspectives of early sociologists, like Emile Durkheim, to live-streamed murders by right-wing extremists, Helfgott's volume is an urgent call to rethink the role digital and social media plays in our lives.
—Randall Blazak, PhD, sociologist, chair of the Coalition Against Hate Crimes, coauthor of *Teenage Renegades, Suburban Outlaws and Editor of Hate Offenders*

This is the book I have been waiting for! In *Copycat Crime*, Dr. Helfgott discusses violent criminal behavior through the lens of copycat crimes, and how such behavior is shaped by our digital culture, technology, and the media. We all love the benefits and pleasures that today's technology and media give us. But we must understand the dark side these influences have on our society—specifically criminal behavior—in ways that are stunning, even terrifying.

Dr. Helfgott, who has researched and studied violent crime and copycat crimes for decades, is unquestionably one of the most preeminent criminologists in the United States. Her theories and research into the causes and evolution of violent behavior and copycat crimes, is essential for everyone to understand but especially for professionals working in the field—from judges, to psychologists, to FBI profilers.
—Mary Ellen O'Toole, PhD, retired FBI special agent, profiler, author of *The School Shooter: A Threat Assessment Perspective*, editor-in-chief of *Violence and Gender;* director of Forensic Science Program, George Mason University

Professor Helfgott has wonderfully integrated scientific theories and findings with case histories in making the case that entertainment and news media can inspire copycat criminal behavior. It is an excellent scholarly read!
—Craig A. Anderson, Distinguished Professor of Psychology, Iowa State University, USA, editor-in-chief of *Aggressive Behavior,* past president of the International Society for Research on Aggression

Helfgott summarizes the research on copycat crime, explores critical incidents, reviews key court cases, and offers recommendations to decrease media-influenced violence. An impressive achievement.
—Peter Langman, PhD, Drift Net Securities, USA, author of *Warning Signs: Identifying School Shooters Before They Strike*

Copycat Crime

How Media, Technology, and Digital Culture Inspire Criminal Behavior and Violence

Jacqueline B. Helfgott

Foreword by Ray Surette

BLOOMSBURY ACADEMIC

NEW YORK • LONDON • OXFORD • NEW DELHI • SYDNEY

BLOOMSBURY ACADEMIC
Bloomsbury Publishing Inc
1385 Broadway, New York, NY 10018, USA
50 Bedford Square, London, WC1B 3DP, UK
29 Earlsfort Terrace, Dublin 2, Ireland

BLOOMSBURY, BLOOMSBURY ACADEMIC and the Diana logo are trademarks of
Bloomsbury Publishing Plc

First published in the United States of America 2023

Copyright © Jacqueline B. Helfgott, 2023

Cover image © xpixel/Shutterstock.com

All rights reserved. No part of this publication may be reproduced or transmitted in any
form or by any means, electronic or mechanical, including photocopying, recording, or
any information storage or retrieval system, without prior permission in writing from
the publishers.

Bloomsbury Publishing Inc does not have any control over, or responsibility for, any
third-party websites referred to or in this book. All internet addresses given in this
book were correct at the time of going to press. The author and publisher regret any
inconvenience caused if addresses have changed or sites have ceased to exist, but can
accept no responsibility for any such changes.

Library of Congress Cataloging-in-Publication Data: 2023001916

ISBN: HB: 978-1-4408-6420-9
ePDF: 978-1-4408-6421-6
eBook: 979-8-216-17108-9

Typeset by by Westchester Publishing Services, LLC
Printed and bound in the United States of America

To find out more about our authors and books visit www.bloomsbury.com and sign up
for our newsletters.

For my daughter, Zalia

Contents

Foreword by Ray Surette — ix

Preface — xv

Acknowledgments — xix

Chapter 1   How Media, Technology, and Digital Culture Have Changed Criminal Behavior and Violence — 1

An overview of cultural changes in technology and mass media that have implications for understanding criminal behavior.

Chapter 2   How Media and Technology Shape Modus Operandi and Signature Elements of Criminal Behavior — 25

Explanation of the continuum of ways in which media and technology shape criminal behavior as modus operandi and signature.

Chapter 3   The Copycat Effect on Criminal Behavior: A Theory of Copycat and Media-Mediated Crime — 43

Review of research on the criminogenic effects of media, technology, and digital culture and development of a theoretical framework for understanding and empirically investigating copycat and media-mediated crime.

Chapter 4	Case Studies of Copycat and Media-Mediated Crime	87
	Significant case studies of copycat and media-mediated crime with reference to a detailed appendix, including a comprehensive list of copycat and media-mediated crime.	
Chapter 5	Copycat Crime in the Courts: Implications for Civil Rights and Criminal Justice	133
	Discussion of how the issues related to copycat crime have arisen in the civil and criminal courts, including landmark civil and criminal cases involving elements of copycat and media-mediated crime.	
Chapter 6	From the Ethical Realm of the Real, to the Aesthetic Realm of the Hyperreal, to the Digital Realm of the Unreal: What the Future Holds and What We Can Do About It	179
	Discussion of what the future holds for the study and understanding of copycat crime, suggestions for future research, and recommendations for reducing the criminogenic effects of media, digital culture, and technology.	

Appendix	219
Notes	255
References	263
Index	315

Foreword

In recent years, the growing number of copycat crime anecdotes have heightened interest in copycat crime, but much of what is found on the phenomena is not theoretically or empirically grounded. I am thus pleased to learn that Dr. Helfgott took on the subject in a rigorous book. I have written on the broad interplay of media, crime, and justice and have contributed some of the existing limited copycat crime research. Related to this book, my interest bridges the media technology transition period that Dr. Helfgott describes in Chapter 2. Beginning in the 1980s I began to write about broad media, crime, and justice issues, and in the 1990s I began to explore the specific phenomena of copycat crime. More recently, I have written about a social media–driven copycat crime meme called "ghost riding the whip" (where people dance beside or sit atop moving driverless cars). Having therefore a long-term curiosity about copycat crime, I am very pleased to write the foreword for *Copycat Crime: How Media, Technology, and Digital Culture Inspire Criminal Behavior and Violence* by Jacqueline B. Helfgott, a book I am thrilled to see.

In this book, Dr. Helfgott explains how the rise of digital social media resulted in the rise of copycat crimes and how the copycat phenomena emerged as a serious criminological and criminal justice concern. Prior traditional media maintained a linear relationship between media content creators, content distributors, and content consumers. In this older legacy media world, consumers were limited to the single passive role as the final depository for content created by others, mostly within large media corporations. In contrast, in the contemporary digital social media world, a web of multimedia relationships coexist. Multiple roles are now available to consumers who can be media content creators, distributors, and evaluators as well as active participatory consumers of content. Despite obvious impacts on society, however, the "rise of new media" has gone under-researched in criminology and criminal justice studies, and until recently, it was rare to find academics interested in studying copycat crime. Continuing the long-term historical trend, most of the crime, justice, and media research has focused on either a violent media-social aggression link, the impact of news media on the processing of criminal cases, or descriptions of the portrait of criminals and criminal justice professionals found in the media. In gist, laboratory studies of exposure to violent media, case studies of newsworthy court cases, and content analysis research have been the norm.

Addressing the associated copycat crime research gap, Dr. Helfgott has actively advanced the understanding of copycat crime, and her research has helped make sense of how the phenomena affects criminology theory and criminal justice practice. This book is the product of her own long-term interest in copycat crime and her teaching about the phenomena. Her applied research in law enforcement and criminal profiling and her theoretical work on criminal psychology, criminal behavior, and typologies of crime bring a unique perspective to the study and understanding of copycat crime. She is the ideal person to write this book.

Providing a foundation for understanding copycat crime, Dr. Helfgott applies the concepts of "edge-sitters," 'hyperreality," and "technology transition" to develop a comprehensive historical base and theoretical model of copycat crime. She describes edge-sitters as those individuals lying between law abiding and criminal behavior who also often float between reality and fantasy. They need only a push to commit crime, and the contemporary media sometimes pushes so that a number of contemporary media-fueled edge "sitters" become criminal "jumpers." In addition, Dr. Helfgott addresses why the impact of contemporary media differs from legacy media's impact through the idea of a media-generated "hyperreality" made up of images, images of images, media loops, virtual interactions, media-mediated messages, and celebrity glorification. Suggesting that the media technological evolution has had a stronger psychological impact than changes in the media's content, the media hyperreality is forwarded as a significant contributor to distorted personal worldviews that many of the extreme copycat offenders are seen to hold.

Professor Helfgott traces the genesis of our current hyperreality to the 1980s as a key transition time when the new digital media technology began to change everything, including crime. Specifically, the media technology of easily accessed digital content first introduced in the 1980s substantially shaped crime and criminal behavior. Harkening back to Durkheim's 1890s concept of anomie and the predictions of the 1970s book *Future Shock* by Alvin Toffler, Dr. Helfgott describes the rapid and

Foreword

pervasive media technology changes in the 1980s that both overwhelmed and socialized edge-sitters. Anomic isolated individuals could withdraw into mediated social groups, ironically alone but deeply networked, and ill-prepared but suddenly inundated with pernicious media content.

Professor Helfgott employs case studies of John Lennon's killer, David Chapman, and President Reagan's attempted assassin, John Hinckley, to make the point that they and many others were ill-equipped to process the media technology that culturally surrounded them in the early 1980s. Particularly important was how digital media presented violence as a realistic graphic art form which began to impact real-world violence in ways not seen previously. Her key point is that human nature did not change due to this media evolution, but human culture was substantially reshaped. Fast-forwarding to 2006, Henry Jenkins forwarded the idea of "convergence culture" to describe the contemporary deep impact of this media evolution. Predicting a mostly positive, democratizing social impact where the sharing of knowledge, media content creation, distribution, and assessment would be enhanced, Jenkins did not foresee the current pernicious effects of media technology exemplified in copycat and performance crime.

In this criminogenic reality, *Copycat Crime: How Media, Technology, and Digital Culture Inspire Criminal Behavior and Violence* is a much-needed book. Dr. Helfgott first introduces readers to the hyperreality era and provides an overview of the technological changes that occurred in mass media technology and digital culture. She addresses important questions such as how these technological changes impact criminal behavior and why understanding the ways in which mass media and digital culture influence criminal behavior matters. Explaining how new media delivers instructional crime models and how media technology shape criminal modus operandi and behavioral crime signatures, she thoroughly reviews the research on the criminogenic effects of different media and discusses the 21st century's celebrity obsession and crime as art.

The book's greatest contribution is to move the discussion of copycat crime from the descriptive to the theoretical, developing a theoretical framework for understanding and empirically investigating copycat crime. A theory of media-related crime is shown to require an interdisciplinary approach. Dr. Helfgott demonstrates how contemporary culture has worked to normalize extreme violence while providing instructional models of that violence. After establishing a theoretical foundation, she offers a set of copycat and media-mediated crime case studies as demonstrative examples of her copycat crime theoretical dynamics. Grounding her work, the real-world considerations and impact separate from crime generation and crime shaping are also discussed with attention to First Amendment and civil rights issues and landmark cases and how research and expert testimony have made their way into case processing, adjudication, and sentencing.

In essence, this book covers what has been largely ignored and situates copycat crime within the broader issues that criminology and criminal justice grapple with. These include the intersection of science, law, ethics, media and popular culture; the social construction of crime; and the administration of justice. Criminologists and criminal justice researchers have been concerned mainly with broad theories of crime such as deterrence, bonding, or strain that can be generally applied to offenders. In contrast, *Copycat Crime: How Media, Technology, and Digital Culture Inspire Criminal Behavior and Violence* reflects on the role and function of the media on a unique subset of offenders. Because of a focus on a small but important set of crimes and offenders, the study of copycat crime has been disparaged as not particularly valuable. However, the media's meaning to people, their impact on victims, the criminal harms they cause, and the benefit knowledge about their relationship to crime offers to society is invaluable for assessment, sentencing, and treatment.

As the 21st century unfolds, the relationship of media and crime is developing in new directions, and Professor Helfgott illuminates important aspects of this continuing evolution. Her book is a welcomed and needed addition to the copycat crime literature and is the first rigorous book in the area. This text brings the idea of copycat crime up to date and thoroughly covers the emerging social and technological landscape. Copycat crime is shown as not monolithic, but a conceptual umbrella that covers a large set of crimes and criminals where media influence ranges from minor aspects of a crime to major triggering and shaping influences and where multiple pathways to copycat crime via various copycat mechanisms exist.

Copycat Crime: How Media, Technology, and Digital Culture Inspire Criminal Behavior and Violence is a valuable contribution and important for any social scientist, criminal justice, professional counselor, and others interested in learning about copycat crime and why it matters. I am confident that this book will stimulate new directions for future theory and research that will advance our comprehension of our rapidly evolving 21st-century media. The persistence of crime as art and a culture of celebrity obsession are guaranteed to continue to generate copycat crimes in the future. Exposure to media content is no longer voluntary and avoidable, and more social media self-surveillance, performance crime, copycat crime,

Foreword   xiii

and mass-mediated crime is coming. Jacqueline Helfgott's book will make the future less surprising and hopefully more palatable.

Ray Surette, PhD
University of Central Florida

References

Durkheim, É. (1893). *The Division of Labor in Society.* Simon and Schuster, 2014.
Jenkins, H. (2006). *Convergence culture: Where old and new media collide.* New York University Press.
Toffler, A. (1984). *Future shock.* V. 553. Bantam.

Preface

Some of my earliest memories involve cartoon characters. Wile E. Coyote and the Road Runner, Bugs Bunny, and the Jetsons. As I grew up, new characters entered—Big Bird, Mr. Rogers, Batman, Superman, Spider-Man, and Wonder Woman, Jeannie and Major Nelson, the Brady Bunch and the Partridge Family, the Bionic Man and Woman, Charlie's Angels, and the families in the ABC Afterschool Specials. I watched Saturday morning cartoons while eating Cap'n Crunch cereal with my brothers after we dug out the prizes out of the boxes. If I had to characterize the cultural "stuff" of my 1960s to 1970s childhood, it would be a mix of comical violence where victims were squashed and instantly reborn, cheerful suburban families dealing with silly mishaps, and a Jeannie in a bottle who was in love with her astronaut "Master" juxtaposed with news stories of lurking predators and missing children.

Depending on when we were born, all of us can identify the cultural "stuff" of our early childhood. In the years since commercial television entered homes in the 1950s, the world has seen a mass media technology boom like never before in human history. In 1962 the Jetsons portrayed video phone calls and robots who cleaned and dispensed food. The violent acts in Saturday morning cartoons consisted of Wile E. Coyote predatorily chasing the Road Runner, his creative acts of violence getting foiled with him getting splattered on a sidewalk in a colorful cartoon blur against the backdrop of crescendoed orchestra music. Fast-forward two generations. The kids who aspired to be the Bionic Man or Bionic Woman are now talking to their grandchildren on Zoom, vacuuming their floors with robots, and Alexa and Siri are ordering their groceries (Natanson, 2017), and they are living in a world where a double amputee can aspire to run a sub-three-hour marathon on prosthetic running blades (Butler, 2018; Webster, 2018) and quadriplegics control robotic limbs with their minds through an implanted brain chip (Ehrenberg, 2012).

Today's kids are not confined to Saturday morning TV cartoons. They have access to all the violence in the world in the palm of their hand, with fictional violence that looks real and real violence that looks fictional. They consume daily news about mass shootings. Watching Wile E. Coyote burn himself up in a self-made bomb explosion has been replaced by media-mediated performance violence. Setting oneself on fire for a social media post and "fire challenging" others to mimic them is the new Saturday morning entertainment (Chiu, 2018).

Technology has changed everything, including crime (Clarke, 2004). Technology has left us all less connected with each other in real life but more connected in virtual life (Turkle, 2011). This movement from real to simulation has implications for understanding how crime and criminal behavior have changed with these technological advances. In 1991 Joel Black published the book *The Aesthetics of Murder*. Black said the book was "about, and inspired by the 1980s," an examination of cases in which young men, John Hinckley and Mark Chapman, committed acts of violence against and the murder of iconic figures (President Ronald Regan and John Lennon, respectively) while under the influence of mass media. Black argued that the 1980s was a unique period in human history when the rise in mass media technology had a particularly negative impact on individuals who were ill-prepared and suddenly inundated with mass media and were particularly vulnerable to its influence. Fiction, he argued, was much more dangerous and held more seductive power than realistic graphic displays of violence. Black wondered in the aftermath of John Lennon's murder and the assassination attempt on President Ronald Reagan how artistic fictions such as *The Catcher in the Rye* and *Taxi Driver* were able to provide "such cogent and compelling models for sociopathic behavior" (p. ix) and why fictional characters portrayed in the media had such an effect on people. *The Aesthetics of Murder* was a groundbreaking book in the study of media-mediated violence examining how art—in all forms—impacts real violence with attention to the shifts in cultural history from art you can hold in your hand in the form of books and paintings to digital art in the form of mass media that travels fast and wide.

This book is the product of a class I teach at Seattle University called *Murder Movies and Copycat Crime* that examines how cultural criminology, media and crime, and copycat crime and cultural artifacts such as TV, music, film, and social media influence criminal behavior. I have been a high media consumer and technology follower throughout my life. I worry that when I die, besides missing my family and friends, what I will miss the most is seeing the amazing new technology that will come after I'm gone and the next episode of whatever show I am currently

Preface   xvii

binging. When my dad died several years ago, I was sad he would miss the *Dancing with the Stars* finale. I watched TV a lot as a child, went to the movies every weekend, and have done my best to purchase and learn the latest technological items as they come out. I was excited when Napster first hit the scene and had a blast when I won the *Monster's Inc.* Boo doll for my daughter at my first eBay auction. However, as a child of the 1960s and 1970s, I did not have my first cell phone until they became affordable to the masses in my late thirties, completed my college applications on a typewriter with no Internet, and did not use my first computer until I was a junior in college. My daughter, who was born in the late 1990s, had a cell phone as a kindergartener. She accesses information from so many different channels that she laughed at me when I asked her if she wanted me to hook up the cable box to the smart TV in her room. It boggles my mind to think about the difference between learning about the world through *ABC Afterschool Specials* from a little box in your living room and the way kids learn today with the world literally and virtually in their hands in the form of a 6 × 3 inch piece of plastic and glass with a bionic chip inside.

The effects of the advances in technology reach every aspect of life. This book examines how mass media and digital culture influence, shape, and change criminal behavior. Human motivations to commit crime have been the same to some extent across human history. However, with most of the theory and data in criminology coming from earlier decades, current theories do not tell us about how media, technology, and culture shape and inspire criminal behavior and violence. Research on cultural criminology (Ferrell, 1999; Ferrell et al., 2015, Ferrell & Hamm, 1998; Ferrell & Sanders, 1995) and media and crime (Surette, 2014a) suggests that crime and criminal justice are intimately tied to, and reflexively related to, culture. The growing body of work on copycat crime, media effects, the contagion effect, and performance crime (Coleman, 2004; Helfgott, 2015; O'Toole, 2014; Surette, 2002, 2013a, 2013b, 2014b, 2015a, 2015b, 2022) suggests that there is much we do not understand about how mass media and digital culture shape criminal behavior. If media that entered culture in the 1980s led to crime committed "under the influence of mass media" and moved us from the "ethical realm of the real" to the "aesthetic realm of the hyperreal" (Black, 1991, p. 138), what is the situation decades later?

This book is my attempt to answer this question. Chapter 1: How Media, Technology, and Digital Culture Have Changed Criminal Behavior and Violence reviews technological changes in mass media technology and digital culture, how these technological changes impact criminal behavior, and why understanding the ways in which mass media and digital culture influence criminal behavior matters for criminology and criminal justice. Chapter 2: How Media and Technology Shape Modus Operandi and Signature Elements of Criminal Behavior explains the continuum of ways in which media and technology shape criminal behavior as modus operandi and signature. Chapter 3: The Copycat Effect on Criminal Behavior: A Theory of Copycat and Media-Mediated Crime reviews the research on the criminogenic effects of different media sources and the impact of celebrity culture on copycat and performance crime and presents a theoretical framework for understanding and empirically investigating copycat and media-mediated crime. Chapter 4: Case Studies of Copycat and Media-Mediated Crimes examines significant case studies of copycat and media-mediated crime with reference to detailed appendix, including a comprehensive list of copycat and media-mediated crime. Chapter 5: Copycat Crime in the Courts: Implications for Civil Rights and Criminal Justice discusses the implications of copycat and media-mediated crime for civil and criminal justice with attention to First Amendment/civil rights and landmark cases. Chapter 6: From the Ethical Realm of the Real, to the Aesthetic Realm of the Hyperreal, to the Digital Realm of the Unreal: What the Future Holds and What We Can Do About It discusses what the future holds, suggestions for future research, and recommendations for reducing the criminogenic effects of media and technology.

Theories and research on criminal behavior have come far since the predigital age but have not kept up to explain how media, technology, and digital culture inspire criminal behavior and violence (Helfgott, 2015; Milivojevic, 2021; Yar, 2012). My hope is that this book will draw attention to the importance of examining the role of digital culture in influencing criminal behavior and violence; highlight the importance of considering media, technology, and digital culture as a risk factor for criminal behavior in criminological theory; and will inspire theory development and empirical research on copycat crime.

Acknowledgments

I want to first thank my daughter, Zalia. Before she was born in the late 1990s, I prided myself on being up on popular culture. Now having parented a child to adulthood, I realize how difficult it is to keep up with cultural goings-on that shape all behavior, especially crime. I am now officially old school. I realized this recently when I picked up a *People* magazine and did not recognize 90 percent of the people in it. Thankfully, Brad Pitt, Jennifer Anniston, and Johnny Depp continue to make the news. I realized this when Zalia was in elementary school when we were in the grocery store parking lot singing along to a song on the radio (Starstrukk by 3OH!3) when I suddenly became aware of the lyrics; when she was in middle school, when I took her to see LMFAO without realizing until the band came out on stage what LMFAO stood for; and when I took her and her friends, Bridget and Lillian, to an impromptu Rihanna concert, which was nothing like the 1980s to 1990s heavy metal/grunge bands I was used to. When Zalia was in high school when I was still watching *Grey's Anatomy* on TV while she was learning all kinds of things on YouTube, I realized there was a digital world that people over a certain age are not part of that plays a central role in what teenagers think about in the critical years when they are developing into adolescence and adulthood. As Zalia moves through her twenties, she too will soon be old school.

Thanks to my family and friends, who provide me everyday support, including helping me out of my spirals when I think to myself, "Who is going to read this?" My mom, Esther Altshul Helfgott, has been a huge support. Having a mother who spends most of her waking hours reading and writing and thinking about how best to construct a sentence has given me tools to think, research, and write that go deeper than what I have learned through academic education. Thanks to my brothers, Ian and Scott, who are a constant support and who were my partners in the TV culture of the 1960s and 1970s, and to my friends and family who put up with having to hear about this book while we were supposed to be having fun doing something else.

I owe a special thanks to two colleagues whose work I have been inspired by for a long time—Dr. Ray Surette and Dr. Mary Ellen O'Toole. In my search for research on copycat crime, I have wondered why more scholars did not focus on the topic of copycat crime. Every time I did a search on the topic, there was Dr. Surette with yet another study. I cold-emailed Ray one day years ago and since have had the opportunity to work with him on several projects and presentations. It was my dream to have him write the foreword to this book, and I am honored that he agreed to do so. It is the mark of a true scholar who kindly accepts invitation from a total stranger to collaborate, knowing nothing about the person other than they are a fan of your work.

Thanks to the authors whose work is cited in this book, in particular Joel Black whose book *The Aesthetics of Murder* has been on my mind since it was published in 1991, Reid Meloy whose work has been a major influence throughout my career, Jeff Ferrell whose work on cultural criminology is central to understanding copycat crime, and the many the authors whose research and writing informed my thinking. Thanks also to Peter Langman for his invaluable help in the final stretch of editing.

Thanks to the many Seattle University students who have helped me with this book, especially students in my *Murder Movies & Copycat Crime* course. The classroom discussions, questions posed, and examples offered by students informed my thinking about how popular culture, media, technology, and digital culture influence crime and the cultural artifacts that make their way into people's thinking. Enormous thanks to the research assistants who helped me with this book—Mary Dillon, who taught me about *Reddit*, *Live Leak*, and ways to access the deep and dark webs; Joshua Bonilla, who assisted with the appendix of copycat crime cases and gave me energy in the final stages of completing the book; and Ashley Catanyag and Michael Britz, who helped research case studies. Thanks to my faculty colleagues at Seattle University Department of Criminal Justice, Criminology, and Forensics, most of all Elaine Gunnison for her friendship and relentless commitment to helping me stay on track to get this book done. Special thanks to my long-time colleagues—Dr. Faith Lutze and Dr. Fran Bernat and my mentor, friend, and former Penn State Professor William Parsonage—who have supported me throughout my career.

And of course this book would not have been possible without the ABC-CLIO/Bloomsbury staff. Thank you to Kevin Downing, Saville Bloxham, Jayati Sarkar, Bridget Austiguy-Preschel, Nicole Azze, and other staff for providing the opportunity to publish this book and for the professionalism and assistance with the many steps throughout the publication process. Thanks also to Debbie Carvalko for her assistance in the early stages of the project.

CHAPTER ONE

How Media, Technology, and Digital Culture Have Changed Criminal Behavior and Violence

Would you drive your car blindfolded if you saw someone do it in a movie? The 2018 Netflix film *Bird Box,* a fictional horror/psychological thriller, had over 45 million viewers in the week it was released. Soon after, news reports surfaced about people mimicking the behavior of the characters in the film who were compelled to drive their cars blindfolded to avoid being harmed by an unknown force that caused people who saw it to commit suicide. Dubbed the "Bird Box Challenge," real people in real life watched *Bird Box* and were inspired to drive blindfolded. Multiple police agencies issued warnings urging the public not to do it. The Portland, Maine Police Department tweeted, "Let's talk 'bird box challenge.' Don't do it. Don't think about doing it. Watch the movie, be happy that's not your reality, but please don't blindfold yourself to relate. Especially not while driving. Most of us have a hard enough time driving safely with unobstructed vision" (Portland Police, 2019).

Driving blindfolded is dangerous, it is a crime, and this bizarre mimicking of fictional behavior in a blockbuster film is an example of the power of mass media, technology, and digital culture to influence people's behavior known as the "contagion" or "copycat effect" (Coleman, 2004; Helfgott, 2015; Surette, 2022). What drove so many seemingly regular people to make the questionable decision to drive their cars blindfolded after watching *Bird Box* and act out in real life the fictional horror depicted in the film? Why were people not content with living in their own reality and felt the need to blindfold themselves while driving "to relate"? Questions like this and others often follow when stories like this appear—*Is it just the edge-sitters?* If millions of people watch a film and only a few of them mimic what they see, then how big of a problem is it? *Anything can set them off*—Aren't those few people already teetering on the edge and literally anything could set them off? *There's nothing we can do about it*—Even if we could establish that media and digital culture play a role in criminal behavior, what can be done about it without limiting freedom of expression, speech, and the press?

Media-Mediated Crime

There is a long list of anecdotal accounts of individuals who have engaged in media-mediated behaviors who mimicked something they read or a character they identified with in a book, TV show, film, video game, social media, or podcast (Helfgott, 2015; Surette, 2022; Surette et al., 2021). In 1980, Mark Chapman channeled the ideas of Holden Caulfield, the fictional character in the book *Catcher in the Rye* when he murdered John Lennon. In 1981, John Hinckley watched the film *Taxi Driver* 15 times before the film became a script for his attempted assassination of Ronald Reagan. Marilyn Manson music, the films *Natural Born Killers* and *The Basketball Diaries*, the video game *Doom*, and news and historical information about Oklahoma City bomber Timothy McVeigh and Hitler made their way into the cognitive scripts of Columbine killers Dylan Klebold and Eric Harris. The film *Natural Born Killers* has been associated with a string of murder sprees (Boyle, 2001; Helfgott, 2015; O'Neil, 2001). Mass shooter manifestos show that many subsequent mass shooters used Columbine as a blueprint for their own violent acts (Helfgott, 2014; Neklason, 2019). One of the most striking examples of digital idolatry-gone-haywire is the incel movement. Incel is a group of individuals who worship mass shooter Elliot Rodger. Incels refer to Rodger as the "Supreme Gentleman Elliot Rodger" and espouse overthrowing "Chads and Stacys"[1] who have made them victims of enforced celibacy (Farrell, 2018). Incel has influenced copycat crimes including the April 23, 2018, mass murder in Toronto, Canada, in which 24-year-old Alek Minassian ran down eight women and two men with a rental van. Prior to the attack, Minassian posted on his Facebook page, "The Incel Rebellion has already begun! We will overthrow all the Chads and Stacys! All hail the Supreme Gentleman Elliot Rodger!" (Branson-Potts & Winton, 2018; Paperny & Saminather, 2018). These crimes are mimetic behaviors inspired by media that have become increasingly problematic with the rise of digital culture.

In another example, two 12-year-old Wisconsin girls, Anissa Weir and Morgan Geyser, lured their best friend 12-year-old Payton "Bella" Leutner into the woods and viciously stabbed her with a knife 19 times. When caught and questioned by police, it was discovered that the girls planned the attack so that they could appease an online fictional character named "Slender Man." Slender Man is a character depicted in the online horror fan site "Creepypasta" on which users generate Photoshopped and video-taped accounts of encounters with monsters and supernatural evil. Weir and Geyser were obsessed with the Slender Man lore and read in Creepypasta that if you killed someone for him, he would come and let you live with him in his house in the woods. Their motive to kill Bella was to be with Slender Man. Weir had even packed photos of her family because, "we were probably going to be spending the rest of our lives [with Slender Man], and I didn't want to forget my family" (Miller, 2015). While Weir told police she knew Slender Man was fiction, Geyser, who was later determined to be schizophrenic, insisted that Slender Man was real. Digital interaction with Slender Man pushed these preteens' fantasy into reality. Weir's brother said that Weir "loved the Slender Man stories, just anything a bit creepy. But I don't see why it changed from dream to reality" (Jones, 2014). Both girls were found "not guilty by reason of insanity" and sentenced to 40 (Geyser) and 25 (Weir) years in a state mental institution for the stabbing. Waukesha Police Chief Russell Jack said, "The Internet has changed the way we live. It is full of information and wonderful sites that teach and entertain. The Internet can also be full of dark and wicked things" (Jones, 2014).

Technology, Culture, and Copycat Crime

Technological advances in media and computer technology have changed how people experience, interact, and behave. As technology has advanced from mechanical and analog to digital culture, we have moved from the "ethical realm of the real," where people engage in real life with real people, to the "aesthetic realm of the hyperreal," where people's primary experience is aesthetic and virtual (Black, 1991, p. x). The *Bird Box* challengers were operating in the aesthetic realm of the hyperreal. So were Hinckley, Chapman, the Columbine killers, and the long list of mass shooters who idolized and mimicked them (Neklason, 2019). They were also exhibiting a phenomenon called the contagion or copycat effect (Coleman, 2004) fueled by other aspects of technologically advanced contemporary culture, including the drive for performance and celebrity. That a police department would have to warn people not to drive blindfolded like a character in a movie reveals how common the copycat effect has become in today's digital culture.

From the Ethical Realm of the Real to the Aesthetic Realm of the Hyperreal

Philo Taylor Farnsworth invented television in 1927. He had utopian hopes for what his invention could do to bring people together across time and space. Farnsworth thought up the idea of television when he was a teenager living on an Idaho potato farm. He wondered, "If we were able to see people in other countries and learn about our differences, why would there be any misunderstandings? War would be a thing of the past" (Eschner, 2017). Almost 100 years later, Farnsworth would likely be surprised at how far beyond television technology has come to be able to see and communicate around the world and to access information across time with a click. Farnsworth grew up in the *ethical realm of the real*—a world that no longer exists, where he interacted in real time and real space with a few kids in a small schoolhouse on an Idaho farm sharing stories and lore contained within a small community. A teenager today living on a farm in Idaho, or anywhere else, has instant access to information and media content from any time and any place with a click of a smartphone and lives in an amplified version of the *aesthetic realm of the hyperreal*. Media-mediated virtual interactions have replaced actual interactions. Old-school fun like riding a bike with no hands, crashing, and getting your chin split open has been replaced with augmented reality computer games with digital personas with hit points that resemble what would happen if a person was actually shot and killed with a sniper rifle, sliced up with a combat knife, or blown up with a flame gun or a microwave pulse emitter; where people who are murdered respawn and come back to life and back for more.

Inventors have had utopian and dystopian predictions about the impact of all media forms going back as far as the telegraph. A prehistory of digital culture encompasses "legacy media" such as radio, telegraph, telephone, newspapers, magazines, radio stations, and other traditional forms of media (Davies & Razlogova, 2013, p. 6). "New media forms" such as communication through mobile devices and social media have supplanted, but have not completely replaced, legacy media. New media companies such as *Vice, Buzzfeed,* and *Vox* have entered the scene (Desjardins, 2016; Wynne, 2017). Livestream citizen video recordings shot on mobile phones and streamed through *YouTube* and *Facebook Live,* independent citizen journalism (Bal & Baruh, 2015; Brown, 2016; Farmer & Sun, 2016; Greer & McLaughlin, 2010; Watson, 2012), blogs, virtual

How Media, Technology, and Digital Culture Have Changed Criminal Behavior   5

reality, online newspapers, digital games, eBooks, podcasts, and social media such as *Facebook, Twitter, Snapchat,* and *LinkedIn* (Penn, 2016) and newer social media such as *TikTok* are now dominant media forms. New media draws public attention in ways legacy media does not with citizen-driven information sharing that dilutes the gatekeeping role of traditional legacy media (Ismail et al., 2019). Rapid transformation of media technologies has created "media microgenerations" defined by narrow age groups characterized by "fresh contact with media technologies during the formative years" that influences media habits and usage, social norms, and (digital) media morality (Bengtsson & Johansson, 2018, p. 96).

A century after the invention of the television, we can see, learn about, and learn from people in other spaces, places, countries, and continents from our own homes in real time. On July 4, 2020, demonstrators protesting for racial justice following the murder of George Floyd who were marching on Interstate 5 in Seattle were violently hit by a driver who bypassed police barricades. Independent citizen journalists livestreamed the protesters on the freeway and caught the hit-and-run in real time from multiple angles. The livestreams included one taken by one of the protesters who was hit showing protesters dancing on the freeway, people shouting "Car, car," followed by horizontal broken screen lines at the moment of impact. Another livestream showed the scene moments after impact before the police and medics arrived, and another from an overpass showed the car careening into protesters sending them airborne and landing on the cement.[2] The protesters who were struck were transported to the hospital in critical condition and one died at the hospital (Bazzaz et al., 2020; Bellisle, 2020; Horne & Sims, 2020). The gruesome details of this tragedy were accessible in real time before major news outlets could get to the scene, citizen journalists filmed the surviving victim in the hospital, and within 24 hours every news source around the world used the images and videos shot by the citizen journalists and bystanders. The media coverage by bystanders and citizen journalists of this horrific incident is an example of the speed at which information travels globally in real time and how violence has become media-mediated cultural performance. This hit and run of the Seattle protesters was one of a cluster of dozens of car attacks that occurred in the United States following the murder of George Floyd by Minneapolis police resulting in social unrest. During this time, images of drivers careening into protesters and memes, jokes, and propaganda about these attacks circulated across social media calling for vehicular attacks on protesters (MacFarquhar, 2020). One meme was a cartoon image of a car hitting people with the phrase "All lives splatter" (Voytko, 2020), a revival of an earlier meme that circulated after the 2017 white supremacist attack in Charlottesville, Virginia, during which a protester was killed when a neo-Nazi drove into a crowd of counter protesters during a white nationalist rally (Gutierrez, 2017).[3]

Violence posted and livestreamed on social media is "performance crime" (Surette, 2015a), a form of media-mediated crime that presents new challenges. Livestreaming of crimes occurring in real time raises another issue unique to the digital age. Where is the line between First Amendment protections against limitations on freedom of speech and public safety? What is the responsibility of social media platforms to make sure that criminogenic social media content that presents a public safety risk is removed? What legal precedent exists with respect to First Amendment challenges to film and video game producers in situations where there have been lawsuits against media producers for inciting crime and violence? Landmark First Amendment cases (O'Neil, 2001) and cases involving law enforcement warrants and gag orders issued to tech companies like Microsoft for data for investigative purposes underscore the "delicate balance between privacy and safety" (Smith, 2019, p. 37).

The Christchurch Mosque mass shooting in 2019 that killed 51 people was livestreamed on Facebook for hours before the video was taken down. During the livestream, moments before the murders, the perpetrator, 28-year-old Brenton Harrison Tarrant, posted a meme endorsing a YouTube star (who unknowingly became entangled in the event[4]), saying "Remember, lads, subscribe to PewDiePie." The meme was referred to as a "satirical Easter Egg" that morphed into a "kind of all-purpose cultural bat signal for the young and internet-absorbed" operating as a "booby trap, a joke to ensnare unsuspecting people and members of the media into taking it too literally" (Roose, 2019). Prior to the murders, Tarrant posted a 74-page manifesto on the website 8chan (a radical offshoot of the white supremacist online forum 4chan). Less than six months later on August 3, 2019, 21-year-old Patrick Crusius killed 22 people in a Waco, Texas Walmart store posting an anti-Latino manifesto on the 8chan site just before he gunned down killed 22 people (Perry, August 14, 2019). In Halle, Germany, the murder of two people outside of a synagogue was livestreamed for 35 minutes on Amazon's Twitch service, leading CNBC reporters to note, "When people want to commit evil, they can broadcast their crimes to an audience using social networks, which can amplify their reach" (Haselton & Graham, 2019). Similarly, Elliot Rodger posted a string of YouTube videos before his mass shooting in Santa Barbara in 2014 that were removed and then reappeared, showing how difficult it is to scour content from the deep web and the darknet (Bartlett, 2016;

How Media, Technology, and Digital Culture Have Changed Criminal Behavior 7

Hill, 2014; Mirea et al., 2019; Rogers, 2019). Then Rodger himself subsequently became a cultural bat-signal for the young and internet-absorbed when the incel movement was spawned on his behalf. Digital culture has become a repository for performance criminals.

Social media and the Internet have replaced the physical spaces in which social learning, association with peers, and cultural conversations have historically occurred. Today, in the aftermath of the 2020 COVID-19 pandemic, digital space, and the aesthetic realm of the hyperreal, have become the dominant realm of human communication and interaction. Fast-spreading violent images, reproduced memes, and other cultural artifacts that circulate via social media that result in subsequent copycat violence illustrate how media, technology, and digital culture spread images and ideas and inspire criminal behavior and violence. However, there is a dearth of theory and research to explain copycat and media-mediated criminal behavior.

Copycat Crime

Copycat crime is "crime inspired by another crime that has been publicized in the news media or fictionally or artistically represented whereby the offender incorporates aspects of the original offense into a new crime" (Helfgott, 2008, p. 177). To be a copycat crime, there must be a pair of crimes linked by the media (Surette, 1998, 2022). Copycat crime can be motivated by a real or fictional media or artistic representation whereby the offender incorporates aspects of the original offense (e.g., method/ technique, choice of victim) into a new crime (Coleman, 2004; Surette, 1990, 1998, 2002, 2013a 2013b, 2022). The copycat effect is sometimes referred to as the "contagion effect," "imitation," "mimesis," and crime "clusters" and refers to the "power of mass communication and culture to create an epidemic of similar behaviors" (Coleman, 2004, p. 1). Identifying copycat crimes can be problematic because media can influence criminal behavior in subtle and not-so-subtle ways, and it is often difficult to know when a crime is or is not a copycat crime (Surette, 2016a).

Two of the most historically infamous copycat criminals are Mark David Chapman and John Hinckley Jr. Chapman and Hinckley were media-obsessed 20-somethings whose crimes were the product of a complicated intertwining of identity disturbance, mimesis, and cognitive distortion. Chapman shot and killed John Lennon on December 8, 1980. Three months later, on March 30, 1981, Hinckley attempted to assassinate President Ronald Reagan, wounding police officer Thomas Delahanty and Secret Service Agent Tim McCarthy and critically wounding Press

Secretary James Brady, who lived in a wheelchair the rest of his life and died in 2014 with his death ruled a homicide caused by the 1981 gunshot wound (Mallonee, 2014). The crimes committed by Chapman and Hinckley were "culturally conditioned, media-mediated events" (Black, 1991, p. 25). Chapman was obsessed with the book *Catcher in the Rye,* saw himself as the book's leading character Holden Caulfield, and when arrested he was found reading the book immediately after the murder. Hinckley was fixated on the film *Taxi Driver,* and with Jodie Foster, who was 12 years old when she played the character Iris, a young prostitute in the film. *Taxi Driver* played such a central role in Hinckley's motivation to commit the assassination attempt that it was shown to jurors in his trial, one of the most notorious insanity defense trials in history.

Catcher in the Rye and *Taxi Driver* are iconic artistic works that played central roles in the mindsets and motivation of Chapman and Hinckley in the commission of their crimes. Hinckley and Chapman were "edge-sitters"—teetering on the edge between law abiding and criminal behavior and reality and fantasy when these cultural artifacts pushed them over the edge. In *The Aesthetics of Murder,* Black (1991) suggests that Hinckley and Chapman came of age during a particularly unique time in history when technology was rapidly advancing, and that they were "artistic illiterates" who were not equipped to handle the onslaught of media that permeated the culture around them. Black suggests that Chapman's and Hinckley's reactions to the media they consumed "[need] to be studied and accounted for" to be able to learn from the cultural conditions that brought about these media-mediated crimes (Black, 1991, p. 25).

Copycat crime is not well understood, and it is difficult to measure its nature and extent (Helfgott, 2015; Surette, 2016a, 2022). Crimes sometimes appear to be mimetic events; however, there is a lack of empirical evidence to support copycat elements. For example, on October 2, 2006, 32-year-old Charles Roberts walked into an Amish schoolhouse in Nickel Mines, Pennsylvania; let all the boys go; ordered all the girls to line up against the chalkboard; and shot the girls ranging in age from 6 to 13, killing five; and then shot himself as the state troopers arrived. Five days before, in Denver, Colorado, 53-year-old Duane Morrison, described after the fact by one of the victims as "an old guy on a mission" (Associated Press, September 28, 2006), entered a Platte Canyon High School classroom with a gun, ordered the girls in the room to line up at the chalkboard, told the boys to leave, sexually assaulted the girls before he let them go, shot one of the girls—16-year-old Emily Keyes—and shot himself as the SWAT team entered. It is not a stretch to wonder about the connection between these two violent acts with such unique elements,

How Media, Technology, and Digital Culture Have Changed Criminal Behavior   9

days apart, five states, and 1500 miles away from each other. There was passing commentary about the potential copycat circumstances of these two crimes (e.g., Gerler, 2007; KLS.com, 2006), but it is striking how little discussion there was about the copycat elements in the aftermath of these two crimes in the popular or academic literature. Mass shootings are particularly influenced by the contagion effect (Jacobson, 2017; Towers et al., 2015). However, it is difficult to know whether and/or how an individual perpetrator was inspired by a crime he or she saw, heard, or experienced through media. The contagion effect can be inferred from the temporal order of mass shooting events that are strikingly similar and clustered in time. However, unless there is evidence directly from the perpetrator or other direct links between a crime and a media source, any connection is only loosely established. Since many mass shooters either commit suicide or are killed by police, "we likely may never know on a case-by-case basis who was inspired by similar prior acts, particularly since the ideation may have been subconscious" (Towers et al., 2015, p. 9).

On the other hand, the manifestos of mass shooters and historical examination of their social media postings prior to their crimes reveal information suggesting that mass media is a powerful influence and inspiration for their crimes. On February 14, 2018, 20-year-old Nikolas Cruz killed 17 students and faculty at Marjory Stoneman Douglas High School in Parkland, Florida. Cruz was expelled from Marjory Stoneman a year before the shooting. Prior to the shooting, he posted about his affinity for firearms on YouTube: "Im [sic] going to be a professional school shooter," "I whanna [sic] shoot people with my AR-15," "I wanna die Fighting killing shit ton of people," and "I am going to kill law enforcement one day they go after the good people" (McLaughlin, 2018). Cruz was inspired by prior school shootings. In a video he posted just prior to the mass murder he boasted, "My name is Nik, and I'm going to be the next school shooter of 2018," "my goal is at least twenty people" (James, 2018), and "Today is the day, the day it all begins. . . . With the power of my AR, you will all know who I am" (Milian, 2018). Less than 48 hours after the attack at Marjory Stoneman Douglas High School, a 15-year-old Florida boy was arrested after he claimed he was planning a follow-up attack to Cruz's mass shooting, posting on social media that he was going to kill people and listing various schools (Corcoran, 2018). Example after example of troubled (mostly young male) individuals have idolized and emulated murderers who came before them to became notorious mass murder icons themselves, such as Elliot Rodger, Adam Lanza, Seung-Hui Cho, and Eric Harris and Dylan Klebold.[5] These individuals have documented histories of lionizing and idolizing mass murderers whose crimes were sensationalized in the media—praising their acts on social media and in manifestos, comparing death tallies, and bragging that they will go down in history as the best of the worst. These media-mediated mass shootings have generated calls for news "blackouts," focusing on the victims, and not using the names of shooters or sharing their manifestos via social media in effort to deny mass shooters the celebrity attention they crave (Tufekci, 2015).

Criminology as a field has just begun to examine how digital culture influences criminal behavior (Milivojevic, 2021). Anecdotal evidence suggests that media and digital culture play a powerful influence on criminal behavior. Many unanswered questions await theoretical development and empirical research: How is digital culture changing the nature of criminal behavior and violence? As technology advances, is copycat crime increasing? Are people who are more technologically sophisticated and/or artistically literate more or less vulnerable to violent media effects? If most people consume violent media and do not mimic the behaviors they see, what explains those individuals who are influenced by media images of crime and violence? Is copycat crime similar to or different from other types of imitative behaviors? What can be learned from anecdotal case studies of copycat crimes? What are the civil and criminal justice implications of copycat crime? As technology advances, how can the criminogenic effects of mass media and digital culture be prevented? Answers to these and other questions are ripe for empirical investigation.

The copycat effect on criminal behavior spans all types of crimes and can play a small or large role ranging from an idea a perpetrator sees in media incorporated into a crime to a step-by-step reenactment of a crime, to a crime committed by a perpetrator who has lost the boundary between fantasy and reality. Criminal behavior is dynamic and constantly shaped by cultural forces. With the extraordinary pace at which culture has changed since the mid-20th century, it is critical for criminologists, psychologists, social scientists, policymakers, legislators, criminal justice professionals, and the public to understand the nature and dynamics of copycat crime. "Nowhere has the blurring of fiction and reality occasioned more confusion and controversy than in the media's depiction of violence" (Black, 2002, p. 111). With the rapid advancement of technology and the nature of digital culture, it is increasingly important to recognize how media, technology, and digital culture inspire criminal behavior and violence.

Early references to the copycat effect appeared in the 1800s involving behaviors thought to be inspired by books. The earliest accounts of the copycat effect date to 1774 when Johann Wolfgang von Goethe's published *The Sorrows of Young Werther* about a young artist involved in a love triangle who commits suicide. Following publication of the book in Europe, so many men shot themselves while sitting at their desks with an open copy of the book in front of them that the book was banned in Germany, Denmark, and Italy (Coleman, 2004). In 1885 Johann Most's book *Revolutionary War Science*—a how-to terrorist manual—was associated with the 1886 Chicago Haymarket Square bombing (Surette, 1998). Gabriel Tarde was the first to theoretically discuss copycat crime in the early 1900s, coining the term "suggesto-imitative assaults" to describe his observation of sensational violent crimes that appeared to be spurred by similar incidents (Surette, 1990, p. 93). Sociologists became interested in suicide copycats in the 1970s. In 1974 sociologist David Phillips coined the term the "Werther Effect" referring to *The Sorrows of Young Werther* copycat suicides.

Suicide contagion occurred after Marilyn Monroe's suicide in 1962. In the month after Monroe's suicide, the suicide rate in the United States increased 12 percent, primarily among young blond women who appeared to use Monroe as a role model in their own suicides. More recently, within days of the Netflix release of *13 Reasons Why*, a drama where a young teen takes her own life, Google queries about suicide rose 20 percent in 19 days with between 900,000 and 1.5 million more searches than usual (Gilbert, 2017). Shortly after, families of suicide victims claimed that *13 Reasons Why* triggered their teens' suicides, providing evidence that their teens had watched the show prior to committing suicide, and the National Association of School Psychologists cautioned that the show romanticizes choices made by the characters and warned that vulnerable youth should not watch it (Kindelan & Ghebremedhin, 2017). Research on suicide contagion suggests that how media covers suicides has a powerful impact in mitigating the copycat effect. Nirvana's Kurt Cobain committed suicide in Seattle in 1994, but this did not result in copycat suicides, which some suggest is the result of the media efforts to refrain from glamorizing his suicide (Jobes et al., 1996). The more attention a suicide gets on social media such as Twitter (Ueda et al., 2017) and the emotional content of the media message in terms of demographic characteristics of the person who commits suicide (e.g., young, female, and famous) (Fahey et al., 2018), the larger and more powerful the contagion effect.

Though first recognition of the copycat effect pertained to suicide contagion, the copycat effect has been increasingly discussed in relation to criminal behavior (Helfgott, 2008, 2015; O'Toole, 2014; Surette, 1990, 1998, 2002, 2013b, 2014b, 2016a, 2022). The growing number of anecdotal accounts of copycat crime has generated interest in scholarly discourse, theory development, and empirical research with a focus on theoretical perspectives explaining the nature and dynamics of copycat crime (Helfgott, 2015), pathways to copycat crime (Surette, 1990, 2013b), how copycat crime can be measured (Surette, 1990, 2016a), social media influence on mass killers (O'Toole, 2014; O'Neill et al., 2016), and what can be done to address this growing social problem (Plywaczewski & Cebulak, 2017). The nature and mechanisms of copycat crime are only beginning to be understood. The extraordinary pace of technological change in the span of a single generation has raised new questions regarding how susceptible we all are to the effects of mass media. We can all access an endless portal of media depictions of fact and fiction, online communities who will nurture and insulate our ideas no matter how distorted, and social media outlets that make everyone a celebrity. "Computers don't just do things for us, they do things to us, including to our ways of thinking about ourselves and other people" (Turkle, 1995, p. 26). As computer technology has advanced, so too has individual and cultural identity.

Social Learning in the Digital Age

In 1961 Albert Bandura conducted a series of social learning experiments at Stanford University known as the "Bobo Doll" experiments. The experiments were designed to examine how social behaviors are acquired through observation and imitation. Bandura studied the behavior of 36 boys and girls from three to six years old. In the experimental condition, 24 of the children watched a male or female who behaved aggressively toward a Bobo doll while the control group watched a nonaggressive model who played quietly with Tinker Toys. The study found that the children who watched the aggressive behavior toward the Bobo doll made more aggressive responses than the children who played with the Tinker Toys, with boys more likely to imitate same-sex models and to imitate more physically aggressive acts than girls. These findings provided support for Bandura's (1977) social learning theory, one of the largest bodies of research in the social sciences, showing that viewing violent media has an imitative influence on aggressive behavior (Anderson, 2003; Anderson et al., 2003a, 2003b, 2007, 2017; Gentile & Bushman, 2012; Lloyd, 2002; Oliver, 2002; Sparks & Sparks, 2002; Surette, 2002, 2013a, 2022).

Fast forward to the 21st century. On June 3, 2003, 18-year-old Devin Moore/Thompson[6] was arrested and brought into the police station for suspicion of auto theft in Fayette, Alabama. Once inside the station, Moore/Thompson grabbed a .40-caliber Glock automatic from a police officer, shot the officer twice in the head, and then shot and killed a second officer and an emergency dispatcher also in the head. Moore/

How Media, Technology, and Digital Culture Have Changed Criminal Behavior 13

Thompson then grabbed keys to a police car and took off in a police cruiser. All three victims were pronounced dead at the scene. Moore/Thompson was captured shortly after. Following his capture, Moore/Thompson reportedly told police that he had been playing the video game *Grand Theft Auto (GTA)—Vice City* for hours prior to the murders and that, "Life is like a video game. Everybody's got to die sometime." At his trial, Moore/Thompson's defense attorneys argued the "*GTA* defense" explaining that he was a compulsive violent video game player who suffered from childhood abuse–related posttraumatic stress disorder, lost touch with reality, and was acting out in real life the virtual violence in *GTA*. The jury rendered a guilty verdict, and on August 10, 2005, Moore/Thompson was convicted of capital murder and sentenced to death (Adams, 2005; "Can a video game lead to murder;" Farrell, 2005). In 2005, a multimillion-dollar lawsuit was filed against the makers and marketers of *GTA*. The victims' families' attorney Jack Thompson argued in the civil suit that Moore/Thompson was trained to do what he did by being given a "murder simulator" and that *GTA* was "primarily a cop-killing game," that Moore/Thompson had played the game for hundreds of hours, and that the video game trained a minor with no prior criminal history for murder. According to Thompson, the video game industry gave Moore/Thompson "a cranial menu that popped up in the blink of an eye, in that police station" (Leung, 2005).

Three years later, a group of six teenage boys—Jaspreet Singh, 17; Samuel Philip, 16; Stephen Attard, 18; Dylan Laird, 17; Gurnoor Singh, 14; and Brandon Cruz, 15, committed a "spree of violence" on the streets of Long Island, New York (Crowely, 2008). The teens became bored while sitting in a park on the evening of the crimes and decided to mug a man sitting at a nearby bus stop. They mugged the man and broke his teeth (Leonard, 2008) and then went on to gather weapons to continue their spree. They carjacked two people and were arrested while committing their third offense. Upon police questioning, it was discovered that their violence spree was inspired by the game *Grand Theft Auto—Liberty City Stories*. In the game, the player virtually becomes the main character who steals cars, assaults people, murders people, and in general commits whatever crime they can in a town called "Liberty City," which closely resembles New York City (Cochran, 2008). "They decided they were going to go out to commit robberies and emulate the [main] character Nico Belic in the particularly violent video game Grand Theft Auto, said Lt Raymond Code of Nassau County Police" (Leonard, 2008).

The cases of Devin Moore/Thompson and the Long Island teens demonstrate a new era moving beyond the hyperreal to the unreal. In the game, players virtually become the main character who commits crimes and respawns if caught by the police. Video games are becoming increasingly more graphic, and teens are growing up with a misrepresentation of the reality of the violence. It should be obvious that in real life perpetrators of crimes do not respawn when they are caught by police; the potential effect of immersion in the virtual world of *Grand Theft Auto* is the blurred boundary between fantasy and reality, in particular for adolescents who are violence-prone and otherwise immersed in hypermasculine and antisocial subcultures. Was the effect *GTA* had on Devin Moore/Thompson and the Long Island teens the same as the Bobo Doll effect on the children in the 1960s Bandura studies? Or is there something different about a teenager who mimics his virtual experience playing a violent video game in real life? Is social learning theory sufficient to explain the copycat effect and the imitative behaviors we are seeing in today's digital age? How have technological advances complicated and changed the mechanisms of social learning that drive the copycat effect?

Violent media exposure has implications for beyond just edge-sitters. TV violence research in the 1960s and 1970s was the most well-funded and most-studied area in the social sciences (Sparks, 1992). Violent media exposure reinforces the notion of violent masculinity as a cultural norm (Gerbner et al., 2014; Katz, 2006) and produces short-term increases in aggression by triggering an automatic inclination toward imitation, enhancing autonomic arousal, and priming existing cognitive scripts (Anderson et al., 2003a). Benign forms of news media coverage on firearm legislation have been associated with increased firearm suicides by adolescents (Niederkrotenthaler et al., 2009), and TV violence exposure increases aggression and social anxiety, cultivates a "mean view" of the world, and negatively impacts real-world behavior (Gerbner, 1994). The National Institute of Mental Health, American Academy of Pediatrics, American Academy of Child and Adolescent Psychiatry, and American Medical Association concluded that TV violence leads to real-world violence (American Academy of Pediatrics, Committee on Public Education, 2001).

In this era of rapid technological change, rather than asking the question of whether media images of crime and violence are criminogenic, we need to ask questions about how media images and digital culture are shaping all behavior—from the ways in which we are "alone, together" as we sit across from each other at a dinner table while we are texting or scrolling through social media on our phones (Turkle, 2011) to how social media offers opportunities for regular people to become "influencers" and "performers." Criminal behavior, like all behavior, operates within this larger cultural context, which means asking new questions about how technology influences crime and recognizing the complex ways in which mass media constructs the reality of crime—creating cultural and sub-cultural meaning and generating new forms of social and legal control (Ferrell, 1999; Ferrell & Sanders, 1995; Ferrell et al., 2015).

New media forms such as video sharing and social media offer opportunities for performance in ways not offered by old media such as print media, television, and film. Black (2002) observes, "It used to be that only movies were on film, now the whole world is" (p. 4). These new opportunities to self-represent offer a global forum for self-celebration, celebrity, and performance. New media forms offer opportunity for instant electronic self-produced media representations. When this intersects with criminal behavior, rather than attending to representations produced elsewhere (as is the case with "old" media), a potential offender can *become* the source of those representations. In this new digital era, "the terms of criminological questioning need to be sometimes reversed: instead of asking whether 'media' instigates crime or fear of crime, we must ask how the very possibility of mediating oneself to an audience through self-representation might be bound up with the genesis of criminal behavior" (Yar, 2012, p. 1).

From the "Ethical World of the Real" to the "Aesthetic Realm of the Hyperreal"

Technological advances have created a digital culture that has completely altered the world around us. With advances in computer technology far surpassing what most expected computers could do in the 1970s, we have moved from a "modernist culture of calculation toward a post-modernist culture of simulation" (Turkle, 1995, p. 20). Technology, media, and popular culture shape offender choices from the decision to commit a crime, the type of crime, and/or the manner in which it is committed to providing a ready-made script for rationalization techniques to neutralize offense behavior. Technology breeds false familiarity, blurs fantasy and reality, and provides a virtual realm that mediates conscience with important implications for the study of criminal behavior (Helfgott, 2008, 2015). Technological advances have created a digital culture in which the boundary between a real-world event and media representation of that event has:

> . . . increasingly become a dotted line through which the real and the simulated share a mass bank of visual references. Within this complex matrix of narrative/visual relationships, images are hyper—and often

confused with one another—and in the mass replication of visual texts, the electronic representation of an event often becomes embedded within the event itself . . . the large-scale dissemination of electronic images leads to a saturated state of hyperconsciousness in which real and simulated events are increasingly determined/defined in mimetic relation to each other. (Tietchen, 1998)

The increasingly technologically complex nature of images and opportunities to interact virtually rather than actually presents unique challenges for all of us in maintaining the boundary between fantasy and reality that have implications for criminal behavior. This "brave new e-world" has created screen-addicted "glow kids" that suffer negative effects from technology addiction, including blurred boundaries between fantasy and reality, developmental disruption, physiological dysfunction, and attention deficit, and psychological disorders (Kardaras, 2016). Black (1991) notes that the dramatic rise in political assassinations in the 1960s and 1970s and other senseless murders in the 1980s attributed to mental illness was the result of the cultural impact of television and must be understood within the "historically unprecedented context of hyperaestheticized mass-culture" (p. 136).

There has been a shift to a postmodernist culture of simulation characterized by blurred boundaries between reality and fiction that is not rooted in physical tangibles. Black (2002) asks, "Have the relatively new recording technologies somehow altered what we take for reality, so that reality is no longer what it used to be? And if so, how is such a transformation itself to be documented?" (p. 2). When we see objects on the screen, we cannot physically touch them. We are left to construct the real from the not-real. Life on the screen "is a place where signs taken for reality may substitute for the real. Its aesthetic has to do with manipulation and recombination" (Turkle, 1995, p. 47). This shift in the way we come to know the world has brought with it a new consciousness—"The social norm in post-industrial society is no longer the ethical world of the real, but the aesthetic realm of the hyperreal" (Black, 1991, p. 138).

Returning to the hallmark copycat crime cases of John Hinckley and Mark Chapman, Black (1991) suggests that Hinckley and Chapman were both "frustrated middle-class youth engaged in a desperate quest for social identity and recognition" (p. 144) who operated "under the influence of mass media" in the realm of the hyperreal (p. 138). Both struggled with making sense of their identities in a quickly changing media-mediated world filled not with reality, but with hyperreality made up of images, images of images, media loops, and celebrity glorification that

How Media, Technology, and Digital Culture Have Changed Criminal Behavior 17

contributed to their already distorted self-view and worldview: "In the world of the hyperreal, identity is contingent upon image, and individuals exist insofar as they are able to identify themselves with an image generated by the mass media" (p. 144). In the 1980s, Hinckley's and Chapman's criminal acts represented "historically unprecedented hyperaestheticized violence" (p. 136). Chapman and Hinckley were "celebrity assassins" immersed in popular culture and the cultural values of fame and notoriety, lacked their own identities, and needed to do something big to someone big in order to matter.

The Chapmans and Hinckleys of today were born into digital culture. New Zealand Mosque mass shooter Brenton Harrison Tarrant was born in the early 1990s at the same time as the World Wide Web. He filmed his mass murder live over the Internet after announcing it via his online manifesto that was filled with pop cultural references and internet memes written in a Q&A format as if he was writing for an audience of journalists. He became "the first accused mass murderer to conceive of the killing itself as a meme . . . he was both inspired by the world of social media and performing for it, hoping his video, images and text would go viral" (Kirkpatrick, 2019). Tarrant's media-immersed crime suggests that we have moved into an entirely new era where the real and the unreal are virtually indistinguishable.

More than 25 years ago, psychologist Sherry Turkle (1995) suggested that the distance between people and machines has become harder to maintain, asking, "Are we living life on the screen or life in the screen? Our new technologies' enmeshed relationships oblige us to ask to what extent we ourselves have become cyborgs, transgressive mixtures of biology, technology, and code" (p. 21). With the technology of today, intimacy is mediated by technology (Turkle, 2011), requiring retraining to communicate in actual face-to-face conversation (Turkle, 2015). Face-to-face conversation means bringing us back from media-mediated hyperreality and digital unreality. Psychologist Nicholas Kardaras (2016) suggests that a growing number of kids have lost the ability to differentiate between reality and fantasy behind their computer screens. Dan Petric shot his mother and father in the back of the head while they were sitting on their living room couch after they took away his computer game *Halo 3*. Petric was 16 years old. His mother died, but his father lived and forgave him. Five years after the crime in an interview from prison in 2013, Petric told reporters, "I'm used to playing these video games and at the end of every round, everything just resets . . . everyone is still there." When he was then asked if he blames the video games, he answered that while he took responsibility, "the game was a catalyst behind the mindset that caused the murder" (p. 163).

Mass Media and Digital Culture—For Good or for Evil?

Criminal behavior is the product of many factors and forces. While continuous playing of a violent video game where murdered victims can respawn can be seen as one of many risk factors for criminal behavior and violence, millions of people play violent video games and do not "copycat" virtual antisocial behaviors they see on their screens. People are differentially impacted by all sorts of cultural artifacts—books, films, TV shows, commercials, video games, and social media. Many people are positively rather than negatively impacted by the media they consume, and the precise psychological role media played is never clear—nor can it be, until we are able to "map a brain like a computer hard drive" (Atkinson, 1999). Rather than asking does media and digital culture cause crime and violence, the more theoretically meaningful and empirically testable question is: *What role does digital culture play as a risk factor for criminal behavior and violence, and how does media make its way into the mindsets of media-influenced perpetrators?* "All human social behavior, including aggressive behavior, is mediated by the cognitions and cognitive processing of participants. This does not mean that the cognitive processes 'cause' social behavior. Rather as mediating processes, they connect biological, environmental, and situational inputs to behavioral outputs" (Huesmann, 1998, p. 73). We may not yet be able to map a brain like a computer hard drive,[7] but integrating criminological theory with research in cognitive psychology can help explain the process by which chronic exposure to a specific media source can influence behavior.

When an individual engages in behavior of any kind, he or she does so within the framework of a sociocultural context and a cultural cognitive script dictated by and inhabited with whatever populates that context. Criminal behavior, like all behavior, is influenced by cultural artifacts and the "stuff" that populates the perpetrator's world and makes its way into that person's cognitive scripts. Cognitive scripts are cultural products—"[a] simple, well-structured sequence of events—in a specified order—that are associated with a highly familiar activity" (Matlin, 2005, p. 275). Once scripts are learned, they serve as nonconscious, automatic guides for future behavior, and repeated priming and use of a set of schemas eventually make them chronically accessible (Anderson et al., 2003a). Aspects of events, experiences, and event sequences become the content of a broader cognitive schema encoded in memory and provide the basis for attributions, judgments, and behavioral decisions. Digital cultural representations have an increasing impact on peoples' cognitive scripts and schemas, make up the "stuff" in people's minds, and in some cases may even be

How Media, Technology, and Digital Culture Have Changed Criminal Behavior   19

more impactful than personal, tangible, physical experiences. What a person knows comes from "all the events you didn't witness but believe occurred, all the facts about the world you didn't personally collect but believe to be true, and all the things you believe to exist but haven't personally seen" (Surette, 1998, p. xvi). The result of this is that in an increasingly digital world, almost everyone's cognitive scripts are media mediated, raising two critical questions: 1) What are the effects of mass media, technology, and digital culture on all of us? How does mass media, technology and digital culture impact criminal behavior and violence generally? 2) What are the effects of mass media, technology, and digital culture on some of us? Who among us are predisposed for media and digital culture to have a negative rather than a positive effect resulting in crime, aggression, and violence, and how does mass media and digital culture influence the decision-making to commit a crime and the modus operandi and signature elements of criminal behavior for those who are predisposed?

Edge-Sitters

Media-mediated crime and violence is predominantly committed by boys and men. Most documented copycat crimes, in particular mass shootings, have been committed by boys and men whose crimes are the product of the dominant cultural script that status and celebrity can be achieved through violence. Some media-mediated crimes have been committed by girls and women,[8] with 9 of 250 active shooter incidents from 2000 to 2017 involving female shooters (Park & Howard, 2019); only 3 percent of all active shooter cases identified from 1966 to 2016 involved female perpetrators (O'Neill et al., 2016). Media construction of violent masculinity as a cultural norm and as a way to assert power is a large part of the picture in understanding how media, technology, and digital culture inspire criminal behavior and violence. The message that power can be achieved through violence made its way into the cognitive scripts of a long list of school shooters such as Michael Carneal, Mitchell Johnson, Andrew Golden (Newman et al., 2004), Columbine killers Eric Harris and Dylan Klebold, Adam Lanza, and virtually every school and mass shooter that has come along since (Neklason, 2019). When it comes to school shootings, one type of shooter stands out—young men who experience humiliation from perceptions of loss of privilege in a school setting merged with fantasies of retribution delivered through "masculinity grounded in violent action" (Tonso, 2009, p. 1278).

Violent masculinity is intimately intertwined with media and culture (Gerbner et al., 2014; Katz, 2006). Adam Lanza, who murdered his mother, himself, and 26 people including 20 children at Sandy Hook Elementary School on December 14, 2012, was fixated on mass shooters and was immersed in violent online gaming communities that insulated him within a virtual fantasy world. Psychiatric problems, hypermasculinity, mass media, and digital culture became a toxic brew that bubbled steadily during his adolescent development, fueling a "gaming-induced psychosis" (Kardaras, 2016, p. 187) that led to one of the deadliest mass shootings in U.S. history. Among Lanza's possessions prior to the murders was a book on the 2006 Amish schoolhouse shooting, a spreadsheet listing mass killings over the years, and digital evidence suggesting that Lanza had a preoccupation with mass shootings, particularly Columbine. For Lanza, after years of living with mental illness, immersion in online communities and video game violence, access to firearms and military gear, and images of violence became "kerosene to throw onto his already burning, obsessive, and turbulent mind." A law enforcement officer said, "The violent games were like porn to a rapist. It was like he was lost inside of one of his own sick games" (Lupica, March 25, 2013).

Elliot Rodger, perpetrator of the May 23, 2014, University of California Santa Barbara mass shooting, was another edge-sitter whose fantasy life and violent behavior were fueled by media. Rodger and his crime subsequently became a digital cultural script—a how-to manual for new edge-sitters to emulate. Rodger killed six university students before committing suicide in a murder rampage. Since the crime, Rodger has become an idol for followers called "incels" who refer to him as Saint Elliot (Hodge, 2019). After the murders it was quickly discovered that Rodger had written a 141-page manifesto entitled "My Twisted World" (DocuCloud.org, 2014) and uploaded multiple videos, including his final video "Retribution," to YouTube and Google+ in which he narrated his social isolation, his misfortune at being a 22-year-old virgin, and contempt for "sorority girls" who were "stuck-up blonde sluts" and the "sexually active men" who were able to have sex with them (Helfgott, 2014). In his manifesto epilogue Rodger concluded:

> I am Elliot Rodger. . . . Magnificent, glorious, supreme, eminent. . . . Divine! I am the closest thing there is to a living god. . . . The ultimate evil behind sexuality is the human female. They are the main instigators of sex. They control which men get it and which men don't. . . . Women are incapable of having morals or thinking rationally. They are completely controlled by their depraved emotions and vile sexual impulses. Because of this, the men who do get to experience the pleasures of sex and the privilege of breeding are the men who women are sexually attracted to . . . the stupid, degenerate, obnoxious men. I have observed this all my life. The most beautiful of women choose to mate with the most brutal of men,

How Media, Technology, and Digital Culture Have Changed Criminal Behavior 21

instead of magnificent gentlemen like myself. . . . My orchestration of the Day of Retribution is my attempt to do everything, in my power, to destroy everything I cannot have. All of those beautiful girls I've desired so much in my life, but can never have because they despise and loathe me, I will destroy. All of those popular people who live hedonistic lives of pleasure, I will destroy, because they never accepted me as one of them. I will kill them all and make them suffer, just as they have made me suffer. It is only fair . . . (Rodger, n.d., pp. 135–136)

Rodger's manifesto and his "Retribution" video he posted prior to acting out his fantasy exemplify a culturally reinforced cognitive script. The "stuff" that populated Rodger's cognitive script is an example of "social-cognitive observational theory gone awry" (Ellison, 2012, p. 523). Rodger's internalization of cultural values—sex as power, virginity as a social stigma—and normalization of violence to solve problems fueled his fantasy and converged with a long history of mental health issues ultimately culminating in extreme homicidal behavior. Rodger was an edge-sitter. His internal dialogue and distorted worldview moved Rodger from "misfit to mass murderer" seemingly overnight and with little overt warning beyond his history of mental health issues—issues shared by millions of people who never commit a crime, yet alone one so heinous and extreme. Posthumously, the idolatry of Rodger by other self-identified involuntary celibates who blame women for their forced celibacy, known as "incels," has, like other online communities,[9] become an insulated breeding ground for Rodger-wannabes whose distorted cognitive scripts are validated, reinforced, and ignited.

Making sense of the point at which an edge-sitter makes the decision to commit a criminal act and what situational, environmental, and cultural risk factors play into this decision is a central criminological question. There is also consideration of whether the move from edge-sitter to the commission of a crime is a decision or a compulsion, the former requiring the person to be cognitively intact and the latter involving some level of diminished capacity or blurred boundary between fantasy and reality. Whether the movement from edge-sitter to criminal involves conscious decision-making or some form of compulsion is of legal importance.

Technology-Related Risk Factors and the Criminogenic Effects of Digital Culture— The Effects on the Rest of Us

With every technological advance, the potential emerges for criminal behavior to change (Clarke, 2004). Media technology and digital culture play a powerful role in the development of cognitive and behavioral scripts (Larson, 2003). Popular culture, television, and film are contemporary forms of myth (Hill, 1992) where stories about good/evil, right/wrong, love/hate are told on movie screens, computer monitors, and smartphones by strangers rather than around campfires by families. Media, technology, and digital culture shape how or whether we see ourselves as victims or perpetrators, who we see as victims or perpetrators, and how safe or dangerous we believe the world around us is. The convergence of culture and technology has created opportunities for media and digital culture to motivate and lay the blueprint for criminal behavior in ways the world has never seen before. Children and adolescents are born into an environment saturated with digital technology and mass media imagery with mixed messages about the meaning of violence, such as parents telling their kids they can't play violent video games while watching the TV news filled with stories about violence and war (Wooden & Blazak, 2001). As technologies become more relevant to targeted audience members, more dominant as an information source, and more entertaining, it is more probable that adolescents will use this information as a tool to understand themselves and others (Lloyd, 2002).

Minimal empirical evidence exists to explain the complex ways in which technology, media, and popular culture influence criminal behavior on an individual level. Most researchers agree that mass media technology presents special challenges for criminology because of its powerful influence on behavior. The imitative effects of violent media are stronger than a story about violence in a book or presented in narrative form from person to person. Electronic media presents a greater concern than print media because there is a larger at-risk pool of individuals who can be criminally influenced (Surette, 1990). Determining whether a violent computer game or movie contributed to a particular criminal act is less a question of causation and more a question of how the influence motivates, shapes, and inspires the behavior in a particular individual:

> It is not simply that the mass media report in certain ways on criminal events or provide fashionable fodder out of which criminal subcultures construct collective styles. For good or bad, postmodern society exists well beyond such discrete, linear patterns of action and reaction. Rather it is that criminal events, identities, and styles take life within a media-saturated environment, and thus exist from the start as moments in a mediated spiral of presentation and representation. (Ferrell & Sanders, 1995, p. 14)

How Media, Technology, and Digital Culture Have Changed Criminal Behavior   23

Exploration of how technology serves as a motivational force for criminal behavior requires interdisciplinary analysis of the socializing properties of technology, media, and popular culture:

> Mass communications, particularly the Internet and television programming, including music videos, can be reconceptualized as opportunities for adolescents to identify cues for social behavior among their peer group as well as cognitively rehearse their own approaches to certain interactions. . . . Without appreciation for the specific "cultural competencies" of the adolescent culture, mass media influences are likely to be overlooked as a significant socialization agent for this population in the new millennium. (Lloyd, 2002, p. 88)

This is even more important to consider when looking at findings reported by Anderson et al. (2003a) from three nationally representative surveys[2] and other studies that have found that virtually all families with children interact with a varied and significant range of media sources and that violent media consumption increases aggression in children and adolescents and not just those who are predisposed to aggression and violence (Anderson & Bushman, 2001, 2018; Anderson & Dill, 2000; Anderson & Murphy, 2003a; Anderson et al., 2009) and that more interactive media such as violent video games increases angry feelings, physiological arousal, and aggressive thoughts and behavior and decreases empathic feelings and helping behavior (Anderson & Bushman, 2001, suggesting that the effects of video game violence is a significant societal concern (Kepes et al., 2017).

Digital culture influences how people commit crimes and has created entirely new forms of crime such as media-mediated mass shootings where offenders utilize media to inform and display the motivations for their crimes (Helfgott, 2014; O'Toole, 2014; Sickles, 2014). Complex influences of technology and culture converge in cases where offenders are inspired by high-tech images of crime and violence that blur the line between fantasy and reality, inspire, provide a vehicle for celebrity through violence, and can help perpetrators stay one step ahead of law enforcement (Helfgott, 2008, 2015). As technology rapidly advances, how mass media and digital culture influence the method by which crime is committed, inspire new forms of crime, and impact the many and the few is of central criminological importance.

CHAPTER TWO

How Media and Technology Shape Modus Operandi and Signature Elements of Criminal Behavior

The 2017 crime drama *Mindhunter,* based on the book *Mindhunter: Inside the FBI's Elite Serial Crime Unit* (Douglas & Olshaker, 1997), depicts the work of the FBI behavioral science unit in the 1970s and early 1980s in the early development of psychological and criminal profiling. The popular *Netflix* series[1] brought renewed attention to the motivations and methods of infamous serial killers. The series features the stories of serial killers who were the subjects of a study funded by the National Institute of Justice conducted by FBI agents John Douglas and Robert Ressler, Boston College psychiatric nursing professor Ann Burgess, and other agents from the FBI behavioral science unit. The stories in *Mindhunter* are drawn from 36 interviews that Douglas, Ressler, and colleagues conducted between 1979 and 1983 with sexually motivated serial killers, the findings of which are reported in the books *Sexual Homicide: Patterns and Motives* (Ressler et al., 1992) and *Crime Classification Manual* (Douglas et al., 2006) and in true crime novels written by Douglas, Ressler, and other FBI agents who were part of the project (Douglas & Olshaker, 1997, 1999; Douglas et al., 2004; Ressler, 1993).

In Episode 2, Season 2 of *Mindhunter,* Ressler's character Bill Tench and Douglas's character Holden Ford seek insight from David Berkowitz, aka

"Son of Sam," to help them investigate Dennis Rader, the BTK Killer. Tench says to Ford, "If you want to learn how to paint, go straight to the artist." There are two important aspects of this idea. First, that the murderer is an artist and second, that other potential murderers are learning and watching the other "artists."

Returning to Black's (1991) aesthetic-critical perspective on murder, consider how artistic and media depictions of murder and other crimes make their way into the minds and behaviors of actual murderers. "Only the victim knows the brutal 'reality' of murder; the rest of us view it at a distance, often as rapt onlookers who regard its 'reality' as a peak aesthetic experience" (Black, 1991, p. 3). This aesthetic experience of murder is the way that most people experience murder unless they are victims themselves or know someone who is—"the extent to which our customary experience of murder and other forms of violence is primarily aesthetic, rather than moral, physical, natural, or whatever term [we] choose as a synonym for the word real" (Black, 1991, p. 3). If most people's experience of murder and violence is aesthetic, how does this help explain how media depiction of crime, violence, and murder influence actual crime, violence, and murder?

There is a reflexive relationship between media depictions of crime and real-life crime. Media and artistic depictions make their way into real-life crime, and real-life crime becomes art in real and fictionalized forms and then feeds back into culture (Ferrell, 1999; Ferrell & Sanders, 1995; Ferrell et al., 2015). In videotaped interviews with police, Gary Ridgeway, aka the Green River Killer, says he followed Ted Bundy and other serial killers in the media (*State of Washington v. Ridgway*, 2004). Dennis Rader, aka the BTK Killer, mentions in interviews that he embraced the acronym BTK because it was like the "Green River Killer" and "Son of Sam" ("Secret confessions of BTK," 2005).

The Continuum of Influence of Media and Digital Culture on Criminal Behavior

In *Mindhunter*, and in real-life, David Berkowitz and Dennis Rader engaged in communiqués with news media (Guillen, 2002). They operated as if the murders they committed were a form of art and reporters covering the crimes were their ticket to fame. The media became a part of the modus operandi of their crimes. Media and technology influence the way crimes are committed and, in some cases, shape the very nature of crimes. The influence of media, technology, and digital culture on criminal behavior and violence can best be understood along a continuum of influence from low to high. On the low end, media and digital culture

How Media and Technology Shape Modus Operandi and Signature Elements 27

give ideas about how to commit a crime, shaping modus operandi. On the high end, media and digital culture become so intertwined with motive that they become a part of the signature and essence of crime itself.

Modus Operandi

Modus operandi (MO) is a Latin term that means method of operation. MO reflects how the offender commits a crime. How the offender commits the crime reflects the experience/state of the perpetrator and the situational/contextual factors that the offender had to work with to successfully complete the crime. "M.O. is a learned set of behaviors that the offender develops and sticks with it because it works, but it is dynamic and malleable" (Douglas et al., 2006, p. 20). MO can change over time as the offender gains experience and runs into challenges that require modifying their method. Offenders may make modifications to their usual way of carrying out a crime as they learn ways to improve their motivational outcome. For example, in the case of a residential burglary, an offender may learn that bringing certain tools to complete a break-in will reduce the necessity of having to break a window. In a serial violent crime such as rape or homicide, the method may change as the offender completes more crimes and through experience learns how to respond to victim reactions.

Technological advances have an impact on the methods used to commit all types of crimes. Old-time safecracking[2] has been transformed into high-tech cyberattacks on banks and financial services companies and sophisticated criminal networks engaged in intercepting logins and transaction authentication codes of people using online banking (Leukfeld & Jansen, 2015). The Internet provides a method through which offenders can target victims. Three-fourths of sex offenders were convicted of crimes against minors they met over the Internet, and almost half reviewed online profiles of minors to identify potential victims (Malesky, 2007). Social media operates as a virtual community through which offenders insulate themselves and get ideas about how to commit crimes. In their study of the MO of Jihadist foreign fighters from the Netherlands, de Bie et al. (2015) found that technology and social media offered Jihadists a virtual forum that replaced close-knit groups, creating a platform to discuss political issues and persuade potential foreign fighters that shaped MO behavior. The incel movement similarly provides insulation for men who see themselves as victims of women who deprive them of sex. For example, incel shaped the motivation and method of Alek Minassian, who posted on Facebook praising incel idol Elliot Rodger minutes before running over pedestrians in a rented van, killing 10 people in Toronto. Minassian called for an "Incel Rebellion" to give himself and his community of "involuntary celibates" access to the women of their choice (Bilefsky & Austen, 2018; Taub, 2018).

Fictional media depictions of crime have been mimicked step by step in cases where the perpetrators have used media as a blueprint for the actual crime. In a 1998 bank robbery in Olympia, Washington, two women and three teenage girls (including a mother and daughter) from Aberdeen, Washington, who watched the 1996 film *Set It Off* starring Jada Pinkett, Queen Latifah, Vivica A. Fox, and Kimberly Elise, committed the robbery, mimicking details from the bank robbery in the film, including calling out the time in five-second intervals (Associated Press, 1998). The women were caught fleeing to Mexico, and it was later discovered that they had watched the film multiple times prior to the crime, and the detectives recovered a videotape of the film in their home.

Technology changes MO behavior by completely altering the nature of some types of crime (e.g., bank robbery and terrorism) and on an individual level provides an instant global information source for ideas about how to commit crimes. Identifying how media, technology, and digital culture influence the method of crime, from providing a minor idea to a step by step blueprint of every aspect of a crime, is important for understanding the nature of the copycat effect on criminal behavior.

Signature

Signature refers to elements of a crime that go beyond the actions necessary to commit it. The signature is the perpetrator's psychological "calling card" (Douglas et al., 2006; Keppel & Birnes, 1997) and applies to extreme crimes where the crime fulfils a psychological need for the offender. Signature analysis has been conducted on infamous cases such as the Jack the Ripper murders showing the rare and individualized elements of crimes committed by the same individual reflecting the psychopathology and fantasy of the perpetrator (Keppel et al., 2005). In serial killer cases, the signature is the behavioral expression of violent fantasy the killer must leave at the scene to satisfy emotional/psychological needs. Signature goes beyond what is necessary to commit the crime and reflects motivation. The signature is "an individualized set of indicators that can point specifically to an offender's personality" (Douglas et al., 2006, p. 19) and reflects individualized behavioral consistency across crimes. Signature elements are used for analysis to link crimes committed by a single offender (Davies & Woodhams, 2019; Harbers et al., 2012; Hazelwood & Warren, 2003).

How Media and Technology Shape Modus Operandi and Signature Elements 29

The copycat effect was a signature element of Chapman's and Hinckley's crimes. Chapman and Hinckley were intimately involved with the stories they consumed from the book *Catcher in the Rye* (Chapman) and the film *Taxi Driver* (Hinckley). These stories and their identification with characters in the stories became a part of Chapman's and Hinckley's cognitive scripts and ultimately became a part of the very nature of their crimes. The signature elements involved in the commission of these crimes were so psychologically complex that the crimes can only be understood through a deep analysis of their motivation. Both Chapman and Hinckley were identity-disturbed individuals who targeted their media heroes and operated under the influence of mass media. "It was not primarily celebrity but identity they were after" (Black, 1991, p. 153). "Chapman and Hinckley were compelled to enact fictions provided by literature and film, without which they would have been incapable of acting out their plans, and possibly even of conceiving them in the first place" (Black, 1991, p. 155). Both Chapman and Hinckley were young men who were overexposed to media images of superstar cult-heroes that provided them with fantasy role models. Both idolized John Lennon and had planned to kill themselves before they turned their violence toward celebrity-others. Hinckley went to Lennon's funeral in New York City and two months later went to the Dakota hotel and stood in the same spot where Chapman opened fire on Lennon, and he brought a gun—the same type of gun that Chapman used to shoot Lennon. "In both Chapman's murder of Lennon and Hinckley's attempted assassination of President Reagan a few months later, an individual with virtually no self-image contemplated suicide, and then abruptly sought to kill a public figure whom he admired and emulated" (Black, 1991, p. 152). Hinckley referenced Lennon's murder in the investigation of his crime, and he had a button of John Lennon in his coat pocket when he shot Reagan. Hinckley had written a paper after Lennon's death describing how he admired Reagan and idolized Lennon and said in the paper, "In America heroes are meant to be killed. Idols are meant to be shot in the back."

Black (1991) observes that it was "no accident" that the era of the hyperreal (when the media came to mediate public reality as it never had before) coincided with the decade in which the president of the United States was a former movie actor. "This is no longer simply a case of life imitating art but . . . of life being indistinguishable from, or unimaginable without, art." Chapman's and Hinckley's acts of violence were motiveless, "quintessentially mimetic acts" designed to "reveal the real" by identity-disturbed individuals who were seeking attention and fame and committed "under the influence of mass media" (p. 138). In these two cases, a popular novel and film were "sufficiently powerful stimulants to trigger a total collapse of these media-junkies' already tenuous sense of the distinction between ethics and aesthetics, reality and fiction" (p. 139), and the acts of violence committed were attempts to restore the distinction between the ethical/aesthetic and reality/fiction. Privately, in the minds of the killers, these seemingly "motiveless" crimes are motivated by a quest for identity and celebrity. "In the world of the hyperreal identity is contingent upon image, and individuals exist insofar as they are able to identify themselves with an image generated by the mass media" (Black, 1991, p. 144).

Chapman's murder of John Lennon is psychologically complex because it involves an individual with an identity disturbance whose crime was the product of a complicated media-mediated cognitive script with a motive that can only be understood by understanding the unique meaning the crime held for Chapman. Unlike media influence of MO behavior in a crime, in Chapman's case, the media he consumed *became* the crime. Lennon was the victim of a media-mediated celebrity assassination. Celebrity murders in the age of mass media are the result of a murderer's identification with a victim who is familiar, yet a total stranger. In Chapman's mind, Lennon was "a false-double who must be destroyed" (Black, 1991, p. 145). Chapman's signature in the murder of John Lennon was his cognitively twisted media-mediated simultaneous quest for identity and celebrity scripted by J. D. Salinger's story in *Catcher in the Rye* and through the other pop culture he consumed. Chapman was fixated on *Catcher in the Rye* and took on the identity of the book's main character, Holden Caulfield, a 17-year-old who goes to New York City for a week after being expelled from prep school, who moves through his world referring to people who he sees around him as "phonies." *Catcher in the Rye* is written in first-person narrative from Caulfield's perspective. In the years leading up to Lennon's murder, Chapman was a Beatles fan who idolized Lennon but then came to view him as a "poser" (Sloane, 2015). Chapman is said to have referred to Lennon as a "bastard" to his wife prior to committing the murder because he was angry at Lennon for preaching love and peace while making millions. Books Chapman read prior to the murder—*Catcher in the Rye* and Fawcett's (1980) *John Lennon: One Day at a Time* made their way into Chapman's cognitive script in the planning of the crime and ultimately became signature elements of John Lennon's murder. In a prison interview three years after the murder, Chapman said that he fantasized prior to committing the crime that when the police came to arrest him, he would shout, "I am Holden Caulfield, the catcher in the rye of the present generation" and would turn into Holden Caulfield. While committing the murder, Chapman was wearing a Russian fur hat with earflaps resembling the

How Media and Technology Shape Modus Operandi and Signature Elements 31

hunting hat Holden Caulfield wore, and he brought with him a copy of *Catcher in the Rye*, writing in the title page, "To Holden Caulfield, From Holden Caulfield, *This* is my statement" (Black, 1991, p. 156).

Hinckley was following a secondary script prepared by Chapman (Black, 1991). Hinckley's attempted assassination of Reagan occurred three months after Chapman's murder of Lennon. Distraught over Lennon's murder, Hinckley went to the murder site, and after he committed his crime investigators found a copy of *Catcher in the Rye* in his hotel room. *Taxi Driver* was the primary script for Hinckley's crime and was for Hinckley what *Catcher in the Rye* was for Chapman—a media catalyst that ultimately became the signature element of Hinckley's crime. Hinckley identified with the film's lead character, Travis Bickel, a New York City taxi driver, and became fixated on actress Jodie Foster, who at the age of 12, played "Iris," a teenaged prostitute. Like Chapman, Hinckley was an identity-disturbed media junkie who identified with Bickel, who, like Holden Caulfield, is a loner who views himself as a savior in a dark, dangerous, dreary world of pimps, whores, and druggies. In the film, Bickel befriends Iris and ultimately kills her pimp after a failed attempt to assassinate a senator. Like *Catcher in the Rye*, the lead character in *Taxi Driver* takes viewers through a first-person narration of a dim journey of the world around him, which he sees as filthy and corrupt, referring to people as "scumbags." In real life, Hinckley attempted to assassinate Ronald Reagan to impress Foster, who on the date of the crime was an 18-year-old college student at Yale University pursuing a degree in literature. Shortly before committing the crime, Hinckley wrote Foster a two-page letter in which he said, "I will prove my love for you through a historic act." When he was arrested, photos of Foster were found in his wallet. It was reported that Hinckley believed Reagan had previously snubbed Foster and his assassination was a way to prove his love for her. An article written in *The Washington Post*, noted, "Today, a psychotic personality may see himself as stepping onto a set ready made for his performance. The character who rescues Jodie Foster in 'Taxi Driver' is a gun nut, an avenger, a lonely figure who longs for a 'clean rain' to sweep the skies of his city and wash away the filth" (Williams, April 1, 1981). Hinckley's assassination attempt on Ronald Reagan was psychologically intertwined with Travis Bickel's desire to clean up the filth and save Iris.

Both Chapman's murder of Lennon and Hinckley's assassination attempt of Reagan are copycat crimes that involved a distinct media-mediated signature that can only be understood by understanding the meaning the crime held for the perpetrators. Unlike crimes such as the *Set It Off*–inspired bank robbery where the perpetrators mimicked the way the crime was committed as reflected in their MO behavior, Hinckley's and Chapman's crimes were psychologically complex in that their own identities, fantasies, and disordered thinking became intertwined with the media they consumed, creating an elaborately personal cognitive script that drove their behavior in ways that made their crimes individually distinct and connected to the personal meaning the crime held for them. The copycat effect on the criminal behavior of Hinckley and Chapman was the signature element of their crimes. This means that the media they consumed did not just give them ideas about how to commit the crime but that the crimes would not have been committed if not for the unique and psychologically complex interweaving of individual characteristics, relationship to media, fantasy development, cognitive script, characteristics of the media source, and cultural factors. While it could be argued that any external information Hinckley and Chapman consumed would have made its way into their crimes and they would have committed some sort of violent crime at some point in their lives, the motives of their crimes can only be understood within the context of the media they consumed, which was intertwined with their crimes. The copycat effect was the signature element of their crimes necessary to understand the meaning the crimes held for them.

The copycat effect impacts criminal behavior along a continuum of influence from low to high (Helfgott, 2015). Mass media and digital culture can influence criminal behavior in a minor way, such as what occurred in the *Set It Off* bank robbery where something a perpetrator saw in a movie was used as part of the MO behavior, or it can be a major influence such as the case of Hinckley and Chapman where the media they consumed was a central and critical factor in the commission of the crime becoming a signature element that characterized the very nature of the crime. On the low end of the continuum, mass media and digital culture act as a "shaper" giving ideas to already active criminals, molding the crime rather than triggering the crime. On the high end of the continuum, mass media and digital culture act as a "trigger" creating crimes that would not otherwise occur (Surette, 1998). (See Figure 2.1.)

Thus, on the low end of the continuum in which individuals get ideas about how to commit a crime from media or popular culture that inform MO behavior. In these cases, the copycat effect has a minor influence on criminal behavior that very likely would have occurred with or without the influence of the media source. On the high end of the continuum are cases in which individuals are psychologically intertwined with media and popular culture, and the motive for their crimes are intertwined with the influencing media source.

LOW ←——→ HIGH

Minor Influence
Modus Operandi

An idea from mass media and digital culture is used to commit a crime as part of the modus operandi. Mass media and digital culture influences crime as a minor shaper giving an idea or ideas to commit a crime that would have occurred regardless.

Major Influence
Signature

Psychologically complex interweaving of individual characteristics with media that becomes a signature element characterizing the nature of the crime. Mass media and digital culture influence crime as a major trigger creating a crime that would not have otherwise occurred.

Figure 2.1 Copycat Crime Continuum

Minor to Major Copycat Effects and the Continuum of Influence on Modus Operandi and Signature

In 1974 William Andrews and Dale Pierre committed a robbery-murder known as the Ogden, Utah "Hi-Fi Murders." Andrews and Pierre robbed a stereo store and during the robbery forced five victims who were in the store to drink Drano before they shot them all in the head. Upon interrogation, Andrews and Pierre told police that they brought Drano to the crime scene because they had watched the Clint Eastwood *Dirty Harry* film sequel *Magnum Force* several times, liked the movie, and decided to take an idea from one of the scenes in the movie to use in the robbery. The scene they mimicked was not exactly like the crime they committed. The *Magnum Force* scene showed a pimp killing a prostitute in the back of a taxi by forcing her to drink drain cleaner, causing her to die immediately. In the Ogden, Utah Hi-Fi murders, the victims choked and vomited, made noise, and did not die immediately, so Pierre then shot each one of them in the head.[3] The medical examiner later determined that it would have taken the victims as long as 12 hours to die just from the Drano (Douglas & Olshaker, 1999).

Andrews and Pierre set out to commit a robbery-murder, and media influenced one part of their method of committing the crime. The media influence in this case was very specific—an idea from a movie that caught the perpetrators' attention and gave them an idea of a method to commit their robbery-murder. However, according to former FBI profiler John

34   *Copycat Crime*

Douglas, media influenced the details and "these two sadistic creeps would have committed this crime regardless of what they'd seen or heard" (Douglas & Olshaker, 1999, p. 107).

In 2012 in Queens, New York, three men (Akeem Monsalvatge, Edward Byam, and Derrick Bunkley) committed a robbery at a Pay-O-Matic. They had committed a similar robbery two years prior, but after watching the 2010 film *The Town* starring and directed by Ben Affleck, they changed their MO to incorporate ideas they saw in the film. In the first robbery, one of the men entered the teller area via the ceiling while his accomplices stood guard, armed, in the lobby while the others gathered around $40,000 from the drawers in the kiosks. In the second crime, the method was more theatrical, incorporating elements of the film. In the 2012 robbery, the men wore high-end special effects masks to hide their identities and accosted an employee by showing her a picture of her home as an intimidation tactic. They wore New York Police Department (NYPD) hoodies and poured bleach on the countertops after stealing $200,000 (Samaha, 2014). *The Town* features the story of a group of bank robbers who kidnap a witness who one of the robbers (Affleck) falls in love with. The film shows scenes of different robberies with details on how the robbers avoided detection from the police. In one of the most iconic scenes, the characters disguise themselves wearing nun masks and habits, show a picture of the teller's home in order to intimidate for compliance, wear police uniforms, and pour bleach on anything they touch to thwart DNA detection. These elements were incorporated into the 2012 Pay-O-Matic robbery but not in the 2010 robbery. After the arrest, the perpetrators indicated when they were interviewed that they were heavily influenced by *The Town* (Algar, 2013). One of the robbers, Monsalvatge, had even gone to a mall and had a custom tee-shirt designed in homage to the film prior to the 2012 robbery. The three men were sentenced to 32 years of imprisonment for the two Queens robberies and found guilty of robbery conspiracy, two counts of robbery, and two counts of using a firearm in connection with the robberies (Huffman, 2017). This case illustrates how an idea from a film can be incorporated into the MO behavior of a crime on the low end of the copycat crime continuum.

Another example of a case that could be considered on the low end of the copycat crime continuum is the week-long violent crime spree committed by Phillip Haynes Markoff in Boston in 2009. Markoff was a 23-year-old Boston University medical student who came to be known as the "Craigslist Killer." The week started with the armed robbery of 26-year-old Trisha Leffler. She had posted a Craigslist ad advertising "to spend some time with a young blonde." She met Markoff in the lobby of

How Media and Technology Shape Modus Operandi and Signature Elements 35

the hotel before allowing him to her room, where he displayed his weapon and robbed her of $800 in cash and $250 in American Express gift cards. He then took Leffler's phone and erased his phone number from her call logs, tied her up with zip ties, and left. Leffler was able to escape from her zip ties and then promptly reported the robbery to the hotel security (Cornwell, 2009). Markoff's next victim was not as lucky. Using the same MO as in Leffler's robbery, Markoff's next victim was 29-year-old Julissa Brisman. Markoff responded to a Craigslist ad Brisman posted advertising massaging services for $200 an hour. Upon entry into Brisman's hotel room, Markoff drew his weapon and began to rob her, but Brisman put up a fight and when she was halfway out the door, Markoff shot her three times, killing her. While this crime is not a copycat crime, it can be considered a media-mediated crime on the low end of the continuum because Markoff used an online site to commit robbery and murder. He targeted victims through online ads and purchased weapons and items used in the crimes on Craigslist. Without the influence of Craigslist, Markoff would not have been able to set up these crimes in the way he did. He used the Internet to cherry-pick ideal victims.

A mass shooting in Thailand on February 9, 2020, that left 28 people dead and 58 people injured offers another example on the low-mid range of the copycat continuum. The perpetrator, Army Sergeant Major Jakrapanth Thomma, had a financial/real estate conflict over a land deal with his superior and his mother-in-law, believing he was owed money he did not receive (Paddock et al., 2020). This conflict culminated in Thomma killing his commanding officer and his mother-in-law at his army base. Thomma then went to a busy shopping mall in the middle of the afternoon, where he shot indiscriminately at mallgoers while posting on Facebook before and during the shooting. Before the shooting, Thomma posted, "Rich from cheating. Taking advantage of other people. Do they think they can spend the money in hell?" During the shooting, Thomma posted a video of himself wearing an army helmet while commenting, "I'm tired . . . I can't pull my finger anymore" while making a trigger motion with his hand. He then posted written updates during the attack such as "Death is inevitable for everyone" and "Should I give up?" Facebook immediately removed the posts, expressed sympathy for the victims, and posted, "There is no place on Facebook for people who commit this kind of atrocity, nor do we allow people to praise or support this attack" (Wongcha-Um, 2020; "Thailand shooting: Soldier kills 21 in gun rampage," 2020).

Thomma mimicked mass shooters who came before him who posted on Facebook during their attacks. However, unlike prior shootings where perpetrators used Facebook Live to post crimes in real time, Thomma used Facebook to communicate while he committed the crime (Rahman, 2020). In this crime, there was a minor-medium-level copycat effect. The perpetrator used Facebook to communicate, and this was woven into the MO of his crime. Thomma may have committed a crime out of anger at his victims in a financial dispute. However, what is important here is the use of Facebook as part of his MO behavior as a mechanism to communicate his crime globally and instantly. Facebook was used on an interpersonal level to communicate what he was doing and on a public level to broadly celebrate his violence. Had Thomma committed this crime a generation ago, the casualties may have been far fewer. It is likely that media outlet for the display of the violence influenced his method of conducting the crime, escalating what in predigital times might have been a double homicide to a mass murder, significantly exacerbating the victim count.

The same can be said about the 2015 Facebook Live murder of WDJB Virginia reporter Alison Parker and photojournalist Adam Ward committed by Vester Lee Flanagan II. Flanagan was fired from WDJB in 2015. Social media posts and correspondence to news media that Flanagan made on the day of the event indicated that Flanagan, who was Black and homosexual, believed he was the victim of discrimination, specifically naming Parker and Ward. This was a crime with high use of social media as a vehicle to broadcast the crime as part of his MO. However, mass media and digital culture were signature elements of his crime. Flanagan claimed to have been angered by the 2015 Charleston, South Carolina church shooting committed by Dylann Roof and described himself as a "human powder keg . . . just waiting to go BOOM" (Cleary, 2017; Shear et al., 2015). Following the murders, ABC News received a 22-page document from Flanagan describing why he killed Ward and Parker. In the fax, Flanagan wrote, "I put down a deposit for a gun on 6/19/15. The Church shooting in Charleston happened on 6/17/15. . . . What sent me over the top was the church shooting. And my hollow point bullets have the victims' initials on them." Throughout the document, Flanagan expressed admiration for previous mass killers, referring to Virginia Tech shooter Seung-Hui Cho as "his boy," expressed admiration for the Columbine shooters Harris and Klebold, and stated that the Charleston church shooting had sent him over the edge. Flanagan's crime involved a complex interplay of a distorted cognitive script that interwove his perspective and feelings of anger and retaliation with his fixation on media depictions of mass shooters using media as both MO and signature. He interwove his admiration for mass shooters with his aggression and anger toward Ward and Parker, which manifested in MO behavior that included committing the crime at his former place of employment, which was a TV

How Media and Technology Shape Modus Operandi and Signature Elements 37

station, while posting live to Facebook. This crime has both MO and signature elements on the medium-high end of the continuum of copycat influence. By his own admission, he was an edge-sitter influenced by a prior crime he saw in the media and then used the media to broadcast his own crime.

Cases at the high end of the copycat continuum include crimes committed by perpetrators who were immersed in a media source that their identities became intertwined with: Chapman's and Hinckley's crimes and other crimes in which perpetrators emulate and identify with media characters. These cases fall on the high end of the continuum because copycat elements define the very nature of these criminal acts. An example of a crime that would fall on the far-extreme end of the copycat continuum is the Dexter Copycat crime committed in Edmonton, Canada, by Mark Twitchell in 2008. Twitchell was a 29-year-old aspiring filmmaker convicted of first-degree murder for the disappearance and death of 38-year-old John Brian "Johnny" Altinger. Twitchell lured Altinger to a garage by pretending to be a woman on the dating website Plenty of Fish, killed and dismembered him, and dumped his body in a storm sewer. Twitchell committed the murder on October 10, 2008; was arrested on October 31, 2008, and was convicted and sentenced to life in prison in 2011. He is currently serving a life sentence with no chance for parole for 25 years in Saskatchewan Penitentiary near Prince Albert, Canada.[4] Twitchell was inspired by the 2006–2013 TV series *Dexter* in what reporters referred to as "a new kind of crime," "murder in the digital age," in "a bizarre tangle of fact and fiction" (Henderson, 2018).

Twitchell was obsessed with the character Dexter Morgan. He ran a Dexter Facebook page in which he wrote about his real-life activities as though he was Dexter. His Facebook followers believed the Facebook page was a Dexter fan page and that the posts were fictional, not realizing that Twitchell was posting about things he was actually doing in real life. Twitchell had no criminal background, was a 1999 graduate of the Northern Alberta Institute of Technology (NAIT), and the people around him had no indication of what he was involved in. A key piece of evidence used in Twitchell's trial was a document that had been deleted but recovered from his computer titled "SKConfessions" (which stood for "Serial Killer Confessions"). In SKConfessions, Twitchell, a self-described psychopath as he wrote in a document police later found titled "Profile of a Psychopath," indicated that SKConfessions was a story of his progression to becoming a serial killer. He described his attempts to lure victims from dating sites, his failed attempt to lure and kill a prior victim, and his subsequent successful murder of Altinger. Additional evidence in his trial included testimony of a witness, Gilles Tetreault, who was his first victim of attempted murder, whom he had also lured from a dating site and attacked with a stun gun before Tetreault escaped.

It is worth examining some of the details of the story in *Dexter* to understand the nature of Twitchell's relationship with the Dexter Morgan character. In the first episode of the series, Miami police detective Harry Morgan finds Dexter Morgan as an infant traumatized and sitting in blood at a crime scene along with his older brother, a toddler. Detective Morgan took Dexter, who he thought was young enough to save to raise as his own, and sent the older brother (who he believed was traumatized beyond repair) to a mental institution. As Dexter grew up, his father recognized that he had psychopathic inclinations that he helped Dexter channel for good rather than evil. As a result of his father's mentorship, Dexter grew up to become a blood spatter analyst with the Miami Police Department who was a serial killer on the side, who killed only people who were evil themselves (including in one episode, his own brother). Thus, the Dexter Morgan character was a psychopath who used his lack of empathy and disordered personality to do "good" rather than "evil." This prosocial presentation of an antisocial and psychopathic personality provided a desirable identity for Twitchell to projectively identify with.[5]

The Mark Twitchell case is similar to earlier cases such as Mark David Chapman's murder of John Lennon and John Hinckley's assassination attempt on Ronald Reagan in that both Twitchell's MO *and* signature were intimately influenced by a media source. Twitchell was fixated on Dexter Morgan the same way Hinckley was fixated on Travis Bickle in *Taxi Driver* and Chapman was fixated on Holden Caulfield in *Catcher in the Rye*. Twitchell assumed Dexter Morgan's identity, interwove the media character into his own fantasy, and committed a crime that can only be understood through the lens of Twitchell's cognitive script that read like a *Dexter* script. Like Hinckley and Chapman, the media source that inspired Twitchell was brought up in his trial. Twitchell's crime was not simply a situation where he took an idea he saw in the media to use as his MO. Nor was he only minimally intertwined with the media content (e.g., as was the case in crimes such as the crime committed by Thomma in Thailand when he used Facebook to broadcast his crime to achieve celebrity). Rather, Twitchell was psychologically intertwined with the fictional character Dexter Morgan similar to the way in which John Hinckley was psychologically intertwined with Travis Bickel and Mark Chapman with Holden Caulfield. Drew Kenworthy, a former classmate of Twitchell's who had gone through the NAIT radio program with him, said of Twitchell. "It was almost like his reality was sort of mixed. You know, his fantasy and reality sometimes might have mixed a little bit . . . I think yeah it's possible for him to have done something like that, to have flipped it; to basically have used media as a tool" (Crime Beat TV, 2008). When Twitchell lured his real-life victim to his garage after catfishing him on the dating site Plenty of Fish, he did so to generate buzz for a "fictional" film about a serial killer he had produced in that same garage two weeks prior. Twitchell blurred the boundary between fantasy and reality in his actions and in his social media posts on his Dexter Facebook page about his activities, and that blurred boundary between reality and fiction became the very nature of his crime. His crime was even more extreme in terms of the copycat effect than the crimes of Hinckley, Chapman, and the *Grand Theft Auto* (GTA) and *Natural Born Killers* (NBK) copycats (Helfgott, 2015) because not only did Twitchell identify with and mimic the character, Dexter, he attempted to film himself doing so and used an online dating site to target his victim. This is an example of an elaborate, methodically planned act of violence that was committed under the influence of mass media and ultimately orchestrated utilizing multiple levels of mass media and digital culture, including Twitchell's filming of the crime, his Facebook fan page devoted to Dexter, and his luring of his victim through the online dating site Plenty of Fish.

Crimes that have a copycat or media-mediated component can be conceptually situated along the continuum from minor influence (shaping MO behavior, where the perpetrator takes ideas from media or digital culture or uses media as a tool to commit the crime) to major influence (the defining signature whereby the perpetrator is psychologically intertwined with, takes on the identity of, and mimics a fictional or actual person in the media). Situating media-mediated and copycat crimes along the continuum offers a heuristic through which to conceptually make sense of the ways in which mass media and digital culture can both shape (give ideas about methods) and trigger (inspire) crime and violence and provide an illustration of the broad manifestation of the influence of media and technology on criminal behavior.

Figure 2.2 shows where different case examples conceptually fall along the continuum from low to high influence.

Where these individual cases fall on the copycat continuum provides important insight into the nature of the crime. With crimes in which technology and mass media play only a minor role, understanding the way in which the media source was involved in the crime may be less important than in cases on the high end of the continuum. Police investigators, prosecutors and defense attorneys, and correctional professionals may not necessarily need to know details about the relationship between

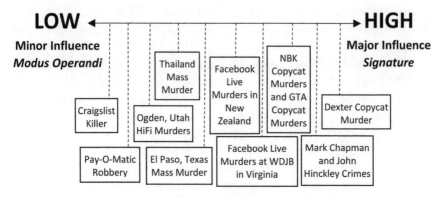

Figure 2.2 Case Examples Across the Copycat Continuum

the crime and the media source in cases that involve low influence because where perpetrators get their ideas is not centrally relevant to criminal investigation, legal determinations, or sentencing. However, in cases where media and digital culture play a major influence, knowing about the relationship between the crime and the media source is critical for adjudication, sentencing, and treatment and management. Additionally, the relationship between the perpetrator and the media source also has implications for the civil justice system in civil lawsuits involving media that has played a central role in a crime.

The Copycat Effect on Modus Operandi and Signature: Why Does It Matter?

So why does it matter whether and how media and digital culture influence MO and signature elements of criminal behavior? What are the implications for criminal justice in terms of police investigations, adjudication and sentencing, correctional management, and potential release/reentry? In identifying the level and intensity of the impact of media and technology, it is important to distinguish between a crime in which the perpetrator simply gets an idea from a movie, social media, the news, or other form of media versus a crime where the media influence is intricately woven into the offender MO, fantasy development, and the very essence of the crime. Situating crimes along the continuum of copycat influence has criminal justice implications for investigation, adjudication and sentencing, and correctional management and treatment, and reentry. Individuals whose crimes fall on the high end of the copycat continuum will engage in behaviors that look very different from those that are only minimally influenced. This information can be used in police

How Media and Technology Shape Modus Operandi and Signature Elements

investigation for the purpose of case linkage; in the adjudication process to understand the nature of the offense, as well as mitigating and aggravating factors in sentencing; and in corrections, management, treatment, and reentry to make decisions about how to manage an individual in custody.

In *Anatomy of Motive*, John Douglas says in his view from many years of observation and research:

> . . . the media can provide criminals with ideas for their crimes (both modus operandi and signature elements), may serve as an influencing factor in those already prone to violent actions, and may desensitize all of us to the real horror that is out there, but except in a few specialized types of cases, the media (and that includes pornography) do not lead otherwise good or law abiding people to commit violent antisocial acts. (Douglas & Olshaker, 1999, pp. 92–93)

So, in the study of criminal behavior, what do we make of the fact that there are cases where individuals get ideas for how to commit their crimes from media, digital, and popular culture on the one end of the continuum to cases where individuals become so completely immersed in some form of media that the media source becomes a psychological road map that drives the very nature of the crime?

Recognizing that the copycat effect can become a signature element of a crime has important criminal justice implications. In law enforcement investigations, identifying MO and signature elements of crimes is part of the investigative process. Identifying elements of a crime that involves methods that the perpetrator has taken from media sources can help direct the investigation and help link cases that involve unknown perpetrators and can also help to understand cultural forces that shape motivations in the case of crimes that have been produced through a contagion effect.

CHAPTER THREE

The Copycat Effect on Criminal Behavior: A Theory of Copycat and Media-Mediated Crime

Theory is needed to better understand the nature of the influence of media, technology, and digital culture on crime; who is influenced; and the factors and forces at play. What is the individual and cultural impact of instant access to images of violence on a global scale? How has the digital space replaced in-person interactions and environments as the place in which social (and antisocial) learning occurs, peer groups are formed, and ideas and ideologies are communicated? How specifically does digital culture influence the development of antisocial behavior, the development of antisocial scripts and schema, and the formation of criminal identity? In what ways does digital culture influence criminal behavior along the copycat continuum? A theory of copycat effect on criminal behavior will help guide empirical research to better understand, predict, and prevent copycat and media-mediated crime. A theoretical road map that guides empirical research to identify how individual, subcultural, cultural, and media-related risk factors interact to produce copycat and media-mediated crime will help sort through obstacles to research investigations that have hindered progress in understanding the effects of media violence on criminal behavior.

Technology as a Risk Factor for Criminal Behavior

Technological advances increasingly define society and culture on a global scale in ways that simultaneously create connection and disconnection (Turkle, 2011). How human beings connect and disconnect, attach, detach, and form social identity is central to theories of antisocial, psychopathy, and violent criminal behavior (Helfgott, 2019). Crime is a product of biological, psychological, sociological, phenomenological, cultural, and routine activity forces (Helfgott, 2008). Criminal social identity develops through a process that involves: 1) a crisis in identity that results in weak social bonds, peer rejection, and poor parental attachment; 2) exposure to an antisocial environment through associations with antisocial peers; 3) the need to identify with an antisocial group to increase self-esteem; and 4) personality traits that moderate the relationship between antisocial environment and development of criminal social identity (Boduszek et al., 2016). Disruption to the way people bond and form peer associations impacts development of both prosocial and antisocial identities.

With every passing decade, digital culture becomes more pervasive and central to human behavior with enormous implications for how we attach and detach as human beings. Unlike generations of the past distinguished by the ethical realm of the real with people, things, and interactions that could be physically seen, felt, and touched, today's world is a vast virtual world with limitless opportunities for exposure to new media to mediate people, communities, information, and environments. The dystopian flipside of digital culture is that instant accessibility to media-mediated images about what everyone is doing is everywhere. This media-mediated hyperreality increases opportunities for images of crime and violence to spread quickly, creates a false sense of intimacy, has the potential to dehumanize and increase conflict, and offers a portal into antisocial environments that is a risk factor for the development of a criminal social identity and media-mediated criminal behavior. Technology has the potential to humanize to increase understanding of others outside of our immediate worlds and also to distance, dissociate, and objectify others as interactions become increasingly media mediated.

Digital Culture and Violence

The shift from the ethical realm of the real to the aesthetic realm of the hyperreal and beyond with the new forms of social media, memes, and global expansion of digital culture has exacerbated the copycat effect on criminal behavior (DeCook, 2018; de Graaf, 2021; Helfgott, 2015; Mohseni

The Copycat Effect on Criminal Behavior   45

et al., 2016; Surette, 2019, 2022). Suicide clusters of the 1980s were replaced by school shootings of the 1990s, which were replaced by media-driven mass shooting contagion in the first two decades of the 21st century. In the first two decades of the 21st century there were more deaths from mass shootings than there were in the entire 20th century (Katsiyannis et al., 2018), and the shooters got younger, death tolls increased, the pace of the shootings faster, and the venue for the shootings more unpredictable (Berkowitz et al., 2019). Mass shootings have become so commonplace that we have a difficult time keeping track of all of them (Bramesco, 2019).

The Internet has abolished most of the constraints of space and time with a few clicks of the mouse (Omand, 2015), and the evolution of smartphone technology in the first decades of the 21st century made it possible for the masses to have the world at their fingertips (Campbell-Kelly & Garcia-Swartz, 2015; Islam & Want, 2014; O'Dea, 2019). In 2020 almost 4.57 billion people used the Internet, representing 59 percent of the global population, with Internet usage in China, India, and the United States ranked ahead of other countries (Clement, 2020). The 1990s cluster of school shootings and the spate of mass shootings the first two decades of the 21st century coinciding in time with the exponential increase in the worldwide digital population begs the question: What role does mass media and digital culture play in contributing to school and mass shootings and other types of crimes over the last generation? This, coupled with research showing that excessive smartphone use is associated with expressive suppression as emotion regulation, and that it is individuals with maladaptive, suppressive emotion regulation who use smartphones for nonsocial rather than social use who have the highest levels of smartphone use (Extremera et al., 2019; Rozgonjuk & Elhai, 2018), suggests that digital technology in the hands of certain individuals can have lethal consequences.

If a Book Made Them Do It, Why Blame Digital Culture?

In 1996, Barry Loukaitis killed two students and a math teacher in Moses Lake, Washington, saying, "This sure beats algebra, doesn't it?"—making reference to the story in Stephen King's novel *Rage* about Charlie Decker, a psychologically troubled high school student who brings a gun to school, kills his algebra teacher, and holds his classmates hostage.[1] In *Rage*, Charlie Decker walks into the classroom as his teacher Mrs. Underwood lectures, "So you understand that when we *increase* the number of variables, the axioms *themselves* never change." When Mrs. Underwood notices him entering, she asks him, "Do you have an office pass, Mr. Decker?" He replies. "Yes" and then takes his gun out of his belt and shoots her in the head. Decker narrates the aftermath: "Mrs. Underwood never knew what hit her, I'm sure. She fell sideways onto her desk and then rolled onto the floor, and that expectant expression never left her face" (King, 1986, p. 29). Loukaitis attributed his motivation to *Rage*, Pearl Jam's music video *Jeremy*, and the films *Natural Born Killers* and *The Basketball Diaries* (Coleman, 2004). *Rage, Natural Born Killers,* and *The Basketball Diaries* were also linked to other mass school shootings in the cluster. Stephen King asked his publisher to remove *Rage* from publication after seeing the effect it had on school shooters. King wrote *Rage* in 1965 when he was still in high school[2] and acknowledged that he wrote the novel in a world very different from the present day: ". . . 1965 was a different world, one where you didn't have to take off your shoes before boarding a plane and there were no metal detectors at the entrances to high schools" (Adwar, 2014).

A question that often arises in conversations about the role of mass media and digital culture in copycat crime is what role digital culture plays if legacy media such as books, magazines, and newspapers inspire copycat crime and violence (Surette, 2015a, 2019). If Loukaitis and other mass school shooters were influenced by a book, then how can it be said that digital culture is any more of a powerful influence than a book or even a story told around a campfire? What role did digital culture play? The answer is that digital culture and mass media allowed the information about the book *Rage* to rapidly and widely spread information about mass school shootings as a way to solve social problems and created an opportunity for performance crime (Surette, 2015a). *Rage* is ranked higher than any other novel as one of top 100 most sought-after books.[3] Used copies of the first printing paperback are on sale online for anywhere between $700 and upwards of $2000 (Adwar, 2014).

Was it the book itself that made *Rage* a favorite of mass school shooters? Or was it the word on the digital street that brought attention to the book, giving troubled edge-sitters a pop cultural facilitator? A similar thing happened with the book *Catcher in the Rye* which became a favorite of celebrity stalker murderers. After Chapman claimed he shot John Lennon in 1980 to be a "somebody" like *Catcher in the Rye*'s character Holden Caulfield, other murderers used *Catcher in the Rye* in their crimes, including Hinckley. In 1989 Robert Bardo shot and killed 21-year-old actress Rebecca Schaeffer who starred in the TV show *My Sister Sam*. After stalking Schaeffer for three years, Bardo traveled to California from his home in Arizona, went to Schaeffer's home with a copy of *Catcher in the Rye* in his back pocket, shot her point-blank in the chest, and then tossed the book onto the roof of another building as if he believed it was evidence after he fled the scene. Bardo was also said to have been emulating a similar crime in which actress Theresa Saldana was stabbed at her doorstep in 1982 by an obsessed fan named Arthur Richard Johnson, who hired a private investigator to find her home address (Fuqua, 2020). Was it the stories in *Rage* and *Catcher in the Rye* that were appealing to these murderers? Was it the spread of information about these books through media and popular culture that made them hot commodities in the minds of already troubled individuals who were searching for identity and celebrity and power? Or was it the result of mental health conditions; personality characteristics; demographics; or social, situational, and environmental circumstances of individuals who could have picked up anything—a book, a TV show, a news story, a film, a video game, or something someone told them—that would have inspired them to commit murder? These questions need to be unraveled to understand copycat crime.

The image of the mass school shooter as an isolated, lone, unpopular, troubled young male whose murderous behavior is a problem-solving strategy and reaction to years of perceived torment and bullying is a powerful message. Mass media and digital culture enable this message to be spread quickly and broadly with deadly consequences. Mass school shootings receive disproportionate amounts of news media coverage (Hoffner et al., 2017; Schildkraut et al., 2018; Silva & Capellan, 2018, 2019), media attention to mass killings generates short-term (Towers et al., 2015) and long-term copycat effects (Lankford & Tomek, 2017), mass media and the Internet disseminate scripts connected with copycat violence (Sitzer, 2013), media images of school shootings offer an "expectable" path of action in the performance of masculinity (Chong, 2012; Gerbner et al., 2014; Katz, 2006), and extreme violent media consumption is a risk factor in school shootings (Meindl & Ivy, 2017; O'Toole, 2000). Mass shootings have involved perpetrators influenced by prior mass shootings and/or media images of violence that permeate digital culture, and when a mass shooting occurs there is an increase in the probability of another event within 13 days, on average (Meindl & Ivy, 2017). Some argue that the study of mass school shooters has taken several wrong turns, in particular the links made by politicians, advocates, and scholars to elements of digital culture such as violent video games (Ferguson et al., 2011). However, the vast amount of research on media effects suggests that media plays an enormous role in what mass shooters think about.

The Broader Consequences of Media Images of Violence

There is also research to suggest that exposure to traumatic events depicted in the media such as the mass shooting in Christchurch, New Zealand can result in PTSD and generalized trauma for all affected from victims and their families and friends, from first responders such as law enforcement, emergency services personnel, and forensic scientists involved in medico-legal death investigation, to broader society (Franklin, 2019). "Media outlets select a handful of events and turn them into stories that convey meanings, offer solutions, associate certain groups of people with particular kinds of behavior, and provide pictures of the world" (Silva & Capellan, 2018, p. 1315).

In Loukaitis's case, *Rage* was only one of several cultural artifacts he mentioned as influences, which included the films *The Basketball Diaries* and *Natural Born Killers*. *Natural Born Killers* (*NBK*), written by Quentin Tarantino and directed by Oliver Stone, has been referred to as "the first mass media production to vehemently condemn the mass media themselves for inducing criminal behavior" (Rafter, 2006, p. 63), "one of the most controversial films of the nineties" (Boyle, 2001, p. 311), "Way cooler than Manson" (Courtwright, 1998, p. 28), and is to date, the most copycatted film of all time. *NBK* has been linked to school shootings—Loukaitis; Carneal in Paducah, Kentucky, in 1997; and Columbine High School in Littleton, Colorado, in 1999 (Brooks, 2002; Lasky, 2012) (all of which were also linked to *The Basketball Diaries*) to a spate of teenage male-female spree murder duos (Boyle, 2001, 2005), a case in which a 14-year-old boy decapitated a 13-year-old classmate because he wanted to "be famous like *NBK*," and other murders dating long after the film came out, including a murder in 2008 in which a 19-year-old strangled his 18-year-old girlfriend after watching *NBK* as many as 20 times[4] (Reynolds, 2015).

Digital culture and media-mediated images have become a primary source of social learning. This is especially true when it comes to crime and violence. Digital images of violence are hot products in the global economic marketplace that travel fast and do not need translation into different languages (Gerbner et al., 2014). Media images of violence are emotionally charged, easily cognitively primed (Bushman, 1998), and appealing to aggressively primed individuals (Langley et al., 1992) with pronounced effects for individuals who show attention problems and impulsiveness (Swing & Anderson, 2014) and low empathy and risk of criminality (Chadee et al., 2017). A generation ago copycat crimes could be considered a relatively rare phenomena committed by psychologically disturbed, media-illiterate individuals who were not digitally sophisticated enough to process media images as fiction. Today, with digital culture comingled with everyday life as a central facilitator for communication and daily information, it is increasingly important to understand how mass media, technology, and digital culture influence criminal behavior and violence.

A Theoretical Framework for Understanding Copycat and Media-Mediated Crime

Criminologists have noted the lack of empirical research on copycat crime, with the designation of a crime as a copycat often made by journalists or others based on statements made by perpetrators during the crime or the investigation or anecdotal reports (Coleman, 2004; Ferrara, 2016; Helfgott, 2015; Surette, 2014b, 2016b). The field of criminology and criminal justice has focused very little research attention toward the topic of copycat crime. A single scholar—Dr. Ray Surette—has produced the bulk of the empirical research conducted to date on copycat crime (Doley et al., 2013; Surette, 1990, 2002, 2013a, 2013b, 2014b, 2015a, 2015b, 2016a, 2019, 2021 2022; Surette & Maze, 2015). Copycat crimes represent approximately 25 percent of all crime (Surette, 2002, 2014b, 2022), and the broader category of media-mediated performance crime, where people commit crime for performance either willingly or unwillingly, has become increasingly pervasive in the new social media reality (Surette, 2015a). With the increasing role media and digital culture play in everyday life, the development of a theoretical framework for the empirical study of copycat and media-mediated crime is long overdue.

A theoretical model of copycat crime is needed to understand the nature and dynamics of media-mediated crimes and to empirically investigate the copycat effect on criminal behavior. Development of a theoretical model and empirical framework for examining copycat crime requires interdisciplinary synthesis of theory and research from multiple disciplines such as psychology, sociology, communications, criminology, and cultural studies to make sense of how social learning, media violence, media effects, social contagion, cultural transmission, celebrity culture, personality theory, etiology, and risk and protective factors for criminal behavior intersect to produce copycat crime. Digital and mass media technologies interact with individual, situational, social, and cultural factors to produce a web of criminogenic influence. Ultimately, mass media and digital culture can be understood as a technology-related risk factor for criminal behavior that produces copycat and media-mediated crime (Helfgott, 2008, 2015).

Development of a theoretical model and empirical framework to investigate copycat crime requires drawing from multiple literatures, including research on media effects (Bushman, 1995, 1998; Bushman & Huesmann, 2006, 2012; Bryant & Zillman, 2002; Felson, 1996; Gentile & Bushman, 2012; Hess et al., 1999; Riddle et al., 2011; Savage, 2003; Sparks & Sparks, 2002; Slater et al., 2003, 2004); the Cultural Indicators Project (Gerbner, 1994; Gerbner et al., 2014); personality theory, violence, and aggression

(Meloy, 1988, 1992); generalized imitation (Meindl & Ivy, 2018); the copycat effect (Coleman, 2004; Fister, 2005; Peterson-Mantz, 2002; Surette, 1990, 2002, 2013a, 2013b, 2014b, 2015a, 2015b, 2016a, 2022; Surette & Chadee, 2020); performance crime (Surette, 2015a); violence contagion (Fagan et al., 2007; Forsyth & Gibbs, 2020; Huesmann, 2012); the aesthetics of murder (Black, 1991, 2002); the psychology of stalking (Meloy, 1998; Orion, 1997; Zona et al., 1998); the phenomenology of crime (Katz, 1988); fantasy development (Ellison, 2012); cultural criminology (Ferrell, 1995, 1999; Ferrell & Hamm, 1998; Ferrell & Sanders, 1995; Ferrell et al., 2015; Wooden & Blazak, 2001); celebrity obsession and culture (Harvey, 2002); video game violence (Anderson & Bushman, 2001; Anderson & Dill, 2000; Anderson & Murphey, 2003); gender, hypermasculinity, violence, aggression, and media (Gerbner et al., 2014; Katz, 2006; Larson, 2003); and violent film analysis (Manning, 1998; Newman, 1998; Shafer, 2009). An integrative theoretical model of copycat crime and media-mediated violence will provide foundation for empirical study of copycat crime, better understanding of the copycat effect on criminal behavior, and has practical implications for policy and practice for crime prevention to reduce technology-related risk factors for criminal behavior.

Key Areas of Theory and Research

Understanding the copycat effect on criminal behavior requires drawing from multiple disciplines and perspectives in criminology and criminal justice, psychology, and media and cultural studies and other fields. Criminology as a field has not yet incorporated copycat crime into mainstream criminological theories, though lines of research and knowledge bases in other disciplines have steadily grown. A theory of copycat and media-mediated violence integrating the limited empirical research on copycat crime with the more developed areas of research in media effects, cultural criminology, hypermasculinity and violence, and risk and threat assessment offers a theoretical framework for empirical investigation of the copycat effect on criminal behavior (Helfgott, 2015).

Media-Mediated Violence Scripts and Schemas

Six decades of media violence research have shown that exposure to media violence increases the likelihood of aggression with effects demonstrated across cultures (Anderson et al., 2017). Methodological challenges have made it difficult to show that violent media directly *causes* aggression and violence, though findings reveal that media violence is a

The Copycat Effect on Criminal Behavior 51

significant factor that contributes to aggression and violence (Bushman & Huesmann, 2012), influences cognitive scripts and schemas (Anderson et al., 2003; Helfgott, 2014; Neklason, 2019), and is a significant public health problem (Browne & Hamilton-Giachritis, 2005).

Children learn complex social scripts (e.g., rules on how to interpret, understand, and handle situations) and schemas (e.g., beliefs, attitudes) from role models they see around them. Parents, teachers, peers, toys, books, fairy tales, songs, magazines, billboards, TV shows, movies, video games, social media, and digital memes help teach the scripts a person is expected to follow in any given culture. Adolescents have "a limited repertoire of 'cultural scripts' or 'strategies of action' that they can draw on to resolve their social problems" (Newman et al., 2004, p. 148). Children and adolescents largely rely on symbolic reality they draw from popular culture in the formation of their cognitive scripts. The media is a primary driver of societal-level social scripts for adolescents (Storer & Strohl, 2017). Criminal behavior is the complex product of the convergence of biological, psychological, sociological, routine activity/opportunity, phenomenological, and cultural factors at a particular time and place for a specific individual. Different people are more or less influenced by different factors and forces. Youth and adults who are high media consumers tend to be more influenced by pop culture, are more technology savvy, and are more likely to weave information from media sources than older people (Helfgott, 2008, 2015).

Individuals who hold cognitive scripts and schemas that involve aggressive fantasies (Gilbert & Daffern, 2017) have the potential to produce antisocial, criminal, and violent behavior are edge-sitters whose antisocial and criminal behavior can be facilitated and exacerbated by media and digital culture (Ferrara, 2016; Helfgott, 2008). These individuals hold cognitions and ideologies shaped by early maladaptive schemas— dysfunctional broad and pervasive patterns of perceiving and relating to the world that consist of emotions, cognitions, memories, and bodily sensations about oneself and others developed in childhood and adolescence that exist and are elaborated across the life course (Tremblay & Dozois, 2009). Maladaptive and distorted cognitive schemas co-occurring with identity disturbance and personality characteristics combined with easily accessible digital antisocial environment is a toxic mix. For these edge-sitters, digital space with like-minded individuals becomes a digitally deviant subculture that offers a community that insulates, isolates, and validates distorted cognitive scripts through a reflexive spiral of media-mediated cognitions and fantasies that can lead to antisocial and criminal behavior in the form of media-mediated copycat crime.

The incel movement is a prime example of how digital culture insulates and validates distorted cognitive scripts as well as the ways in which media and digital culture affect violence-prone individuals immersed in hypermasculine subcultures (Bosman et al., 2019; Elise, 2014a, 2014b; Helfgott, 2014). Incels find a community that supports their view that women who won't have sex with them are called "Stacys" and men who are successful alpha men who have sex with the "Stacys" are called "Chads" (Hines, 2019), and where their misogynist disordered cognitive scripts find validation and reinforcement. Incel-related violence has been rising since the mass shooting by incel-hero Elliot Rodger and has been linked to the deaths of at least 53 people (Tomkinson et al., 2020). Incel killers are considered a dangerous threat to society and university communities (Richter & Richter, 2019). Research using a sample of 18- to 30-year-old heterosexual men in the United States found that the stress of living up to the norms of masculinity and endorsement of incel traits are associated with using powerful weapons against enemies and violent rape fantasies (Scaptura & Boyle, 2020).

Cultural artifacts such as literature, art, film, mass media, computer games, and popular culture make their way into these sorts of cognitive scripts. Digital culture exacerbates the ways that pop culture enters cognitive scripts globally spread through individuals, communities, and subcultures. Technologies are "human creations that facilitate structuring of opportunities to solve real-life problems" that operate as physical and ideational tools (Lee & Daiute, 2019, p. 5). Digital culture enables ideas and images to make their way in a split second around the world with a power of influence like never before seen in the history of humankind. It is increasingly important to understand how the speed at which digital information is transferred and how the salience and aesthetics of these images facilitate and exacerbate the copycat effect on criminal behavior.

Generalized Imitation and Contagion

How media and digital culture make their way into individual and cultural scripts is a matter of two conceptually distinct phenomena—general imitation and contagion. Generalized imitation, rooted in social learning theory (SLT), is the learned ability to perform behaviors that are like observed or described behaviors, even when performance is delayed. People learn behaviors from three sources—direct (family, peers, and other close influential people), community (people in a geographical community or neighborhood), and the media (news, television, Internet) (Bandura, 1977). General imitation is a product of social learning and the

The Copycat Effect on Criminal Behavior 53

human tendency to mimic others' modeling behaviors whether models are people they know from real-world experience or people they see in media and digital culture.

The learned ability to mimic behaviors is a skill acquired at an early age and gradually strengthened through life experiences. Neuroscientists have discovered that mirror neurons promote mimicry and long-term imitation. The mimicry of aggressive behavior requires only a simple mirror representation of an observed act (Bushman & Huesmann, 2012). Generalized imitation does not mean that the imitator will always or ever perform an exact copy of the model's behavior, but rather a behavior with similar characteristics. If someone were to watch a violent film and then engage in similar violent behavior at a later time in the future and that person's likelihood of engaging in violent behaviors increased as a result of watching someone else engage in violence, then imitation could be said to be an important contributing factor.

The General Aggression Model (GAM) is a comprehensive, integrative framework for understanding human aggression that has been applied to understand media violence effects. The GAM explains media violence effects with focus on social, cognitive, developmental, and biological factors, including elements from theories of aggression including social learning theory, script theory, and social interaction theories and posits that human aggression is influenced by knowledge structures (beliefs and attitudes, perceptual schemata, expectation schemata, and behavioral scripts) that affect social-cognitive phenomena ,including perception, interpretation, decision, and behavior (Allen et al., 2018). The General Learning Model (GLM) is a model of behavioral learning that examines behavior at two levels—the acquisition of personal characteristics that influence behavior developed over the long term and how an individual's personal characteristics play out within the context of situations. This model explains media violence with attention to how repeated exposure influences attitudes, stereotypes, beliefs, schemas, and scripts in some individuals. Once the feelings and attitudes are internalized, these learned characteristics influence how the individual responds in any given situation—what feelings they experience, what cognitions are activated, and how physiologically aroused they become. Media can influence the individual's characteristics through long-term violent media exposure, and short-term exposure to media can provide cues for behavior in the moment (Warburton & Anderson, 2022).

Correspondence between a media consumer and a media character and the level of media consumption affect how repeated exposure to media violence will become internalized and integrated into cognitive scripts and ultimately result in generalized imitation. People are more likely to imitate those who are demographically like themselves, competent, of high social status, who are seen being rewarded (Meindl & Ivy, 2017). Research on media imitation of aggression in girls shows that the correlation between violent television viewing and aggressive fantasies in girls is stronger if the individual identified with a female character (Moise & Huessman, 1996). Cultivation theory (the theory that long-term exposure to media shapes perception) plays an additional role in the degree to which a person will imitate a media source. Social learning, cultivation theory, the GAM, and the GLM offer important information to explain why some individuals are more susceptible to violent media effects than others.

Copycat Crime

While much has been made in the media about the topic of copycat crime (e.g., Ferguson, 2018; Ferrera, 2016) and there has been some scholarly work and documentaries on the subject (e.g., Claroni et al., 2016; Coleman, 2004; Enos, 1999; Surette, 2022), empirical research on copycat crime is extremely limited with most of the empirical research on copycat crime conducted by Surette (2002, 2013a, 2014b, 2015a, 2016a, 2019, 2021, 2022) and colleagues (Surette & Maze, 2015; Surette & Chadee, 2020; Surette et al., 2021). Empirical findings from this work offer a starting point for further study that, guided by theory, provides a framework for examination of the many unanswered questions and aspects of copycat and media-mediated crime.

In one of the first empirical examinations specifically focused on copycat crime, Surette (2002) surveyed 68 incarcerated male serious and violent juvenile offenders and found that 26 percent indicated they had committed a crime they had seen or heard about in the media with the most common copycat practice being borrowing media crime techniques. That same year, a dissertation study conducted by Peterson-Manz (2002) used a different methodological approach comparing homicides from 1990 to 1994 (9442 cases) with news reports of murder, finding that the number of homicides was significantly greater in the two weeks following front-page news articles covering homicide.

One of the primary research questions on the topic of copycat crime centers on whether mass media directly *causes* crime and violence or whether media and digital culture operate as a risk factor or as a shaper of criminal behavior that would have been committed either way. Surette (2013a) examined two competing perspectives on copycat crime—whether the media operates as a "trigger," directly causing crime, or a "catalyst or rudder," shaping rather than generating crime. The study simultaneously examined the effects of "real world crime models" that explain crime as a product of social learning through the real world, examining risk factors such as delinquent peers and criminogenic family members as compared with "media crime models" that explain crime as a product of social learning through media with a direct criminogenic effect of media exposure. The results suggest that the media operates as more of a "rudder" than a "trigger" for crime. The findings also reveal that young male offenders exposed to both real and media crime sources are at particularly high risk for copycat criminal behavior. Thus, the media-copycat link was found to be tied to both real-world *and* media models:

> The media-copycat link is associated with both exposure to real world crime models and pro-criminogenic attitudes toward media crime content. It is not felt to be due to independent exposure to media modeled criminality. That is, pre-inclined offenders who were also exposed to real world criminality are hypothesized to seek out media crime models and extract crime instructions. These results did not support strong direct media exposure trigger effects on these inmates. Instead, a model of media influence where the media operate as stylistic catalysts is more supported. The media is best conceived as a rudder for crime more than a trigger. (Surette, 2013a, p. 407)

This finding is important because it sheds light on how mass media and digital culture operate as a technology-related risk factor for criminal behavior among other risk factors such as demographic factors, environmental and situational factors, and criminogenic factors. The study found that it was younger males with real-world crime models "who read less and spent more time web-surfing and playing electronic games and who perceived the media as a good source of knowledge on how to commit crimes and were interested in media crime content were most likely to have copycat histories" (Surette, 2013a, p. 407).

Surette and Chadee (2020) extended research on copycat crime prevalence from the previous focus on incarcerated individuals to nonincarcerated adults and found that 10 percent of the nonincarcerated general population have considered committing a copycat crime and about 5 percent have attempted one. This finding raises the question: If 10 percent of the general (nonincarcerated) population would consider committing a copycat crime, are these individuals already crime-prone, or are media and digital culture providing a vehicle for social learning that may move the needle from media as a shaper and rudder to more of a trigger? As digital culture becomes the primary space in which social, emotional, and learning now occurs (Walker, 2020), this question becomes even more important.

Much of what is known about copycat crime comes from anecdotal accounts where an individual perpetrator is linked in the media. Columbine killers Klebold and Harris were said to have been influenced by multiple forms of media, including the computer game *Doom*, the films *Natural Born Killers* and the *Basketball Diaries*, and the music of Marilyn Manson. The black trench coats they wore resembled Leonardo DiCaprio's character's jacket in *The Basketball Diaries*, and information gleaned in Klebold and Harris's "Basement Tapes" (Gibbs and Roche, 1999), including documented references to *NBK* (Klebold, 2016), suggests a media-crime link. However, the question of what evidence is needed to establish a crime as a copycat crime is an important one for the purposes of empirical research. Surette (2016a) offers a tool to determine whether a crime is in fact a copycat crime. For example, in the UK murder of 2-year-old James Bulger by Robert Thompson and Jon Venables, two 10-year-old boys, the crime was said to be a copycat of the film *Child's Play 3*. There was evidence that Venable's father had rented the film; however, the father denied that the boys had ever seen it (Kirby, 1993; Nowicka, 1993).

Surette's (2015a) research on performance crime and social media provides a building block to better understanding how mass media and digital culture operate as risk factors for new criminal behaviors committed for performance and celebrity. While there is a long history of offenders communicating with police (Guillen, 2002), only the crime of terrorism has been committed predominantly for the express purpose of performance. The advent and rise of social media have created an entirely new form of crime as performance:

> "Performances" are no longer rare events that are place and time bound to physical stages and scheduled broadcasts; they are now ephemeral renditions constantly created and repeatedly distributed in millions of social media interactions. The irony is that legacy media performances were created for wide heterogeneous audiences, but access was limited by time, place and medium. In contrast, new media performances are usually created for small homogeneous audiences, but access is often unbounded due to their digital nature. In this new social media reality, the altered nature of a performance has had significant effects on criminal justice. (Surette, 2015a, p. 197)

Performance crime is a new technology-driven form of crime in which motivation for the crime is to achieve celebrity and notoriety. While

The Copycat Effect on Criminal Behavior 57

terrorism has historically been committed as performance, the motive underlying the performance element of terrorism is very different. Terrorism is an ideologically motivated crime that requires an audience to terrorize in order to get a particular ideological point across. The performance element of terrorism could be considered then to be the modus operandi—the method by which the crime is committed motivated by ideology. Contrary to terrorism, performance crime is solely motivated by the desire for celebrity, notoriety, and the use of crime to achieve identity.

Another product of technological advance and digital culture is the role of the "meme" as a media source for crime mimicry. A copycat crime meme is a digital example of performance crime that involves "purposeful recording, sharing, and uploading of criminal performances to a waiting audience" (Surette, 2019, pp. 18–19). Surette (2019) examined the role of the viral "copycat crime meme" called "ghost riding the whip" using *Google Trends* and *YouTube* posting analysis, examining the longevity of the meme, its diffusion across social media, and traits that made it successful.[5] The "ghost riding the whip" is the precursor to copycat crime memes that have become widespread in the years since (e.g., "Bird Box Challenge," "All Lives Splatter"). The ghost riding meme originated in 2004 in Oakland, California, as part of the "hyphy" hip-hop movement that generated impromptu public gatherings that revolved around car stunts. The "ghost riding the whip" meme depicted drivers exiting their cars and dancing on top or beside a moving driverless vehicle with the objective to create the illusion of a ghost driving the car, or "whip." This meme spread from the small Oakland community to mainstream teens and adults across the United States within a three-month period via social media. Thousands mimicked the meme, committing reckless moving vehicle violations. Viral video memes like the "ghost riding the whip" present a new media form that spreads quickly through social media and fills a social need to participate in a culture of "networked individualism" within which participants "construct and highly value their digital identities" through a visual social media community (Surette, 2019, p. 4).

The "ghost riding the whip" meme contained successful traits that exacerbate the copycat effect: Flawed masculinity, humor, simplicity, and attractive ghost riders wearing expensive clothing and bling. The "ghost riding" meme spread faster and longer through social media than did memes spread from earlier periods through 19th-century and 20th-century legacy media such as newspapers and television. Whereas legacy media memes have historically spread outward and downward (spreading and then declining), the ghost riding meme spread outward but not downward, "diffusing up from a lower economic class to a middle class accompanied by an urban to suburban spread" (Surette, 2019, p. 17). The ghost riding the whip meme illustrates the difference between digital culture and legacy media. Surette's study also found that reading was a possible insulator of copycat crime—the more a respondent read, the less likely they were to report past copycat behaviors, while new interactive media (e.g., engaging with the Internet, playing a video game) was significantly related to copycat behaviors, with increases in both media-related activities positively correlated with increased copycat scores.

Empirical research conducted by Surette offers a starting point for systematic examination of the copycat effect on criminal behavior to better understand how mass media and digital culture influence crime. Understanding how individual, cultural, and media factors influence and/or exacerbate the copycat effect is critical to understanding criminal events that involve mimetic behaviors with implications for criminal justice practice and has implications for law enforcement (e.g., investigation, interrogation, and case linkage), the courts (criminal and civil), and corrections (treatment, management, and reentry). Many unanswered questions remain.

Media Effects

Media effects research has focused on key theoretical areas. Six theoretical mechanisms have been identified in the literature that contribute to the knowledge base on the influence of violent media (Perse, 2001; Sparks, 2016; Sparks & Sparks, 2002):

1. **Catharsis:** Media violence provides a cathartic outlet that allows viewers to engage in fantasy aggression that reduces the need to carry out aggressive behavior.
2. **Social Learning:** Media characters serve as role models. If people see aggressive characters being rewarded rather than punished for the behavior, they will be more likely to imitate the behavior.
3. **Priming:** Exposure to violent media images plants aggressive and violent cues in people's minds, making them easily cognitively accessible. These cues interact with the viewer's emotional state and can increase the likelihood of aggressive behavior.
4. **Arousal:** People become physiologically aroused when they view media violence in a way that intensifies the emotional state of the viewer.
5. **Desensitization:** The more violent media a person consumes, the more dulled a person's sensitivity to violence will become. This can contribute to aggressive behavior by reducing the recognition that aggression and violence are behaviors that should be curtailed.

6. *Cultivation and Fear:* Viewing violent media cultivates a particular social reality and induces high levels of fear that can persist for days, months, or years after the initial exposure.

All six of these theoretical areas have been explored at length in the media effects literature, and all but catharsis theory is empirically supported. Research from the Cultural Indicators Project on the effects of TV violence (Gerbner, 1994; Gerbner et al., 2014) coupled with the media effects research suggests that the "scientific debate over whether media violence increases aggression and violence is essentially over" (Anderson et al., 2003, p. 81) and no one is immune to the powerful effects of media violence. However, the underlying psychological processes, magnitude of media-violence effects, and the factors that mediate media violence effects remain underexplored.

Existing research has examined the impact of media violence on aggression. Studies that have specifically focused on criminal aggression yield different results and have failed to support the causal link between viewing violent media and criminal behavior (Savage, 2004). Meta-analyses of studies of the effects of media violence on criminal aggression show statistically significant effects, but effect sizes are smaller than those found between media violence and general aggression (Savage & Yancey, 2008). Various factors likely play a role in how viewing violent media influences criminal behavior, including viewer characteristics, social-environmental influences, the nature of media content, and the level and interaction with the media source (Helfgott, 2008, 2015).

Violence can be understood from risk factor and etiological perspectives (Andrews & Bonta, 2016; Rutter, 2003). Etiology refers to cause, while risk factors increase the likelihood that the outcome will occur. Understanding how digital culture operates as a risk factor for copycat and media-mediated crime and the role digital culture plays in existing theories of criminal behavior is critical. Violent media images have long-term effects for children and short-term priming effects for adults (Bushman & Huesmann, 2006); can increase a hostile worldview, physiological arousal, aggressive thoughts and behavior, and angry feelings (Bushman & Huesmann, 2012); and are particularly impactful for adolescent males, who tend to have less social disinhibition to aggression, view more violent media, and exhibit increased physical and verbal aggression in response to violent media exposure (Wiedeman et al., 2015). The risk factors for criminal behavior and violence include individual risk factors (e.g., being male, low IQ, hyperactivity, history of violent victimization, early aggressive behavior, personality characteristics, and personality disorder symptoms); family risk factors (e.g., low parental involvement, low emotional attachment to parents or caregivers, parental criminality or substance abuse); peer risk factors (e.g., delinquent peers, social rejection by peers); and community risk factors (e.g., high social disorganization and transiency) (Andrews and Bonta, 2016; Reising et al., 2019). Individual protective factors include individual factors (e.g., intolerance toward deviance, high educational aspirations, positive social orientation); family protective factors (e.g., connectedness to family, shared activities with parents, involvement in social activities, and consistent presence of a parent during key times throughout the day); and peer protective factors (e.g., close peer relationships, membership in a peer group that does not condone antisocial behavior, and involvement in prosocial activities) (Lösel & Farrington, 2012; Ttofi et al., 2016).

Violent media consumption is one of many risk factors for aggression, criminal behavior, and violence. Hostile attribution bias, being male, prior involvement in a physical fight, prior physical victimization, and parental media involvement combined with media violence exposure can increase the likelihood of aggression combined with other risk factors. "Exposure to violent media is not the only risk factor for aggression, or even the most important risk factor, but it is one important risk factor" (Gentile & Busman, 2012, p. 149). Some risk factors are large (e.g., substance abuse), some are moderate (e.g., being male), and some are small (e.g., media exposure). Media violence is a lower risk factor than substance abuse, being male, and weak social ties but a greater risk factor than low IQ, abusive parents, antisocial peers, and coming from a broken home (Donnerstein, 2011; Sparks, 2016). All risk factors play an important role in increasing the likelihood of criminal behavior and violence.

To understand how the risk and protective factors model plays out in the development of criminal and antisocial identity, it is important to examine how criminal identity develops. Criminal identity develops from a complex interplay between important psychosocial factors including identity disturbance that weakens social bonds, exposure to a antisocial environment and peers, a need to identify with antisocial and criminal groups to protect self-esteem, and moderating personality traits (Boduszek et al., 2016). As digital culture becomes the social space within which increasing numbers of people communicate, engage, and interact with others—through the aesthetic realm of the hyperreal rather than the ethical realm of the real—individuals with identity disturbance and moderating personality traits become exposed to antisocial environments populated with antisocial peers and join groups that insulate, isolate, and validate distorted cognitive scripts and schemas that fuel the copycat effect on criminal behavior and violence.

One of the obstacles to theory and research on copycat crime has been resistance, in culture and in science, to recognizing media as a risk factor for crime and violence. Sparks (2016) asks, "Why is there such resistance to what the science of media effects has clearly revealed?" (p. 129). Much of this resistance is rooted in the common claim that many people consume violent media but only a small few mimic what they see. Even in cases where it can be established that the perpetrator identically mimicked something seen in the media, with other risk factors for crime, it is challenging to establish a causal or strong connection between watching a violent film or playing a violent video game and committing a violent act. However, if most scholars agree that the evidence converges showing that exposure to media violence increases aggressive behavior, "why has scholarly and public debate on this topic produced so much controversy?" (Sparks & Sparks, 2002, p. 277).

There are disconnections in scholarly literature that explain resistance that has stalled research on copycat crime. First, it is difficult to unravel the findings from the large number of studies on media violence. Some authors completely deny any causal role, others identify media as a significant risk factor, and the large body of research establishing a connection between media and aggression (but not media and criminal aggression) make it difficult to sort out the complexities in the media-crime-violence relationship that could advance systematic empirical research. Second, making sense of the complex media-crime-violence relationship requires pulling from multiple and divergent disciplines and lines of research, requiring scholars to step outside of their traditional disciplinary demarcations—in some cases way outside—to include cultural studies, media studies, cultural criminology, and alternative research methods such as autoethnography and narrative criminology (Earle, 2021, Ferrell & Hamm, 1998; Rice & Maltz, 2018) and creative mixed-method research design (Helfgott, 2018). Examination of the media-crime-violence relationship requires an integrated theoretical framework pulling from psychology, criminology, cultural criminology, cultural studies, media studies, computer science, science and technology, literature, and the arts.

Media effects scholars have identified reasons why people deny media effects (Strasburger et al., 2014):

1. "The Third-Person Effect"—People think media has a stronger effect on others than on themselves.

2. "Faulty Reasoning"—People believe that since they consume violent media and have not mimicked what they see, this proves there is no effect, even though research shows small effect sizes (equivalent to risk factors that are often thought of as playing a causal role in crime such as delinquent peers and abusive parents).

3. "Refusal to Believe the Evidence"—Refusal to believe thousands of research studies to "buck the establishment" to promote themselves and their research.

4. "Cognitive Dissonance"—Psychological discomfort holding two dissonant thoughts at the same time—that media is fun and entertaining and that it can also cause harm.

5. "Psychological Reactance"—The unpleasant tension from the idea that someone is trying to limit one's freedom by restricting media.

6. "Catharsis Theory"—The idea that violent media serves a cathartic function, purging negative unhealthy emotions even though research has consistently shown that the catharsis hypothesis is not supported.

7. "Hollywood Denials"—Media makers in the entertainment industry highlight violent media that has not shown any negative media effects and refuse to take responsibility for harmful effects, which has a high economic cost.

8. "A Lot of Media Are Good for Children and Teenagers"—High-quality media available for children such as *Sesame Street* and other programming shows that media critics are overly negative and shortsighted.

9. "The Media Themselves Don't Often Report on Negative Effects"—The media downplays the negative effects of violent media. In fact, media contributes to more harm than does exposure to asbestos and secondhand smoke.

Thus, while media effects scholars have arrived at a consensus on the effects of media violence,[6] resistance remains.

Taking together the research on media violence on aggression and violence in the laboratory studies (keeping in mind that studying media effects on real-life violent behavior is much more difficult), the media effect on violence is small and the effect on aggression is small to moderate (U.S. Office of the Surgeon General, 2001). Violent media accounts for 10 to 15 percent of the variance in aggressive behavior (Boxer et al., 2009; Sparks, 2016). This means that 85 to 90 percent of the variance is attributable to something else. In statistical terms however, for one factor to account for 10 to 15 percent in explaining aggressive behavior is extraordinary. The average effect sizes of exposure to media violence on aggression range from small ($r = 0.13$) to large ($r = 0.64$). Studies on the effect of media violence on violent behavior is more limited, with smaller effect sizes from $r = 0.06$ to $r = 0.13$ in cross-sectional studies and from $r = 0.00$ to $r = 0.22$ in longitudinal studies. Table 3.1 shows exposure to TV violence in relation to other risk factors for violence for children and adolescents.

The most important point here is that small statistical effects can translate into large social problems with tragic consequences. Media violence critics note that if one person out of millions of violent media consumers is inspired to mimic violence, this small statistical effect is unpreventable. However, if one person out of millions is inspired to mimic media violence and murders one or many people, it is imperative to study what happened to develop predictive models and preventive measures. If that 0.13 effect size was the risk factor that was the edge-sitter's tipping point that led to harm to a single victim, let alone many victims, understanding that risk factor is of enormous value and a public safety imperative.

Cultural Criminology

The branch of criminology most suited to understanding the intersection of media, technology, and digital culture is cultural criminology (Ferrell, 1995, 1999; Ferrell & Hamm, 1998; Ferrell & Sanders, 1995, Ferrell et al., 2015; Ilan, 2019). Cultural criminology examines the reflexive relationship between culture, crime, and criminalization from multidisciplinary and interdisciplinary perspectives. Cultural criminology views crime and its control as "cultural products" (Hayward & Young, 2004, p. 259). Cultural criminology recognizes that the response to crime must be understood within a world "always in flux" and with recognition that "human culture has long remained in motion." This view considers the "plethora of cultural referents carried by the globalized media" that influence techniques of neutralization and motivations for crime. From the perspective of cultural criminology, ". . . the very modus operandi of the criminal act itself, all emerge today as manifold, plural, and increasingly global" (Ferrell et al., 2015, p. 6).

With its focus on the reflexive, reciprocal, dynamic, and evolving relationship between crime and culture, cultural criminology considers how cultural (and subcultural) artifacts, symbols, aesthetics, and values make their way into motives and methods for criminal behavior in an increasingly digital and global environment. Examination of aspects and elements of culture such as the aesthetics of crime and violence, celebrity culture, and hypermasculinity are critical to the development of a theory of copycat and media-mediated crime.

Copycat Crime

Table 3.1 Effect Sizes of Early and Late Risk Factors for Violence at Ages 15 to 18
(Adapted from U.S. Office of the Surgeon General, 2001, p. 87)

Early Risk Factors (age 6–11)	Effect Size (r =)	Late Risk Factors (age 12–14)	Effect Size (r =)
Large Effect Size ($r > 0.30$)			
General offenses	0.38	Weak social ties	0.39
Substance use	0.30	Antisocial, delinquent peers	0.37
		Gang membership	0.31
Moderate Effect Size ($r = 0.20–0.29$)			
Being male	0.26	General offenses	0.26
Low socioeconomic status/poverty	0.24		
Antisocial parents	0.23		
Aggression	0.21		
Small Effect Size ($r < 0.20$)			
Psychological condition	0.15	Psychological condition	0.19
Hyperactivity	0.13	Restlessness	0.20
Poor parent-child relations	0.15	Difficulty concentrating	0.18
Harsh, lax, or inconsistent discipline	0.13	Risk taking	0.09
Weak social ties	0.15	Poor parent-child relations	0.19
Problem (antisocial) behavior	0.13	Harsh, lax discipline; poor monitoring, supervision	0.08
Exposure to television violence	0.13	Low parental involvement	0.11
Poor attitude toward, poor performance in school	0.13	Aggression	0.19
Medical, physical	0.13	Being male	0.19
Low IQ	0.12	Poor attitude toward, performance in school	0.19
Other family conditions	0.12	Academic failure	0.14
Broken home	0.09	Physical violence	0.18
Separation from parents	0.09	Neighborhood crime, drugs	0.17
Antisocial attitudes, beliefs, dishonesty	0.12	Neighborhood disorganization	0.17
Abusive parents	0.07	Antisocial parents	0.16
Neglect	0.07	Antisocial attitudes, beliefs	0.16
		Crimes against persons	0.14
Antisocial peers	0.04	Problem (antisocial) behavior	0.12
		Low IQ	0.11
		Broken home	0.10
		Low socioeconomic status/poverty	0.10
		Abusive parents	0.09
		Other family conditions	0.08
		Family conflict	0.13
		Substance use	0.06

Crime as Art

One of the most central elements of the copycat effect on criminal behavior is the power of artistic depictions of crime and violence as influences for criminal behavior. The view of crime as art, in culture, and in the minds of individual perpetrators is a critical piece in understanding the copycat effect on criminal behavior. "Violence needs art" (Appelbaum, 2017, p. xiii) to tell about its nature, who the victims and the perpetrators are, and the stories in which it occurs. Violent crime is a rare event, and most people's experience with violence is media mediated. America and other cultures have become so media-saturated that artistic depictions of violence have taken on a life of their own. Images of violence with no stories or moral context—scrolling screens of scenes of violence on the Internet or social media is an example of the "aestheticization" of violence. The aestheticization of violence allows an audience to take on an aesthetic attitude toward violence and to admire through art violence for the sake of itself apart from its moral consequences (Appelbaum, 2017, p. 16).

The aestheticization of crime and violence plays a key role in copycat crime. Aestheticized media-mediated crime and violence exacerbate the "unprecedented role played by the media in contemporary society as a mimetic mechanism" (Black, 1991, p. 144). When crime and violence are presented without (or with ambiguous) context as entertainment on a digital and global scale, the potential for blurred boundaries between fantasy and reality is high. Aestheticization of crime and violence in ways that glamorize violence send a powerful message that criminals are worthy of attention, and the more horrific and extreme the crime is, the more notoriety the perpetrator will receive. Global consumer culture exacerbates the power of aestheticized violence and "with the rise of electronic media, society has become increasingly established as a society of spectacle, commodity signs and representations" (Penfold, 2004, p. 290). When certain individuals consume (and are repeatedly exposed to) media violence in a culture where violence and violent offenders have superstar status, this is a volatile mix. Disciplines and perspectives through which crime and violence are traditionally explored—law, philosophy, sociology, psychology, criminology, etc.—fall short of their ability to help understand how artistic depictions of crime and violence make their way into the cognitive schemas and scripts and motivations and methods of individuals who mimic the aestheticized violence they consume. An aesthetic-critical approach offers an alternative, morally neutral lens through which to understand murder and violent crime that offers a phenomenological description rather than a prescriptive assessment of copycat or media-mediated crime (Black, 1991).

The case of Dennis Rader, aka "the BTK Killer," exemplifies this convergence of influence of aesthetic depictions of violence, celebrity culture, and real-world media-mediated murder. Rader tortured and murdered 10 people over a 30-year period while watching his own crimes play out in the media. Rader's primary motivation for murder was driven by deviant sexual fantasy, sadism, psychopathy, and narcissism—the cat and mouse game he played with the media reveals his fascination with the cultural lore of the serial killer and his view that becoming a serial killer would make him a "somebody." His "mentors" were H. H. Holmes, Harvey Glatman (Ramsland, 2013), and Jack the Ripper (Leblanc, 2016). He engaged in communication with the news media during his offense period (Guillen, 2002). He followed his own crimes in the news, studied criminal justice to stay a step ahead of investigators, and was caught only because he decided to contact the media himself because there was too long of a lull in media attention to his crimes (Hansen, 2006). His desire to perform a grandiose public persona in the face of being sentenced to 10 consecutive life sentences could be seen in his 30-minute speech reminiscent of an Academy Awards acceptance speech (Krishnamurthy, 2018).

Another example of copycat murder inspired by aestheticized violence is the case of James Holmes, who on July 12, 2012, clad in full body armor and armed with multiple guns including an assault rifle, murdered 12 people and injured 70 others at the Aurora Cinemark theater in Colorado during a screening of the film *The Dark Knight Rises*. Holmes was wearing a shirt that said, "Guns don't kill people, I do" and had brightly dyed orange hair resembling the Joker character in the film. Sandy Phillips, whose daughter Jessica was murdered by Holmes in the shooting, joined surviving victims and other parents of victims to write a letter to Warner Brothers asking them to not show the 2019 film *Joker* in Aurora, Colorado, and to donate proceeds to a gun advocacy group. *Joker*, like *The Dark Knight Rises*, depicts the Joker, Batman's arch-nemesis, engaged in scenes of extreme violence. Phillips explained her concern about potential effects of the film on violence saying, "My worry is that one person who may be out there—and who knows if it is just one—who is on the edge, who is wanting to be a mass shooter, may be encouraged by this movie. And that terrifies me" (Parker, 2019).

How the aesthetics of violence impact that one edge-sitter is central to understanding copycat crime. Much of what has been written on the aesthetics of violence has come from perspectives of literature scholars (e.g.,

The Copycat Effect on Criminal Behavior

Appelbaum, 2017; Black, 1991, 2002). The aesthetic perspective has important implications for criminology and criminal justice and the development of a theory of copycat and mimetic violence. New media forms such as the Internet and social media present an opportunity for instant electronic media representations that are self-produced (Black, 2002). From a cultural criminology perspective, attention to the media effects of aestheticized violence *and* the self-representation of crime and violence in aestheticized images is key to understanding the relationship between crime and digital culture. In the examples of Dennis Rader and James Holmes, both perpetrators internalized aestheticized images of violence as part of their own cultural scripts, and in turn, their crimes became aestheticized when publicized in the media, allowing them to gain global notoriety. An even more pronounced example of this is the case of Elliot Rodger, whose cultural script was influenced by media and popular culture and then he himself (his manifesto, his video images documenting his mindset and his motivation, and the play-by play news footage on his crime and its aftermath) became aestheticized violence as an icon for the incel movement, which was then used as a script for subsequent perpetrators (Vice Staff, 2022).

Celebrity Obsession

Mass media technology has altered the public relationship to celebrities, and social media has made celebrities out of everyone. Celebrities seem familiar because of the amount of time we spend watching them in various forms of media. This voyeuristic relationship between the public and celebrities is culturally supported and reinforced. Social media such as YouTube, Facebook, LinkedIn, Instagram, Tik Tok, and BeReal blurs the boundaries between celebrities and noncelebrities, making regular people into media icons. "Cybersocializing is marked by pseudo-relationships that promote getting to know people from afar" (Ellison, 2012, p. 524). With these new forms of media, celebrity obsession applies to noncelebrity regular people who are social media users and influencers who become celebrities. Obsessional following, stalking behavior, and surveillance activities are sanctioned in American popular culture through TV, films, music, comics, jokes, visual art, and advertisements (Marx, 1995). Popular magazines buy photos of celebrities while they are grocery shopping for thousands of dollars from the paparazzi (sometimes called the "stalkerazzi"), who are willing to engage in risky behaviors with sometimes fatal consequences, which is telling about public interest in entertainment voyeurism.

Despite known cases of harm and death resulting from obsessed fans and paparazzi, there has been little research attention to how media technology creates new targets for criminal victimization. Media depiction of a real person or character creates a familiarity with strangers. The more visible and accessible a person is, the more likely they are to be a crime target. From a routine activity perspective, "Any activity that separates those who are prone to violence from each other, or from potential victims, is likely to decrease the incidence of violence" (Felson, 1996, p. 116). TV and other forms of media can reduce crime if potential offenders stay at home, consuming their media, and away from potential victims and vice versa. However, media technology brings individuals figuratively into our worlds who we would otherwise not know—and this overexposure to media celebrities and the pseudo-familiarity that many people experience with them add an entirely new dimension to the notion of routine activity. Media technology does physically separate people; it also reduces virtual distance and increases accessibility, creating a new type of victimization target.

Virtual familiarity with strangers increases the likelihood of stranger-victims. Individuals who suffer from attachment pathology take familiarity with celebrities too far, developing elaborate fantasies and a "narcissistic link" between themselves and the object of their admiration that can turn dangerous or deadly (Meloy, 1992, 1998; Zona et al., 1998). Celebrity stalking perpetrators often have criminal, psychiatric, and drug abuse histories and show evidence of a range of *Diagnostic and Statistical Manual of Mental Disorders* (DSM) mental health and substance use and personality (primarily cluster B) disorders, though most are not psychotic at the time of their offense (Meloy, 1998). An example of celebrity stalking that resulted in murder is the case of singer, songwriter, actress, and YouTuber Christina Grimmie. Grimmie was murdered by a fan at age 22 on June 10, 2016, at a post-concert "meet and greet" after a concert in Orlando, Florida, while she was signing autographs. The fan, 27-year-old Kevin James Loibl, traveled to the concert from St. Petersburg and arrived with two handguns and a hunting knife. Loibl shot Grimmie four times and then shot himself after being tackled by Grimmie's brother immediately after the murder. Grimmie became famous doing cover songs on YouTube and released her debut EP in 2011 and her second in 2016. Her YouTube followers were in the millions, and she became a contestant on the competition TV series, *The Voice,* winning third place. After Grimmie's murder, the investigation revealed that Loibl had an "unrealistic infatuation" with Grimmie. Stalkers, some of whom may be psychotic, may misinterpret the

The Copycat Effect on Criminal Behavior   69

familiar tone often used in social media (Wilson et al., 2018). According to YouTuber, media artist, and video essayist Ian Danskin:

> Internet fame simultaneously creates the sense that a person is a celebrity but also that that person is your friend. Having those two things happen at the same time (not only is this person famous and getting judged by the rules of famous people, but also you have an intimate access to them and judge them in the way you would if your friend was acting badly) is weird. (Stokel-Walker, 2019)

YouTubers, like Grimmie, are seen as "known" and accessible by their fans. Regular social media posting and the closeness and directness of the video posts exacerbate media-mediated familiarity and create intense virtual intimacy.

This media-mediated simultaneous idealization and familiarity have consequences for both edge-sitters and the public. The rise in digital culture in the 21st century has the power to exacerbate the aesthetic realm of the hyperreal to entirely new levels. In the post–COVID-19 world, more and more people are isolated from others and insulated within their social media environments, interacting with each other digitally on an everyday, global level. In a world where 47 percent of Millennials indicate that they turn to YouTube for improved mood and health rather than turning to a friend (Stokel-Walker, 2019), the increasingly aestheticized way that human beings relate to one another blurs the boundary between what is real and what is digital for an increasing number of people. With legacy media, media violence impacted a smaller number of edge-sitters who already had the propensity to commit crime and violence. Media violence today moves faster, further, and has a more powerful impact on more than just edge-sitters.

To understand the nature and dynamics of celebrity stalking violence, it is helpful to examine cases that occurred during earlier legacy media time periods. Actress Theresa Saldana who starred in the 1978 film *I Wanna Hold Your Hand* and the 1980 films *Defiance* and *Raging Bull* was stabbed multiple times with a hunting knife by a fan on March 15, 1982, outside of her West Hollywood home in broad daylight. Saldana survived the attack and founded the Victims for Victims organization. Saldana later told a judge, "I will never forget the searing, ghastly pain, the grotesque and devastating experience of this person nearly butchering me to death, or the bone-chilling sight of my own blood splattered everywhere." Saldana's attacker was a Scottish drifter named Arthur Jackson who become obsessed with her after seeing Saldana in *I Wanna Hold Your Hand*

and *Defiance*. Jackson entered the United States illegally and enlisted a private detective to track Saldana down. The subsequent investigation revealed that he wrote in his diary that he was on a "divine mission" to win Ms. Saldana by "sending her into eternity." After he attacked Saldana he spent 10 years in prison and during that time wrote Saldana a letter saying he regretted using a knife in the attack because "a gun would have given me a better chance of reunion with you in heaven" (Grimes, 2016).

In a case a few years later in 1989, 21-year-old actress Rebecca Schaeffer, star in the 1980s sitcom *My Sister Sam* was shot dead at her own front door by obsessed fan Robert Bardo in 1989. Bardo was a fan of Schaeffer, had sent her letters and gifts, and tried to meet Schaeffer at the studio where she worked (Weisholtz & Caulfield, 2019). Bardo copied the method Jackson had used to stalk Saldana and hired a private investigator to obtain Schaeffer's address from the California Department of Motor Vehicles. (In both cases the perpetrators obtained the actresses' addresses through the California Department of Motor Vehicles.) Saldano's and Schaeffer's cases led to the California Drivers Policy Protection Act and to the development and enactment of stalking laws and specialized stalking units within law enforcement agencies (Brownfield, 2019; Harvey, 2002; Orion, 1997).

Other celebrities have been similarly stalked in situations where an individual has a pathological fixation on a celebrity that ends in violence. The Hinckley and Chapman cases were celebrity stalking copycat crimes. Hinckley was fixated on actress Jodie Foster, and Chapman (and Hinckley) idolized John Lennon. Hinckley sent detailed letters to Foster while she attended Yale and indicated to authorities after the assassination attempt that his primary motivation was to win Foster's affection. Mark Chapman murdered John Lennon in the culmination of Chapman's slowly unraveling obsession with Lennon and his conflated cognitive script that intricately interwove elements of popular culture (John Lennon's image) and literature (*Catcher in the Rye*), with Chapman's disordered search for identity (Black, 1991; Jones, 1992). Other celebrities have been the victims of celebrity stalkers, becoming targets of offenders who formed obsessive media-mediated pseudo-relationships with them. David Letterman was the victim of two serious celebrity-related stalking offenses. One offense involved a female stalker, and the other the attempted kidnapping for ransom of his son ("Heartfelt Thanks from Letterman," 2005; Wolf, 2005). Other victims of obsessional stalkers include Madonna, Brad Pitt, Jennifer Aniston, Steven Spielberg, Gianni Versace (Harvey, 2002), Whitney Houston, Sharon Gless, Janet Jackson, Suzanne Sommers, Paula Abdul, Justine Bateman, Cher, Olivia Newton-John, Vanna White, Kathie Lee Gifford

(Orion, 1997), Avril Lavigne (Sullivan, 2004), Uma Thurman (Hartocollis & Eligon, 2008), Sandra Bullock, Harry Styles, and Selena Gomez (Brownfield, 2019).

Modern society is a world of celebrity culture. Social media influencers and content creators, pop stars, sports stars, TV and film stars, and football managers achieve status and become "new gods" to be followed and worshiped. And increasingly social media has created an opportunity for everyday people to act and feel like celebrities even if they never achieve the status of having hundreds, thousands, or millions of followers. For those with obsessive characteristics ranging from simply obsessed persons to persons suffering advanced paranoid disorders, these "new gods" continue to supply new targets for harassment, stalking, and even death (Harvey, 2002, p. xiv). Celebrity culture brings opportunities to make a Nobody into a Somebody. Celebrities, and to a lesser extent anyone (famous or not) who makes it onto the TV news, Internet, YouTube, Tik Tok, or other media form, have increased exposure, increasing the likelihood of becoming a victim of celebrity stalking, doxing, or other offenses. The celebration of violence in culture; the glorification of mass killers, serial murderers, and "lone wolf" terrorists; and the speed at which information is globally disseminated via digital culture create a powerful force of influence for violence-prone, at-risk edge-sitters who turn violent characters they see in the media into idols they emulate.

The role of celebrity obsession is central to the copycat effect on criminal behavior and violence. The copycat effect is evident in a third of lone wolf terrorist attacks (Hamm & Spaaij, 2015), the incel movement and the violence it unleashed was born from the idolization of mass killer Elliot Rodger (Tomkinson et al., 2020), and in just over two decades, over 100 copycat shooters have been inspired by the Columbine killers (Frazin, 2019). The celebrity obsession phenomenon helps to better understand copycat crime in two ways. First, media plays a central role in crime involving celebrities and copycat crime. Both find inspiration in a media source and are driven by and dependent on the cultural power of fame and notoriety. Second, technology gives potential copycats wide access to information that validates and can be used to mimic the behavior of notorious offenders and well-publicized cases, in particular those involving celebrities. There are tribute web pages devoted to celebrity stalkers such as Mark David Chapman and spree killer Andrew Cunanan that detail their methods and beliefs available for anyone who may be an aspiring celebrity stalker (Harvey, 2002). Copycats of celebrity stalking incidents are crimes that most clearly and blatantly reveal the role of media and the quest for notoriety. Sarah Lockett, a news reporter for Meridian Television in England, was stalked by Jeremy Dyer, a fan, who sent her over 80 letters from 1998 to 1999 and was sentenced to prison for two years for harassment. The letters included numerous references to the well-publicized celebrity murder of BBC news reporter Jill Dando. Dando was shot in the head at close range at her doorstep in 1999 (Harvey, 2002). Barry George, a media-obsessed celebrity stalker, who had a history of obsession with celebrities (including Princess Diana and Freddie Mercury, lead singer from the band Queen), was eventually convicted of the murder but later acquitted on appeal, and the killer remains unknown (Lusher, 2019). The letters by Dyer to Lockett specifically referenced the Dando murder with threatening passages such as "You looked a bit miserable on the Monday show. I suppose you would be considering Jill Dando just got her brains blown out by a probable stalker" (Harvey, 2002, pp. 149, 151). Dyer used the Dando murder to threaten his victim and to validate and reinforce his own stalking behaviors. Visibility made Dando and Lockett targets of celebrity stalkers whose fantasies and behaviors were influenced by the cultural emphasis on fame and celebrity voyeurism and facilitated by media technology. The cultural forces that make it appealing to become a notorious celebrity killer are crucial to understanding copycat crime.

Violent Masculinity

Fame-seeking mass shooting perpetrators are overwhelmingly young white males who perceive themselves as victims who exhibit grandiose behaviors, mental illness, and suicidal tendencies (Silva & Greene-Colozzi, 2019). The role of masculinity and the depiction of violent masculinity in the media (Gerbner et al., 2014; Katz, 1988, 2006; Walsh & Gentile, 2003) are cultural elements that exacerbate the copycat effect. Images of violent masculinity play a key role in the glorification of media violence, conveying the idea that male violence is power.

In the aftermath of the Columbine shooting, the FBI's National Center for the Analysis of Violent Crime invited 160 educators, administrators, law enforcement officers, mental health professionals, prosecutors, academic experts, and people who personally knew school shooters from 18 schools involved in the study that had had mass shooting incidents to a symposium on threat assessment and school shooters. The product of the symposium was a report titled, "The School Shooter: A Threat Assessment Perspective" (O'Toole, 2000). The report noted that "there is no magical number of traits or constellation of traits which will determine what students may present a problem" (p. 15). The report listed four prongs with 46 associated elements, including personality traits and

The Copycat Effect on Criminal Behavior 73

behaviors, family dynamics, school dynamics, and social dynamics, including media-related elements such as fascination with violence-filled entertainment, negative role models, absence of limits or monitoring of TV and Internet use, media and technology, and copycat effect.

What the FBI school shooter report did not note was that the majority of the mass shootings were committed by males. A review of 185 mass shooters from 1966 to 2010 shows that 96 percent are male (Lankford, 2015). Recent research has highlighted the role of hegemonic masculinity in mass shootings, specifically toxic masculinity, exaggerated masculinity, violence against women, machismo, and power depicted in the media (Follman, 2019; Issa, 2019; Silva & Greene-Collozi, 2019; Silva et al., 2021). Hegemonic masculinity is the idealization of traditional and dominant male identities that involve challenges to manhood and/or failures in achieving an idealized male identity that encourages some men to engage in violence as a form of corrective action (Kennedy-Kollar & Charles, 2013; Messerschmidt, 2018). Hegemonic masculinity is a critical element of a culture of violent masculinity that contributes to violent crime. While not all copycat crimes are violent crimes committed by boys and men, the prevalence of male perpetrators in copycat mass and school shootings highlights the importance of media depictions of violent masculinity as a part of culture that contributes to the copycat effect.

Phenomenology of Crime

No single theoretical perspective is more important in understanding the continuum of copycat influence and its importance in criminology and criminal justice than phenomenological criminology as described in Katz's (1988) *Seductions of Crime*. Crimes that fall on the extreme end of the copycat crime continuum are those in which the perpetrator's behavior is rooted in a complex cognitive script that has meaning for that individual. These individuals engage in crime that makes little sense to others and is precipitated by elaborate fantasy, stimulated by, and intertwined with media or digital muses. At that moment when the edge-sitter moves from sitting on the edge fantasizing about and contemplating a criminal act to action, they are compelled to do so by a force that is difficult to explain and only understood from a phenomenological framework:

> To believe that a person can suddenly feel propelled to [commit a] crime without any independently verifiable change in his background, it seems that we must almost believe in magic. And indeed this is precisely what we must do. . . . The particular seductions and compulsions they experience

may be unique to crime, but the sense of being seduced and compelled is not. . . .

A sense of being determined by the environment, of being pushed away from one line of action and pulled toward another, is natural to everyday, routine human experience. . . . We are always moving away from and toward different objects of consciousness, taking account of this and ignoring that, and moving in one direction or the other between the extremes of involvement and boredom. Indeed, to one degree or another, we are always being seduced and repelled by the world. (Katz, 1988, pp. 4–5)

Katz's phenomenological perspective recognizes that the positivist search for deterministic forces does not adequately explain that space in between risk factors for criminal behavior and criminal acts. He asks:

. . . Can we really see any novel causal forces in the black box between background factors and subsequent acts? After we have refined correlations between problematic acts and explanatory background factors, is there anything more to say other than that those whose actions do and those whose actions do not line up with predictions just "choose" to act that way? (p. 5)

The "more to say" is that crime holds meaning for the people who commit it, in the moment, and in the unique cognitive scripts that, especially in the case of copycat crimes, become a propellant for the criminal act. Joined with Black's (1991) aesthetic-critical perspective in *The Aesthetics of Murder,* the phenomenological perspective explains what happens in that seemingly inexplicable space between those who have risk factors for violence and choose not to act and the edge-sitters with the same risk factors who are compelled by their risk factors or those with no risk factors who are propelled by the aesthetics and the meaning the act holds for them in the moment of the crime.

From this perspective the decision to commit a criminal act that makes little sense from a cost/benefit perspective, that defies explanation, and that is not solely explained by risk factors or scientifically established determinants of crime can be explained by aesthetics and the existential meaning and subjective experience a criminal act holds for the individual who commits that act. "By pacifying his subjectivity, a person can conjure up a magic so powerful that it can change his ontology. . . . As unattractive morally as crime may be, we must appreciate that there is genuine experimental creativity in it as well. We should then be able to see what are, for the subject, the authentic attractions of crime and we should then

The Copycat Effect on Criminal Behavior 75

be able to explain variations in criminality beyond what can be accounted for by background factors" (Katz, 1988, p. 8).

Thinking about copycat crimes from aesthetic-critical and phenomenological perspectives allows for understanding beyond traditional etiological and risk factor models of criminal behavior. For example, how do we make sense of aesthetically motivated perpetrators who defy traditional explanation? For example, mass murders are inherently aesthetic in that they are generally performed publicly for an audience and target strangers as victims. While only 4 percent of murderers commit suicide, 38 percent of mass shooters committed suicide by their own hand, with 48 percent dying in the aftermath of the crime, suggesting that mass shooters are a unique category of murderers. Mass shooters who die are statistically different from those who do not in that they armed themselves with more weapons, killed more victims, and often struck at different locations than those who survived their attacks (Lankford, 2015).

Fundamental differences between suicidal and nonsuicidal mass shooters from the start and differences in outcomes of their attacks reflect differences in motivation. For example, the Connecticut Police Department believed Adam Lanza committed suicide because he was an avid violent video gamer, and in gamer code, if somebody else kills you they get your points. This is a very different reason for committing suicide than the traditional motivations for homicide-suicides of histories that include depression and mental illness. Evidence found in Lanza's home, including his murder of his mother in their home and evidence found in his bedroom, including the video games *Grand Theft Auto, Call of Duty, School Shooter* and the book *Amish Grace: How Forgiveness Transcended Tragedy* (Kraybill, Nolt, & Weaver-Zercherbook, 2007) about the 2006 Amish school shootings suggest that violent gaming and prior mass shootings influenced his motivation for his crime.

Officers who attended the International Association of Police Chiefs presentation by Colonel Danny Stebbins from the Connecticut State Police spoke of what they learned about a seven- foot-long, four-foot-wide, nine-point-font spreadsheet found in Lanza's home that required a special printer to print it out that read like a mass murder scoresheet:

> We were told [Lanza] had around 500 people on this sheet. . . . Names and the number of people killed and the weapons that were used, even the precise make and model of the weapons. It had to have taken years. It sounded like a doctoral thesis . . . that was the quality of the research. . . . We keep calling them mass murderers, but there should be a new way of referring to them: Glory killers. . . . They don't believe this was just a

spreadsheet. They believe it was a score sheet. . . . This was the work of a video gamer, and that it was his intent to put his own name at the very top of that list. They [Connecticut police] believe that he picked an elementary school because he felt it was a point of least resistance, where he could rack up the greatest number of kills. . . .They believe that [Lanza] believed that it was the way to pick up the easiest points. It's why he didn't want to be killed by law enforcement. In the code of a gamer, even a deranged gamer like this little bastard, if somebody else kills you, they get your points. They believe that's why he killed himself. . . . He had been planning this thing forever. In the end, it was just a perfect storm: These guns, one of them an AR-15, in the hands of a violent, insane gamer. It was like porn to a rapist. They feed on it until they go out and say, enough of the video screen. Now I'm actually going to be a hunter. . . . The fascination [Lanza] had with this subject matter, the complete and total concentration. There really was no other subject matter inside his head. Just this: Kill, kill, kill. . . . It really was like he was lost in one of his own sick games. (Lupica, 2013)

To understand Lanza's "own sick game" requires the aesthetic and phenomenological perspectives to illuminate the meaning of his crime and the aesthetics of his violent act. His adulation and emulation of the Columbine killers and other mass murderers and his experience with and mimicry of video game violence made its way into his unique cognitive script that can only be understood phenomenologically.

The Nature and Mechanisms of Copycat Crime

The copycat effect of criminal behavior is in many ways no different than the copycat effect of prosocial behavior and can be partially explained through social learning theory. People, in particular children, imitate what they see in both positive and negative ways. What is the difference between harmless and prosocial acts of imitation and the car theft/murder committed by a teen who plays *Grand Theft Auto* for hours on end? We are all influenced to some extent by popular culture. The extent to which technology has made media and popular culture such an enormous part of everyday life exacerbates the powerful influence of media images. However, imitation is too simplistic a process to fully understand copycat crime. The salient role of technology and media in contemporary life coupled with the elevation of the criminal (specifically serial and mass murderers) to star status and the value placed on public recognition that has been reinforced by American popular culture together contribute to the particular phenomenon of copycat crime.

The Copycat Effect on Criminal Behavior

The volume of crime and violence in digital culture has the potential to increase the copycat effect, not because of the violence itself, but because of its glorification and the message that committing violence is one route to fame and notoriety. According to Surette, "the news media's emphasis on drama, violence, and entertainment and the entertainment media's emphasis on themes of violent criminality appear to work together to foster copycat crimes . . . simply for notoriety" (Surette, 1998, p. 139). There is an enormous disparity between the number of murders displayed in popular culture and the actual extent of the phenomenon in real life (Jenkins, 1994). There are serial killer board games, trading cards, and serial killer art. In the 1980s and 1990s dozens of serial killers were featured on popular magazine covers, and films about them were instant box office smashes (Campbell, 2002). The serial killer in film has replaced the Western in American genre fiction as a "new mythic monster." This elevation of the serial killer to mythical figure has elevated the status of the serial killer to a supernatural being and has blurred the boundaries between fantasy and reality for the public, policymakers, and criminal justice professionals. Even police have been known to release offenders because they did not fit the media stereotype of a serial killer (Epstein, 1995).

Actual serial murderers and school shooters mimic and/or alter their behavior based on media stories of actual or fictional killers. Two of the most notorious serial killers in history Gary Ridgeway, the Green River Killer, and Dennis Rader, the BTK Killer, followed other serial killers in the media. Columbine school shooters, Harris and Klebold, boasted on video about inflicting "the most deaths in U.S. history" to one-up other school shooters and Timothy McVeigh's actions in the Oklahoma bombing (Cullen, 2004). The 2002 D.C. Sniper shootings by John Muhammad and Lee Malvo inspired a series of sniper attacks around the world, and Lee Malvo himself was said to have watched the film *The Matrix* over 100 times to prepare himself for the sniper attacks (CNN Transcripts, 2003). Just days before the eighth anniversary of the Columbine murders, Seung-Hui Cho mailed a video of himself to NBC News ranting about Columbine killers Klebold and Harris before going on to murder 32 students and professors on the Virginia Tech campus later that day (Cullen, April 20, 2007), committing the ultimate one-up of his Columbine predecessors. Aaron Ybarra, who was convicted and sentenced to 112 years in prison for gunning down and killing two students and injuring three others at Seattle Pacific University in 2014 (Green, 2016, 2017), wrote in his journal two weeks prior to the mass shooting incident that Virginia Tech shooter Seung-Hui Cho and Columbine killer Eric Harris were his idols.

He said of Harris, "He just made everything so exciting. He made hate so exciting" (Walker & Mallahan, 2016). Clearly, the behavior of the most extreme serial killers and mass murderers in recent times has been shaped by media and popular culture.

The copycat effect influences criminal behavior as a shaper or a trigger along a continuum ranging from media influences that play a minor role influencing modus operandi, to media influences that are a major trigger for severely psychopathologically disturbed individuals who are isolated, personality-disordered media junkies for whom pop cultural imagery plays a critical role in the formation of violent fantasy. Excessive media coverage of mass murders glorifies perpetrators and develops role models for edge-sitters to idolize. Most of the perpetrators of mass shootings after Columbine idolized the Columbine killers and/or other killers whose crimes received high media coverage (Silva & Greene-Colozzi, 2019). Media images glorifying murder incite and inspire edge-sitters whose motives are aesthetic and phenomenological. The symbiotic relationship between perpetrators and media images of the perpetrators who came before them validates, informs, and embellishes their cognitive scripts. Individual, environmental, situational, and media-related factors interact to influence whether an individual or group of individuals will mimic criminal behavior they see in the media and popular culture (see Figure 3.1).

Individual-level criminogenic factors such as emotional development, personality and/or mental state, cognitive schema, social alienation, use/abuse of facilitators (drugs, alcohol, pornography), history of abuse and/or family dysfunction, and social/physical isolation increase or decrease the likelihood of mimetic violence and influence the extent to which an individual psychologically connects to a particular media source. The presence of social-environmental variables that interact with a psychological predisposition to aggression exacerbates the potential for violent media exposure to be a risk factor for violent behavior (Grimes et al., 2008). For violence-prone individuals who heavily consume violent media, such consumption has an exacerbating influence, with its greatest effect on boys who exhibit lower academic performance, who are aggressive-prone but who become more aggressive after viewing violent media. However, the violent media–aggression–violence relationship is complex because aggression and violence-prone boys consume more violent media (Courtwright, 1998).

The copycat effect involves a combination of influences of media content, social context, and individual predisposition that presents in the

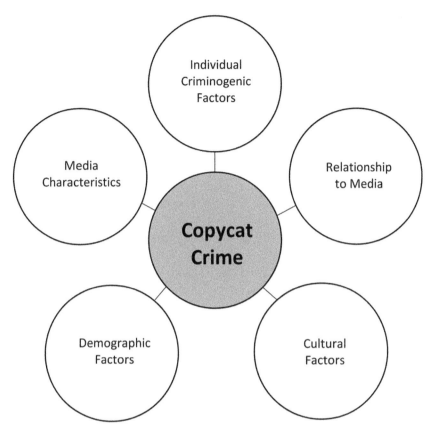

Figure 3.1 Factors that Exacerbate the Copycat Effect

form of distinct pathways. Surette (2013b, 2022) proposes a theoretical model of copycat crime, hypothesizing that there are three paths to copycat crime: Path 1 (central systematic processing where all relevant and available information is assessed before making a decision where the individual actively scrutinizes all available information); Path 2 (heuristic peripheral where decisions are made with incomplete information and only readily available information is accessed and used); and Path 3 (narrative persuasion) where media information is simply absorbed, reflecting entertainment education theory and research on the impact of media communicated stories. This model explains copycat crime in terms of different pathways that aid in understanding the role of individual characteristics and cognitive mechanisms.

Offender Characteristics, Media Effects, Cultural Facilitators, and Copycat Crime

Films such as *Natural Born Killers* and *The Matrix* and video games such as *Grand Theft Auto* that have been associated with more than a single copycat crime raise questions regarding the potential for a specific media source to trigger the copycat effect in individuals who would not otherwise commit violent acts. From a prevention standpoint, it is important to understand the characteristics of these media sources and the ways in which media characteristics are criminogenic and how they interact with other risk factors that exacerbate the copycat effect on criminal behavior and violence. While most people who consume violent media, with or without criminogenic features, do not go out and commit a violent act, when a specific media source is associated with multiple copycat cases, questions arise regarding elements of that media source; how the media source interacts with certain individuals; and how media characteristics interact with risk factors for copycat crime such as demographic characteristics, individual criminogenic factors, situational-environmental factors, and cultural factors. Identification of how particular media sources exacerbate the copycat effect for both the subset of individuals who are violence-prone and those who are less violence-prone is critical in violence prevention, threat assessment, and threat management (Meloy & Hoffman, 2014).

This raises the question of what individual-level factors make a person prone to the copycat effect. Meta-analyses support the General Aggression Model (GAM)—that repeated exposure to violent people and situations increases aggression by altering an individual's affective state, priming aggressive cognitions, and inducing physiological arousal, and viewing violent acts teaches behaviors that are then aggressively acted out (Anderson & Bushman, 2001, 2002; Anderson & Dill, 2000; Bushman, 2016). The effects of violent media can be best understood from a risk and resilience framework that considers factors that facilitate and inhibit violence and media effects (Gentile & Bushman, 2012). Individual-level factors influence media violence effects—individual affinities; readiness to respond; personality traits; disposition toward characters in media; and selective attention, avoidance, perception, and memory all play a role. "Unexplained variance can be appreciated as representing the opportunity for researchers to explore the importance of individual differences in the media effects process" (Oliver, 2002, p. 520). The interaction between risk and resiliency factors ultimately explains who is prone to the copycat effect on criminal behavior and the process by which particular risk factors operate with resiliency factors to produce media-mediated violence.

The Copycat Effect on Criminal Behavior   81

Individual-level factors interact with media and situational-environmental and cultural influences to produce different types of behaviors. Some violence-prone individuals who have a proclivity for violent media may possess characteristics that make them resilient to media effects, while others who are not violence prone may be influenced by environmental or cultural risk factors. A person's relationship to media, such as trust in media as a source of information, level and extent of media consumption, media literacy, artistic literacy, identification with perpetrators in media depiction, and susceptibility to "mean world syndrome" (Gerbner, 1994; Gerbner et al., 2014), influences the extent to which a particular media form will influence a person's cognitive scripts and, in turn, behavior. Demographic factors such as age, sex, socioeconomic status, and race/ethnicity play a role in the type of media, characters, and images a person is likely to identify with.

Media-related factors can exacerbate the copycat effect. Over- or under-attention to certain crime stories; a "language of violence" (Newman, 1998; Young, 2009) that glorifies and legitimizes violence (e.g., depicting individuals who engage in violence who get away with their behaviors at the end of the story; presentation of violent perpetrators as appealing and attractive); a presentation that blurs boundaries between fantasy and reality; "media looping" (showing and reframing an image in another context) (Manning, 1998); and a wide range of content factors related to the specific media source such as genre confusion, special effects, instant reincarnation/spawning, lack of consequences for violent acts, presentation of crime as fun, depiction of criminals as superhuman, and appeal of offender character, all play a critical role in whether or not a particular media source is likely to influence a specific individual (Helfgott, 2015).

Cultural factors also play an important role in exacerbating the copycat effect. Cultural values placed on fame and notoriety, cultural relationship to crime and violence, violent masculinity as a cultural norm, the extent to which peers and peer subcultures support or reject media as a legitimate source of information, social/cultural acceptance of a particular media source, and moral panics are aspects of culture that decrease or increase the importance of media on the individual level.

A synthesis of theory and research on the aesthetics of violence, media affects, social learning and the psychology of mimetic criminal behavior, and analysis of case studies of known copycat offenders reveals risk factors for copycat crime. These factors can be organized into six categories of individual-level factors and cultural-environmental factors (see Figure 3.2). Individual characteristics such as age and sex and criminogenic factors are associated with criminal behavior more generally (some more

Demographic Characteristics

- Age
- Sex
- Race
- Education

Criminogenic Factors

- Mental Disorder
- Personality disorder
- Developmental failure in attachment/human bonding/lack of identity
- Cognitive schema of viewer/Extremist beliefs
- Social isolation and alienation
- Aggressive traits/use of aggression as approach to conflict resolution

Relationship to Media

- Trust in media as a source of information
- Media literacy
- Artistic literacy
- Identification with perpetrators featured in media source (with respect to gender, age, race/ethnicity, lifestyle, personal aesthetic, beliefs, habits, experiences, characteristics, etc.)
- Extent to which viewer uses media as a source of information
- Forms of media sources used and level of interaction with source

Media Characteristics

- Imagery and storyline that blurs boundaries between fantasy and reality
- Demographics of characters
- Appeal an physical attractiveness of characters
- Positive response to violence and crime (e.g., happy ending for criminals)
- Media Loops
- Language of violence -- how crime and violence is contextualized, weapons, validation and tolerance for antisocial behavior.

Situational-Environmental Factors

- Situational Factors
- Environmental Influences
- Opportunity

Cultural Factors

- Cultural values placed on fame and notoriety
- Cultural relationship to crime and violence
- Extent to which others support/reject media as a legitimate source of information
- Social/cultural acceptance of particular media source
- Moral panics

Figure 3.2 Factors that Influence the Copycat Effect

The Copycat Effect on Criminal Behavior 83

than others). However, it is the particular interaction between these factors and the individual's relationship to media that is critical in creating the propensity for copycat criminal behavior. Other individual and demographic factors such as race/ethnicity and socioeconomic status may play a role in the characters, themes, and media forms with which an individual is likely to identify.

Research suggests that age and emotional development play a role in an individual's reaction to violent media content (Lloyd, 2002). There is strong evidence to suggest that exposure to violent media such as video game violence produces short-term changes in brain activity (Hummer et al., 2010). Aggressive youth seek out violent media and that media violence predicts aggression in a mutually reinforcing, downward spiral (Slater et al., 2003). Personality and situational variables (school alienation, peer victimization, sensation seeking, and dispositional receptivity to arousing stimuli) moderate the relationship between violent media and aggression, and some individuals are more suggestible than others and more susceptible to pathological fantasy and dissociative symptomatology (Terhune et al., 2011), which may play a role in the individual response to violent media. The younger and less emotionally developed, the greater the media exposure, the greater the number of moderating personality and situational variables, and the more suggestible, the greater the likelihood of a relationship between violent media and aggressive behavior.

Research on criminal behavior, in particular media-related crimes such as celebrity stalking (Meloy, 1998), shows that failure in developmental bonding, formation of disordered identity, diagnosis with axis I mental disorders and axis II/cluster B personality disorders, social isolation and alienation, disordered cognitive schema, and aggressive traits play a role in copycat criminal behavior. These findings are further supported by anecdotal evidence that suggest that most known copycat offenders were under age 25 when they committed their offenses and that these individuals are socially alienated individuals who possess a range of developmental, identity, and mental health issues exacerbated by situational factors such as peer associations, immersion in various forms of media, lack of parental supervision, and access and availability of firearms.

Identification of risk factors for the copycat effect on criminal behavior requires interdisciplinary integration and attention to the complex interplay of individual, developmental, situational, environmental, and cultural factors. Gaziano (2001) suggests that a primary element in understanding individual effects of media violence is powerlessness at the level of the individual, families, and society, along with lack of self-efficacy, that children of parents who feel powerless often grow up to feel powerless themselves, and these individuals are more likely to be attracted to violent media and its effects. Shim (2004) found that children's TV viewing was predicted by parental education and the number of peers they have, while violent game playing was predicated by parenting practices, including harsh discipline and media parenting, and that different predictors are present for different age, sex, and race/ethnicity subgroups. Multiple risk factors have been identified for youth violence such as family transiency and disruption, substance abuse, poor information processing and problem-solving skills, lack of parental supervision, inability to deal with negative feelings, lack of attachment, and lack of economic opportunity, among others. Risk factors associated with crimes that have involved a mimetic component such as school shootings include family stresses, access to guns, obsession with violence in some form of media, feelings of inferiority, and expressed wishes to commit violent acts with exposure to violent media—"yet another ingredient in an already volatile mix" (Gaziono, 2001, p. 220). Theory and research examining the interrelationship between early childhood and adolescent development, personality, and childrearing lend support for the identification of a cluster of risk factors that exacerbate the copycat effect on criminal behavior.

This complex and unique interaction between these demographic, criminogenic, and media-related factors distinguish the propensity for copycat criminal behavior. Exposure to media violence has been empirically identified as a risk factor for aggression (Gentile & Bushman, 2012), and individual-level factors such as high trait aggressiveness have been associated with both choosing violent media and increased aggression following viewing violent media (Bushman, 1995). Other individual-level factors have been attributed to aggression such as sex (with male adolescents producing more violent imagery in response to violent media) (Hess et al., 1999) and males hold a more hostile view of the world after playing violent video games (Anderson & Dill, 2000). Riddle et al. (2011) found that individuals with vivid memories give higher prevalence estimates of real-world crime and violence, supporting a memory-heuristic processing model that may also play a role in media violence effects on aggressive and violent behavior. Recent research examining dispositional factors and media effects has found that a genetic disposition for attention deficit/hyperactivity disorder (ADHD)–related behaviors are associated with greater violent media use (Nikkelen et al., 2014). The interaction between individual-level factors and the media source is just beginning to be

The Copycat Effect on Criminal Behavior 85

examined. Shafer (2009) examined the degree to which viewers morally disengage from actions of violent fictional characters, and frequent exposure and affinity for violent media is correlated with moral disengagement. Anderson and Murphy (2003) suggest that the effect of violent video game violence might be greater when the game player controls a same-sex violent game character. In addition, the degree to which an individual trusts and uses media as a source of information about the world (Helfgott, 2008), the extent to which the individual identifies with characters depicted in the media source (Gerbner, 1994; Katz & Jhally, 1999), artistic illiteracy (Black, 1991), and media illiteracy (Gerbner, 1994) interact with media-related influences and the nature of the media content and presentation (Manning, 1998; Newman, 1998) to produce copycat crime.

Examination of the interaction between individual-level factors and characteristics of the media source requires further exploration. Future research is needed to determine how specific types of media interact with individual-level characteristics such as demographic characteristics, personality, trait aggressiveness, and psychopathy-level in an era of a rapidly changing and global digital media environment. The creators of violent media are engaged in rapid market-driven ante-upping. For example, violent video games such as *Grand Theft Auto* and *Call of Duty* that have been considered the most extreme and interactive forms of media violence on the market in recent years pale in comparison with Internet-based games such as *RapeLay* where the player follows a mother and her daughters into a subway station with the goal of stalking and raping them (Ellison, 2012).

The exponential increase in violent media combined with the degree to which digital media has saturated everyday life on a global scale has the potential to result in the blurring of boundaries between fantasy and reality through repeated exposure to media violence and the influence of violent media on preconscious scripts. Cultural saturation of social media can disrupt or break human connections that inhibit violence for most people. "Lack of face-to-face interactions in the pseudo-relationships of the virtual world can have a cruel downside" (Ellison, 2012, p. 524). Empirical research is needed to answer questions such as: What individual-level characteristics are empirically associated with attraction to the more extreme forms of media violence? Do the more extreme and repulsive forms of media violence have a different effect on different individuals (e.g., the more extreme and realistic, the more repulsive and non-criminogenic to the average media consumer, but perhaps the more attractive and criminogenic for a small subset of psychopathologically disturbed individuals who are utilizing the media as facilitators to act out their elements of a highly developed violent fantasy life)? Do sex, age, race/ethnicity, and/or other demographic factors play a role in an individual's reaction and processing of these extreme forms of media violence? Do prosocial outcomes of digital media technology counteract the antisocial outcomes (e.g., the use of social media as a platform to speak out against violence or as memorial to violent crime victims)? These and other unanswered questions highlight the need for ongoing research and theory development.

CHAPTER FOUR

Case Studies of Copycat and Media-Mediated Crime[1]

Copycat crime case studies offer real-life examples of how media and digital culture influence criminal behavior. With the lack of empirical research on the copycat effect on criminal behavior, case studies offer rich anecdotal information for retrospective analysis to generate hypotheses for empirical research. These case studies illustrate how media, technology, and digital culture inspire criminal behavior and violence; who is susceptible to the copycat effect; individual, environmental, and cultural factors that exacerbate the copycat effect; and the range of media sources that make their way into modus operandi (MO) and signature behavior across the copycat crime continuum.

The copycat effect plays a role in all types of crime and affects all types of people. For most people, the effect of media violence contributes to the "mean world syndrome"—the more media a person consumes, the more dangerous that person will perceive the world to be (Gerbner, 1994; Gerbner et al., 2014). For others, the copycat effect is an all-consuming blurring of the boundary between reality and fantasy, fact and fiction. The copycat effect can explain a range of criminal behavior: from the vigilante whose violence is rooted in fear of crime, to perpetrators who get ideas from media for their MO giving them new ideas about ways to commit crimes they may have already planned to commit, to those who commit crimes for performance to gain notoriety and celebrity, to those who operate under the "influence of mass media" through a distorted identification with a character they idolize and identify with in the media. It is important to understand how this aesthetic hyperreality influences individual edge-sitters who possess risk factors for criminal behavior and have a preexisting propensity for antisocial behavior, criminal behavior, and violence, as well as those who do not have these risk factors. Case studies of known copycat crimes illustrate how the copycat effect influences criminal behavior across the continuum of copycat crime and how technology interacts with other risk factors to produce copycat and media-mediated crime.

Idolatry, Identity, and the 1980s Chapman and Hinckley Cultural Copycat Cluster

Technology in the 1980s was cable TV, VHS video, cassette tapes, the Walkman, fax machines, typewriters, camcorders, MTV, and the evening news. Computers and cell phones were on the scene, though they were clunky, and few people had them in their personal homes. Only people who worked at universities and businesses had email, and there was no Internet available for public use. Television viewing increased from the 1960s and 1970s. With the increased use of videocassette recorders and rapid development of satellite and cable transmission, television became the most popular mass communication medium, strengthening its position as an integral part of American life. Next to working and sleeping, watching television was the activity Americans spent most of their time doing (Xiaoming, 1994). We were unwinding from the intensity of the civil rights movement and the Vietnam War and the cultural unrest of the 1960s and 1970s. A Hollywood movie star became president. The term "yuppies" was popular; Michael Jackson, Madonna, and Prince were at the top of the music charts; *E.T.* was the top-grossing film of the decade; and by the end of the decade the Cold War ended and the Berlin Wall fell.

Murder and the aesthetic presentation of murder in the 1980s were distinctly different from decades prior. Serial murder became a moral panic, with a significant increase in the number of sensationalized cases with every year breaking records in the number of reported cases and victims (Jenkins, 1994). Ted Bundy was executed, and the Green River Killer, the BTK Killer, and the Golden State Killer operated under the radar. The "bizarre, quasi-political, media-mediated violence of the 1980s" needs to be understood "in the historically unprecedented context of hyperaestheticized mass culture" (Black, 1991, p. 136) where "categories of meaning and madness were increasingly being determined by the media . . . . It was no accident that the decade of the presidency of former movie actor and television host Ronald Reagan coincided with a hyperreal phase of mass culture when the media (literature, film, TV, and all the other arts) came to mediate as never before the general public's sense of reality'" (Black, 1991, p. 137).

Case Studies of Copycat and Media-Mediated Crime 89

Catcher in the Rye: Mark David Chapman

Mark David Chapman believed himself to be Holden Caulfield, the main character of J. D. Salinger's (1945, 1946, 1951) *Catcher in the Rye.* At the age of 25, he murdered John Lennon in 1980 after years of fixation on both Lennon and Caulfield. In an interview with Jim Gaines three years after he murdered Lennon, Chapman recounted his motivation for the murder (Gaines, 1987). Chapman was a Beatles fan who idolized John Lennon. Chapman became disillusioned with Lennon over time, and according to a high school friend, became angry when he heard Lennon proclaim in a 1966 interview with the *London Evening Standard* that the Beatles were "more popular than Jesus." Chapman was a devout Christian and destroyed Beatles albums, and his friend said he changed the words to "Imagine" to "Imagine if John were dead." Chapman moved to Hawaii after high school, became depressed, and attempted suicide. He got married to Gloria Abe in 1979 while living in Hawaii and began working as a security guard in a condominium and going to the local library. During that time, he read two books, *John Lennon: One Day at a Time* (Fawcett, 1980) and *Catcher in the Rye* (Salinger, 1945, 1946, 1951). After reading the books, Chapman's hatred of Lennon became more intense. Reflecting on reading *Catcher in the Rye*, Chapman explained how he became enamored with the leading character in the book, Holden Caulfield. "I really identified with him . . . his plight, his loneliness, his alienation from society." Eventually, Chapman's thinking became a blurred mix of fiction and reality as he came to see Lennon through the eyes of Holden Caulfield. Just as Caulfield narrated the world around him, calling people he encountered "phonies" and "morons," Chapman came to see Lennon as a "poser" who did not espouse his ideals and virtues (Sloane, 2015).

Chapman decided to leave Hawaii and fly to New York City on October 29, 1980, with a .38-caliber gun. When he found out he could not legally buy bullets in New York City, he flew to Atlanta to meet an old police officer friend, who gave him some bullets. Chapman returned to New York, had second thoughts, and called his wife in Hawaii and told her he was planning to kill Lennon. His wife did not alert the police because he told her he would seek counseling. Chapman returned to Hawaii but after a few weeks decided to return to New York armed and ready to murder Lennon. He said when he was there the second time, "I couldn't stop it." After spending two days in New York waiting on the sidewalk outside Lennon's apartment, on December 8, 1980, Chapman crossed paths with Lennon, who he said was "very kind" to him when he asked him to autograph a copy of his latest album *Double Fantasy.* Chapman said, "I was just so excited to see him." Just over five hours later that night at 10:30 p.m. he fired five shots, hitting Lennon in the back four times. After shooting Lennon, Chapman just stood there. A bystander took the gun from his hand and kicked it across the pavement and then the police apprehended him. Though his attorney attempted to argue that Chapman "had touches of schizophrenia and paranoia," Chapman chose to plead guilty. Chapman has been denied parole eight times, most recently in 2014, and his wife has stood by him for 25 years. To the question of why he did it, Chapman has said, "Shooting Lennon was an answer to all of my problems, I guess. . . . It was to cancel all my past, to give me an identity" (Sloane, 2015).

Chapman's identity entanglement with Holden Caulfield was a key motivational element in his murder of John Lennon amidst a backdrop of what was going on around him during this historical time. In his book *Let Me Take You Down,* based on interviews with Chapman in prison, Jones (1992) describes Chapman as a "troubled, self-absorbed, and emotionally unfulfilled child" who grew up amid America's divisiveness over the Vietnam War in a "confused and hypocritical world" who was "desperate for recognition" (p. xv):

> Since John Lennon was just "an image on a screen" in the mind of Mark David Chapman, the former Beatles fan found it relatively easy to incorporate the superstar into an intricate narrative that controlled his life. To justify the act of murder, Chapman also found it necessary to transform himself into the fictional character Holden Caulfield. According to the *Catcher* script, as Chapman interpreted it, Lennon's blood would give him an identity as *The Catcher in the Rye* of his generation. His new identity would, in turn lend an aura of literary dignity to the desperate and cowardly act of shooting a man in the back. (Jones, 1992, p. 243)

Similarly, Black (1991) notes that it took a "violent act of self-creation" for Chapman to "transform the anonymous individual from a Nobody to a Somebody" (p. 144). Chapman reached adulthood "at a time when identity, and indeed reality itself, had become in large part a fabrication of mass media" (p. 153). "To be somebody is to be Somebody—to be a media personality, to have one's personality mediated by the media. . . . Chapman was the man who would be king in a hyperreal world where media coverage defines and confers existence—existence, however, which is no longer anything more substantial than image" (Black, 1991, pp. 153–154).

Chapman wrote a letter to *The New York Times* after Lennon's death, maintaining that the motive for his murder of John Lennon was contained in *The Catcher in the Rye.* On the night he killed Lennon, Chapman wrote in a Bible in his hotel room "Holden Caulfield" and added Lennon's name

Case Studies of Copycat and Media-Mediated Crime   91

to the Gospel According to John. He also picked up a copy of *Catcher in the Rye* and wrote in the title page, "Holden Caulfield, From Holden Caulfield," followed by the words "*This* is my statement." On the way to kill Lennon he wore a Russian fur hat with earflaps like the hunting hat Caulfield wore, and called it his "people shooting hat."

Black (1991) suggests that Chapman was compelled to enact a fiction provided by literature and film to achieve both identity and celebrity and that he would have been incapable of acting out his plan, or even conceiving of it in the first place, without his fascination with Lennon as a cultural icon and his engulfment with the character Holden Caulfield. Lacking an identity of his own, Chapman's murder of John Lennon was a way of playing the identities of a fictional antihero and an actual media star identity off each other, perhaps to see which one was more real. In interviews after his trial, Chapman expressed concern about being a phony, asking his psychiatrists if they thought he was a phony, and maintained that every generation needs a catcher in the rye who speaks out against phoniness and corruption (Black, 1991, pp. 156–157). In his parole board hearing in 2010, Chapman said, "I felt that by killing John Lennon I would become somebody and instead of that I became a murderer and murderers are not somebodies" (Virtanen, 2012). From Black's perspective, "In the hyperreality of the 1980s, such practices of appropriating, simulating, exchanging, and denying media images and narrative fictions became an indispensable means of fashioning a social identity. In a narcissistic culture awash in inauthenticity, murder seemed to offer a desperate means of clarifying the real (Black, 1991, p. 158).

Taxi Driver: John Hinckley, Jr.

Four months after Chapman murdered John Lennon, on March 30, 1981, 26-year-old John Hinckley, Jr. attempted to assassinate Ronald Reagan. Hinckley fired six shots from a .22-caliber firearm loaded with explosive Devastator bullets in the direction of President Reagan as he was exiting the Washington Hilton Hotel in Washington, D.C. He hit four people, including President Ronald Reagan, White House Press Secretary James Brady, Secret Service Agent Tim McCarthy, and Washington, D.C. police officer Thomas Delahanty. President Reagan was struck underneath his left arm and suffered a broken rib, a punctured lung, and internal bleeding. McCarthy was struck by a bullet in the chest that then passed through his right lung, doing minimal damage, and lacerated his liver. Delahanty was shot in the lower left of his neck, and the bullet was lodged near his spinal column. The bullet was later removed. Brady suffered severe injuries when struck in the head, with the bullet entering his forehead and exiting the side of his head. He sustained significant brain damage from the incident, and his death in 2014 was ruled a homicide as a result of the attack (Feaver, 1981; Hermann et al., 2015). The incident led to the signing of the Brady Bill that requires a waiting period and a background check on people purchasing a handgun. Hinckley was determined to be not guilty by reason of insanity (NGRI) and served 38 years at the St. Elizabeth's Mental Hospital in Washington, D.C. He was released at age 63 to live with his 90-year-old mother in Williamsburg, Virginia, in 2019 and now lives a quiet life where he is running an antiques and books business, plays music, and does art. He lives under restrictions barring him from the Internet and from owning a gun and is one of the most closely watched Not Guilty by Reason of Insanity (NGRI) patients in history (Cohen, 2016; Cole, 2019).

In Hinckley's trial details came out to show that he lived a solitary existence with no social relationships outside of his family. His early childhood was said to be normal by all appearances and then he dropped out of high school and went to Hollywood to try to make it as a musician with no success. While in Hollywood, Hinckley watched the 1976 film *Taxi Driver* (Scorsese, 1976) 15 times at the Egyptian Theatre. He became psychologically immersed in the story and Travis Bickel. The main character in *Taxi Driver* became Hinckley's reality. Travis Bickle is a loner who attempts to assassinate a political candidate to impress a political campaign worker played by Cybill Shepherd. Later in the film, Bickle meets and becomes obsessed with protecting Iris, a child prostitute played by Jodie Foster. At the end of the film, Bickle kills Iris's pimp in a bloody shootout, which is open to interpret as to whether it is real or a figment of Bickle's imagination (Hough, 2020); a voice-over plays showing Iris's father reading a thank-you letter to Bickle for saving his daughter accompanied by a screen view of a newspaper article with the tag line "Parents Express Shock, Gratitude," painting a picture of Bickle as a New York hero, leaving open to interpretation as to whether this is reality or a figment of Bickle's imagination (Hough, 2020).

Hinckley heavily identified with Travis Bickle, the main character played by Robert De Niro, and developed an obsession with Jodie Foster. He wore an army jacket, boots, and flannel and drank peach brandy, popped pills, and purchased weapons like Bickle. He told his parents he had a fictional girlfriend named "Lynne Collins" like Bickle did in the film when he wrote to his parents claiming Betsy the political campaign worker was his girlfriend (Capps, 2013). He wrote letters to Foster, physically stalked her, and eventually began taking a class at Yale in New

Case Studies of Copycat and Media-Mediated Crime   93

Haven, Connecticut, where Foster attended to be closer to her. In letters to Foster, Hinckley detailed how he would hang around her dormitory to be near her. Just before the attack, he wrote an unsent letter to Foster that said, "Jodie, I would abandon this idea of getting Reagan in a second if I could only win your heart and live out the rest of my life with you, whether it be in total obscurity or whatever."

Chapman's murder of Lennon and *Catcher in the Rye* was a secondary script for Hinckley. Chapman and Hinckley were young, isolated men seeking identity and celebrity who turned suicidal fantasies into homicidal acts while operating under the influence of mass media. Both Chapman and Hinckley imitated Bickle's pose in *Taxi Driver*, taking photos with guns to their heads. Both became entangled in the identities of fictional characters who sought celebrity by being saviors. "Hinckley became caught up in an ongoing interplay between art and real life whereby literary and cinematic fictions repeatedly mediated actual events, and vice versa" (Black, 1991, p. 160).

From Ethical Reality to Aesthetic Hyperreality

The Chapman and Hinckley cases epitomize media-mediated copycat crimes of the 1980s. Culturally this was a time of fast-moving media technology where the ethical realm of the real collided full-force with the aesthetic realm of the hyperreal. Media consumers were not yet technologically sophisticated, yet the pace at which media contributed to the communication of meaning and messages and symbols of politics, pop culture, and violence was relentless. Lone, isolated young men like Chapman and Hinckley who lacked identity were exposed to mass media and popular culture at a time when life became indistinguishable from and unimaginable without art. "In the new media mediated 'reality' thoroughly awash in art-as-advertising and advertising-as-art, acts of violence like those of Chapman and Hinckley need to be studied as media-simulations, as quintessentially mimetic acts" (Black, 1991, p. 138).

Chapman's and Hinckley's motivations for murder are not explainable through traditional motives such as greed, retaliation, or power. Their acts of violence were media-mediated mimetic acts. Their cognitive scripts were connected to each other and to cultural scripts that sent them messages about how to gain power and celebrity. The masculine savior themes in their cognitive scripts were reinforced by cultural artifacts (*Catcher in the Rye* and *Taxi Driver*) that cemented ideas that led them to believe that they would be celebrated Somebodies if they proved themselves through violence. The sequence of and connections between their crimes and the media they consumed that inspired their violence offer a telling example of the power of media and popular culture to influence lonely, isolated, violence-prone edge-sitters. Chapman and Hinckley were keen consumers of pop culture—identity-less men searching for identity in a culture that sold the idea that you could be the catcher in the rye of the generation if you take down the phonies and are willing to do something bold and violent. Chapman and Hinckley operated in the crux between the ethical realm of the real and the aesthetic realm of the hyperreal. Media and pop culture populated their fantasies and became their crimes through which they were convinced they would achieve identity and celebrity through violence.

Natural Born Killer *Copycats of the 1990s: Media Characteristics that Exacerbate the Copycat Effect*

In the 1990s, the Internet, pagers, cell phones, and computers were becoming available to mainstream consumers. Print newspapers declined. Celebrity magazines were popular. TV viewing continued to increase, with more heavy users of television found among the socially disadvantaged. People who did not watch television became a "vanishing breed" (Xiaoming, 1994). Blockbuster Video became the go-to place on a Friday night, launching its 1000th store and becoming the top video rental company in the United States (Olito, 2020). Media and popular culture were awash with grunge and Generation X. Bob Dole campaigned for president and lost on a Hollywood-bashing platform accusing films like *True Romance* and *Natural Born Killers* of being films "that revel in mindless violence and sex" (Campbell, 2015). Popular culture was given a criminal flair with songs like "Cop Killer" and groups like N.W.A. that were criticized by President George Bush for inciting violence, with calls to boycott commercial availability by the police (Ferrell & Sanders, 1995). Rodney King, the LA riots, O. J. Simpson, and the Unabomber were in the news; Princess Di died in a car crash while being chased by paparazzi; and the president of the United States, Bill Clinton, had an affair with Monica Lewinsky in the Oval Office. The 1990s was "defined by fracture, anxiety, and nervousness" (Ewen, 2020).

The 1990s also brought school shootings involving teen and preteen shooters (Ferguson et al., 2011) with the decade ending in the Columbine massacre. The 1990s was the heyday of the "culture of control" (Garland, 2001) characterized by draconian criminal justice policies such as three strikes, mandatory sentencing, sex offender registration and civil commitment, and the idea of the "superpredator" (Pizarro et al., 2007). Serial

Case Studies of Copycat and Media-Mediated Crime

murder, mass murder, and school shootings dominated the real and fictional media. Female empowerment through violence became part of the cultural discourse in literature, popular culture, and the news. Lorena Bobbitt and Mary Kay Letourneau[2] were in the nightly news, *Thelma and Louise* (1991) and *The Last Seduction* (1994) were on the screen, Lara Croft became one of the most popular action stars in computer gaming (Moltenbrey & Donelan, 2002), and Aileen Wuornos became history's most notorious female serial killer (Shipley & Arrigo, 2004; Stockton, 2018). Journalists and scholars raised awareness and attention to girl gangsters (Sikes, 1996), female rage (Valentis & Devane, 1994), and the rise of the violent female who was "Deadlier than the Male" (Kirsta, 1994).

The 1994 film *Natural Born Killers* (*NBK*) directed by Oliver Stone with screenplay written by Quentin Tarantino (Stone, 1994) has been linked to over a dozen murders in the United States, Canada, and Europe and to mass shootings, including Columbine. To date, no other film has been linked to so many real-life crimes. *NBK* inspired so many copycat crimes that the film has been called the "ne plus ultra of copycat-killing source material" (Atkinson, 1999). *NBK* and the crimes the film inspired offer a case study in media-related factors that enhance the copycat effect. The influence of the film suggests that features of a media source can exacerbate the copycat effect on criminal behavior for more than just edge-sitters.

NBK is loosely based on the real-life story of 19-year-old Charles Starkweather and 14-year-old Caril Ann Fugate, who went on a road-trip murder spree across Nebraska and Wyoming between December 1957 and January 1958 killing 11 people including Fugate's mother, stepfather, and half-sister. Prior to *NBK*, other films loosely based on the Starkweather-Fugate murders spanned decades of cinema (Sergeant, 1996).[3] Oliver Stone insisted that he did not intend the film to be a celebration of violence. Rather, according to Stone, *NBK* was a satire of the violence he saw around him in the 1990s media landscape. The film is "the first mass media production to vehemently condemn the mass media themselves for inducing criminal behavior" (Rafter, 2006, p. 63). Stone said of *NBK*, "Its violence was satiric. I had a history of making films with realistic violence, and I thought it was clearly not literal, but metaphoric, over-the-top, not even close to real" (Lattanzio, 2019).

The story in *NBK* follows Mickey and Mallory Knox, a young, attractive, visually eclectic couple on a road-trip-serial-mass murder spree across the Southwest that results in over 50 murders. The film is shot in 18 different formats, including animation, 16 mm and 35 mm cameras, back projection, and High 8 with approximately 3000 rapid-fire cuts.

Throughout the film, flashbacks are shown (that the film's animator calls "psychological landscapes") depicting Mickey's and Mallory's childhoods comprising a range of visual genres including superhero/villain animation, TV sitcoms, and news-like sequences including a depiction of childhood sexual abuse to the theme of *I Love Lucy*, acts of female aggression to the tune of female metal band L7, psychedelic mushroom trips, and heavy/industrial metal music background music by Nine Inch Nails (Kiselyak, 1996). In the end of the film, there is a prison riot scene (with images strikingly similar to the horrific real-life images of the 1980 New Mexico Prison riot) shot in the famous real-life Illinois Stateville Prison in which (in the director's cut edition) the prison warden (played by Tommy Lee Jones) is attacked by rioting inmates who thrust his severed head in the air on a broomstick. The final scene shows the couple executing TV reporter Wayne Gayle (played by Robert Downey, Jr.) while he begs for his life. The postcredit images show a domesticated Mickey and pregnant Mallory in a floral dress riding off into the sunset in a motor home with a bunch of kids.

One notable aspect of the film is female empowerment violence depicted in the character Mallory Knox. Mickey and Mallory bonded through the power and fame they achieved throughout their murder spree. The psychological landscape in Mickey's background suggests that he is a "natural born" killer. The landscape in Mallory's background suggests that she is the victim of sexual abuse at the hands of her father. She uses violence throughout the film as readily as Mickey does, more so in some incidents. In multiple places throughout the film, she unleashes her violence on men who sexualize her. Her response after shooting men in a barrage of overkill is "How sexy am I now flirty boy?"[4]

Natural Born Killers: Benjamin Darras and Sarah Edmondson

The most notorious of the *NBK* cases in the United States was the 1995 murder spree in Louisiana and Mississippi committed by 18-year-olds Benjamin Darras and Sarah Edmondson. The Darras and Edmondson case was notorious for several reasons. The case involved the teenage daughter of an Oklahoma Supreme Court justice, niece of the state attorney general, granddaughter of a former congressional representative, and great-niece of a former Oklahoma governor. The case involved two notable victims—William Savage, a businessman and Louisiana cotton gin manager and friend of author John Grisham, and Patsy Byers, a convenience store clerk who was left for dead and rendered quadriplegic and went on to launch a First Amendment civil suit against *NBK* director

Case Studies of Copycat and Media-Mediated Crime   97

Oliver Stone that went to the U.S. Supreme court (O'Neil, 2001). John Grisham wrote a scathing essay blaming Oliver Stone for inciting violence and triggering Darras and Edmondson, who previously had no history of violence (Grisham, 1996). Byers died of cancer in 1997 a day before she was scheduled to videotape her testimony against Edmondson. Her death was unrelated to her shooting injuries; however, her paralysis delayed her cancer diagnosis (Baldwin, 2010).

Darras and Edmondson's crime/murder spree began on March 6, 1995, when they went on a road trip after watching *NBK* multiple times over a period of days while consuming hallucinogenic drugs. They originally planned to attend a Grateful Dead concert in Memphis, Tennessee but got the date wrong. Darras and Edmondson left Darras's home in Tahlequah, Oklahoma, in Edmondson's white 1986 Nissan Maxima without telling anyone where they were going. They brought Edmondson's father's .38-caliber revolver with them, and as they drove through Oklahoma, Arkansas, Mississippi, and Louisiana Darras spoke about reenacting scenes from *NBK* by killing people at random. According to Edmondson, Darras talked as if he were fantasizing from the movie (Kunich, 2000). On March 7 they went to Hernando, Mississippi, and stopped at Producers Gin where William Savage was working as manager. Darras shot Savage twice in the face at point-blank range, left with $200 and credit cards, and got back on the road. An insurance representative making a routine call found Savage's body later. On March 8 Edmondson and Darras traveled 300 miles south to Ponchatoula, Louisiana, where they drove to a Time Saver convenience store. Darras stayed in the car and Edmondson went in. Patsy Byers was a clerk at the store. Byers's murder was caught on the store surveillance camera showing that Edmondson came into the store, grabbed three chocolate bars, walked to the register, and shot Byers in the throat while she was standing at the register. When Byers fell to the floor, Edmondson screamed, left, and then returned a few minutes later and went behind the cash register to try to open it. Byers, who was lying on the floor with her spinal cord severed, heard Edmondson say, "Are you dead yet? No? How do you open this?" Darras and Edmondson traveled back to their homes in Oklahoma and were caught four months later after Edmondson told an ex-boyfriend about the crimes, who was later pulled over by police for speeding and told the police about the murders. Edmonson and Darras testified against each other, confessed, pled guilty, and told investigators they were inspired by *Natural Born Killers*.

Darras and Edmondson were convicted and sentenced to 35 years each for the Byers shooting. Edmondson pled guilty to armed robbery,

98   *Copycat Crime*

attempted second-degree murder, and the use of a firearm during a violent felony. Darras pled guilty to armed robbery in Louisiana and testified against Edmondson. Edmondson was released on parole in 2010 after serving 11 years, and her parole will end in 2025 (Baldwin, 2010). Darras was also sentenced to life for Savage's murder and is serving his sentence in Mississippi. Edmondson testified that during the road trip Darras spoke openly with her about killing people like Mickey did with Mallory, including mentioning coming upon a remote farmhouse and murdering all its occupants and then moving on to the next slaughter. Edmondson also said that after Savage's murder Darras said that the murder made him feel powerful and he made fun of the noise Savage made when he shot him. Edmondson's explanation for shooting Byers was that Sara thought she "saw a demon" (a reference to a scene in *NBK*) (Ahrens, 1995; Brooks, 2002; Grisham, 1996; Spearman, 20194).

Other *NBK* Copycats

There were two *NBK* copycat cases in Paris, France, involving teenage couples influenced by *NBK*. Florence Rey, age 19, and her boyfriend, 22-year-old Audry Maupin, killed four people in a violent spree on October 4, 1994. Also in Paris, 18-year-old Veronique Herbert and her boyfriend, 17-year-old Sebastian Paindavoine, stabbed a 16-year-old in March 1996 closely mimicking a scene in the film (Lichfield, 1998; O'Neil, 2001).

In October 1994, six months before Darras and Edmondson's murders, 19-year-old Florence Rey and her 22-year-old boyfriend, Audry Maupin, killed three police officers and a taxi driver during a car chase in Paris that left Maupin dead. Both were said to have connections to anarchist movements. Rey was convicted and sentenced to 20 years in prison. *NBK* was released in Europe at the Venice Film Festival on August 29, 1994, a month before the murders. Rey described the shootings as "fate" (a line from the film), and the pair was dubbed "France's Natural Born Killers" (Boyle, 2001).

Soon after the Rey trial, Herbert and Paindavoine were tried in Paris for the murder of 16-year-old Abdeladim Gahbiche. Herbert was said to be obsessed with *NBK*. It was uncovered during her trial that she lured Gahbiche to his death with the promise of sex, mimicking an *NBK* scene where Mallory leaves Mickey in a hotel room after getting into an argument with him because he flirted with a woman who is bound and gagged in the corner of the room whom they had abducted. Mallory leaves the hotel in anger and goes to a gas station where she lures a young male gas

Case Studies of Copycat and Media-Mediated Crime

station attendant into the garage while she does a dance for him. He lies down on the hood of a car in the garage expecting Mallory to lie on top of him, at which time she steps back and shoots him multiple times. In Herbert's case, she, rather than her boyfriend Paindavoine, was the primary perpetrator and ringleader in the case. Herbert received a 15-year sentence and Paindavoine received a 12-year sentence (Lichfield, 1998; O'Neil, 2001).

NBK has been connected to school shootings and other crimes dating up to 15 years after the release of the film. In 1994, a 14-year-old boy was accused of decapitating a 13-year-old girl. The boy told police he wanted to be famous "like the natural born killers" (Brooks, 2002; Patten, 1997). Twenty-one-year-old William Sodders of Rock Point, New York, was turned in by his father for killing a local firefighter; his father told police that the son was obsessed with *NBK* and that he shot the firefighter with a stolen 9-mm for the thrill (Patten, 1997). In Salt Lake City, Nathan Martinez wore tinted round sunglasses, shaved his head like Mickey Knox, and shot his stepmother and 10-year-old sister. When arrested he told police how much he loved *NBK* (Patten, 1997). A teenager in Georgia accused of shooting an 82-year-old Florida man to death shouted at TV cameras, "I'm a natural-born killer!" In 1995, four individuals in their twenties killed a truck driver in Georgia after seeing *NBK* 19 times. One of the co-defendants in a Massachusetts murder case in 1995 bragged to his girlfriend that he and his accomplice are "natural born killers" (Kunich, 2000; Schweizer, 1998). In 2007, 13 years after *NBK*'s release, 12-year-old Jasmine Richardson and her 23-year-old boyfriend Jeremy Allen Steinke murdered Richardson's parents and 8-year-old brother in Alberta, Canada. During their 2007 trial, it was discovered that the couple had a fixation with death and Goth subculture, had watched *NBK*, and that Steinke watched the film while high on cocaine and got the idea to "rescue" Richardson as Mickey had done in the film. Richardson was convicted of three counts of first-degree murder, becoming the youngest person in North American history to receive this sentence (Shapiro, 2007).

School shooters including Barry Loukaitis in Moses Lake, Washington, in 1996; Michael Carneal in Paducah, Kentucky, in 1997; and Columbine killers Klebold and Harris in 1999 all made reference to *NBK*. Loukaitis loved *NBK* and wore clothes emulating Mickey Knox on the day of the shooting (Kunich, 2000; Pankratz & Ingold, 2003). He had watched *NBK* seven times and had told friends he wanted to go across the country killing people like the movie. Columbine killers Harris and Klebold had notebooks filled with references to *NBK*. A year before the Columbine massacre they made entries in each other's 1998 yearbooks referring to "the holy April morning of *NBK*" (Newman et al., 2004). In Klebold's journal he wrote, "I'm stuck in humanity. Maybe going '*NBK*' (gawd) with Eric is the way to break free" (Klebold, 2016, p. 166).

What Was It About *NBK*?

With so many perpetrators referring to *NBK* before or after committing acts of violence, the film is an important case study in media elements that exacerbate the copycat effect. The psychedelic, psychological background landscapes and use of multiple film formats create genre confusion, especially for developing adolescents and youth. Gratuitous violence, presentation of serial murder as fun, justification for violence in the childhood histories of the main characters, use of violence as a form of feminist empowerment, appealing characters who were in love, the happily-ever-after ending, and excessive media looping contribute to a swirl of aesthetic elements that blur the boundary between fantasy and reality (Helfgott, 2008, 2015). Oliver Stone himself said at the film's premier, "The most pacifist people in the world said they came out of this movie and wanted to kill somebody" (O'Neil, 2001, p. 157). Identifying what made this film so influential in the minds of these copycat offenders is an empirical question of great importance for future research.

There are several elements of *NBK* that likely exacerbated the copycat effect. First, *NBK* is full of media loops. A media loop involves showing and reframing an image in another context (e.g., an instant replay, a clip of a real-life event within a fictional film, or footage from an original news story replayed within the context of another news story) (Manning, 1998). *NBK* is riddled with media loops of images of past criminal events—the 1966 Charles Whitman spree murder at the University of Texas, the Manson murders, the Rodney King beating, Richard Ramirez, the Menendez brothers, O. J. Simpson, and Lorena Bobbitt trials move back and forth from the fictional characters/storyline to real-life violent media events—"even to a generation raised on MTV and Sega games, this is the cinematic equivalent of staring into a strobe light for two hours" (Patten, 1997, p. 3).

The entire film in fact was a complex "copycat loop"—a media loop that shows/reframes an image of a copycat crime in another context (Helfgott, 2015, p. 56). *NBK* itself is a "copy" of the real-life 1958 Starkweather-Fugate murder spree (Sergeant, 1996). Copycat loops, even more than other types of media loops, distort and blur the boundary between reality and fantasy while glorifying mimetic violence, creating cognitive

Case Studies of Copycat and Media-Mediated Crime 101

confusion that makes violence look appealing to individuals who may or may not have risk factors for violence, in particular youth in various stages of rebellion and development.

The appeal of the *NBK* characters is another risk factor for copycat violence. *NBK*'s main characters Mickey and Mallory Knox are physically attractive, cool, and make murder look fun. Films and media images that ask the audience to identify with violent characters by making them likable while glamorizing and making excuses for the violence they engage in exacerbate the copycat effect. In *NBK* we see road-tripping characters who are madly in love. They take a day off from murdering people to get married in the middle of their violent spree. They become media heroes, escape from prison, and ride off happily ever after in a Winnebago with a bunch of kids and one more on the way. This depiction of young love on the run is rich for inclusion into violent scripts of edge-sitters with the great potential to fuel fantasy for others who may never have thought of committing a violent act.

The depiction of female empowerment–related violence mixed with the sexualization and infantilization of Mallory Knox and her depiction as a victim of incest in her childhood also exacerbates the copycat effect, especially for female-identified viewers. *NBK* depicts female violence that is simultaneously contradictory and confusing, empowering and infantilizing. Mallory Knox is portrayed as a victim of sexual assault and incest who is rescued by bad boy Mickey, who murders her parents (with her help) and is carried off into the sunset. Mallory Knox evolves into a killer with fragmented emotions who, if sexually harassed or devalued, responds with violence. What is so contradictory about her character is that she is physically small, emotionally vulnerable with Mickey, and simultaneously portrayed as a victim and predator. In theatres during the opening night of the film, audiences cheered as Mallory broke necks and shot men dead after they humiliated or sexualized her. Like her character, her violence horrified and empowered audiences and became the inspiration for a string of unprecedented violent female copycats (Helfgott, 2008, 2015).

The *NBK* copycats involved female murderers, resulting in media coverage that focused on the deadlier-than-the-male notion of violent female offenders that entered cultural discourse in the early 1990s. The way Mallory Knox was depicted in *NBK* is consistent with how female violent offenders are presented in real life. When a man commits a violent act, in fantasy or reality, he is more likely to be depicted as a violent "natural born killer" than his female counterpart. "Mickey fills a recognizable (male) space in Western culture" while Mallory must be explained and understood (Boyle, 2001, p. 315). Oliver Stone chose Woody Harrelson as the actor for the part of Mickey Knox because Harrelson's real-life father is in prison for murder. The *NBK* copycats were unique in that the film inspired violence in male-female duos. In *NBK* and in the real-life *NBK* copycats, the female perpetrators were as instrumentally aggressive and violent as their male counterparts. However, they were depicted in the media as expressively motivated, with their crimes explained away in ways that their male partners' crimes were not. The media referred to Rey, who was convicted of armed robbery, attempted murder, and the murder of four people including three police officers, as "a timid girl of 19" who "committed un crime d'amor fou, and her charismatic, stubborn, angry boyfriend will go down in popular legend as France's rebel without a cause" (Marlow, 1998). The news media, like the fictional world of *NBK*, attempted to understand the female killer while depicting the male killer as naturally violent:

> It is inconceivable, even within the fictional world of *NBK*, that the violent woman could be "naturally born" while male violence is so pervasive as to require neither comment or analysis. Representing Mickey and his fictional counterparts as "natural born killers," as inherently evil or monstrous, ignores their agency, choice and hence responsibility for their actions. To this extent, Oliver Stone *and* the international press are equally culpable as they help to perpetuate the normality and apparent inevitability of male violence. (Boyle, 2001, p. 314)

The masculinization of violence in *NBK* presents male violence as natural, normal, expected, and invisible. This gendered presentation of violence in the film carries a particular language of violence that provides a gendered justification for violence that works in tandem with cultural gender stereotypes with implications for the copycat effect. Mickey Knox's character validates the notion of the male natural born killer, and Mallory Knox provides a role model for female victim retaliatory violence.

The many copycat perpetrators associated with *NBK* draw attention to media characteristics that exacerbate the copycat effect. *NBK*'s central theme according to Stone was to hold a satirical mirror up to society to self-examine the media-mediated violence of the times. However, the film's satire seemed to pass without reflection by the public. This failure to collectively understand the main point of the film can be viewed as a "social dream" (Reiber and Green, 1989). *NBK* evoked strong reaction for graphic violence by film critics, politicians, and the public, but did not evoke comment to Stone's intended satirical theme. This is what largely

Case Studies of Copycat and Media-Mediated Crime 103

made *NBK* so appealing to copycat criminals. On its surface, the film was a glorious display of unabashed violence. Less overtly (or unconsciously), it was a virtual reflection of the bizarre cultural glorification of celebrated violence and infamy. This message directly appealed to and validated the psyches of would-be copycats who (like many of the film's critics) were unable to process the deeper satirical substantive message. With the number of *NBK* copycats, it could be hypothesized then that the film was a trigger, not a shaper, and that Darras and Edmondson were under the influence of Mickey and Mallory Knox and would not have committed the murders, or as many murders, had they not watched *NBK*. In his essay "Unnatural Killers," John Grisham (1996) emphatically argues that although Darras and Edmondson were troubled teens who had both spent time in psychiatric facilities and had abused drugs, they were "confused, disturbed, shiftless, mindless . . . but they had never hurt anyone before" (p. 349) and it was *NBK* that incited the violence.

When a media source influences not one, or two, but over a dozen copycat crimes, even years after the film was released, this begs the question—*What is it about the media source that exacerbates the copycat effect?* While Stone emphasized that *NBK* is satire examining the reflexive relationship between media and violence in culture in the 1990s, Grisham argued that *NBK*'s "relentlessly bloody story" was designed to shock, numb, and make murder look fun, sending the message that the more you kill, the cooler you are. You can become famous, get your face on a magazine cover, and get away with it. For Grisham, there was a direct causal link between *NBK* and the Darras-Edmondson murder spree:

> A case can be made that there exists a direct causal link between the movie Natural Born Killers and the death of Bill Savage. Viewed another way, the question should be: Would Ben [Darras] have shot innocent people if not for the movie? Nothing in his troubled past indicates violent propensities. But once he saw the movie he fantasized about killing, and his fantasies finally drove them to their crimes. (Grisham, 1996, p. 350)

This question—*Would Darras and Edmondson have gone on their murder spree had they not seen NBK?*—requires empirical examination. In the case of the school shooters such as Loukaitis who was inspired by multiple media sources, including Stephen King's story *Rage* and Pearl Jam's song "Jeremy" and Klebold and Harris whose crime was also associated with the film *Basketball Diaries* (Kalvert, 1995), Marilyn Manson, and *Doom,* what role did *NBK* play amidst the many different mass and pop cultural artifacts that made their way into these individuals' cultural scripts? The *NBK* copycats generate questions that need to be empirically examined within a theoretical framework that makes sense of the intersection of media effects, culture, hypermasculinity, individual-level characteristics, and features of specific media sources.

Simulated and Virtual Reality at the Turn of the 21st Century: *Lost Inside* **The Matrix** *and* **Grand Theft Auto**

At the turn of the 21st century, hysteria over Y2K turned out to be a big nothing (Uenuma, 2019) to be shockingly overshadowed by the September 11, 2001, attacks. The horrific media images of the violence unleashed on 9/11 changed global approaches to terrorism and led to widespread cultural acceptance of law enforcement, governmental, and private surveillance in the United States (Hughes, 2012; Kondrasuk, 2004; Lyon and Haggerty, 2012). TV households with cable or satellite had an average of 130 channels (a 400 percent increase from the decade prior) with TVs outnumbering people in U.S. homes (McAdams, 2009) and the greatest growth in TV viewing time of any decade since Nielsen began keeping track in 1949–1950. Americans watched 32 percent more TV from the birth of television to the first years of the 21st century (Madrigal, 2018). By 2009–2010, television viewing hit an all-time peak with the average American watching 8 hours and 55 minutes per day. The number of movie tickets sold (from 1980 to 2019) in the United States and Canada hit its peak in 2003 (Statistica, 2020a). *The Dark Knight* and *Avatar* were top grossing films. Camera phones became commercially available, and Myspace and Google launched. The Gulf War ended, and the Human Genome Project was completed. Al Gore lost the presidency to Bush, and Obama became the first Black president. Steve Jobs unveiled the iPhone. The Xbox 360 was released, and *Grand Theft Auto (GTA)* (released in 1997 as a 2D game) moved to a 3D immersive experience with *GTA 3, GTA Vice City, GTA San Andreas GTA 4*, and *GTA 5. GTA 5* became the highest grossing media title to date, with 90 million units sold, historically surpassing any movie, album, book, or other video game (Connor, 2018). Computer games moved to fully immersive 3D environments, improving the characters and animations of the 1990s, and *World of Warcraft* became a mass phenomenon.

Not Guilty by Reason of *The Matrix*

The film trilogy *The Matrix* (Wachowski & Wachowski, 1999, 2003a, 2003b) is associated with a half dozen copycat murders, including the 2002 Washington, D.C. sniper spree murders. In two cases, Tonda Lynn Ansley

Case Studies of Copycat and Media-Mediated Crime   105

in Ohio in 2002 and Vadim Mieseges in San Francisco in 2003, attorneys used the "*Matrix* Defense" to argue that their clients were not guilty by reason of insanity, a result of losing touch with reality while lost inside the *Matrix* (Bean, 2003; Campbell, 2003; Coleman, 2004; Stern, 2003). The *Matrix* copycat cases illustrate the increasing recognition of the power of media to inspire violence and a notable shift in the aftermath of Hinckley's NGRI verdict that resulted in widespread insanity defenses.

The premise of the *Matrix* trilogy is that the real world is an illusion created by an evil computer. Most of its inhabitants dream away their lives while prefabricated experiences are forcefully pumped into them through a cord at the back of the skull. Keanu Reeves plays the main character "Neo" who is one of only a few humans who have unplugged the cord and fought their way out of The Matrix. The blurred boundary between reality and fantasy in *The Matrix* has the potential to influence individuals with preexisting mental health conditions whose lives are "fractured" and "without meaning" through the story of a "reality-itself-as-conspiracy, a worldview with a natural appeal to the alienated, the paranoid, and the otherwise unbalanced" (Schone, 2003).

On February 17, 2003, 19-year-old Joshua Cooke murdered his adoptive parents, 51-year-old Paul and 56-year-old Margaret Cooke, in Fairfax, Virginia. In interviews after his conviction, Josh described the feeling he had the day of the murders. The morning of the murder he felt "off." He had the habit of playing violent video games for up to six hours a day. His favorite games were *Grand Theft Auto III, Doom,* and *BloodRayne.* He was listening to "Bodies" by Drowning Pool on repeat. "Let the bodies hit the floor, let the bodies hit the floor." Cooke purchased a Remington 870 Express Super Magnum a few days prior with money he earned from working at a local Jiffy Lube. He previously worked at Blockbuster and CVS, had no close friends, had never been on a date, got poor grades, and just weeks prior to the crime learned he could not join the Marines because of his poor eyesight. He purchased the gun because of its similarities with the weapon the character Neo used in *The Matrix.* Cooke watched *The Matrix* so many times he wore out his VHS video tape of the film and had to buy a new one. He purchased a wardrobe like Neo's—an identical black, floor-length cape-like trench coat, black boots, and wrap-around sunglasses and wore the outfit when his parents were not around while playing *The Matrix* soundtrack full-blast on his headphones.

On the evening of February 17, Cooke picked up the weapon while listening to "Bodies" while staring at his poster of *The Matrix* on his bedroom wall and said he wanted to end his and his parents' lives.

Prior to shooting, he had a flash that reminded him of *The Matrix*. He loaded his weapon and went downstairs to where his parents were located. He first approached his mother and as she turned around, shot her in the chest. His father, who was working on a computer in the same room and on the phone with Cooke's older sister who was in college, ducked under the desk. He approached his father and shot him six times, went upstairs to reload his weapon, returned, and gave the final shots to the heads of his parents. Paul was shot seven times and Margaret was shot twice in the chest and face. Cooke then grabbed his father's phone, told his sister he had to hang up and call somebody, and then called 911 and said, "I just shot my parents. I just blew them away with the shotgun—12-gauge Super Magnum. Get your asses over here" and called again a few minutes later asking them why they were not there yet (Perl, 2003).

Joshua Cooke had no prior history of violence. He was immersed in virtual reality, just as Neo is in the film. When describing the murders, Joshua told his lawyers,

> It was like a video game . . . like I was in a virtual reality. It was like I was watching myself. . . . I don't know. I kinda went into a zone. I had no emotion at the time. I felt like I was kind of a zombie. . . . And then I looked at my shotgun, and I felt like there was nothing left in my life. No future for me. I had all this anger building up, and I guess I just felt like doing something. Anything. There was no sense behind it. It was just senseless. (Perl, 2003)

Cooke's attorney initially planned to argue the insanity defense but refrained when psychologists assessed Joshua and determined he was mentally sound during the commission of the crime. The case drew media attention to the idea of "the *Matrix* Defense."

Cooke was convicted of two counts of first-degree murder and two felony gun charges, and his obsession with *The Matrix* was raised in his sentencing hearing. Cooke's aunt said, "He was compassionate. It's unbelievable to me. It's not the Joshua we knew . . . I just can't put the two people together." When asked about his motivation for the crime Cooke said,

> Dressing as Neo became an important break from that life . . . I felt like it was drawing attention to me, like, "Hey, he looks like the guy in The Matrix." "He looks like one of those guys from the Columbine shooting." . . . Any kind of attention was good—negative or positive. I just wanted it. I didn't have any kind of love or understanding for Dylan Klebold, the guy in

Case Studies of Copycat and Media-Mediated Crime

Columbine. But I just thought if I resembled them, so maybe somebody would point at me, and people would look at me and say, "Look at him.". . .

I felt like nobody wanted me, and maybe if I could get some kind of attention, any kind of attention, somebody might come up to me and talk to me. (Perl, 2003)

In Cooke's mind, mimicking Neo helped him transform from a Nobody to a Somebody. Throughout Cooke's trial and sentencing, it was discovered that his biological father was schizophrenic, and at least one psychologist indicated that he was likely schizophrenic but that his condition was masked with no outward signs of delusions but that he suffered from a "detachment from the self." The psychologist explained, "People are scarcely real to him . . . video games are a community he could relate to . . . he suffered from 'attachment failure' and the murders of his adoptive parents were a 'deflected suicide' resulting from subconscious self-loathing that aimed instead at the only available targets—'Let me destroy the mirrors' so 'I won't have to look at the self.'"

Cooke was sentenced to 40 years in prison without possibility of parole. During his sentencing hearing, psychologists (including Dr. Brad Bushman, who served as an expert witness on the effects of video game violence) presented expert testimony suggesting Cooke understood the act he committed. However, his early trauma and mental health issues made him susceptible to influence from *The Matrix* and virtual violence in video games. One psychologist testified, ". . . as far as the self, it was as if it was the action of another" (Perl, 2003).

The Matrix also played a key role in the insanity defense of Lee Boyd Malvo. In 2002, Malvo was 17 years old when he and John Allen Muhammad went on a cross-country robbery and killing spree ending in Maryland, Washington, D.C., and Virginia. When all was said and done, Muhammad and Malvo had killed 17 people and wounded 10. Malvo was sentenced to six consecutive life sentences without parole, and Muhammad was sentenced to death and executed in 2009. Malvo told detectives to watch *The Matrix* to understand the motives behind the shootings. During his trial, the film and Malvo's drawings of Neo and lines he had written in a journal from the film were presented. It was argued that Malvo's accomplice, John Allen Muhammad, was seen by Malvo as Neo's mentor Morpheus in the film (Kiehl, 2003).

In 2000, Vadim Mieseges, a 27-year-old exchange student from Switzerland who had formally been institutionalized in a mental hospital, murdered a woman he was renting a room from. He told police the woman was giving off evil vibes and feared he would be sucked into *The Matrix*.

He confessed to police that he skinned and dismembered his landlady and scattered her body parts around San Francisco, putting her torso in a dumpster in Golden Gate Park. A judge accepted his insanity plea, and he received NGRI based on the argument that his preexisting paranoia had turned deadly under the influence of crystal meth and *The Matrix*.

In 2002, 36-year-old Tonda Lynn Ansley shot and killed a university professor, Sherry Lee Corbett, who she rented a room from in Ohio. After the murder, Ansley told police she was living in *The Matrix*. She said that her landlord and three other people she was thinking about killing, including her husband, had been controlling her mind and making her have "dreams that I've found out aren't really dreams" (Schone, 2003).

Grand Theft Auto Copycats: The Case of Devin Moore/Thompson and Others

On June 7, 2003, 18-year-old Devin Moore/Thompson allegedly played *GTA: Vice City* for hours before stealing a car and gunning down two police officers and a 911 dispatcher in Fayetteville, Alabama. When Moore/Thompson was captured, he said to police, "Life is like a video game. Everybody's got to die some time." At trial, it was revealed that he was a compulsive violent video game player who played GTA for months prior to the murders and suffered from childhood abuse–related posttraumatic stress disorder (PTSD). Moore/Thompson's attorneys argued the "*GTA* defense"—that he had lost touch with reality and was acting out the virtual violence in GTA. Despite his attorney's efforts, the *GTA* defense was unsuccessful, and Moore/Thompson was sentenced to death in 2005 ("Can a Video Game Lead to Murder?" 2005). On the day of the crime, Officers Arnold Strickland and James Crump apprehended Moore/Thompson on suspicion of stealing a vehicle. Upon performing intake procedures in police headquarters, Moore/Thompson grabbed Officer Strickland's .40-caliber Glock automatic while he was being fingerprinted and shot Strickland twice. Officer Crump ran to the scene and was met in the hallway by Moore/Thompson who shot him three times. Moore/Thompson continued down the hallway where he found 911 dispatcher, Leslie "Ace" Mealer, and fired five shots at him. Moore/Thompson grabbed a set of keys to a patrol car, fled the scene, and was apprehended in a nearby town 45 minutes away (Leung, 2005; Smith, 2005). Prior to the murders, Moore/Thompson had been a super-fan of the video role-playing games *Grand Theft Auto III* and *Grand Theft Auto: Vice City* (Leung, 2005). He reported that he played the game every day, especially in the months leading up to the murders.

Case Studies of Copycat and Media-Mediated Crime

In addition to Moore/Thompson's case, six teenage boys mimicked *GTA: Liberty City Stories* and went on a violent spree in Long Island, New York, committing an armed robbery and carjacking (Crowely, 2008; Leonard, 2008). When police questioned the teens, they said their violence was inspired by the GTA Liberty City, which closely resembles New York City. The teens wanted to emulate the main character, Nico Belic, in the game (Cochran, 2008).

The Combined Effect of Media and Mental Illness

The Matrix and *GTA* cases illustrate how mass media can operate with other risk factors to produce a lethal cocktail of influence for violence. In *The Matrix*, Malvo's, Mieseges's, and Ansley's cases, preexisting psychiatric conditions exacerbated and facilitated by media contributed to their acts of violence. Dr. David Shostak, expert witness for the defense in the Joshua Cooke case, explains the role of violent media as one of a number of risk factors for violence. "Would it have happened if he hadn't had access to [violent media]? I can't say. Did it make it more likely? There's a good chance. But it was in combination with many other very potent variables." These cases illustrate the complex ways that media influences violent behavior for individuals with mental health issues. In these cases, *The Matrix* could be said to have provided the narrative but not a motive. *The Matrix* was not the causal factor leading to the violence but was one of the scripts in the minds of the perpetrators that operated as a simulated reality catalyst for their violence.

The *GTA* games provide opportunity for first-person virtual violence in what has been called a "murder box"—an enclosed screen space "where social and psychic desires that demand sexual and violent interactions [draw] on a new-found world of dark delights" (Atkinson & Rodgers, 2016, p. 1304). For Moore/Thompson and the Long Island teens, *GTA* offered a place within which to form ideas about the world becoming part of their social learning environments, entered their cognitive scripts, and with other risk factors present, moved their fantasy violence to real life. The violence in *GTA* conceals the reality of violence, providing a space where violence is entertainment; an interior temporary world where a player "can choose to go crazy, to take a kind of psychopathic holiday," where everyday rules and conventions are suspended for the time they are in the game (Atkinson & Rodgers, 2016, p. 1304). People can play *GTA* while "thinking outside the murder box" choosing to mix in prosocial behaviors amidst the violence in the games (Denham & Spokes, 2019). For individuals for whom the connection between reality and fiction is already tenuous, ideas and actions that become habit while immersed in the virtual worlds of extreme violence can transfer to the real world. Violent video games are "places of social exception" that move beyond the focus of media effects:

> To play in these spaces is to experience certain forms of freedom from inhibitions—both social and psychological—and an inevitable subjugation of others encountered in these spaces as cannon fodder, expendable or necessary collateral damage. It is here that extreme forms of conduct are normalized as staple reference points for playful engagement. . . . The emptiness of law in these spaces is of course simulated and thereby allows an increased capacity to play with lawlessness, to test it and discover its coded limits. . . . For video games, it does indeed seem that exceptionality from normative and pro-social order itself becomes the norm. (Atkinson & Rodgers, 216, pp. 1302–1303)

It may be difficult for some players such as Devin Moore/Thompson and the other *GTA* copycats to move back and forth between actual and virtual worlds without some element of blurred boundaries. The questions become: Would Moore/Thompson have killed three police officers if he had never played Grand Theft Auto? Would he have stolen a car in the first place? Would the Long Island teens have been as inclined to move their violence from Liberty City to Long Island had the violence in the game been less realistic?

Performance Crimes of the 2010s: Livestreamed Murder

From 2010 to 2020 mass media and digital technology surpassed the wildest dreams of those who grew up in the 1960s, 1970s, 1980s, and 1990s. The most striking advance in mass media and digital culture was social media. From 2010 to 2020 *Facebook, YouTube, Instagram, Snapchat, LinkedIn,* dating sites, *Twitch, TikTok,* and many other social media sites became the mainstay of culture, with an estimated 3.6 billion people using social media worldwide (Statistica, 2020b). The decade started with Barack Obama as president and ended with Donald Trump. There were over 200 mass shootings during the decade, more than any other decade in American history (Steinkoler, 2017). #MeToo, Black Lives Matter, cancel culture, and livestreamed images of police violence against Black lives culminated in the largest protest movement in American history (Loofbourow, 2020).

By 2010, Facebook became the world's most popular social media platform and most popular online activity, with 2.45 billion users (Iqbal,

Case Studies of Copycat and Media-Mediated Crime

2020). Facebook mobile apps were launched in 2008 on iOS and in 2010 on Android, expanding its use exponentially. In 2016 Facebook Live was launched enabling livestream broadcasting through the mobile app. Facebook Live became a feature of social life, allowing anyone to livestream videos used to document police violence (Hern, 2017) and other forms of violence, including mass murder (Grygiel, 2019). In 2017 Facebook creator Mark Zuckerberg acknowledged the harm from violent social media and committed to better address public safety and vicarious victimization. In 2018 Facebook was sued for causing PTSD to staff charged with moderating violent images (Garcia, 2018). This decade was characterized by a cultural interplay between mainstream voyeurism and broadcasting of violence and murder through social media.

One of the earliest Facebook-related murders occurred in 2008. On February 18, 2008, Wayne Forrester murdered his wife, Emma Forrester, in their home in New Addington, Croydon, United Kingdom. Three days after their separation, Emma changed her relationship status on Facebook to "single" and posted that she was newly single and looking to date new men (Bracetti, 2011; Cheston, 2008). Her husband repeatedly called Emma's parents complaining to them about the Facebook entries, saying that they made her look like a fool. While intoxicated on alcohol and cocaine, Forrester broke through her bolted door and stabbed her multiple times with a kitchen knife and a meat cleaver ("Man murdered wife over Facebook posting," 2008). Social media provides public access to otherwise private information that can carry a criminogenic media-mediated element and provides a portal into the personal details of the lives of noncelebrities, making otherwise private information public to potential perpetrators. Just how celebrity stalkers create media-mediated fantasies and fixations about their victims, social media makes public details of everyday life that have historically been private for all but the most famous of celebrities. This digital access to information about both noncelebrities and celebrities alike is a critical aspect of the aesthetic realm of the hyperreal.

Social media as a vehicle by which noncelebrities can publicly broadcast information has taken hyperreality to an entirely different level. TV, films, the Internet, video games, and other forms of media play a role in influencing copycat crime; social media provides an influence *and* a vehicle for perpetrators to publicize their crimes in real time, often before site administrators have the time to take down posts. Access to information made possible by social media is one form of media-mediated crime where media plays a small but important role in MO behavior. The murder of Emma Forrester by her husband who was angered by her social media posts about their relationship status sits along the less extreme side of the copycat crime continuum influencing MO behavior. In this case, the perpetrator used a computer to find out information about his wife. His digital interaction with a media-mediated version of his wife became a surrogate for actual interaction with her that ultimately influenced his decision to murder her.

Luka Rocco Magnotta: Broadcasting Murder Online

At the other end of the copycat continuum is the case of Luka Rocco Magnotta. On May 25, 2012, an 11-minute video titled, "1 Lunatic 1 Ice Pick," was uploaded to Bestgore.com, a now-defunct Canadian shock site that made available highly violent real-life news, photos, and videos. The video depicted a naked male tied to a bedpost who was being stabbed repeatedly with an ice pick and a kitchen knife by someone whose face was not visible. The video showed the unknown assailant dismembering the male victim, performing necrophiliac acts on the corpse, slicing the victim's flesh, and encouraging a dog to chew on the body. The owner of Bestgore.com was indicted for publicly posting the snuff film and sentenced to six months of house arrest (Cotter, 2016). On May 29, 2012, a package containing the victim's left foot was sent to the national headquarters of the Conservative Party of Canada, and another package containing his severed hand was intercepted by the Canadian post in a package addressed to the Canadian Liberal Party. A janitor in Montreal discovered the victim's torso in a suitcase that was left outside of an apartment building, and other body parts were sent and intercepted by police. Police identified the victim as a 33-year-old international student from Wuhan, China, who was an undergraduate engineering and computer science student at Concordia University in Montreal.[5] Canadian police were able to identify a primary suspect, 30-year-old Eric Clinton Kirk Newman, also known as "Luka Rocco Magnotta."

After a worldwide manhunt that involved the help of crowdsourced Internet sleuths, Magnotta was caught, convicted of first-degree murder, imprisoned, and details of his escalation to graphic social media–mediated performance murder were revealed (West & Wells, 2012). He will be eligible for parole in 2034. After his capture, details revealed his twisted past involving public displays of animal torture posted on social media including a series of videos on *YouTube* entitled, "1 boy 2 kittens" in which he suffocated two kittens with a vacuum cleaner, and "Python Christmas" where he fed a kitten to a 17-foot-long albino Burmese python while dressed as Santa Claus (Hopper, 2012).

Case Studies of Copycat and Media-Mediated Crime 113

Magnotta's crimes were distinctly motivated by a quest for celebrity status through the performance of extreme violent behavior for an audience. In a bizarre cultural twist, Magnotta was controversially named Canadian Newsmaker of the Year by Canadian media, causing a major controversy (The Canadian Press 2012) and his story was featured in the three-part 2019 *Netflix* documentary, *Don't F**k With Cats* (Hegedus, 2019). Magnotta has stayed in the news media even while in prison. In June 2015 he posted an online dating website Inmates Connect, Inc., for prisoners looking for his "Prince Charming." He asked to remove his profile in July 2015 saying he found what he was looking for and got married at the maximum-security prison in Port Cartier, Quebec (The Canadian Press, 2017). For Magnotta, social media and performance were integral signature elements of his crime.

Vester Lee Flanagan: The Murder of Alison Parker and Adam Ward

On August 26, 2015, 41-year-old Vester Lee Flanagan (known by his news name Bryce Williams), a former employee of a local Roanoke Virginia CBS-affiliate news channel WDBJ-TV, murdered his former coworkers, 23-year-old reporter Alison Parker and 27-year-old cameraman Adam Ward during a live television broadcast, fled, and killed himself while being chased by police. Flanagan was fired from WDBJ in 2013 after he displayed volatile behavior towards coworkers claiming racial bias. Parker and Ward were conducting a live interview at 6:45 a.m. with Vicki Gardner, head of the Smith Mountain Lake Regional Chamber of Commerce. Flanagan approached the three after the segment began and fired 15 shots with a Glock handgun. Ward and Parker were killed; Gardner survived with injuries. The murders were broadcast on live television (Hermann et al., 2015).

Flanagan recorded the shooting from his first-person perspective (Gambino & Swaine, 2015) and posted the video recording on Facebook and Twitter with messages saying that he was upset with Ward and Flanagan for making complaints and racist comments about him. Flanagan was tracked down after the shooting and purposefully crashed his car and was discovered with a self-inflicted gunshot wound and died in a local hospital (Bacon, 2015). About two hours after the murders, ABC News received a 22-page document from Flanagan describing why he killed Ward and Parker:

> Why did I do it? I put down a deposit for a gun on 6/19/15. The Church shooting in Charleston happened on 6/17/15. . . . What sent me over the

top was the church shooting. And my hollow point bullets have the victims' initials on them. (Cleary, 2017)

Throughout the document, Flanagan expressed admiration for the Columbine and Virginia Tech killers and said that his anger over the Charleston church shooting committed by Dylann Roof sent him over the edge.

Steve Stevens: The Murder of Robert Goodwin, Sr.

On Easter Sunday, April 16, 2017, 74-year-old Robert Godwin, Sr. was walking down a Cleveland, Ohio street at 2 p.m. when he was confronted by 37-year-old Steve Stevens. Stevens recorded himself driving up to Godwin, Sr. and asked, "Can you do me a favor? Can you say the name Joy Lane?" Godwin responded, "Joy Lane?" and Stephens replied, "Yeah, she is the reason this is going to happen to you." Stephens then shot and killed Godwin while saying to the camera, "This is going to be called the Easter Sunday Joy Lane Massacre" (Selk et al., 2017). The investigation determined that Stephens chose Godwin at random after Stephens had a conversation with his girlfriend, Joy Lane, who raised an issue about his gambling addiction and told him if he didn't stop, she would leave him. After Stephen's initial Facebook post of the video of him murdering Godwin, Stephens went on Facebook Live and explained why he had shot Godwin and how he had also killed 13 other people, though no other murders were corroborated by police (Silverstein, 2017). Stephens was found a few days later in Erie County, Pennsylvania, where after a police chase, Stephens ended up shooting himself inside his own car (Selk et al., 2017). The case sparked discussion around the regulations Facebook imposes on users posting video footage (Yan & Simon, 2017).

Derek Medina: The Murder of Jennifer Alfonso

Facebook has become a portal for information that might otherwise be private and a forum for performance crime. In August 2013, 33-year-old Derek Medina murdered his wife, 27-year-old Jennifer Alfonso. They had been arguing in an upstairs bedroom of their South Miami, Florida home while Alfonso's 10-year-old daughter from a previous marriage was in the house but was not injured. Closed-circuit television (CCTV) footage showed parts of the killing with Medina arguing with Alfonso in the kitchen, leaving the kitchen, returning with a gun, and then shooting Alfonso eight times. The footage shows Medina with his cell phone. When he was holding his phone, he was making a Facebook post of his deceased

Case Studies of Copycat and Media-Mediated Crime 115

wife's body with the caption, "RIP Jennifer Alfonso." The image and caption reportedly stayed online for five hours before being removed by Facebook. After his initial post, he posted again saying, "I'm going to prison or death sentence for killing my wife love you guys miss you guys take care Facebook people you will see me in the news my wife was punching me and I am not going to stand anymore with the abuse so I did what I did I hope u understand me," Medina then reportedly went to visit family before turning himself into authorities (Ford, 2015; Newcomb, 2013).

Amanda Taylor: "The Selfie Killer"

On April 4, 2015, 24-year-old Amanda Taylor repeatedly stabbed her father-in-law, 59-year-old Charlie Taylor, with a bayonet-style knife and then her accomplice, 32-year-old Sean Ball, hit Charlie Taylor over the head with a tire iron in Ellett, Virginia. After the murder, Taylor posed with the knife in front of her father-in-law's bloodied deceased body, posted it on Instagram calling herself the "Brunette Bomber," and sent it to a crime blogger asking her to post it on her website. The blogger called the police and assisted in helping locate Taylor as she called her multiple times after the murder from burner phones. During her flight from the crime scene to Tennessee, Taylor took a selfie of a revolver in her lap with the comment, "Alright. It's about that time. I'm going to go find my husband in hell and finally be at peace" (Hemraj, 2021). In an interview from prison two years later, when questioned about why she posted the postmurder selfie to social media, Taylor said, "I was just really excited and I was like hey I'm gonna take a picture so I can post it and show everyone. It was just something that I, it made me really happy" (Smith, 2017).

Eight months prior to the murder in August 2014, Taylor's husband Rex committed suicide by hanging himself in his father's home. Amanda and Rex had met in the ninth grade, got married at age 19, and had a young daughter and son. The pair were said to be fascinated with serial killers and murder. Rex had an opioid addiction, and Taylor believed his father was responsible for his suicide because he supplied him with drugs. After Rex's suicide, Taylor met Ball, who had a romantic interest in her. The pair murdered Charlie Taylor, went on a spree to murder more people, and fled to Tennessee. Taylor turned on Ball while they were on the run after he refused to help her kill two college students and shot him in the face before they both were caught by police in North Carolina. When Taylor shot Ball, she pointed the gun at him and said, "I want you to know before you die that I used you for your guns and your car and I hope you die." After she shot Ball, she took a photo of his face and later told the police when they asked her why she took the picture that she wasn't sure if she shot his eyes out or what and she thought it would be easier to look at the cell phone photo afterwards than to look at his actual face. Ball survived, and both were arrested and convicted of murder. Taylor was convicted of first-degree murder and sentenced to life in prison, and Ball was convicted of second-degree murder and was sentenced to 60 years with 41 years to serve on a suspended sentence (Exclusive Prison Interview: Amanda Taylor Talks, 2019).

"Boonk Gang" Instagram Crime Posts

On April 18, 2017, the "Boonk Gang" Instagram page was launched. The first video featured the page's creator, John Robert Hill, age 20, going behind the counter of a Popeye's Chicken and stealing a box of fried chicken while yelling, "I'm a fucking savage!" In only a few short months, that video reached over 1.1 million views. Following that video, Hill, also known as "Boonk," would repeatedly post videos of himself committing petty theft at various establishments. After Hill reached 1 million followers on Instagram, he posted a video of himself in a Chik-fil-A restaurant removing his clothes (Caldwell, 2018). Other crimes included receiving a tattoo and running out of the tattoo parlor without paying, taking a cookie dispenser from a Subway, carjacking an Uber driver, and thefts from local fast-food restaurants (Spyrou, 2017)—all filmed and posted to his Instagram, creating content and notoriety through his public posting of crimes he committed.

On May 17, 2017, he was arrested at a Dunkin' Donuts for stealing a tray of donuts. A more serious charge came in 2018 when police were tipped off to Hill having unregistered assault weapons and nonprescribed narcotics. His home was searched via a warrant and the weapons and drugs were found and he was booked and released on a $35,000 bond ("Calabasas," 2018). Hill became Instagram famous, reaching over 5 million views after posting X-rated graphic content of himself with a woman having sex in various positions until his site was eventually shut down for violating Instagram policies. His followers said after his site was shut down, "Must you post literally everything on social media?"; others said, "I couldn't stop myself from watching his stories" (Benitz, 2018).

Live-Streamed DUI

On December 28, 2015, 28-year-old Dustin Rittgers decided to drive his car while intoxicated, drinking whiskey, while Facebook livestreaming.

In the video, Rittgers is seen nodding to music, swerving his vehicle, and taking multiple swigs of whiskey from a bottle. One of the people viewing his livestream commented, "Dude, really!!!" to which he responded, "I am a good driver, don't worry." Another viewer reported the behavior to the police. Rittgers was caught and charged with operating a vehicle while intoxicated, following too closely in a vehicle, refusing to take a field sobriety test, lane straddling, and having an open container of alcohol in his vehicle (Woods, 2015). It was later reported that this was Rittgers's third charge for driving under the influence (Sukosd, 2015). Sheriff Zach Scott of the arresting police department in Franklin County, Ohio, said, "This situation shows the power of social media. Social media led us straight to this suspect to stop him before he was able to hurt himself or others. Social media is another crime fighting tool we use to keep Franklin County residents safe" (Long, 2015).

These acts of murder and other crimes on Facebook are performance crimes. Perpetrators who are willing to show themselves live on camera on social media in the act of committing crimes with murder weapons dripping with blood, leaving a surveillance trail and leading police right to them are motivated by the desire for attention, celebrity, and status.

The Copycat Effect on Mass and School Shootings from 2010 to 2020

From 2010 to 2020, there were 68 mass shootings in the United States. Rapid technological advances in handheld mobile phones (Islam & Want, 2014) and findings that have examined the media contagion and copycat effects on mass shootings and their broader cultural implications (e.g., Cross & Pruitt, 2013; Katsiyannis et al., 2018; King & Jacobson, 2017; Langman, 2018; Lankford & Tomek, 2017; Meindl & Ivy, 2017; Schildkraut et al., 2018; Silva & Capellan, 2018, 2019; Silva & Greene-Colozzi, 2019; Towers et al., 2015, 2018) call for examination of the role of digital culture in mass shootings.

On December 14, 2012, 20-year-old Adam Lanza shot and killed his 52-year-old mother, Nancy Lanza, while she slept. He then went to Sandy Hook Elementary School in Newtown, Connecticut, and shot 20 children between the ages of six and seven and six adults and then shot himself. He used a semiautomatic rifle and two handguns that belonged to his mother, who previously worked at Sandy Hook Elementary as a teacher's aide who was said to be a gun enthusiast (ABC News, 2012).[6] The Connecticut State Police investigation uncovered more than 1000 pages of documents, including hundreds of pages of Lanza's writings in a spreadsheet detailing violence committed by 400 mass murder perpetrators methodologically organized by number of people killed with 17 columns including weapon type, nature of location, day of week, and fate of the shooter. Lanza was an isolated teenager with a history of mental health issues including obsessive-compulsive disorder, anorexia, and solipsism/malignant narcissism. His few social interactions were in video game arcades and online gaming chat rooms. He was described by his mother as experiencing social paralysis and held a worldview that reflected disdain for relationships, intolerance of peers, contempt for anyone carrying a few extra pounds, and a belief that certain aspects of living are worse than death. Themes revealed in the analysis of the evidence collected after the crime describe a picture of a young man whose thinking and emotional experience were characterized by isolation, obsession, scorn for others, yearning for connection, an ambivalent sexual identity, and fascination with murder (Altman, 2018; Kovner & Altimari, 2018).

Lanza offers a case study in how mass media and digital culture operate to insulate and further isolate troubled edge-sitters—his behavior a product of the evolution of violent fantasy and an aggressive script that culminated into mass violence. Lanza's mother had communicated with school staff about helping Lanza, who she said had Asperger syndrome and sensory processing disorder, be more social. According to the Newtown School District chief of security, Lanza was recruited into his high school tech club to get him to be more social after his mother expressed concern that she was failing to "bring him out of his little world" (Childress, 2013). He spent most of his time in his mother's basement with blacked-out windows turning into what a psychiatrist called a "homebound recluse" (Rojas & Hussey, 2018). Lanza stockpiled mass murder memorabilia and newspaper clippings, first-person-shooter video games, and photos of deceased people covered in blood and wrapped in plastic in his bedroom, where he spent almost all of his time before the shooting (Curry, 2013). Among the computer games found in Lanza's bedroom was one called *School Shooter*, a first-person-shooter game in which the player enters a school and shoots students (Pilkington, 2013). Lanza's "near complete attachment to the Internet or the television" left him living in a "distinctly noisy solitude" that led him on a path where he came to see mass violence to "make a name" for himself to become "someone" (Steinkoler, 2017, p. 217).

Lanza was obsessed with Columbine and mass murder. In the years since Columbine, 8 out of 10 mass shooters directly referred to Harris and Klebold and saw them as heroes. Lanza regularly posted on a blog about school and rampage shootings (Steinkoler, 2017) and hundreds of images, videos, and documents relating to the Columbine massacre were

Case Studies of Copycat and Media-Mediated Crime   119

on his computer (Pearce, 2013). Lanza's fixation on Columbine was similar to the central role Columbine played in the minds of other mass shooters such as Seung-Hui Cho, who committed a mass shooting at Virginia Polytech Institute in 2007, killing 32 people, who said in a video recording he sent to the press that he was a martyr seeking revenge for the Columbine killers (Follman & Andrews, 2015; Langman, 2017; Sedesky, 2013).

Santa Barbara mass shooter Elliot Rodger, who murdered 6 people and injured 14 others on May 23, 2014, has been described as "the most dangerous possible shooter for an age of media saturation" who seems "less like a person than like a character from an artsy slasher flick meant to comment on inequality, misogyny, gun violence, and online alienation" (Klein, 2014). Rodger began his murder spree by stabbing his three roommates to death, one of whom was stabbed 94 times. He then drove his BMW to the Alpha Phi Sorority house where he knocked on the door and when no one answered, walked across the street and began shooting at three female University of California, Santa Barbara (UCSB) college students who were walking by the house, two of whom died and one left injured. He then drove to a deli, got out of his car, shot a UCSB student, got back in his car, and drove at high speed continuing to shoot until he crashed his car in a police chase. The police discovered him dead by a self-inflicted gunshot wound to the head.

Media played an integral role in the fantasy development, planning, and performance of Rodger's crime. He researched on the Internet how to stab his roommates and rehearsed before he committed the murders (Naranjo, 2015). During the week before the murders, he uploaded multiple YouTube videos including his final video "Retribution," and 13 minutes prior to the murders emailed his manifesto "My Twisted Life" to his parents and therapist. Rodger's videos showed him having a running dialogue with the camera talking about how sad, depressing, alone, and unfair his life was because he was a 22-year-old virgin and how despite his $300 Giorgio Armani sunglasses and BMW, none of the beautiful girls he saw around him wanted to be with him. He described himself as "gorgeous" and "magnificent," a "nice guy," and said he could not understand how he was still a virgin, why "beautiful blonde girls" would not go out with him and have starved him of sex, enjoyment, and pleasure, how flawed female attraction is because women are attracted to "stupid-obnoxious-looking douchebags" and how "twisted" and "cruel" "you girls" make the world. In one of the videos, he talks to the camera while drinking a latte, sitting in his car, watching a sunset saying, "There's no beautiful girl in that passenger seat to enjoy it with me because you girls have something against me. I don't know what it is." The series of videos Rodger posted the week before his crimes offer a window into his thinking, culminating with his final 7-minute video "Retribution" and his manifesto, "My Twisted World" (DocuCloud, 2014), which became public shortly after the murders.

In his final video "Retribution," Rodger talked about his "day of retribution" when he would have his "revenge against humanity" for the rejection he experienced by "blonde girls" who did not give him sex. He discussed being a virgin at age 22 and explained how torturous it had been for him to "rot in loneliness" during his college years. He says, "I am going to enter the hottest sorority house of UCSB . . . and I will slaughter every single spoiled stuck up blonde slut I see inside there." He says, "I will take great pleasure in slaughtering all of you," describing himself as the "true alpha male" proclaiming, "If I can't have you girls, I will destroy you. You denied me a happy life, and in turn, I will deny you all life. It's only fair. . . ."

The videos and the release of Rodger's manifesto offer a look inside the mind of an edge-sitter who operated under the influence of mass media. Between Rodger's own video posts and those generated during his commission of the crimes, there was a rush of digital information about the antecedents and consequences of his crimes, offering a cognitive road map explaining how media depictions of misogyny, celebrity, sex, and entitlement became intertwined in Rodger's expectations and beliefs about the world around him. Rodger's behavior was media-mediated to an extent historically not seen before, illustrating the complex ways in which mass media and digital culture inform and motivate edge-sitters and operate as a vehicle for attention and celebrity. Rodger's murders and the role of media and digital culture as a signature element in his crimes show the cultural forces at play that become embedded in the cognitive scripts of individuals who are predisposed to the copycat effect and how the Internet is used to publicly share videotaped narrations and communication of motives, thought processes, and feelings of omnipotence (Helfgott, 2014).

Less than two weeks after Rodger's murders, on June 5, 2014, 27-year-old Aaron Ybarra opened fire at Seattle Pacific University (SPU). The day before the shooting, Ybarra visited the university to survey the campus and gain information on escape routes. The day of the shooting he entered the campus armed with a shotgun, a large hunting knife, and live shotgun rounds. Ybarra encountered 19-year-old Paul Lee, an SPU freshman. Ybarra approached Lee and showed him his weapon. When Lee did not appear threatened by Ybarra, Ybarra shot and killed him. Ybarra later said

Case Studies of Copycat and Media-Mediated Crime 121

he was offended that Lee did not take him seriously. Another student, Thomas Fowler, was hit with pellets from the same shot but was not critically injured. The investigation revealed that Lee was shot in the back of the head at close range and that Ybarra tried to shoot another female student, but the weapon misfired. He then continued into Otto Miller Hall, where he told a student that he had just shot a man outside for disrespecting him. Ybarra then saw another student, 22-year-old Sarah Williams, coming down the stairs and shot, injuring her in her torso. Shortly after, Ybarra was pepper-sprayed by a student school monitor named Jon Meis, who tackled and disarmed Ybarra, which was later shown in a released CCTV video. Ybarra was held down by Meis and taken into custody by the Seattle Police Department (Cruz, 2014; Mallahan, 2016).

While in police custody, Ybarra revealed that he was inspired by the Columbine shooting and Isla Vista shooting, committed by Elliot Rodger just two weeks prior (Green, 2017). Ybarra told police that he admired Columbine killer Eric Harris, "He just made everything so exciting. He made hate so exciting" (Walker & Mallahan, 2016). Ybarra claimed that he didn't choose specific targets and would only shoot at those who disrespected him, similar to the tactics of and sentiments expressed by Elliot Rodger and the Columbine shooters. Ybarra wrote in his journal on the day of the attack, "This is it! I can't believe I'm finally doing this! So exciting. I'm jumpy. Since Virginia Tech and Columbine, I've been thinking about these a lot. I use to [sic] feel bad for the ones who were killed, but now Eric Harris and Seung-Hui Cho became my Idols. And they guided me til today" (Langman, 2014, p. 2). What is particularly illustrative in this case is the less than two-week proximity between this shooting and the mass shooting committed by Rodger. Like Columbine and the Santa Barbara shootings, the SPU shooting was committed by a man expressing the desire to make others suffer for his own pain who was emulating earlier mass shooters he saw in the media and idolized. Ybarra was an edge-sitter who fantasized about and planned mass murder emboldened by the heavy mass media coverage of Rodger's murders in Santa Barbara, inspiring him to finally follow through on his plan of committing his own mass murder.

Several years later, the Marjory Stoneman Douglas High School (MSD) mass shooting in Parkland, Florida, on February 14, 2018, became one of the deadliest mass shootings in America. The perpetrator, Nikolas Cruz, who had been expelled from the school a year earlier, was dropped off by an Uber at MSD at 2:19 p.m., just before school dismissal time. He entered a building armed with an AR-15–style semi-automatic rifle, activated the fire alarm, and fired randomly at students and faculty. He continued to shoot for six minutes, killing 17 students and faculty. The victims were Alyssa Alhadeff, 14; Scott Beigel, 35; Martin Duque, 14; Nicholas Dworet, 17; Aaron Feis, 37; Jaime Guttenberg, 14; Chris Hixon, 49; Luke Hoyer, 15; Cara Loughran, 14; Gina Montalto, 14; Joaquin Oliver, 17; Alaina Petty, 14; Meadow Pollack, 18; Helena Ramsay, 17; Alex Schachter, 14; Carmen Schentrup, 16; and Peter Wang, 15.

Cruz posted about firearms on his social media accounts, and following his expulsion his posts became increasingly disturbing. He commented on a YouTube page, saying, "Im [sic] going to be a professional school shooter" (McLaughlin, 2018). He also made comments saying: "I whana [sic] shoot people with my AR-15," "I wanna die Fighting killing shit ton of people, I am going to kill law enforcement one day they go after the good people" (McLaughlin, 2018). Cruz was apparently playing a game of who can kill the most people in a school shooting with the goal of becoming as famous as the previous shooters he was trying to emulate. Cruz pleaded guilty, and after a lengthy sentencing hearing including gut-wrenching testimony from victims and victims' family members, as well as testimony about his dysfunctional family life, mental health issues including fetal alcohol spectrum disorder and antisocial personality disorder, and his birth mother's drug and alcohol addiction while pregnant with him as mitigating factors, he was spared the death penalty and sentenced to life without the possibility of parole on November 3, 2022 (Andone et al., 2022).

The Influence of Social Media and Digital Culture on Criminal Behavior During the COVID Pandemic, the George Floyd Protests, and the Insurrection—2020–2022

School closures brought on by the COVID pandemic in 2020 slowed mass school shootings, but 2020 was one of the deadliest years for mass shootings in other locations (Jackson, 2020). The intersection of fear and stress over the pandemic that shut the world down in March 2020; the murder of George Floyd on May 25, 2020, and the subsequent protests and riots with calls to defund the police; the U.S. presidential election that resulted in the ousting of Donald Trump; and the insurrection at the U.S. Capitol on January 6, 2021, occurred within a new and extreme media-mediated cultural environment characterized by bombardment by mainstream media, citizen journalists, and social media influencers. As the COVID pandemic required people around the world to minimize contact with other human beings, it accelerated digitalization creating a cultural environment that turned the aesthetic realm of the hyperreal into the aesthetic realm of the unreal.

Case Studies of Copycat and Media-Mediated Crime

During the pandemic people around the world decreased their in-person activities and increased their digital activities in virtually every area of life (Vidal et al., 2021). The impact of this sudden shift from in-person interactions where people obtain information first-hand (the ethical realm of the real) to almost completely digital interactions where people obtain information and interact with each other through a media-mediated digital environment (the aesthetic realm of the hyperreal) created a world in which we were all watching each other, learning from each other, and interacting with each other as if we were watching ourselves and everyone else on a giant movie screen. The impact this accelerated digitalization had on criminal behavior and the copycat effect is enormous and historical.

When the COVID pandemic hit in March 2020, the world ceased or reduced social interactions and activities in the workplace, dining out, going to the movies, physical fitness activities, and virtually every area of life. "The 'stay-at-home' mandates brought about the most wide-reaching, significant, and sudden alteration of the lives of billions of people in human history" and with this came a drop in crime rates resulting from this stark change in routine activities (Stickle & Felson, 2020, p. 526). On the other hand, this drop in the crime rates was not the same for all types of crime, and though crime initially fell in response to the pandemic, with the addition of the murder of George Floyd and the social movement for racial justice, some types of crime, specifically violent crimes and homicides, rose to levels not seen in decades. A study of crime in 32 cities found that there was a cyclical pattern in the homicide rate over time:

> The rate began to increase in the beginning of 2020 and rose sharply immediately after George Floyd's May 25 murder, which sparked nationwide protests against police violence. Homicide levels remained elevated through the summer, before decreasing through the late fall of 2020 and first three months of 2021. Even with that decline, however, the number of homicides during the first quarter of 2021 was 24% greater than during the same period in 2020 and 49% greater than the same period in 2019. In the 24 cities for which homicide data was available, there were 193 more homicides in the first quarter of 2021 than during the same timeframe the year before, and 324 more than the year before that. (Rosenfeld & Lopez, 2021, p. 5)

The study concluded that this historic (30 percent) rise in homicide rates "was likely attributable to the pandemic, social unrest, and other factors that combined to create a 'perfect storm' of circumstances" (Rosenfeld & Lopez, 2021, p. 6).

While the 2020 homicide rate was still half of what the homicide rate was in the mid-1990s (11.4 deaths per 100,000 residents in those cities versus 19.4 per 100,000 in 1995), the suddenness of the increase in violent crime to levels not seen in three decades is historically remarkable because of the pace at which the rise in crime took place. Preliminary analyses suggest that the convergence of factors including COVID, the George Floyd protests, the defund the police movement, and the mass exodus of police were potential factors in the sudden rise in crime (Thompson, 2021). However, the degree to which the increase in violence appeared to turn on a dime on a local, national, and even global scale begs the question: What role did digital culture play in contributing to the violence surge?

Instant access to information on social media and digital platforms has created increasingly intense and complex violent media loops. Media loops occur when an image is shown within another image (Manning, 1998). An example of a simple media loop is an instant replay in a sports game, and an example of a more complex media loop would be when images of real-life violence are shown within a fictional context, such as the psychological landscapes used in the film *NBK* where images of real-life news events (e.g., beating of Rodney King, the Menendez brothers, Lorena Bobbit, and O. J. Simpson trials) were shown as a backdrop interspersed throughout the film.

Violence Involving Police and Protestors

During the unrest triggered by the killing of George Floyd in May 2020, online comments involving anti-police slogans surged over 1000 percent on Twitter and nearly 300 percent on Reddit, and left-wing networks such as the Socialist Rifle Association and the Redneck Revolt grew at tremendous speed (Timberg & Stanley-Becker, 2020). While the numbers in these groups are much smaller than the numbers of right-wing extremist networks, the pace of their growth during a short time in 2020 following the murder of George Floyd is a case study in how mass media and digital culture influence criminal behavior and violence.

The role of digital culture as one of the potential factors in this dramatic rise in violent crime is national, and in cities like Portland and Seattle are important to consider and explore given the role online coordination played nationally and locally in 2020. The rate of violence in Portland, Oregon, rose 950% from 2 homicides in 2020 to 21 in the first quarter of 2021 (Rosenfeld & Lopez, 2021), and Seattle saw a 525% spike during the Capitol Hill Autonomous Zone/Capitol Hill Occupation Protest (CHAZ/CHOP) protests (Eustachewich, 2020). In Portland, a statue

Case Studies of Copycat and Media-Mediated Crime

of George Washington was taken down by protesters and spray painted with "ACAB," "Fuck cops," and "F12." In Seattle, the CHAZ/CHOP movement was erected so protesters could implement autonomous self-rule and oust the police, creating territorial markers with spray painted ACAB, 1312, and FTP memes. The riots in Portland, Seattle, and across the United States involved anarcho-socialist online/real-world hybrid militias and weapons enthusiast groups who engaged in "real-time online coordination of offline rioting and anti-police" (Finkelstein et al., 2020, p. 4). These violent anarcho-socialist networks grew rapidly and reached record levels of participation during the COVID pandemic and social protests and actively played an online role (through Reddit, Instagram, and private chat groups) in preparing for and coordinating real-world, real-time riots as "subcultural forums" that incubated dehumanization and demonization of police, seditious political ideas, conspiracy, hate, and violent insurgency (Finkelstein et al., 2020, p. 7). For example, the Portland Youth Liberation Front (YLF) lionize Willem Van Spronsen, embrace the radical Northwest/1999 Seattle World Trade Organization (WTO) legacy of the "black bloc," dress in black to avoid identification, and describe themselves as a decentralized network of autonomous youth collectives dedicated to direct action towards total liberation. The Portland YLF, with over 20,000 followers on Instagram and 30,000 followers, grew in membership over 50 percent during a two-week time period from July 15 to August 1, 2020. The YLF leveraged social media to offer tactical advice, disseminate graphics and memes, and engage in cyberswarming (Finkelstein et al., 2020).

Central to the MO of the Portland YLF and other online/real-world hybrid militias is the use of instructional memes that show mobs attacking police with projectiles, committing arson, and blinding officers with high-powered lasers. Images from real-time attacks on police as well as violence by police are then posted online to recruit and reinforce the acts of members. On July 25, 2020, these groups organized riots in four cities targeting police precincts and courthouses with fireworks, projectiles, arson, and explosives using advanced communication capabilities and sophisticated division of labor in a coordinated campaign with the hashtag "#J25" that had hundreds or thousands of retweets/comments with riots declared simultaneously in four cities: Portland, Oregon; Seattle, Washington; Eugene, Oregon; and Richmond, Virginia (Finkelstein et al., 2020).

The Insurrection

Social media and digital culture played a role in the 2020 presidential election and the insurrection that occurred on January 6, 2021, in much of the same ways that it played a role in coordinating and inspiring violence among protesters in the aftermath of the murder of George Floyd and the resulting protests.

> The storming of the U.S. Capitol was one of the most extensively and closely documented events in modern history. Around the world, people watched the violence unfold in real time, via livestreams, selfies and social media posts. Rioters uploaded videos and commentary of themselves entering the building. (Cockerell, 2021)

The groundwork for the role social media played in inspiring the 2021 insurrection was laid by Donald Trump during his run as the president of the United States from 2017 to 2021 (Guynn, 2021). Trump was a prolific Twitter user, often posting inflammatory tweets to communicate with the public. Some have suggested that his use of Twitter was a mouthpiece to divide, conquer, rile people up, and fragment democracy (Mosley & Hagan, 2021) and that the January 6, 2021, insurrection was the culmination of "brazenly divisive rhetoric by the White House—and decades of white supremacist sentiment" (Michallon, 2021). Social media was used for a "coordinated disinformation campaign" that created a "big networked effect" (Rash, 2021). Emerson Brooking, resident fellow at the Atlantic Council's Digital Forensic Research Lab and co-author of *Like-War: The Weaponization of Social Media,* said on the day of the insurrection, "Today's tragic attack on the U.S. Capitol is the result of a years-long process of online radicalization. Millions of Americans have been the target of disinformation and conspiracy theories until they can no longer tell the difference between reality and fiction. This moment has been building since 2016 . . . President Trump lit the fuse" (Guynn, 2021).

The 2021 insurrection is reminiscent of *The Turner Diaries* (Macdonald, 1978), one of the most prominent historical copycat crime influences. *The Turner Diaries* was written by neo-Nazi leader William Luther Pierce using the pseudonym Andrew Macdonald and is one of the most influential texts among right-wing extremists offering a "blueprint for how to enact a violent insurrection" (Alter, 2021). The book, which describes the bombing of the FBI headquarters with a homemade truck bomb, has been associated with at least 40 terrorist attacks and hate crimes (Alter, 2021), inspiring more than 200 murders since its publication in 1978 (Berger, 2016). One of the most notorious crimes inspired by *The Turner Diaries* was the 1995 Oklahoma City bombing committed by Timothy McVeigh, who was executed at the Federal Complex in Terre Haute, Indiana, in 2001 (Thomas, 2001). Photocopied pages from *The Turner Diaries* were

Case Studies of Copycat and Media-Mediated Crime

127

found in McVeigh's getaway car after the bombing and were presented during his trial. Prosecutors argued that *The Turner Diaries* was a blueprint for the Oklahoma City bombing (Michael, 2009).

Many of the ideas put forth in *The Turner Diaries* proliferate on online far-right media via memes on social media and in chat rooms. After the 2021 insurrection, users on sites such as 4chan, Stormfront, and Telegram celebrated the violence, likening it to a mass hanging that occurs in *The Turner Diaries* called "the Day of the Rope." Insurrectionists posted photos of the book while livestreaming the assault, and rioters made references to erecting gallows outside the Capitol, stringing up, and hanging politicians. Historian Kathleen Belew said about *The Turner Diaries*, "It's a book that has been used to kill a lot of people, over and over" and "People should understand that's what it is." The week following the insurrection, Amazon removed *The Turner Diaries* from its website along with QAnon products and books and suspended the far-right–friendly social media website Parler from its web service (Alter, 2021).

Fictional novels have long influenced far-right propaganda movements.[7] Digital culture has given these novels and their ideas new life through memes and posts online in social media and chat rooms, showing up in messages by far-right groups such as the Proud Boys and referenced by the insurrectionists. In the days prior to the insurrection, all social media platforms (platforms popular with extremists such as Parler, as well as major online forums including Facebook, Instagram, Twitter, YouTube, TikTok, and Reddit) were inundated with violent rhetoric against elected officials fueled by then President Trump's claims of voter fraud. Trump supporters posted on Facebook and Instagram to promote the January 6 march on the Capitol extensively and to organize bus trips to Washington, D.C. Over 100,000 Facebook users posted hashtags affiliated with the "Stop the Steal" movement prompted by baseless claims of election fraud, including #StopTheSteal and #FightForTrump (Dwoskin, 2021). TikTok videos with hundreds of thousands of views encouraged viewers to arm themselves with guns. Posts on Parler warned of a second civil war, and QAnon social media accounts suggested that Black Lives Matter and Antifa activists planned to kill Trump supporters, urging followers to arm themselves for "Independence Day." The extremist group the Boogaloos put out a call to "Burn down DC," and one Twitter user asked, "Whos running arms and ammo to dc for when the fun starts." On a message board called TheDonald (formed after the group was banned from Reddit) encouraged violence, "Start shooting patriots. Kill these (expletive) traitors." As of 4:23 p.m. EST on the day of the insurrection, posts involving calls for violence had 128,395 engagements (Guynn, 2021).

The renewed attention to *The Turner Diaries* after the January 6, 2021, insurrection illustrates the power of the copycat effect. The book has been described by author Talia Lavin as "not art," a "manifesto disguised as a thriller-style novel," "the far-right version of a Marvel movie" (Michallon, 2021). The violent acts committed during the insurrection mimicked acts depicted in the novel with specificity. Violence against journalists and mass hangings depicted in the book were echoed in the insurrection when rioters scrawled "Murder the Media" on a door at the Capitol and erected a noose outside.

Following the insurrection, Facebook indefinitely banned Trump for inciting violence while also saying that the events on the day of the insurrection were largely organized through other social media platforms "that don't have our abilities to stop hate" (Timberg et al., 2021). As more companies like Amazon and social media networks attempt to shut down extremist conversations, information sharing, hate speech, and calls for violence, there could be a return to books and other legacy media to spread ideology (Alter, 2021).

In addition to playing a role in inspiring and coordinating the insurrection, social media provided a digital theater for the rioters to perform, broadcast, celebrate, and display their behaviors in real time for a worldwide audience. Reminiscent of the 2019 Christchurch, New Zealand mass shooting that was livestreamed on Facebook, the insurrection rioters posted play-by-play real-time video streams on YouTube, Facebook, and lesser-known outlets such as DLive (Karimi, 2021). News accounts following the insurrection reported:

> You got the feeling they all thought they were in a movie. . . . The insurrectionists who stormed the Capitol wrote, directed, and starred in their own films, scaling walls, bellowing from podiums, mugging for their buddies' glamour shots. Hungry for attention, having written a blockbuster movie of their own devising patterned on the ones they've watched all their lives, they gave out their names, the better to see them in lights. (Wilkinson, 2021)

The live feed broadcasting of the insurrection inundated news feeds on mass media and social media around the world. On Twitch, an Amazon-owned platform known for broadcasting video game play that has over 7 million channels, the channel Woke displays different livestreams presented in a single feed, allowing viewers to watch over a dozen different streams simultaneously—"The feel of the channel is a little like the oft-depicted image of one person sitting in front of many televisions, all tuned to different things" (VanDerWerff, 2021). The chaos of insurrection and subsequent protests was livestreamed on Woke.

The performance crime aspect of the insurrection is evidenced by the carelessness of the rioters; their blatant willingness to post their illegal activities (including posting on social media about which Congress members should be targeted first with maps of the layout of the Capitol building and talk of bringing weapons and ammunition); posing for selfies and videos in offices and the House and Senate Chambers; stealing in the Rotunda; destroying federal property; and showing attacks on Capitol Police officers by rioters with hockey sticks, crutches, and pepper spray on their personal social media pages. The rioters' thirst for celebrity and desire to perform superseded their concerns about getting caught. As a result, the FBI was able to track down and charge many of the rioters through public images, viral memes, and real-time videos they posted themselves (Khavin et al., 2021).

Another issue to consider in unraveling elements of the copycat effect in the insurrection was the power of politically driven violent rhetoric, transmitted through the media, as a force of influence and insulation. From Trump's claims of the stolen election to the calls for violent takeover by far-right extremist groups is a form of "stochastic terrorism" (Amman & Meloy, 2021). Stochastic terrorism was first used by mathematician Gordon Woo to suggest a quantifiable relationship between the goal of perpetuating fear through mass media's coverage of the violence and the seemingly random acts of terrorism. Stochastic terrorism is the

> . . . interactive process between the originator of a message, its amplifiers, and one or more ultimate receivers. A charismatic public figure, or perhaps an organization, lobs hostile rhetoric against a targeted out-group or individual into the public discourse to further some political or social objective. An unrelated consumer of the rhetoric absorbs and reacts with anger, contempt or disgust, often mirroring the speaker's emotional state, and adding his own fear and anxiety to that cocktail of negative emotionality. . . . The speaker's rhetoric may range from bombastic declarations that the target is a threat by some measure, to "jokes" about violent solutions, or to the shared problem posed by the target—always stopping short of requesting or directing an attack for reasons of plausible deniability. Social and news mass media outlets are exploited to spread and amplify the message. . . . Once he reaches his personal tipping point, a consumer of the rhetoric, unknown to the speaker, mounts an attack against the targeted out-group or individual. (Amman & Meloy, 2021, p. 3)

The concept of stochastic terrorism, and the centrality of media as the amplifier of a message to incite violence, is important in understanding the copycat or contagion elements of the insurrection.

Stochastic terrorism does not exist independently of the power of mass media and digital culture as an amplifier and call to action. In the insurrection, a political leader—President Donald Trump—used the media to signal violence in such a way that it was "hidden in the noise of extremist rhetoric" (p. 9). This rhetoric resonated with primed receivers who were compelled to react through violence. Media-mediated politicized rhetoric, as is the case with other types of copycat crimes, operates as both a "trigger" directly causing crime and a "catalyst or rudder" shaping rather than generating crime. A small group of individuals would likely commit a crime no matter what. In these cases the media operates as a mechanism that shapes MO behavior. Media and rhetoric can also operate as a trigger for individuals susceptible to "poliregression"—the regression of a large group under the influence of a narcissistic leader. In the case of the Capitol insurrection, individual rioters fell into two groups—those who were intent on committing crimes and those who were caught up in the rhetoric and the mob mentality of the group (similar to the incel followers of Elliot Rodger or the shooters who have emulated the Columbine killers). Individuals who belonged to groups such as the Oath Keepers likely engaged in planned, purposeful violence with media operating as a shaper or rudder, while many others were triggered by media-mediated stochastic narcissistic rhetoric that led them to engage in a carnival of poliregressed defensive violence. These rioters were operating under the influence of stochastic terrorism that put them in a psychological "freeze, flee, or fight" reaction to a perceived imminent and existential threat.

The role digital culture played in the 2020 George Floyd protests and the 2021 U.S. Capitol insurrection is a stark contemporary illustration of the copycat effect. Even more illustrative is the concern of the contagion of the Capitol riots in Europe shortly after the insurrection. The head of misinformation tracking firm Europe at NewsGuard, Anna-Sophie Harling, said, "If ever there was a sign that American tech platforms were having an impact on international discourse in a way that has no borders, this [the Capitol riots] is." Factual incidents and occurrences suggest that there was a contagion of violence that spread to Europe following the insurrection. The Dutch National Coordinator for Terrorism and Security published its quarterly threat assessment on April 14, 2021, *DTN 54*. In the report, the Capitol riots were singled out as a trigger event for right-wing extremist violence in Europe with overlap between the Boogaloo

Case Studies of Copycat and Media-Mediated Crime

movement and the ideas of the UK-based Feuerkrieg Division, noting that ". . . events in the U.S. can have an inspiring effect." The report also noted that two young men who were arrested for suspicion of far-right extremism were part of the American online network The Base, noting that the Capitol riots were not the trigger for the event—the Christchurch, New Zealand attacks were—but the fear of geopolitical events and the contagion element of global triggers was noted to raise awareness to the issue. One hour into the Capitol insurrection, political leader Thierry Baudet issued a tweet supporting Trump, and representatives of his and other right-wing populist parties issued statements that were viewed as a call to action against the government in response to COVID-related mandates and curfews. Over 12,000 people in the Netherlands subscribe to QAnon-related Facebook sites, and numerous calls to action and attempts to rally the masses promoting conspiracy theories, QAnon slogans, and antigovernment sentiment to come to public places in Amsterdam or prominent demonstration sites in The Hague were made. Spontaneous riots erupted in over 20 villages and cities in the Netherlands leading to over 570 arrests and 12 people injured. The riots appeared to erupt spontaneously, and protesters referred to the Capitol riots (de Graaf, 2021). This almost immediate contagion effect of the violence in the U.S. Capitol shows the power of mass media and digital culture to influence violence on a global scale. Significant advances over the last decade in mass media and information technology and changes in the global media landscape require continued examination of the copycat effect and the role of mass media (via the Internet, social media, and TV) in influencing violence (Nacos, 2009).

Copycat crimes over the past 50 years offer insight into how technological advances influence criminal behavior. From the 1980s when the ethical realm of the real collided full-force with the aesthetic realm of the hyperreal influencing lone, isolated young men like Chapman and Hinckley, to the 1990s *NBK* and mass school shootings at a time of rapid technological advancement, to the simulated and virtual reality of the 2000s exemplified by *The Matrix* and GTA copycats, to the increasing role of social media and rise of performance crime exemplified by cases such as Luka Magnotta and Elliot Rodger in the 2010s, to the global contagion of extremist violence in the technology-saturated 2020s, with every decade, media and digital culture has become more complex and exacerbates the copycat effect on criminal behavior. For a comprehensive list of copycat crime cases throughout history, see Appendix.

Today, copycat crime is the product of a complex, reflexive, and chaotic interplay between real life, online life, virtual reality, and augmented reality, with increasingly blurred boundaries between what is real and what is not real. Everyone can be a celebrity. We are all watching and being watched. We are not bound by time or scheduled broadcasts. Social media provides a vehicle for performance with instant global digital self-distribution while simultaneously offering a tool for law enforcement through self-surveillance of those who publicize their crimes on social media. The changing technological environment has shifted audiences from passive to active participants with performance as a central feature of media content (Surette, 2015a, 2016b). Media, technology, and digital culture influence criminal behavior in ever-changing ways.

CHAPTER FIVE

Copycat Crime in the Courts: Implications for Civil Rights and Criminal Justice

The growing number of cases of criminal behavior and violence that involve mass media and digital culture and the copycat effect present unique challenges for the civil and criminal courts. Social media is increasingly used as evidence in law enforcement investigations and in court (Lane & Ramirez, 2021). In criminal courts, the influence of media on criminal behavior has been a question of practical significance in adjudication, insanity defense cases, and sentencing. In the civil courts, lawsuits have been waged against media producers arguing that films, music, video games, and social media incite violence and contribute to specific criminal acts. The question "What role did media play in influencing crime and violence?" is of critical and practical importance in the civil and criminal courts.

Legal decisions in criminal and civil courts must be made in real time and have practical implications. Theory and research that provide insight and empirical evidence to understand how media and digital culture influence criminal behavior and violence are necessary to answer legal questions about responsibility and culpability. Landmark criminal cases include Mark Chapman's murder of John Lennon and the role the book *Catcher in the Rye* played in his motivation for the crime, the trial of John Hinckley where the jury was shown the film *Taxi Driver* to understand Hinckley's mindset and motivation when he attempted to assassinate

President Ronald Reagan, and more recent attempts to use *The Matrix* and *Grand Theft Auto* defenses (Bean, 2003; Leung, 2005; Montgomery, 2012). Landmark civil cases have attempted to hold media producers, directors, and distributors responsible for inciting violence. Civil lawsuits filed in the aftermath of Columbine and other school and mass shootings (Frontline, 2000; Steinlage, 2020), the *Natural Born Killers* incitement case against Oliver Stone and Warner Brothers (Kunich, 2000; O'Neil, 2001), and lawsuits against violent video game creators and distributors reflect judicial decisions that determine where free speech ends and responsibility begins in cases involving the effects of media violence. Examination of the ways in which media has been used to explain the motives and methods of perpetrators in the criminal courts and actions taken against the media producers, directors, and distributors in the civil courts provide important insight into how the courts (and culture) view the role of media and digital culture in inspiring crime and violence.

Social scientists have investigated the connection between media and violence since the 1960s (Proman, 2004), the relationship between media and aggression has been long established (Gerbner, 1994; Gerbner et al., 2014), and empirical evidence over the past 30 years on the General Aggression Model (GAM) suggests that mass media and digital culture are risk factors for aggression and violence (e.g., Anderson & Bushman, 2018; Anderson et al., 2017; Bushman, 2016; Bushman & Huesmann, 2012; Grossman & Paulsen, 2018). However, in the courts, questions have been raised regarding the causal link between media violence and criminal behavior (e.g., Draper, 2019; Ferguson et al., 2008, 2011, 2017; Markey & Ferguson, 2017). Social science operates on the process of scientific discovery and endless hypothesis testing. Scientific research and public discourse on the effects of digital culture and mass media on criminal behavior and violence continue to accumulate. However, legal decisions must be made in real time based on the existing theory and empirical research to date.

The First Amendment, Responsibility, and Harm

The effect of media and digital culture on criminal behavior is an issue of practical concern in the civil and criminal courts. Landmark criminal cases have presented evidence on media violence and the copycat effect to establish legal defenses such as not guilty by reason of insanity (NGRI), diminished capacity, and as a mitigating factor at sentencing in defense arguments. Prosecutors have argued that evidence of mimicry of media violence that influences modus operandi behavior establishes premeditation

Copycat Crime in the Courts: Implications for Civil Rights and Criminal Justice   135

and instrumental violence. Civil cases brought forth by victims and families of victims have involved incitement, negligence, and wrongful death lawsuits against media creators, producers, and distributors. How criminal and civil court decisions involve media effects illustrates the historical and legal demarcation of criminal and civil responsibility in cases that involve media-influenced crime and violence. In the criminal courts, examining the ways in which copycat crime appears in legal arguments provides insight into how the law views criminal defenses that argue that defendants are operating under the influence of mass media. In the civil courts, judicial decisions about negligence and responsibility of media creators, producers, and distributors help to understand where the courts draw the line between First Amendment protections and negligence, responsibility, and harm.

In 1992 a PBS TV documentary was aired titled *Rage, Rights, Responsibilities* (Ganguzza, 1992). The documentary featured a Socratic seminar narrated by Fred W. Friendly facilitated by Harvard Law School Professor Charles Ogletree. Professor Ogletree posed hypothetical cases to a distinguished panel of movie, TV, and music producers; performing artists; media violence activists; police; and scholars[1] engaging them in a discussion about media violence, its impacts, rights, and responsibilities. The issues raised included the line between art and incitement, the responsibility of media producers, the role of parents in educating their children about media, and First Amendment issues. The *Rage, Rights, and Responsibilities* seminar was held the year the song "Cop Killer" was released by Ice T's band Body Count (Body Count, 1992) and was funded by the Warner Music Group, the company responsible for distributing "Cop Killer" (Goodman, 1992). "Cop Killer," a song about retaliating against police brutality, generated extreme backlash from media-violence critics and politicians, including then-President George H. W. Bush, was subsequently banned and removed from the Body Count album, and the controversy nearly ruined Ice T's career. Three decades later the song is still not publicly available on streaming platforms because of the controversy (Germaine, 2021). The *Rage, Rights, and Responsibilities* seminar highlights issues that continue to be at the center of legal decisions involving the media-crime relationship.

In the *Rage, Rights, and Responsibilities* seminar, Professor Ogletree begins by telling panelists about a new movie called "The Michael Stormer Story." a psychological thriller that examines the motivations of Stormer, who engages in violent crimes and cannibalism. Ogletree asks the panelists: Would you act in/produce this movie? Would you allow your children to watch the movie? Who is responsible if someone mimics the movie?

Panelist actor Richard Dreyfus tells Professor Ogletree that, yes, he would be willing to act in the Michael Stormer movie.

Nadine Strossen, president of the American Civil Liberties Union says:

> . . . Mr. Wolf said earlier that he thinks one of the great movies of the last half century was *Taxi Driver* and yet we know that Mr. Hinckley said that he was inspired by that movie to try to assassinate a president of the United States, so if we are going to be reduced as individuals to seeing only that material that will not motivate anybody to go out and commit a crime, then we are not going to see anything at all. I think we are really here talking about individual responsibility. By all means, hold the Hinckleys, hold all the other actual criminals responsible for their acts, but don't scapegoat Hollywood, don't scapegoat art.

Professor Ogletree then asks Jeff Ayeroff, president of Virgin Records, "I have a group I want you to hear . . . a powerful rap group called Black Nightmare Messengers—interested?" Ayeroff says, "Yes . . ." Professor Ogletree adds, "The song is called 'Dirty Looks' . . . no more pencils, no more books, no more teachers, dirty looks.[2] . . . They are saying we are tired of teachers. . . . How will you market this?" Professor Ogletree asks panelist Michael Franti, founder of the band Disposable Heroes of Hiphoprisy, "Is it a problem? . . . What if the message is saying to off teachers. . . . They are literally saying, 'off teachers.'" Franti responds, "I would have to hear the whole thing and consider based on what the artists are trying to convey . . . I'm against killing, but I feel every artist has the right to say what they want to say, but I may not put it on my record label." Professor Ogletree asks panelists, "Would this song get people to kill teachers?" Dr. Prothrow-Stith, public health leader and professor of medicine, responds:

> I think it's obviously not likely to cause young people to kill teachers. However, the impact on all of us is probably very small and the impact on a small number of kids is probably very large.

Professor Ogletree asks music producer David Harleston, president of Def Jam Recordings, "Would you release the song?" Harleston replies:

> . . . in my view, there is absolutely no empirical evidence that that song is going to lead to the killing of teachers. Moreover, I caution everyone not to conclude when you're looking at a rap lyric that says, 'no more teachers, no more books, off the teacher,' that what they're talking about is killing the teacher. Art, poetry, lyrics are very rarely to be literally interpreted. I have really no problem with that lyric.

Copycat Crime in the Courts: Implications for Civil Rights and Criminal Justice 137

The conversation turns to the issue of race, censorship, and hate speech. Professor Ogletree asks, what if it is not "offing teachers," but "offing cops." Houston Police Officer Mark Clark says yes, this is going too far. Ogletree then tells panelists, there's a new band, "even hotter than the Black Nightmare Messengers, called the New Plague and their plague is Blacks and Jews." He asks Harleston, "Would you sign them?" Harleston says, No ". . . because I make a personal political judgement as to whether or not I am going to sign an album that is conveying something that I don't support, regardless of how successful it is." Ogletree follows, "You support killing teachers and cops but not blacks and Jews?" Michael Franti says, "If the Aryan Brotherhood wants to make a record, I'd give them a rope to hang themselves."

Professor Ogletree then asks panelists, what if the record is out and teachers are killed, do you bear any responsibility? Harleston replies:

> I'd want to know what his family experience is, what his personal history is . . . I'm worried about our looking at music and film and television and blaming it for problems that . . . this country simply doesn't want to acknowledge.

The *Rage, Rights, and Responsibilities* seminar is a time capsule that articulates the central issues of importance that have historically defined cultural and legal discourse on media violence effects and criminal and civil responsibility that holds to this day. The issues discussed in the seminar regarding the influence of media violence and the line between incitement and the responsibilities of media producers are issues that have arisen in landmark cases. Issues raised in the discussion, such as whether and how media violence influences real-life crime and violence, where the line is between art and exploitation, who bears responsibility when media violence incites actual violence, and how First Amendment protection of freedom of speech can be balanced with public safety interests, continue to be raised in the courts.

Copycat Crime in the Courts

Theory and research on violent media effects and copycat crime has made its way into criminal and civil court cases. In the criminal courts, research presented by expert witnesses on the effects of violent media on defendants has been used in adjudication, insanity defenses, and sentencing. In the Hinckley case, the jury was shown the film *Taxi Driver* to provide insight into his mindset (Low et al., 1986). In the case of Mark Chapman, though Chapman was ultimately convicted of murdering John Lennon, the jury was presented with details on the book *The Catcher in the Rye* to show Chapman's fascination with and mimicry of the character Holden Caufield (Black, 1991; Jones, 1992). In other cases, prosecutors have attempted to introduce films as evidence, such as in the case of Mechele Linehan, who received a 99-year sentence in 2015 for murdering her fiancé, who was said to be influenced by the film *The Last Seduction* (Associated Press, 2015). In other cases, the entire defense has been named after a film such as in the cases involving the "*Matrix* defense" where defense attorneys argued that *The Matrix* contributed to the diminished capacity of the defendants said to have become lost inside the film (Bean, 2003).

In the civil courts, legal challenges have been raised regarding the role of media in inciting violence in liability cases involving wrongful death, injuries, and negligence. Mass shootings before and after Columbine resulted in subsequent wrongful death and injury lawsuits. Other crimes such as serial and spree murders such as those committed by individuals who were said to have been influenced by films such as *Natural Born Killers* (*NBK*) or video games such as *Grand Theft Auto* have resulted in incitement lawsuits that (in the case of *NBK* and director Oliver Stone) have made it to the U.S. Supreme Court. Movie, TV, video game, and music directors, producers, and distributors have been named in these lawsuits.

Under the Influence of Mass Media: Copycat Crime in the Criminal Courts

In the criminal courts, landmark cases have involved defendants whose behaviors have allegedly been influenced by violent media. Most of these cases have involved defense attorney arguments that the defendant committed a crime under the influence of mass media as part of an NGRI defense, a diminished capacity defense, or as a mitigating factor. Prosecutors have raised the issue of media violence effects as part of an argument that copycat elements show premeditation or at sentencing to suggest that the copycat effect on criminal behavior is a mitigating or aggravating factor. How the courts have decided in these cases has important relevance for determining how media effects on criminal behavior are viewed by the courts and gaps in theory and research on copycat crime where more research is needed to answer legal questions.

Mark Chapman/*Catcher in the Rye*

Mark Chapman murdered The Beatles member John Lennon on December 8, 1980. Just hours before the murder, Chapman had met

Copycat Crime in the Courts: Implications for Civil Rights and Criminal Justice 139

Lennon when he signed his album. Later, shortly before 11 p.m. when Lennon and his wife, Yoko Ono, were returning to their residence at the Dakota Apartments in New York City, Chapman fired five shots into Lennon's back and then calmly opened *The Catcher in the Rye* and read from the book until police arrested him. Lennon died on the way to the hospital. When Chapman was arrested, he was carrying the pistol he used to shoot Lennon and a copy of the book by J. D. Salinger, *Catcher in the Rye* which was taken into evidence by the police (Jones, 1992). During his trial, Chapman's defense team argued that Chapman was NGRI. However, during the trial Chapman pleaded guilty, saying it was the will of God. He was sentenced to 20 years to life and has been denied parole 11 times.

The Catcher in the Rye's main character, Holden Caulfield, travels to New York City and narrates the story, expressing disdain for the "phoniness" he sees around him and views himself as the savior of innocent children, as the "Catcher in the Rye" (Jones, 1992). In a letter to *The New York Times* after Lennon's murder, Chapman said that the motive for killing Lennon was contained in *The Catcher in the Rye*. He told a defense psychiatrist while awaiting trial, "Everybody's going to be reading this book" and "With the help of God-almighty media. And I'm going to use it like it's never been used before" (Black, 1991, p. 156). On June 22, 1981, Chapman pled guilty and at his sentencing hearing he read from *The Catcher in the Rye* the passage that he said explained his crime:

> I keep picturing all these little kids playing some game in this big field of rye and all. Thousands of little kids, and nobody's around—nobody big, I mean—except me. And I'm standing on the edge of some crazy cliff. What I have to do, I have to catch everybody if they start to go over the cliff—I mean if they're running and they don't look where they're going I have to come out from somewhere and catch them. That's all I'd do all day. I'd just be the catcher in the rye and all. I know it's crazy, but that's the only thing I'd really like to be. I know it's crazy. (Salinger, 1945, 1946, 1951, p. 173)

Chapman told the court that he committed the murder to be Somebody like Holden Caulfield (Whitfield, 1997).

In Chapman's mind, idolization of Lennon turned to disdain, and he murdered Lennon to save the world from phoniness and to be, as he said to the police who arrested him, "the Catcher in the Rye" (Jones, 1992, p. 49).

When the parole board asked about the role of *The Catcher in the Rye* and Holden Caulfield in the murder of John Lennon, Chapman told the parole board, "I identified with that character's isolation, loneliness and I got very wrapped up in that book" (New York State Department of Corrections and Community Supervision Board of Parole, 2020, p. 16). The parole board member then read the passage from *The Catcher in the Rye* that Chapman had brought up in his sentencing hearing and asked, "Enlighten us with that. I don't understand why you chose that passage and why did you do that at sentencing?" Chapman replied,

> Well, I think psychologically I look back at it now and I haven't heard or read that for years. This guy wants to save the world. In my twisted way at that time in my thinking, I'm not thinking that what I did was good, but I'm thinking, you know, maybe there's something I can do now that's important and this is my heart. This was my—this is my horrible evil self. Just a way to try to make up for it and trying to say I'm not really a bad person. That's the best explanation that I can give at that time. (New York State Department of Corrections and Community Supervision Board of Parole, 2020, p. 16)

The parole board ultimately did not grant Chapman parole, stating:

> The sentencing comments have been reviewed and weighed. It is noted that instead of apologizing in open court, you oddly read out loud a passage from the novel. . . . During the interview you stated you committed this murder to seek glory. You said "infamy brings you glory." This panel finds your statement disturbing. Your actions represented an evil act. The fact that today, almost forty years later, you can still speak of what you did as something that you felt was a positive and in your mind gave you "glory" at the time, is disturbing for this panel. When considering all relevant factors, it is in the best interests of society, as well as yourself to continue to be incarcerated. (New York State Department of Corrections and Community Supervision Board of Parole, 2020, pp. 38–39)

The role that *The Catcher in the Rye* played in Chapman's mind when he was 25 years old and the relevance of the book at his sentencing and his parole hearing 40 years later at age 65 attest to the intertwining of the story with Chapman's motivation and thought processes about his crime at the time and throughout his life.

John Hinckley, Jr./ *Taxi Driver*

In the trial of John Hinckley, Jr. the film *Taxi Driver* was played for the jury to illustrate the links between the film and Hinckley's thought processes and behaviors that followed the film like a script. The defense

Copycat Crime in the Courts: Implications for Civil Rights and Criminal Justice 141

argued that Hinckley was diagnosed with schizophrenia and major depressive disorder. The prosecution argued that Hinckley was diagnosed with narcissistic personality disorder. Ultimately, the jury was swayed by the defense and ruled that Hinckley was NGRI.

Taxi Driver was a central part of John Hinckley's trial. The film was played for jurors during which Hinckley was observed watching the film intently. Hinckley's defense team argued that he suffered from schizophrenia, schizotypal personality disorder, and major depressive disorder. Expert witnesses for the defense testified that Hinckley's inner world was compelling him to commit the assassination attempts (on President Carter who he had stalked months prior on October 2, 1980, and ultimately President Reagan on March 30, 1981), which was ultimately the product of psychosis. Hinckley was psychologically immersed in the *Taxi Driver* script and took on the "Travis Bickle parallel" (Low et al., 1986, p. 56) in attempt to feel more competent and stable. The defense ultimately argued that Hinckley's acts were motivated by his own inner world. The prosecution argued Hinckley suffered from narcissistic personality disorder, mixed personality disorder, schizoid personality disorder, and dysthymic disorder; that he knew what he was doing and was motivated by a desire for fame and a fascination with assassination; and that his obsession with Jodie Foster was "just like any other man with a fantasy" (Low et al., 1986, p. 87).

Chapman's murder of John Lennon was noted in the closing argument of Hinckley's defense as a stress factor for Hinckley's assassination attempt. When Hinckley traveled to Washington, D.C. to commit the assassination he had with him in his suitcase a copy of *The Catcher in the Rye, Strawberry Fields Forever: John Lennon Remembered, Romeo and Juliet* and *Ted Bundy: The Killer Next Door* (Wilber, 2011). Hinckley created a lengthy audiotape on New Year's Eve, 1980 that was played in court in which he lamented over John Lennon's murder and his love for Jodie Foster in which he said, "John Lennon is dead. The world is over. . . . My obsession is Jodie Foster . . . I love her. I don't want to hurt her . . . I think I'd rather just see her not, not on earth, than being with other guys . . ." (Low et al., 1986, p. 98). Hinckley then traveled to New York City to attend John Lennon's funeral in February.

Dr. William Carpenter, Jr., one of the defense experts, testified that Hinckley identified with Bickle and mimicked many of his attributes including wearing an army jacket, becoming fascinated with guns, and keeping a diary, suggesting that Hinckley had lost his own identity and took on Bickle's. Carpenter testified that Hinckley became obsessed with Jodie Foster, who he had contacted while she was a student at Yale, leaving her letters and poems in her mailbox and calling her on the phone twice and recording her. In addition to Hinckley's fixation with *Taxi Driver* and Foster, Dr. Carpenter testified that Hinckley was devastated by John Lennon's death and traveled to New York City to be among the mourners; and in the month before his assassination attempt also traveled back and forth between New Haven, Connecticut, where Foster was and New York City. In a final trip to New Haven, he left Foster a love note that stated, "Jodie, after tonight John Lennon and I will have a lot in common. Its [sic] all for you" (Low et al., 1986, p. 27), and in another communication he said, "I love you six trillion times. Wait for me. I will rescue you" (p. 99).

While all the defense experts in the Hinckley trial did not agree on Hinckley's specific diagnosis (which ranged from borderline personality disorder to schizotypal personality disorder to schizophrenia), all testified that he was psychotic at the time of the offense. In the defense's closing arguments, defense attorney Vincent Fuller said of Hinckley:

> He lives in a world where the only reality is that which he makes for himself. That which he defines for himself. . . .
>
> I should go back to a moment in 1976, briefly, and recall to your mind that it was this period that he was alone in Hollywood, that he saw the movie "Taxi Driver," and he made identification, sympathized with Travis Bickle. I can't quite call him a hero. You saw the movie. Characterize him as you will. . . .
>
> But John Hinckley saw him as a loner, as he, Hinckley was a loner. Isolated. Angry at what he saw in the outside world. Unable to establish any relationship in that world that he saw. (Low et al., 1986, p. 95)

Fuller followed this by saying that Hinckley's behavior showed that, rather than being entitled, as the prosecution suggested, he was "almost paralyzed" and that he had played Russian roulette holding a gun to his head and taking a photo in late 1979 or 1980, "much like the likeness of the character Travis Bickel from Taxi Driver" (Low et al., 1986, p. 95). Fuller continued, "Ladies and gentleman of the jury, I submit to you that the mental problem that the defendant was suffering from [at] the end of 1979 and by early 1980 was so deep, so deeply rooted in himself that it would take hours and hours of psychiatric examination to ferret it out" (Low et al., 1986, p. 96). Ultimately, the defense experts concluded that Hinckley was psychotic, withdrawn into his own inner world in an "internal frenzy, an internal confusion . . . all built upon false premises, false assumptions, false ideas" (Low et al., 1986, p. 101).

Copycat Crime in the Courts: Implications for Civil Rights and Criminal Justice   143

In contrast, prosecution expert psychiatrist Dr. Park Dietz concluded that Hinckley was not psychotic at the time of the offense and that he met the criteria for dysthymic disorder, narcissistic personality disorder, and schizoid personality disorder. The prosecution, led by Assistant U.S. Attorney Roger Adelman, argued that the defense was using the film *Taxi Driver* as an excuse, that Hinckley was ultimately responsible for his behavior, and that his crime was the result of multiple stressors he experienced, including his failure to establish a relationship with Jodie Foster, the death of John Lennon, and his previously failed psychiatric treatment with a local psychiatrist his parents had sent him to named Dr. John Hopper. In his closing argument, Adelman said, ". . . Mr. Hinckley put the blame for what happened on March 30 on his parents, on the Secret Service for not protecting the President properly. On Dr. Hopper. On Jodie Foster. On 'Taxi Driver'" (Low et al., 1986, p. 111).

The *Matrix* Defense

Over 20 years after the Hinckley trial, in a completely new legal landscape after reforms were put into place restricting the use of the insanity defense following controversy over Hinckley's NGRI verdict (Callahan et al., 1991; Finkel, 1989; Simon & Aaronson, 1988), *Taxi Driver*–style arguments were raised in murder trials involving individuals who were said to have been lost inside *The Matrix* (Wachowski & Wachowski, 1999, 2003a, 2003b, 2021). *The Matrix* is a series of four films beginning with *The Matrix* (1999) followed by three sequels, *The Matrix Reloaded* (2003), *The Matrix Revolutions* (2003), and *The Matrix Resurrections* (2021).

Matrix-inspired murders resulted in cases in which defense attorneys attempted to use "*The Matrix* defense" (e.g., Bean, 2003; Kiehl, 2003; Schone, 2003). Perpetrators of gruesome murders indicated in the aftermath of their crimes that their crimes were inspired by *The Matrix*. Mass school shootings, including Columbine and Marjory Stoneman Douglas High School in Parkland, Florida, have been associated with *The Matrix* (Roberts, 2018; Young, 2009). Lee Boyd Malvo, one of the two perpetrators in the 2002 Washington, D.C. Beltway sniper attacks who is currently serving multiple life sentences, idolized Neo, the main character in *The Matrix,* and drawings and writings by Malvo with references from *The Matrix* about freeing one's mind were found in his cell (Kiehl, 2003).

In 2000, San Francisco State University computer science student Vadim Mieseges murdered Ella Wong, a hospital administrative assistant he was subletting a room from. He said he was "sucked into the Matrix."

He led police to body parts in Golden Gate Park where Wong's torso was found in a trash bin and other body parts were found in park garbage cans. Mieseges came to the attention of law enforcement not because of the murder, but because he was acting erratically at a local mall where he was observed speaking in gibberish and acting strangely (Hanley, 2000). He was found by mall security officers wandering through a Macy's department store after he took a wooden dowel from a mannequin and put it in his belt as if it were a sword. He waved the dowel at the officers, kicking and biting them as they tried to arrest him while shouting "Those are my TVs!" while being taken away (Van Derbecken, 2000). The security officers found a knife, marijuana, and methamphetamine on him. While being arrested he told police he had killed and chopped up Wong. It was later found that he came to the United States from Switzerland in 1996 where he said he was previously institutionalized and prescribed medication for attention deficit disorder. Mieseges told police that he had skinned and disemboweled Wong and then cut her up and scattered her parts around the city (Hanley, 2000). While in custody, a judge ruled Mieseges mentally unfit to stand trial, and he was sent to the Atascadero State Hospital for further examination (Curiel, 2000). In 2002, the trial court found Mieseges NGRI and he was court-ordered to be committed to the state hospital for a maximum term of 25 years to life. In a later appellate court decision, the court noted that Mieseges believed drug abuse was the source of his issues and described a history of drug use, psychiatric hospitalization, and suicidal thoughts, psychotic delusions, and assaults. In treatment in the years following his psychiatric hospitalization after the murder, he was diagnosed with "PTSD, attention deficit disorder, amphetamine induced psychotic disorder in full sustained remission, amphetamine dependence, opiate dependence, alcohol abuse, cannabis abuse, hallucinogen abuse, and personality disorder not otherwise specified with antisocial and obsessive-compulsive traits" (*People v. Miesegaes*, 2014, pp. 1–2).

In February 2002, Lee Boyd Malvo and John Allen Muhammad committed a series of coordinated sniper attacks on the Washington, D.C. Beltway. Malvo was 17 at the time and Muhammad was 41. During the attack, 10 people were killed and 3 were injured. Muhammad was sentenced to death and was executed in 2009. Malvo was tried on two counts of capital murder and weapons charges. *The Matrix* was linked to these murders shortly after the crimes. The main character in *The Matrix* is a computer programmer whose real name is Thomas A. Anderson, who secretly operates as a hacker by the name of Neo. The movie is about a dystopian future in which all humanity is trapped inside a simulated

Copycat Crime in the Courts: Implications for Civil Rights and Criminal Justice 145

reality controlled by machines. Neo discovers the truth and joins a rebellion against the machines with others who have been freed from The Matrix, including his mentor, captain of the *Nebuchadnezzar*, Morpheus, played by Laurence Fishburne, in an us-against-them mission to save humanity. The D.C. Sniper murders have been referred to as "one of the worst copycat crimes in our nation's history." Anthony Meoli, author of *Diary of the D.C. Sniper* (2014), says, "I don't think most people realize that this was a copycat crime related to *The Matrix*." During the crime spree, which caused a nationwide manhunt, Malvo and Muhammad dropped a tarot card near a suburban Maryland school near where they shot a 13-year-old boy (Miller et al., 2006). It was the Death card and written on it was "For you Mr. Police. Call me God." Dr. J. Buzz Von Ornsteiner, also interviewed for the *Copycat Murders* docuseries, said that Malvo and Muhammad had a need for attention and glorified the murders they committed.

Malvo reported having watched *The Matrix* with Muhammad over 300 times. Malvo's attorneys mounted an insanity defense, arguing that he committed the crimes under the control of Muhammad and that Malvo's troubled childhood and mental instability made him vulnerable to indoctrination by Muhammad. While Malvo's obsession with *The Matrix* was not a core element of Malvo's insanity defense, experts for the defense testified that the film influenced his thinking. A social worker testified about Malvo's interest in *The Matrix* noting that she saw Malvo in the role of the hero, Neo, who brings about a societal change, and Muhammad in the role of Morpheus, who was Neo's mentor (Associated Press, 2003, December 8). A clinical psychologist who evaluated Malvo and testified at his trial planned to play a 12-minute clip from *The Matrix* in addition to clips of violent video games that Malvo and Muhammad played together as part of her testimony to show that he did not have the capacity to understand the difference between right and wrong. However, the judge ultimately did not allow the film clip to be admitted as evidence (Associated Press, 2003, December 9).

In July 2002, Tonda Lynn Ansley walked up to her landlord, Sherry Lee Corbett, on an Ohio street, told her she wanted to talk to her, and shot her with a handgun. Corbett was a professor at nearby Miami University who was renting Ansley her house. Ansley had known Corbett for eight years and helped Corbett work on homes she renovated and rented, including to Ansley. Ansley told police that Corbett, Corbett's partner Robert Sherwin who was also a Miami University professor, and several other intended victims including her ex-husband, were controlling her mind, trying to brainwash her, and making her have "dreams I've found out aren't really dreams" (Schone, 2003). When police questioned her, she made references to *The Matrix*. She said she had been experiencing dreams where Corbett, Sherwin, and her ex-husband appeared as vampires and were trying to kill her and that she soon discovered that the dreams were real, that the three had been drugging her, and she was being drawn into *The Matrix*, "They commit a lot of crimes in *The Matrix*. . . . That's where you go to sleep at night and they drug you and take you somewhere else and then they bring you back and put you in bed and, when you wake up, you think that it's a bad dream" (Bean, 2003; Jackman, 2003, May 17). She also told police that she had to kill Corbett, Sherwin, and her ex-husband before they killed her and that they wanted to kill her because they were trying to silence her for uncovering that they were committing arson and fraud. Ansley's attorney said that *The Matrix* allowed her to awaken and see the reality of her dreams. "It resonated with her. . . . Things that you don't think are real—really are in *The Matrix*." Psychiatrist Dr. John Kennedy said, "Someone who is already psychotic could use *The Matrix* as evidence of an alternative universe" (Cooper, 2007, p. 167).

Ansley was indicted for aggravated murder but was then declared incompetent to stand trial. Her attorneys later filed an NGRI plea. The judge ordered a psychiatric evaluation after Ansley petitioned to act as her own attorney which the judge denied. She was ruled competent, but Ansley waived her right to a jury trial following a series of independent psychological evaluations that declared that she did not understand the difference between right and wrong, saw almost everyone around her as conspiring against her, and that she killed Corbett because she believed she was protecting herself and her son. Ansley was placed in the custody of a maximum-security psychiatric hospital (Cooper, 2007). In 2010, Ansley was allowed unsupervised four-hour day passes out of the mental health facility once or twice a week but is barred from the city of Hamilton, Ohio, where she committed the murder (Roppel, 2010).

Oakton, Virginia teenager, 19-year-old Joshua Cooke murdered his adoptive parents in the basement of their home on February 13, 2003. Cooke's father was on the phone with his teenage sister during the entire shooting and she thought she heard her mom say, "Josh, you wouldn't." After the murders, Cooke picked up the phone with his sister on the other end and when she asked to talk to her dad, Cooke told her he had to call somebody and hung up the phone. Cooke then called 911 twice and told the dispatcher, "I just shot my parents. I just blew them away with a shotgun. Get your asses over here" and "I will not be armed when they get here. I don't want to be shot by police." His mother was shot two times

Copycat Crime in the Courts: Implications for Civil Rights and Criminal Justice   147

and his father was shot seven times with a 12-gauge shotgun. When police officers arrived, Cooke was standing in the driveway, drinking a Coke (Jackman, 2003, June 25).

Cooke's defense team attracted attention because they filed a motion saying that he may not have known the difference between right and wrong. His defense attorneys claimed that he believed he was living in a computer simulation, couldn't distinguish between reality and the digital world, and "harbored a bona fide belief that he was living in the virtual reality of 'The Matrix'" (Bean, 2003). Cooke underwent a month-long psychiatric evaluation and was ultimately determined to be mentally competent and able to tell the difference between right and wrong. Cooke felt strongly about accepting responsibility for the crime and made the decision to plead guilty, so a trial did not occur. However, elements of the influence of *The Matrix* and of violent video games were raised at Cooke's sentencing hearing. After Cooke pled guilty, his attorneys requested postponement of his sentencing and sued to unseal his adoption records. It was then discovered that Cooke's biological parents and brother (who had not been adopted by the Cookes) suffered from schizophrenia. Both his parents were prostitutes, and his father repeatedly beat his mother, which led to both parents being declared unfit when Cooke was one year old. Upon discovery of this familial mental illness, Cooke's attorneys argued that his inherited mental illness and early childhood trauma made him particularly susceptible to the negative influence of *The Matrix* and playing violent video games for hours on end and that this should be considered a mitigating factor in his sentencing. Psychologist Brad Bushman, author of many peer-reviewed articles on the impact of violent films, TV, and video games (e.g., Bushman, 1995, 1998; Bushman & Huesmann, 2006, 2012), testified for the defense that exposure to violent media has physiological effects, including increased aggression and anger and likelihood of violent behavior, as did child psychologist David Shostak, who testified that the murders were "deflected suicide." The prosecutor in the case, Robert Horan, rejected the media violence stating that millions of people saw *The Matrix* and played violent video games and did not go out and kill anyone. Cooke was sentenced to 40 years in prison, at the high end of the 26- to 46-year sentencing guideline (Cooper, 2007).

Since his sentencing, Cooke has done public interviews shedding light on what he was thinking at the time of his crime. In a 2013 interview from prison with journalist Piers Morgan, Cooke said about himself and the role of media in his crime, "I don't blame anyone but myself. . . . These things do contribute, and they accumulate, especially with someone who may have psychological issues like I know I've had. You can become a ticking time bomb. . . . Nobody just snaps overnight . . . it builds up over time" (CNN, 2013, August 24). Cooke offered details on the day of the crime in an interview clip included in the documentary, *A Glitch Inside the Matrix* (Ascher, 2021).

Cooke's account of his crime highlights the elements of the case his defense team attempted to initially mount:

> So, when I met my lawyers for the first time in Fairfax jail, they asked me about my crime and . . . and I told them I said, "I did my thing just like Neo in *The Matrix*. Like I was in virtual reality." And that really took them by surprise. They weren't expecting that. I also told them that the moment of my crime, I had also felt a tinge of remorse, because it was two strong things at the same time, that I was entering the world, or exiting the world of the Matrix. And then real life, with what I did to my parents. My lawyers later went to my house, and they went upstairs to my room, and they saw my enormous Matrix movie poster on my wall. And they saw my black trench coat laying out on my bed, smoothed out on my bed. They saw my black boots. The ones like Neo wore. And they began to think that they may have an insanity defense. They said that I, quote, "Harbored a bona fide belief that I was living in the virtual world of *The Matrix* at the time of the murders." That was part of my defense . . .

On October 2, 2003, Cooke was sentenced to 40 years in prison and he is due to be released in 2043 when he is 62 years old (Jackman, October 2, 2003).

Cooke's defense team's pretrial motion claiming he was under the influence of *The Matrix* drew a lot of media attention. While ultimately, Joshua Cooke pled guilty to the crime, one of his attorneys, Rachel Fierro, appeared on the national news defending the insanity defense strategy (Cooper, 2007). In an interview with CNN, reporter Sophia Choi posed the common question raised when a movie or other form of media is linked with a violent crime to Cooke's attorneys, "Millions of people have seen this movie and not used it as a defense, and they haven't actually killed anyone. Millions have seen it. So how can you use this as a defense?" Fierro responded that after reviewing the facts of the case it was clear that "Joshua Cook was obsessed with the movie" and at the time of the offense, he was in possession of many of the props from the movie, including a 12-gauge shotgun used by the main character Neo. Choi also brought up a statement from Warner Brothers in which the company expressed condolences to the victims but said, "Any attempt to link these crimes with a motion picture or any other art form is disturbing and irresponsible" and

Copycat Crime in the Courts: Implications for Civil Rights and Criminal Justice   149

asked "Do you think Warner Brothers is responsible for your client's behavior?" To this Fierro replied:

> No. I'm not saying that the movie made him kill his parents. I'm saying that to Joshua Cook [sic],[3] the movie was more than just entertainment. To Joshua Cook, it had an influencing factor to his decisions. But it was certainly only one of many other elements that contributed to his decision. Obviously, the movie impacts people differently and to Joshua Cook, it was more than entertainment. And that's why we've petitioned the court for a psychiatrist, to be able to evaluate his mental health. (CNN, May 20, 2003)

Years after the trial, Fierro said she recognizes how controversial the *Matrix* defense was but maintains that Cooke's behaviors can be explained only by "something out of the ordinary" (Cooper, 2007, p. 173).

Cooke's accounts of the role of violent video games and the movie *The Matrix* show that he was obsessed with the film to the point where ideas from the movie became embedded in his thinking and ultimately his behavior. While Cooke did not mention *The Matrix* to police when he was arrested, the association appeared in his attorneys' pretrial motion and in his accounts following his sentencing. He said in a letter he wrote in 2005, "I would pretend, when Neo shot his enemies, that *I* was killing *my* enemies." Cooke reported having a fascination with violent video games and that he bought a black trench coat, boots, and a shotgun like the gun Neo used. He said he was obsessed with games, including *Grand Theft Auto, Doom, Quake, Metal Gear Solid,* and *Max Payne* and played them constantly staying in his room for hours, peeing in a cup, stashing food, and when he got angry with someone in real life, he would go into virtual reality and hunt and kill and unleash his anger on them, and that the video games were so life-like that at times it almost seemed real (Cooper, 2007).

In these *Matrix*-inspired cases, defense attorneys used the defendant's fixation on *The Matrix* to mount an insanity defense. In three of the cases the insanity defense was successful, and the perpetrators were determined to be NGRI. Tonya Lynn Ansley received a NGRI verdict in 2002 and in 2010 was granted unsupervised day release from the mental health facility (Roppel, 2010). In Ansley's case the county prosecutor who handled her case said that the movie had a role in the killing in her mind because of her "warped perception" and her mental illness. That the *Matrix* defense was used and was successful in most of these cases is surprising given the rarity of the use and success of the insanity defense.[4] Cases involving *The Matrix* succeeded for two reasons: 1) the film's premise that humans are living in an artificial virtual reality created by machines and 2) the film focuses on the idea that there are humans (the chosen few) who are aware of the manipulated world within *The Matrix* and those who are not. In the successful NGRI cases, the defendants believed themselves to be one of the chosen who know about the Matrix, and their acts of violence were motivated by their attempt to protect themselves and others from the evil machines taking over the world (Cooper, 2007).

Grand Theft Auto: A Murder Simulator?

The video game *Grand Theft Auto* (GTA) and its sequels have been linked to crimes ranging from theft, carjackings, kidnapping, and robberies to rape and capital murder (Markey & Ferguson, 2017) and has been referred by some as a "murder simulator" (Blain, 2015; Leung, 2005).[5] GTA is a video game series produced by Rockstar Games. The first of the series, *Grand Theft Auto*, was released in 1997, followed by *Grand Theft Auto 2* in 1999, *Grand Theft Auto III* in 2001, *Grand Theft Auto: Vice City* in 2002, *Grand Theft Auto: San Andreas* in 2004, *Grand Theft Auto IV* in 2008, and *Grand Theft Auto V* in 2013. A series of expansion packs and handheld games have also been produced (Andrea, 2022). Like the *Matrix* defense, the *Grand Theft Auto* defense has been used to argue diminished capacity and as a mitigating factor at sentencing.

The case of Devin Moore/Thompson is one of the most notable cases associated with the GTA games in part because of what he told police at the time of his arrest, "Life is a video game; everybody has to die sometime" (Associated Press, 2005). Moore/Thompson was convicted of six counts of capital murder and was sentenced to death following a jury recommendation by a vote of 10 to 2. The trial court's decision was appealed in 2012 and 2018 (*Devin Darnell Thompson v. the State of Alabama*, 2012, 2020). Moore/Thompson's attorneys attempted to use the "*Grand Theft Auto* defense" arguing that Moore/Thompson's many hours of playing GTA led to a dissociative state and posttraumatic stress disorder (PTSD), which contributed to his commission of the offense. There is a mission in the game that depicts an escape from a police station, killing officers, and escaping in a police cruiser, exactly what Moore/Thompson did in his crime (Leung, 2005). His defense argued that the many hours he played GTA "rendered him in a dissociate state at the time of the murders" (*Devin Darnell Thompson v. State of Alabama*, 2020, p. 27). At trial, the court allowed Moore/Thompson's experts to testify regarding PTSD and that he was in a dissociative state at the time of the murders, but did not allow experts to testify that he reverted to scripted behavior learned through

Copycat Crime in the Courts: Implications for Civil Rights and Criminal Justice   151

daily, prolonged, and repetitive video game playing prior to the commission of the crimes. The court held that the scientific research on the impact of violent video games on an individual's conduct was not a viable defense because it had not gained general acceptance in the scientific community and did not then meet the criteria for admissibility under *Frye v. United States* (1923).

In a 2018 appeal of his capital sentence, Moore/Thompson's attorneys argued that the post-conviction court erred in dismissing his prior appeal in 2012 for ineffective trial counsel because the judge presiding over the post-conviction appeal was not the same judge who presided at his trial. The appeal also argued that the trial counsel failed to present evidence on Moore/Thompson's mental health and youthful offender status and that the attorneys failed to ask questions in the voir dire process regarding whether potential jurors had seen the *CBS 60 Minutes* program depicting graphic details of Moore's case. In addition, the appeal argued that the post-conviction court erred in dismissing Moore/Thompson's claim that his trial counsel was ineffective "for failing to conduct an adequate investigation and to hire experts to support his video-game defense" and specifically that his trial counsel should have called experts such as communications professor Dr. Brad Bushman and psychology professor Dr. John Murray. The state replied:

> [Thompson] has failed to plead facts that, if true, would show a reasonable probability that experts more well-versed in the video games and violence theories would have been permitted to testify by the trial court. As discussed above, the dubious video game violence theory was properly excluded by the trial court and has not been backed up by credible research or accepted by courts or the scientific community. There is no reasonable probability that experts more well-versed in the questionable video game violence research would have been able to demonstrate to the trial court that the link between violent video games and behavior during a dissociative state caused by PTSD was sufficiently established that it had gained general acceptance in the scientific community. Thus, his allegations must be summarily dismissed . . . (*Thompson v. State*, 2020, p. 26)

On direct appeal, it was argued that the circuit court erred by preventing Moore/Thompson from presenting his defense by not allowing his experts to testify that his frequent playing of GTA rendered him in a dissociative state at the time of the murders and thus he reverted to programmed behavior.

Thus, in the case of Devin Moore/Thompson, the argument of the *Grand Theft Auto* defense and the notion that playing GTA contributed to his dissociative state and PTSD was ultimately unsuccessful at trial and in the appellate courts. In addition, the appeal charged that Moore/Thompson's trial counsel should have presented an expert to testify concerning the adverse effects of violent video games and its effects on him given his age and early childhood trauma. In 2018, the appellate court affirmed the post-conviction court's dismissal of the petition (*Thompson v. State of Alabama*, 2020).

Other Cases That Have Admitted Evidence on Copycat Crime in the Criminal Courts

In addition to cases in which copycat crime is used as a defense strategy, both prosecutors and defense attorneys have relied on evidence of copycat crime to support various aspects of their cases. For example, prosecutors have introduced evidence that defendants have mimicked fictional characters in films to show premeditation and influence of modus operandi and defense attorneys have used evidence on copycat crime as a mitigating factor to reduce culpability.

In a 2007 trial, Mechele Linehan, who was referred to in the news media as a "stripper-turned-soccer-mom," was convicted of plotting with another man who wanted to marry her to kill her former fiancé Kent Leppink in a murder-for-hire scheme that prosecutors said was pulled directly from the 1994 film *The Last Seduction*. In *The Last Seduction*, the film's main character, Bridget Gregory, played by Linda Fiorentino is a femme fatale who carries out an elaborate scheme to convince a man who is in love with her to kill her fiancé. In the 1990s Linehan had worked as a stripper in Alaska, was reported to have had three fiancés at one time, and conspired with one of them, John Carlin III, to kill Leppink to receive $1 million in life insurance money. Leppink wrote a letter to his parents shortly before he was shot dead on an Alaska trail on May 2, 1996, on a deserted road 90 miles south of Anchorage saying that Linehan would probably be responsible if he died suspiciously. Linehan moved to Washington state after the murder, got married to a doctor, and had two children. She was arrested 10 years later in 2006 and sentenced to 99 years in 2007. In 2010 the appellate court overturned the conviction and granted a new trial. The defense successfully argued that the jury should not have been allowed to read Leppink's letter and Superior Court Judge Philip Volland should not have allowed prosecutors to introduce evidence that Linehan admired and was inspired by the lead character in *The Last Seduction* which prosecutors used to argue premeditation (D'Oro, 2010). Linehan's conviction was overturned, she was released from prison, and in 2011 her murder indictment was dismissed (Yager & Smith, 2015).

Copycat Crime in the Courts: Implications for Civil Rights and Criminal Justice 153

In *U.S. v. Monsalvatge* (2017), the U.S. Court of Appeals, Second Circuit reviewed the district court conviction by jury of three individuals who committed two armed robberies—Akeem Monsalvatge, Edward Byam, and Derrick Dunkley. The U.S. Court of Appeals considered whether the district court abused its discretion in admitting into trial evidence four clips from the 2010 movie *The Town* directed by and starring Ben Affleck. Monsalvatge, Byam, and Dunkley were convicted of robberies at the Pay-O-Matic that occurred two years apart in 2010 and 2012 employing a modus operandi (MO) very similar to the method used in the film. At trial, the state introduced three of the four admitted film clips over the objections of the defendants stating that the clips (lasting a total of one minute, seven seconds) explain why the MO changed between the two robberies because the defendants altered their MO behavior in the second robbery in a manner resembling the film. The clips were allowed into the trial because of the similarity between the fictional robberies in *The Town* and the 2012 robbery committed by the defendants in addition to the fact that there was evidence that one of the defendants had special-ordered a t-shirt that featured an image from the film. The film clips were a small part of the jury trial, which included overwhelming evidence, and the trio was convicted of the robberies. The U.S. Court of Appeals upheld the court's admission of the film clips stating:

> In February 2010, when the first robbery occurred, The Town was still seven months away from its wide-release date. But, by the second robbery in February 2012, the film had long been available to the public. The 2012 robbery bears a remarkable—even obvious—resemblance to multiple aspects of the clips from The Town. In fact, nearly every distinctive aspect of the 2012 robbery can be traced to the film. The robbers' disguises, with minor differences, appear to combine the navy-blue police jacket with a hood and text detail on the front left side of the jacket in Clip 1 and the sunglasses and badge in Clip 4. The idea for special-effects masks imitating real skin is in Clip 3. The idea to use bleach to eliminate traces of DNA is in Clip 2 (and the effects of using bleach are explained in Clip 1). Threatening an employee by revealing knowledge of a home address is in Clip 4. That is every key facet of the 2012 robbery. Taken individually, each of these elements might not be sufficiently distinctive to raise a connection to the film. But taken together, as they occurred here, the attributes of the 2012 robbery are clearly connected to the film. (*U.S. v. Monsalvatge*, 2017, pp. 5–6)

The court noted that the film clips did not have a strong impact on the jurors given the overwhelming evidence in the case, and the defendant Monsalvatge provided insufficient explanation about how inviting the jury to speculate that the 2012 robbery was a copycat crime would impact the jury. The court ruled that the district court's ruling to admit movie clips was not arbitrary or irrational because the clips were relevant to the issues and the defendants, they were short and narrowly tailored, and the court provided instructions to minimize the potential for prejudice and that the clips represented Hollywood and not the Brooklyn Federal Court:

> Our courtrooms are not movie theaters. But we cannot assume that our jurors—whom we routinely ask to pore over the violent and often grisly details of real crimes—are such delicate consumers of media that they would so easily have their passions aroused by short film clips of the sort at issue here. In this case, the district court acted well within its discretion in permitting the jury to see one minute and seven seconds of relevant Hollywood fiction during the course of a four-day criminal trial in real-life Brooklyn federal district court. (*U.S. v. Monsalvatge*, 2017, p. 6)

U.S. v. Monsalvatge upheld the district court's decision because any element of unfairness of presenting the video clips in terms of prejudicing the jury was outweighed by the demonstrative value of the clips in explaining the MO behavior of the defendants.

Copycat crime was introduced in court in a very different way in *State v. Majors* (2020). Surette's (2002) research on copycat crime among violent juvenile offenders was cited in the dissent in an Iowa Supreme Court review of the lower court sentencing decision to suggest mitigated responsibility that should be factored into sentencing in the case of 17-year-old Jarrod Dale Majors who was convicted of home invasion and attempted murder in Bedford, Iowa. Majors had become obsessed with his 30-year-old neighbor Hollie Peckham who lived across the street with her 32-year-old husband, Jamie Peckham, and their 22-month-old twins. On May 30, 2002, Majors entered their home wearing a ski mask and gloves with a knife in his waistband and a roll of duct tape on his wrist holding a .22-caliber rifle with a plastic soda bottle taped to the barrel to act as a makeshift silencer. Majors pled guilty and was sentenced and convicted on January 22, 2003, to 25 years with a mandatory minimum of 17.5 years before parole. He was resentenced twice over the course of his incarceration, and both times the court upheld the sentence. In 2020 when Majors was 35, the Supreme Court of Iowa reviewed the district court decision to affirm the sentence, arguing that the court abused its discretion by imposing the mandatory minimum prison term before parole eligibility on the defendant's second resentencing and whether defense counsel provided constitutionally deficient representation. The Supreme Court affirmed the district court resentence. In the dissent (by Justice Appel joined by Justice Wiggins), the issue of whether Majors should have been seen as a child or an adult when he was only 15 days from his eighteenth birthday was raised, citing academic research on the changing adolescent brain, life course criminology, violence risk assessment, and copycat crime. Justice Appel said, "Majors is a poster child of the influence of the media" because he got the idea to put a plastic bottle on the end of his rifle as a makeshift silencer from a Steven Segal movie. Surette's (2002) article, "Self-Reported Copycat Crime Among a Population of Serious and Violent Juvenile Offenders" was used to support the argument that media influence is not unusual in juveniles and that the fact that Majors had mimicked a movie was evidence that he was more like a child than an adult.

Media Violence, The First Amendment, and Civil Liability: The Civil Courts

The issue of media violence and copycat crime has made its way into the civil courts in cases naming movie, music, video game producers and others in incitement, wrongful death, and negligence lawsuits. Landmark cases show how the courts have responded to these challenges (*Davidson v. Time Warner*, 1997; *James v. Meow Media, Inc.*, 2000; *McCollum et al., v. CBS, Inc. et al.*, 1988; *Olivia N. v. National Broadcasting Company*, 1981; *Rice v. Paladin Enterprises, Inc.*, 1997; *Yakubowicz v. Paramount Pictures Corp.*, 1989). The issue of copycat crime and violent media effects has also been raised in legal challenges to keep violent media footage from public view in an attempt to prevent copycat crime and to protect public safety (e.g., *Jane Does 1 through 15, Appellant v. King County*, 2014). Civil legal challenges by plaintiffs who argue that media incited violence against media distributors over the last 50 years have been largely unsuccessful, ruling in favor of the defendants under the protection of the First Amendment (Germaine, 2001; Surette, 2022).

The First Amendment prohibits the government from restricting speech and the press:

> Congress shall make no law respecting an establishment of religion, or prohibiting the free exercise thereof; or abridging the freedom of speech, or of the press; or the right of the people peaceably to assemble, and to petition the Government for a redress of grievances. (U.S. Const. amend. I)

The First Amendment protection extends to all artistic and creative works including violent entertainment. Ultimately, the purpose of the First

Amendment is "not to protect the speech we welcome, but rather to protect the speech we choose to hate" (Wellstood, 2000, p. 221).

The First Amendment protection is not absolute. The court has excluded some categories of speech from First Amendment protection, including obscenity, incitement, fighting words, and "true threat."[6] For example, rap music (such as Ice T's "Cop Killer," NWA's "Fuck tha Police," and 2 Live Crew's "As Nasty as They Wanna Be") has been targeted with legal challenges of obscenity, incitement (Ferrell et al., 2006, 2015; Hudson, 2009), and true threat (*Commonwealth v. Knox,* 2018). In *Davidson v. Time Warner, Inc.* (1997), the wife of a state trooper who was murdered by 19-year-old Ronald Ray Howard who was listening to Tupac Shakur's album *2Pacalypse Now* just before the murder, filed suit against Time Warner, the album's producer. Howard was driving a stolen car while listening to the album that includes songs with lyrics that portray killing police officers. The lawyer for the state trooper's widow said the lyrics read like "pages out of a cop-killing manual" (Phillips, 1992). The court ruled that the album was protected under the First Amendment (Firestre & Jones, 1992; Germaine, 2001).

The incitement exclusion to the First Amendment is the primary exclusion sought in copycat crime cases. Legal challenges that have argued that media content incites violence are required to meet the Brandenburg test. The Brandenburg test was established in the U.S. Supreme Court case *Brandenburg v. Ohio* (1969), a case that determined when inflammatory speech intended to promote illegal behavior can be restricted. In Brandenburg, Ohio, Ku Klux Klan leader Clarence Brandenburg gave a rally speech in front of local TV cameras and armed Klansman saying, in part, "If our president, our Congress, our Supreme Court, continues to suppress the white, Caucasian race, it's possible that there might have to be some vengeance [sic] taken." Brandenburg was found guilty of violating Ohio state law prohibiting advocating crime, violence, or "unlawful methods of terrorism" as a means of accomplishing political reform. The U.S. Supreme Court overturned his conviction, holding that the Ohio court violated Brandenburg's First Amendment protection of freedom of speech because the rally was not intended to incite specific acts of violence. The court said that speech, press, or assembly "merely to advocate" falls within the First (and Fourteenth) Amendments, "except where such advocacy is directed to inciting or producing imminent lawless action and is likely to incite or produce such action" (*Brandenburg v. Ohio,* 1967). In the over 50 years that the Brandenburg test has been used, there have been calls for staunch adherence to the test to preserve the integrity of the First Amendment (Firestre & Jones, 2000), recommendations for additional criteria to identify "camouflaged incitement" (Crump, 1994), and discussion of the difficulties in proving the

Copycat Crime in the Courts: Implications for Civil Rights and Criminal Justice 157

intent requirement and need for clarification on the application of imminence and likelihood (Calvert, 2019).[7] However, the Brandenburg requirement of intent, imminence, and likelihood continues to govern incitement law (Rosenwald, 2021; Ross, 2021; Surette, 2022).

Early Cases That Set the Stage for Media Violence Civil Litigation

Lawsuits by family members of victims of suicide and homicide said to be inspired by violent media have argued that media producers were negligent in the distribution of violent media. In *McCollum et al., v. CBS, Inc et al.* (1988), the parents of suicide victim 19-year-old John McCollum filed suit against CBS Records and Ozzie Osbourne alleging that the song and Osbourne's music aided, advised, or encouraged creating an "uncontrollable impulse" in John McCollum to commit suicide on October 24, 1984, when he shot himself in the head with a .22-caliber handgun while listening to Osbourne's album "Speak of the Devil," which was the proximate cause of his death. John McCollum was found the next morning still wearing his headphones with the stereo running, with the needle on the revolving record. Prior to the suicide he had been listening to other albums including *Blizzard of Oz* and *Diary of a Madman*. One of the songs on the *Blizzard of Oz* album is the song "Suicide Solution" that conveys that suicide is the only way out with a line that is repeated. The parents alleged that the words and music of Ozzie Osbourne "demonstrate a preoccupation with unusual, antisocial and even bizarre attitudes and beliefs," convey that "life is filled with nothing but despair and hopelessness and suicide," and seek to appeal to and profit from troubled adolescents like their son who had severe emotional problems and problems with alcohol abuse.

In *McCollum*, the court said that music and lyrics, like all media, is accorded protection under the First Amendment of the Constitution of the United States, except where such media dissemination "is directed to inciting or producing imminent lawless action and is likely to incite or produce such action." The court concluded that to find culpable incitement, the court had to find that Osbourne's music was directed and intended to bring about the suicide of listeners and likely to produce this result. The court concluded:

> . . . there is nothing in any of Osbourne's songs which could be characterized as a command to an immediate suicidal act. . . . Moreover, as defendants point out, the lyrics of the song on which plaintiffs focus their

158 Copycat Crime

> primary objection can as easily be viewed as a poetic device, such as a play on words, to convey meanings entirely contrary to those asserted by plaintiffs . . .
>
> Merely because art may evoke a mood of depression as it figuratively depicts the darker side of human nature does not mean that it constitutes a direct "incitement to imminent violence." . . . Moreover, musical lyrics and poetry cannot be construed to contain the requisite "call to action" for the elementary reason that they simply are not intended to be and should not be read literally on their face, nor judged by a standard of prose oratory. Reasonable persons understand musical lyrics and poetic conventions as the figurative expressions which they are. No rational person would or could believe otherwise nor would they mistake musical lyrics and poetry for literal commands or directives to immediate action. . . . To do so would indulge a fiction which neither common sense nor the First Amendment will permit.

Thus, the court concluded that Ozzie Osborne and CBS Records had no liability for John McCollum's suicide because there was no incitement or intent to influence the suicide (*McCollum et al., v. CBS, Inc et al.,* 1988).

In the McCollum case, the court noted the long history of reluctance to impose liability on media producers dating back to similar cases such as *Zamora v. Columbia Broadcasting System* (1979) and *Olivia N. v. National Broadcasting Company* (1981). In the Zamora case, the Zamora family (15-year-old Ronny Zamora and his parents) alleged that when Ronny Zamora was 5 years old, he became involuntarily addicted and "completely subliminally intoxicated" by extensive viewing of TV violence, which contributed to his development of a sociopathic personality, desensitized him to violent behavior, and influenced him to shoot and kill his 83-year-old neighbor Elinor Haggart. In the Olivia N. case, the plaintiff alleged that the film *Born Innocent* incited a group of minors to rape her with a bottle when she was nine years old with a bottle on a beach in San Francisco. The minors were said to have watched the film and had discussed a violent scene in the film in which four girls who are residents of a state-run home violently attack another girl in a bathroom raping her with a plunger.

In a 1989 lawsuit against Paramount Pictures and Saxon Theatre Corporation brought forth by the father of 16-year-old Martin Yakubowicz, who was killed in 1979 outside of a theater in Boston showing the film *The Warriors* (*Yakubowicz v. Paramount Pictures Corp.,* 1989), the plaintiff alleged that the film incited the perpetrator, Michael Barrett, who consumed alcohol he had brought into the theater while watching the film and then stabbed and killed Yakubowicz after leaving the theater. The

Copycat Crime in the Courts: Implications for Civil Rights and Criminal Justice 159

lawsuit alleged that Paramount Pictures and the Saxon Theatre Corporation knew of the violence and the threats of violence perpetrated by gang members at showings of the film after its release in Boston and California. Citing previous landmark cases, the court ruled:

> "The Warriors" is a work of fiction portraying the adventures of one New York City youth gang being pursued through territory controlled by hostile gangs. Although the film is rife with violent scenes, it does not at any point exhort, urge, entreat, solicit, or overtly advocate or encourage unlawful or violent activity on the part of viewers. It does not create the likelihood of inciting or producing "imminent lawless action" that would strip the film of First Amendment protection. Brandenburg v. Ohio, supra. The movie does not "purport to order or command anyone to any concrete action at any specific time, much less immediately." McCollum v. CBS, Inc., 202 Cal. App. 3d 989, 1001 (1988). See Olivia N. v. NBC, 126 Cal. App. 3d 488, 496 (1981), discussing Weirum v. RKO Gen., Inc., 15 Cal. 3d 40 (1975). Therefore, we hold that the defendant Paramount did not act unreasonably in producing, distributing, and exhibiting "The Warriors," because such expression is protected by the First Amendment. Accordingly, Saxon, too, did not act unreasonably in exhibiting "The Warriors." "[I]t is simply not acceptable to a free and democratic society . . . to limit and restrict . . . creativity in order to avoid the dissemination of ideas in artistic speech which may adversely affect emotionally troubled individuals." McCollum v. CBS, Inc., supra at 1005–1006. We thus conclude that summary judgment for the defendants is proper on counts one, two, and four. (*Yakubowicz v. Paramount Pictures Corp.*, 1989)

Thus, the argument that *The Warriors* incited the violence resulting in the murder of Martin Yakubowicz did not meet the criteria necessary, specifically it did not meet the Brandenburg criteria for intent, imminence, or likelihood.

In *Pahler v. Slayer* (2001), the parents of Elyse Pahler who was brutally murdered by three teenage boys who listened obsessively to the heavy metal band Slayer, filed a lawsuit against the band arguing that the band's songs gave instructions on how to stalk, rape, torture, murder, and commit necrophilia. Elyse Pahler was murdered by Joseph Fiorella, Jacob Delashmutt, and Royce Casey, who were sentenced to 25 years to life for the murder. A year after the murder, one of the perpetrators (Fiorella) said he had studied the Slayer lyrics as if they held deep meaning and told a police counselor about the murder: "It gets inside your head. It's almost embarrassing that I was so influenced by the music. The music started to influence the way I looked at things." Elyse's father said about the music, "There's a whole generation of children out there that are being fed this music. It's like feeding a child a little poison every day. . . . We're saying, 'Enough is enough'" (Waxman, 2001).

Court decisions in civil lawsuits seeking to place blame on media producers for violent acts have been overwhelmingly unsuccessful. Judicial decisions have utilized U.S. Supreme Court Justice Oliver W. Holmes's famous dissenting opinion in *Abrams et al., v. United States* (1919) known as the "marketplace of ideas"—that the free trade of ideas in society advances ultimate truth. The marketplace of ideas theory is also referred to as "the search for truth" theory of the First Amendment, which exempts incitement from constitutional protection only in cases when speech is likely to produce imminent lawless action (Campbell, 2000). In *Abrams et al., v. United States* (1919) the U.S. Supreme Court upheld the conviction and 20-year prison sentence of several individuals who were Russian immigrants to the United States for circulating two leaflets thrown from a window in New York City denouncing the U.S. war effort on Russian soil against Germany. In his dissent, Justice Holmes said:

> . . . the principle of the right to free speech is always the same. It is only the present danger of immediate evil or an intent to bring it about that warrants Congress in setting a limit to the expression of opinion where private rights are not concerned. Congress certainly cannot forbid all effort to change the mind of the country. Now nobody can suppose that the surreptitious publishing of a silly leaflet by an unknown man, without more, would present any immediate danger that its opinions would hinder the success of the government arms or have any appreciable tendency to do so.
>
> . . . But when men have realized that time has upset many fighting faiths, they may come to believe even more than they believe the very foundations of their own conduct that the ultimate good desired is better reached by free trade in ideas—that the best test of truth is the power of the thought to get itself accepted in the competition of the market, and that truth is the only ground upon which their wishes safely can be carried out. That at any rate is the theory of our Constitution. It is an experiment, as all life is an experiment. Every year if not every day we have to wager our salvation upon some prophecy based upon imperfect knowledge. While that experiment is part of our system I think that we should be eternally vigilant against attempts to check the expression of opinions that we loathe and believe to be fraught with death, unless they so imminently threaten immediate interference with the lawful and pressing purposes of the law that an immediate check is required to save the country. I wholly disagree with the argument of the Government that the First Amendment left the common law as to seditious libel in force. History seems to me against the notion. . . . (*Abrams et al., v. United States,* 1919)

Copycat Crime in the Courts: Implications for Civil Rights and Criminal Justice

A century later in the cases involving violent media, judicial reliance on Justice Holmes's marketplace of ideas concept is steadfast. The courts have consistently decided in favor of the media, unwilling to overrule First Amendment protections of freedom of speech whether political pamphlets, gangsta rap and death metal (Reilly, 2009), or violent television, films, and video games (Cooper, 2007; Surette, 2022). However, examination of landmark cases illustrates the central issues at play and sheds light on what the future may hold for challenges that will most certainly continue at an even greater pace given the speed with which digital culture has created an entirely new world from the world in which the McCollum and Zamora families and Olivia N. filed their cases against media producers in the 1970s and 1980s.

A Manual for Contract Killers: The Case Against Hitman and Paladin Press

To date, only one court ruling has held a media source liable, standing in opposition to the others. In *Rice v. Paladin Enterprises, Inc.* (1997), the U.S. Court of Appeals, Fourth Circuit held that the book *Hit Man: A Technical Manual for Independent Contractors* by Rex Feral (1985) assisted James Perry in committing the murders of Mildred Horn, her eight-year-old quadriplegic son Trevor, and his nurse Janice Saunders by providing detailed instructions on how to commit a murder and was not protected under the First Amendment. The court held Paladin Enterprises, the publisher of *Hit Man,* liable in the wrongful deaths of Mildred and Trevor Horn and Janice Saunders, who were murdered on March 3, 1993, by Perry who offered his services as a professional killer to Mildred Horn's ex-husband, Lawrence Horn, following detailed instructions that he read in *Hit Man* on how to solicit a client and plan, execute, and conceal a murder. Lawrence Horn hired Perry to kill his ex-wife and son to acquire $2 million that was held in a trust fund that his son had received as a settlement for injuries that had left him paralyzed for life.

The court reviewed and published excerpts from the 130-page book and noted that portions of the book were omitted from the court opinion to minimize the danger to the public from repeating the passages. The court did, however, publish long excerpts of the book to illustrate the distinct nature of the book's passages. The court also listed the specific instructions that Perry followed in detail in the solicitation of a client and the planning, commission, and concealment of the murders.

The court found that Paladin Enterprises knew that the instructions in the book might be used by murderers, that it intended to provide assistance to murderers and would-be murderers, that it aided and abetted Perry in the murders of Mildred and Trevor Horn and Janice Saunders, and that long-established caselaw provides that speech that constitutes aiding and abetting is not protected by the First Amendment. In its decision, the courts detailed the specific instructions that Perry had followed, including requesting expense money, choosing the victims' home as the location of the murders, using a rental car to reach the victims' location, establishing a base at a motel in close proximity to the "jobsite" before committing the murders, using a made-up license plate number, using an AR-7 firearm, how to construct a homemade silencer, and how to shoot at close range shooting the victims in the eyes. The court articulated that while speech advocating lawlessness has long enjoyed protections under the First Amendment under *Brandenburg v. Ohio* (1969), speech that so clearly prescribes conduct does not necessarily enjoy First Amendment protection:

> Hit Man does not merely detail how to commit murder and murder for hire; through powerful prose in the second person and imperative voice, it encourages its readers in their specific acts of murder. It reassures those contemplating the crime that they may proceed with their plans without fear of either personal failure or punishment. And at every point where the would-be murderer might yield either to reason or to reservations, Hit Man emboldens the killer, confirming not only that he should proceed, but that he must proceed, if he is to establish his manhood.

The court also noted that the book is so effectively written that the book's protagonist seems to be present in the planning, commission, and cover-up of the murders the book inspires, as if the book's protagonist and reader are in a criminal partnership and that the publisher specifically marketed the book to target a specific audience. Ultimately, the court concluded that the district court had misread *Brandenburg* and erred in its decision to rule in favor of the defendant Paladin:

> After carefully and repeatedly reading Hit Man in its entirety, we are of the view that the book so overtly promotes murder in concrete, nonabstract terms that we regard as disturbingly disingenuous both Paladin's cavalier suggestion that the book is essentially a comic book whose "fantastical" promotion of murder no one could take seriously, and amici's reckless characterization of the book as "almost avuncular," . . . The unique text of Hit Man alone, boldly proselytizing and glamorizing the crime of murder and the "profession" of murder as it dispassionately instructs on its commission, is more than sufficient to create a triable issue of fact as to Paladin's intent in publishing and selling the manual . . .

Copycat Crime in the Courts: Implications for Civil Rights and Criminal Justice

> Any argument that Hit Man is abstract advocacy entitling the book, and therefore Paladin, to heightened First Amendment protection under Brandenburg is, on its face, untenable . . . this book constitutes the archetypal example of speech which, because it methodically and comprehensively prepares and steels its audience to specific criminal conduct through exhaustively detailed instructions on the planning, commission, and concealment of criminal conduct, finds no preserve in the First Amendment . . .

The court ultimately held that the district court had misperceived the nature of the speech in *Hit Man*, that the speech is protected advocacy under *Brandenberg*, and that plaintiffs cause of action against Paladin Enterprises for aiding and abetting the murders was not barred by the First Amendment.

Mass School Shooting Lawsuits

In the 1990s a rash of school shootings were associated with media violence. On February 2, 1996, 14-year-old Barry Loukaitis killed two students and a math teacher in Moses Lake, Washington, saying afterwards. "This sure beats algebra, doesn't it?" in reference to the Stephen King novel *Rage*. Loukaitis said he was inspired to commit the murders by *Rage*, Pearl Jam's video for the song "Jeremy," and the films *The Basketball Diaries* and *Natural Born Killers* (Coleman, 2004). On December 1, 1997, 14-year-old Michael Carneal killed three students and wounded five others at Heath High School in Paducah, Kentucky. Carneal told police after the shooting that he was an avid player of *Mortal Kombat* and *Doom* and was also a big fan of the film *The Basketball Diaries* (which included a dream scene in which the main character played by Leonardo DiCaprio shoots teachers and students). And on April 20, 1999, 18-year-old Eric Harris and 17-year-old Dylan Klebold murdered 12 students and a teacher, wounded 24 others, and then committed suicide at Columbine High School in Colorado. Klebold and Harris were avid players of the video game *Doom* and were fans of the films *The Basketball Diaries* and *Natural Born Killers,* which became "the pop cultural artifact most associated with the Columbine massacre" (Cullen, 2010, p. 197).

The attorney for families of the victims in the Paducah, Kentucky murders said the families didn't care about the money—they wanted to get as much insight into the murders as possible, naming 50 defendants in the original lawsuit, including Carneal's parents, school officials, and fellow students who had advance knowledge about the crime, and agreed to a $42 million settlement. Later Breen and media violence crusader Jack

Thompson filed a $130 million lawsuit against 25 media producers they believed influenced Carneal's behavior during the shooting, including a pornographic website, the producers and distributors of *The Basketball Diaries*—Time Warner, Inc., Polygram Film Entertainment Distribution, Inc., Palm Pictures, Island Pictures, and New Line Cinema—and the creators and distributors of the violent video games *Doom, Quake,* and *Castle Wolfenstein,* including Atari, Corporation, Nintendo of America, Sega of America, Id Software, and Sony Computer Entertainment (Cooper, 2007).

The courts ultimately ruled that the media producers and distributors could not be held liable and that criminal behavior is not the likely outcome of viewing violent media and media producers cannot foresee the actions of everyone who uses their products. In *James v. Meow Media* (2000), the court noted the case *Watters v. TSR, Inc.* (1989) in which Johnny Burnett committed suicide after playing the role-playing board game *Dungeons & Dragons.* In the *Watters v. TSR, Inc.* case, Burnett's mother said that her son was a devoted player of the game and that he was incapable of separating the fantasies of the game from reality, which resulted in his losing his independent will and he was driven to self-destruction. In *James v. Meow Media,* the court held that both the cases of Burnett and Carneal "stretch the concepts of foreseeability":

> Reasonable people would not conclude that it was foreseeable to Defendants that Michael Carneal, a boy who played their games, watched their movie, and viewed their website materials, would murder his classmates. Even accepting the pleaded facts as true, that Michael Carneal was an avid consumer of violent video games, nihilistic movies, and obscene internet materials and was influenced by all of these events, does not make the murders foreseeable to the Defendants. Just as Johnny Burnett's suicide in Watters was unforeseeable to the distributors of the game, Dungeons and Dragons, so was Michael Carneal's killing spree unforeseeable to the Video Games, *Basketball Diaries,* and Internet Defendants. The fact that Michael Carneal chose to kill his classmates rather than himself does not make his actions any more foreseeable. (*James v. Meow Media,* 2000)

The court also noted other landmark cases, including *Davidson v. Time Warner* (1997) regarding Tupac Shakur's 2Pacalypse Now, *Zamora v. CBS* (1979) regarding TV violence, and *McCollum v. CBS* (1988) regarding Ozzie Osbourne's "Suicide Solution." in their ultimate decision.

After Columbine, victims and victims' families also filed lawsuits against the school district, the sheriff's department, the perpetrators' parents, and video game creators and movie distributors and producers. In the lawsuits against media, the victims and victims' families alleged that

Copycat Crime in the Courts: Implications for Civil Rights and Criminal Justice   165

the video games and the movies incited Harris and Klebold to commit the mass shooting. The U.S. District Court in Colorado held that the perpetrators' violent acts were not foreseeable and were the cause of the deaths; that under Colorado law intangible ideas, thoughts, and expressive content in video games and movies are not "products" under the liability doctrine; and that video games and movies are protected under the First Amendment (Steinlage, 2020).

In the 2016 Pulse Nightclub mass shooting in Orlando, Florida, victims sued social media platforms used by ISIS to spread violent, hateful messages that inspired the perpetrator to become radicalized, which influenced him to commit the mass shooting. The lawsuit sought to hold Twitter, Facebook, and Google liable, alleging that the companies aided and abetted the shooting by giving the perpetrator access to radical jihadist content. The district court dismissed the case for a number of reasons including that the requirement that the defendant's actions were the proximate cause of the injuries were not met, which on appeal, was subsequently affirmed by the U.S. Court of Appeals. The appellate court observed that if the plaintiff's argument was accepted, "Defendants would become liable for seemingly endless acts of modern violence simply because the individual viewed relevant social media content before deciding to commit the violence" (Steinlage, 2020; Zoppo, 2021).

Natural Born Killers and the Case Against Oliver Stone and Warner Brothers

The 1994 film *Natural Born Killers* (*NBK*) is one of the most controversial films in history and has been linked to more crimes than any other single media source. The film has been referenced by perpetrators of mass shootings and violent crime sprees in the United States and Europe by school shooters and male/female duos who emulated the film's lead characters Mickey and Mallory Knox, who committed over 50 murders on a love-fueled road trip. The film has been associated with high-profile cases in United States, including the murders of William Savage and Patsy Byers by Benjamin Darras and Sarah Edmondson, and in Europe, including the murders of five people committed by Florence Rey and Audry Maupin in 1995 in Paris, France, and the murder of 16-year-old Abdeladim Gahbiche by Veronique Herbert and Sebastien Paindavoine in 1998, also in Paris, France (Boyle, 2001; Kunich, 2000; Lasky, 2012; O'Neil, 2001).

The film has been noted in the criminal trials of individual perpetrators who have been said to have copycatted the film (e.g., *Commonwealth v. Obrien*, 2000; *State v. Taylor*, 2003) as well as other cases including a case in which inmates sued Stateville Correctional Center ("Stateville") asserting unconstitutional treatment by reason of the filming of scenes for the film inside the institution, which was ultimately dismissed by the court and deemed frivolous (*Walker v. Peters*, 1994). In criminal cases the issue of *NBK* and its influence has been raised by defense attorneys, who have made reference to the film as evidence of the defendant's state of mind providing evidence that the defendants were fascinated with the film (*Commonwealth v. Obrien*, 2000), and by prosecutors, who have noted the film's influence to argue premeditation. For example, in *State v. Taylor* (2003), the prosecution presented expert testimony and evidence to establish premeditation, arguing that the defendant critiqued a bank robbery featured in a scene in *NBK* and discussed how he would commit a bank robbery and that his bank robbery scheme and plan to make a run for the Mexican border was "as if the entire episode were an out-take from the defendant's favorite movie, Natural Born Killers" (*State v. Taylor*, 2002, p. 4).

The civil case against Oliver Stone, the director of *NBK*, and Warner Brothers, the film's distributor, went further than any other case since *Paladin*. The lawsuit came on the heels of much political and public attention to the issue of violent media effects after the concerns and legal challenges raised in the aftermath of Columbine and other mass school shootings in the 1990s (Rubenstein, 1999). For three decades prior to the *NBK* civil lawsuit, civil litigation by victims of copycat crimes against creators and disseminators of violent media including books, television shows, films, magazines, and other media were largely unsuccessful. That pattern changed with the lawsuit over *NBK* against Oliver Stone and Warner Brothers (O'Neil, 2001). The case, *Byers v. Edmondson* (2002), was the final decision in a two-year-long legal challenge.

The *NBK* lawsuit was filed by the family of Patsy Byers against Oliver Stone, Warner Brothers, Ben Darras and Sarah Edmondson, and their families and insurance carriers. Patsy Byers's family claimed that Stone, the film's producers, and the movie theaters that showed the film were liable for producing a film that glorified violence and for distributing a film that they knew or would have known would incite some individuals to commit a crime such as shooting Patsy Byers. Patsy Byers worked at a convenience store in Ponchatoula, Louisiana. On the evening of March 8, 1995, she was working at the store when teenagers Sarah Edmondson and Benjamin Darras robbed the store and engaged in a shootout that left Byers seriously wounded. Byers, who was 35 years old at the time of the attack, became a paraplegic and three years later died of cancer. During the trial of Edmondson and Darras, it became clear that the two had been obsessed with the film *NBK* (O'Neil, 2001). On July 26, 1995, Byers filed

Copycat Crime in the Courts: Implications for Civil Rights and Criminal Justice

suit against Darras and Edmondson seeking damages for injuries she sustained as a result of the shooting (*Byers v. Edmondson*, 1998, 2002).

The *Byers v. Edmondson* (1998) lawsuit against Stone and Warner Brothers argued that Edmondson and Darras engaged in a crime/murder spree that culminated in the shooting of Byers as a result of watching and becoming inspired by the film *Natural Born Killers*. The Louisiana Circuit Court found that the petition made sufficient allegations to remove *NBK* from First Amendment protection based on the argument that it incited imminent lawless activity. The substantive issue in *Byers v. Edmondson* (2002) in the appeal was whether *NBK* is protected speech under the First Amendment. The court indicated that motion pictures are protected under the First Amendment; however, there are limitations to the freedom of speech protection, citing a 1957 case that said that "unconditional phrasing of the First Amendment was not intended to protect every utterance" (*Roth v. United States*, 1957).

The *Byers v. Edmondson* case focused on two elements that limit the First Amendment protection—incitement and obscenity. Regarding incitement, the court concluded that "based on our viewing of the film, nothing in it constitutes incitement," indicating that while the film depicts the killing spree by Mickey and Mallory Knox, the film also portrays how their violence is glorified in the media. The court also noted that the live action video; images switching from color to black and white; sitcom laugh tracks; scenes that included facial distortions, slow motion, and oblique camera angles; and news and cartoon clips place the film in "the realm of fantasy" and that "the violence in the film is presented in the format of imagery and fictionalized violence." Thus, the court concluded that though the film included an abundance of violent imagery, the depiction of violence in the film does not rise to the level of incitement and that the film does not encourage or command unlawful or violent activity on the part of viewers. The court also noted the concept of "copycat" actions citing *Rice v. Paladin Enterprises, Inc.* (1996) highlighting the absence of intent on the part of media publishers or producers:

> [I]n virtually every copycat case, there will be lacking in the speech itself any basis for a permissible inference that the speaker intended to assist and facilitate the criminal conduct described or depicted. Of course, with few, if any, exceptions, the speech which gives rise to the copycat crime will not directly and affirmatively promote the criminal conduct, even if, in some circumstances, it incidentally glamorizes and thereby indirectly promotes such conduct . . .

The court followed:

> After viewing Natural Born Killers, we are convinced that the present case presents such a copycat scenario. . . . Edmondson and Darras may very well have been inspired to imitate the actions of Mickey and Mallory Knox, but the film does not direct or encourage them to take such actions. Accordingly, as a matter of law, we find Natural Born Killers cannot be considered inciteful speech that would remove it from First Amendment protection.

Thus, the court determined that *Natural Born Killers* is not inciteful speech and that though the plaintiffs went to great lengths to demonstrate intent on the part of the defendants, especially Oliver Stone, because the court determined that *NBK* itself is not inciteful speech, the intent of Stone and Warner Brothers is not essential to the disposition.

With respect to the obscenity element, Byers did not argue that the film met the legal definition of obscenity established in *Miller v. California* (1973). To constitute obscenity, there must be independent proof, measured based on contemporary community standards, that 1) the average person would find that the work, taken as a whole, "appeals to the prurient interest"; 2) the work "depicts or describes, in a patently offensive way, sexual conduct specifically defined by applicable state law"; and (3) the work, "taken as a whole, lacks serious literary, artistic, political or scientific value." Rather, Byers argued that "[t]here is no reason why senselessly violent speech like [Natural Born Killers] cannot also be labeled as obscene, as it does precisely the same thing." The court declined to extend the obscenity exception to the First Amendment in the case based on prior recognition by the Louisiana court (in *State v. Johnson*, 1977) that the First Amendment "does not permit a violence-based notion of obscenity."

The *Byers v. Edmondson* case was originally dismissed by the 21st Judicial District Court in Amite, Louisiana, but then was reinstated on appeal and involved two years of depositions, going to the U.S. Supreme Court in 1999 before the case was ultimately remanded and dismissed in 2001. By the time the case landed in the Louisiana Court of Appeals, more than a dozen copycat shootings had been linked to *NBK*. A source for the plaintiff's counsel was author John Grisham, who had been a friend of Edmondson and Darras's first victim, Bill Savage. Grisham wrote a scathing article attacking Stone, accusing him of intentionally producing a film that would cause copycat violence (Black, 1998; Grisham, 1996). The Court of Appeals ruled that the case had to go to trial because the plaintiff alleged that Stone had intentionally created a film that would cause

Copycat Crime in the Courts: Implications for Civil Rights and Criminal Justice 169

impressionable viewers to mimic the violence depicted in the film (O'Neil, 2001).

The lawsuit against Oliver Stone and Warner Brothers was the first case of its kind against a film/media producer alleging incitement to violence to make it to the U.S. Supreme Court. Oliver Stone said:

> The lawyers told me this is a huge victory, but I don't think so. I sympathize with the Byers family, but it is Sarah Edmondson who shot Patsy Byers. It's depressing that a suit that should have been thrown out on the first pass could result in such a waste of time, energy, and money. We've created a new legal hell where everyone is entitled, and no one is responsible.

Stone's attorney followed, "Litigation of this type chills creative activity," and a spokesperson from Warner Brothers who produced *NBK* added, "Today's decision is an affirmation of the rule of law that we don't hold moviemakers and songwriters and authors liable for the criminal misdeeds of people who don't understand what they're watching, hearing or reading" ("Natural Born Killers lawsuit finally thrown out," 2001).

Violent Video Game Lawsuits

In the wake of school shootings in the 1990s and subsequent lawsuits that found violent video games to be protected under the First Amendment, state legislators began to explore ways to limit childhood exposure to video game violence and states across the country enacted laws restricting the sale of violent video games to minors. These attempts to legislate restrictions on violent media were met by lawsuits brought against states by media companies. Civil lawsuits against violent video game creators and distributors also continued.

In reaching decisions about the media effects of violent video games, the courts have relied on experts and research from the social sciences to aid in legal decisions from two general camps—1) media violence influences real-world violence and 2) media violence has no causal influence on real-world violence. Two experts and their colleagues have been particularly prolific in conducting research, publishing findings and commentary, and providing expert testimony on violent video game media effects, on opposite sides of the issue: 1) Craig Anderson and colleagues, including Ohio State University Communications and Psychology Professor Dr. Brad Bushman, have argued that while there is no linear relationship between media violence and real-world violence, evidence suggests that mass media has substantial effects, and 2) Christopher Ferguson and colleagues, including Villanova University Psychology Professor Patrick Markey, have argued that there is no causal relationship between violent media and real-world violence.[8]

Dr. Craig Anderson and his colleagues' research on media violence and the General Aggression Model (GAM) (Allen et al., 2018; Anderson & Bushman, 2018) laid groundwork for subsequent research on priming effects of media violence and the General Learning Model (GLM) (Warburton & Anderson, 2022). Dr. Anderson is seen as one of the highest-ranking media and violence scholars and is listed among the top 200 "Eminent Psychologists of the Modern Era" (Diener et al., 2014). Dr. Anderson has provided expert testimony in numerous court cases, and his research has been used to support arguments made by politicians, media violence activists, and family members of victims of mass shootings that have been associated with media violence. He testified before the 2000 U.S. Senate after the Columbine massacre (United States Senate Hearing 106–1096, March 21, 2000) and a 2018 meeting held by then-President Donald Trump at the White House after the school shooting in Parkland, Florida (Kain, 2018).

The purpose of the 2000 U.S. Senate hearing was to examine the role of video game violence given the thousands of studies that have shown the effects of violent television and films, with questions posed about the interactive nature of violent video games. Questions were posed in the hearing including ". . . is it really the best thing for our children to play the role of a murderous psychopath? Is it all just good fun to positively reinforce virtual slaughter? Is it truly harmless to simulate mass murder?" (p. 5). Dr. Anderson testified in the hearing that "there is one clear and simple message" that parents, policymakers, and educators need to hear and that is "playing violent video games can cause increases in aggression and violence" and "there are good reasons to expect that the effects of exposure to violent video games will be even greater than the well-documented effects of exposure to violent television and movies." Anderson concluded by saying that many factors contribute to any given act of violence and that, for the purposes of the hearing, "high exposure to media violence is a major contributing cause of the high rate of violence in modern U.S. society" (p. 33).

The work of Anderson and colleagues on violent media effects (e.g., Anderson & Bushman, 2018; Anderson et al., 2017; Anderson et al., 2020; Barlett et al., 2009; Bushman et al., 2015a, 2015b; Kepes et al., 2017; Warburton & Anderson, 2022) has been used in the courts to support arguments that suggest that violent media is one factor that contributes to aggression and violence and media influence is large enough to be of

Copycat Crime in the Courts: Implications for Civil Rights and Criminal Justice

consequence as an influence for real-world aggression and violence. Anderson has provided expert testimony to courts and governmental hearings presenting research findings and meta-analyses on media effects and video game violence.[9] The research conducted by Anderson and his colleagues aligns with the consensus among media psychologists and communications scientists that exposure to media violence increases aggression in children, whether it is causal and whether it is a major factor in real-world violence (Bushman et al., 2015).

Dr. Christopher Ferguson is a clinical psychologist, co-author of the book *Moral Combat: Why the War on Violent Video Games Is Wrong* (Markey & Ferguson, 2017a, 2017b), and author of numerous op-eds, news articles, and peer-reviewed articles on the link between violent video games and violence (e.g., Ferguson, 2013a, 2013b; Ferguson et al., 2020; Ferguson et al., 2011). Dr. Ferguson is an outspoken critic of the work of Anderson and colleagues and has given numerous media interviews, written op-eds, and published research findings conveying the position that the claim that violent video games influence real-world violence is a moral panic and is unsupported by science (e.g., Ferguson, 2013a, 2013b, 2014, 2015; Ferguson et al., 2017; Ferguson et al., 2020). He argues that the link between media violence and aggression is overstated, is not supported by empirical research, and that there is no causal link between violent video games and real-world aggression and violence (Markey & Ferguson, 2017a, 2017b). Ferguson further contends that empirical research has failed to support a causal relationship between violent video game playing or media/cultural influences and real-world aggression and violence (Ferguson, 2013a, 2013b, 2014; Ferguson et al., 2020), emphasizing the lack of evidence of a causal link between media violence and aggressive behavior and real-world violence. Ferguson's work reflects the controversy and politics around the media violence debate, data, and research design limitations. He challenges the tendency for researchers, policymakers, politicians, and the public to focus on idiosyncratic elements such as media and cultural misogyny in cases of violence such as mass shootings, suggesting that focusing on idiosyncrasies (the consumption and influence of violent media) distracts from commonalities (anger, resentment, and mental illness) when ultimately the cause of violence is chronic mental illness (Ferguson, 2013, 2014).

Ferguson chairs the News Media, Public Education and Public Policy Committee of the American Psychological Association (the views of whom do not represent an official position of the APA). In 2013, the APA established a task force to provide a declarative summary of the violent video game research. The task force conducted a meta-analysis of existing studies on the association of violent video games and aggression and lack of prosocial outcomes and concluded that "violent video game use has an effect on aggression"; the media effect of violent video game play "is manifested both as an increase in negative outcomes such as aggressive behavior, cognitions, and affect and as a decrease in positive outcomes such as prosocial behavior, empathy, and sensitivity to aggression"; and violent video games as one risk factor of many that increases the likelihood of aggressive and violent behavior (APA, 2015, p. 16). Dr. Ferguson and his colleagues on the APA News Media, Public Education and Public Policy Committee conducted an independent evaluation of the APA's 2015 resolution on video game violence and issued a statement highlighting the lack of research to support the causal link between the use of violent video games and societal violence (Ferguson et al., 2017). Ferguson and colleagues maintain that the consensus among media effects scholars reported by the APA task force regarding the link between violent video games and real-world aggression and violence does not acknowledge the debates and inconsistencies in the scientific literature and misinforms the public (Elson et al., 2019; Ferguson et al., 2020).

The empirical research and issues raised by Anderson and colleagues and Ferguson and colleagues lie at the center of key cases involving violent video game violence. Two cases exemplify where the civil courts stand on the issue: *Strickland v. Sony Corporation of America, et al.* (2005) and *Brown v. Entertainment Merchants Association* (2011). These cases highlight the issues raised in two types of civil lawsuits focused on violent video games: lawsuits brought by the families of victims of violence against the violent video game creators and distributors and lawsuits brought by video game companies against states that have placed restrictions that the video game companies have argued violate First Amendment protections.

In *Strickland v. Sony Corporation of America, et al.* (2005), the families of the Fayette County, Alabama police officers who were murdered by Devin Moore/Thompson sued the Sony Corporation, GameStop, Wal-Mart, and Take-Two. The plaintiffs alleged that the companies violated or conspired to violate the federal "sexual material harmful to minors laws" by "designing, manufacturing, marketing, distributing, and/or selling" *Grand Theft Auto III* and *Grand Theft Auto: Vice City* to minors, including Moore/Thompson when he was a minor. The plaintiffs further alleged that Moore/Thompson had purchased these games from GameStop and Wal-Mart, that the games had a rating of "M" meaning they were for sale only to individuals 17 years old or older, and that the stores did not have adequate policies to prevent the sale of these games to minors, including to Moore/Thompson, which was a criminal act. After playing the game,

Copycat Crime in the Courts: Implications for Civil Rights and Criminal Justice

Moore/Thompson carjacked a car and was arrested, and while being booked, took Officer Strickland's gun from its holster and shot Officer Strickland, Officer Crump, and Dispatcher Mealer. The plaintiffs argued that Moore/Thompson would not have murdered Strickland, Crump, and Mealer if not for having played the *Grand Theft Auto* games. The U.S. District Court for the Northern District of Alabama held that the federal law the plaintiffs alleged was violated is part of the Child Online Protection Act (COPA), which applies to material harmful to minors sent via the Internet. However, the law has no bearing on the sale of video games to minors by a traditional store. The court ruled that the plaintiff's complaint was insufficient to create jurisdiction in federal court and remanded the case back to the Circuit Court of Fayette County, Alabama.

In *Brown v. Entertainment Merchants Association* (2011), the U.S. Supreme Court considered whether a California law imposing restrictions on violent video games comports with the First Amendment. The court held in a 7–2 decision (Justices Thomas and Breyer dissenting) that California's attempt to legislate violent video games violated the First Amendment (Clements, 2012). In the landmark case *Roth v. United States* (1957), the U.S. Supreme Court stated that "the First Amendment was not intended to protect every utterance." During the 20th century, the Supreme Court identified specific exceptions to the First Amendment, including obscenity, fighting words, defamation, and child pornography. "The unprotected utterance most often at question in video game violence litigation is that of obscenity" (Clements, 2012, p. 665). In a series of cases (e.g., *Interactive Digital Software Association v. St. Louis County, Missouri*, 2002; *American Amusement Machine Association v. Kendrick*, 2000), the courts held that the violence in video games does not constitute obscenity and that perceived violent speech is inherently different from sexually explicit speech in the eyes of society.

The opinion in *Brown v. Entertainment Merchants Association* made it clear where the courts stand on the issue of video game violence and emphasize the gaps in the empirical research and flawed methodology that are insufficient to establish a causal link between playing violent video games and violent behavior. The court stated:

> The State's evidence is not compelling. California relies primarily on the research of Dr. Craig Anderson and a few other research psychologists whose studies purport to show a connection between exposure to violent video games and harmful effects on children. These studies have been rejected by every court to consider them, and with good reason: They do not prove that violent video games cause minors to act aggressively (which

would at least be a beginning). . . . They show at best some correlation between exposure to violent entertainment and minuscule real-world effects, such as children's feeling more aggressive or making louder noises in the few minutes after playing a violent game than after playing a non-violent game.

The court concluded:

California's effort to regulate violent video games is the latest episode in a long series of failed attempts to censor violent entertainment for minors. While we have pointed out above that some of the evidence brought forward to support the harmfulness of video games is unpersuasive, we do not mean to demean or disparage the concerns that underlie the attempt to regulate them—concerns that may and doubtless do prompt a good deal of parental oversight. . . .

The court indicated in the ruling that California's legislation legitimately straddles the fence between addressing a serious social problem and helping parents control their children. The court noted that when a social problem such as video game violence affects First Amendment rights, the solution must be pursued by means that "are neither seriously underinclusive nor seriously overinclusive"—that there are many forms of violent media not addressed by the legislation and the law abridges the First Amendment rights of young people whose parents and/or guardians see violent video games as harmless, stating that "the overbreadth in achieving one goal is not cured by the underbreadth in achieving the other. Legislation such as this, which is neither fish nor fowl, cannot survive strict scrutiny." Thus, the court's decision in this case centered on the importance of empirical findings that establish a causal link between video game violence and violent behavior.

The *Brown v. Entertainment Merchants Association* (2011) decision reflected the court's determination that the empirical evidence presented by experts, including Anderson and colleagues, does not support a causal link between video game violence and violent crime. The work of Anderson and colleagues and Ferguson and colleagues were cited in this case. Ultimately, the court did not consider the research by Anderson and colleagues supporting a relationship between violent media and aggression to be sufficient in establishing a causal link between video game violence and real-world violence. Justice Thomas noted in his dissent that the Court "is far too quick to dismiss the possibility that the experience of playing video games (and the effects on minors of playing violent video games) may be very different from anything that we have seen before." He

Copycat Crime in the Courts: Implications for Civil Rights and Criminal Justice

noted that any assessment of the experience of playing video games must take into account the characteristics of those games and the games of the future.

> Today's most advanced video games create realistic alternative worlds in which millions of players immerse themselves for hours on end. These games feature visual imagery and sounds that are strikingly realistic, and in the near future video-game graphics may be virtually indistinguishable from actual video footage. . . . Persons who play video games also have an unprecedented ability to participate in the events that take place in the virtual worlds that these games create. Players can create their own video-game characters and can use photos to produce characters that closely resemble actual people . . . the means by which players control the action in video games now bear a closer relationship to the means by which people control action in the real world. . . .

Justice Thomas went on to provide a litany of examples to illustrate the unique characteristics of violent video games that include mass murder with victims killed with "every imaginable implement"; victims who are "dismembered, decapitated, disemboweled, set on fire, and chopped into little pieces" who beg for mercy and cry in agony; and graphic violence that shows severed body parts and "gobs of human remains" with "no antisocial theme too base for some in the video-game industry to exploit" such as games in which players can take on the identity and reenact the mass murder carried out by the Columbine and Virginia Tech killers. Justice Thomas concluded:

> When all of the characteristics of video games are taken into account, there is certainly a reasonable basis for thinking that the experience of playing a video game may be quite different from the experience of reading a book, listening to a radio broadcast, or viewing a movie. And if this is so, then for at least some minors, the effects of playing violent video games may also be quite different. The Court acts prematurely in dismissing this possibility out of hand.

Justice Thomas concluded that violent video games present a "significant social problem" and observed that the Court was untroubled by the interactive nature of violent video games and that he did not agree with the Court decision that the interactive nature of video games is nothing with the view that all literature is interactive. Justice Breyer also dissented, concluding, "The freedom of speech, as originally understood, does not include a right to speak to minors without going through the minors'

Public Access to Violent Media Content: Balancing Public Right to Know with the Potential for Copycat Violence

In addition to civil lawsuits against media creators, producers, and distributors and by media companies against states that have attempted to violate their First Amendment protections, lawsuits have been brought forth that have challenged public disclosure and the right of media companies to access video footage of actual violence, on one hand, and the responsibility of media companies to restrict violent media content, on the other.

The issue of whether a surveillance video of a shooting is protected under the First Amendment was raised in *Does 15 15 2014 v. King County LLC KCPQ TV Q13 TV LLC TV 100* (2014). The June 5, 2014, Seattle Pacific University shooting committed by Aaron Ybarra was followed by a civil suit that pit the news media against the victims and Seattle Pacific University. Seattle news media outlets—*The Seattle Times, KING 5, KOMO News,* and *KIRO 7*—fought in court to obtain footage of the shooting. Seattle Pacific University turned over surveillance video footage of the shooting to the Seattle Police Department and the King County Prosecuting Attorney's Office. The news media organizations and an individual made a public records request for the footage. Seattle Pacific University and certain students objected to the public disclosure of the surveillance video (Herz, 2016; Williams, 2015). Victims and witnesses of the shooting filed suit to object to the public disclosure of the video footage. The university and victims of the shooting argued, in part, that the release of the video of the shooting would have a substantial likelihood of threatening public safety by 1) enabling future individuals to successfully evade the surveillance security system and 2) by publicly releasing video of the shooting that would potentially lead to copycat crimes.[10] The court ruled that the plaintiffs failed to meet the burden to show that the public disclosure of the video surveillance would have a substantial likelihood of threatening public safety and concluded that the trial court did not err in ruling that the video could be publicly released.

Similarly, shortly after the mass shooting in a Tops grocery store in Buffalo, New York, where 10 people died and 3 were injured (11 of whom were Black) there was speculation that the social media platform Twitch could be sued for removing the livestream of the Buffalo mass shooter under a new censorship law that makes it illegal for any social media

Copycat Crime in the Courts: Implications for Civil Rights and Criminal Justice 177

platform with over 50 million U.S. monthly users to block, ban, or remove content (Masters, 2022; Smith, 2022). The Buffalo shooter, Payton Gendron, livestreamed to Twitch as he was driving up to the store and during the shooting. He could be seen in the rearview mirror wearing a helmet and heard saying, "Just got to go for it," before pulling up to the store where customers are seen walking through the parking lot as he drives up (Stelter & Paget, 2022). Twitch removed the livestream of the shooting in under two minutes with only 22 concurrent users having seen the footage, much faster than what occurred in prior events such as the Christchurch mosque shooting that was livestreamed on Facebook, or the gunman who livestreamed an attack outside a German synagogue (Grayson, 2022; Noack et al., 2019). The Texas law HB 20, went into effect on May 12, 2022, after the Fifth Circuit Court of Appeals decided in favor of Texas Attorney General Ken Paxton in a lawsuit over a law banning many websites and apps from moderating posts by residents in Texas. While the Texas law does not apply in New York, however, the controversial law was approved by a Republican legislature and is an example of a new conservative "anti-tech consensus" that many on the political right would like to see widely implemented (Robertson, 2022). On May 31, 2022, the U.S. Supreme Court blocked the Texas social media law in response to an emergency application to the court after many in the tech industries, including Amazon, Google, Twitter, NetChoice, and the Computer and Communications Industry Association (CCIA) and others who opposed the law, warned that the law would allow hate speech to run rampant on online social media platforms. Counsel for NetChoice said the Texas law is a "constitutional trainwreck" that amounts to (in the lower district court's words) "burning the house to roast the pig" and that it is unconstitutional overreach allowing government to direct what private companies do in terms of carrying certain types of speech (Feiner, 2022).

Implications for Future Legal Decision-making

At the heart of criminal and civil court cases has been the question of the causal role of violent media; the rapidly changing nature of media and digital culture; the responsibility of media creators, producers, and distributors to control violent media effects; and the First Amendment protections that set the boundaries for speech and artistic and creative media content. The question that continues to be raised in legal discourse is: If millions of people consume media violence and do not act out violently as a result, then how can media violence be used as a criminal defense or as grounds for civil liability? Judicial decisions involving media violence and copycat crime have shown that the courts have been extremely hesitant to consider the notion that media violence inspires real-life crime and violence and except in rare cases. Criminal defenses suggesting that defendants are acting under the influence of media such as "*The Matrix* defense" or the "*Grand Theft Auto* defense" have been largely unsuccessful. In the civil courts, while lawsuits against media directors, producers, and distributors have gone further than they have in the past such as the *NBK* lawsuit against Oliver Stone and Warner Brothers, the courts have consistently decided in favor of media defendants, ruling that violent media is protected under the First Amendment.

Criminal cases, such as the case of John Hinckley and *The Matrix* defense case of Tonda Lynn Ansley, that have been successful at trial have been successful because defense attorneys have effectively argued that the defendants were operating under the influence of mass media. In these cases, defense attorneys argued that the defendants were in a state of psychosis, and used their relationship to media to establish that the defendants had lost the distinction between reality and fantasy and met the criteria for the insanity defense (based on the law of insanity for the state in which they lived or the time period in which they went to trial). To date, in the civil courts, it has been a book publisher (Paladin Press) and not a movie director or a violent video game creator who has been at the losing end of a First Amendment lawsuit—a case that was decided because of the establishment of intent and the specificity of the violent message and instructions on how to commit a contract killing that the court determined was not protected under the First Amendment.

As Justice Thomas stated in his dissenting opinion in *Brown v. Entertainment Merchants Association* (2011), the court decisions to date may be premature in dismissing the possibility that the characteristics of new media such as violent video games may be so different that the effects of using these forms of violent media may be very different from reading a book, listening to the radio, or watching a movie. It is unclear what the future will hold. Current legal challenges to social media companies such as Facebook, Twitch, and Twitter in the aftermath of livestreamed violence and global hate speech on both sides of the issue[11] will be telling in drawing the legal lines between harm resulting from violent media and First Amendment protections of free speech, including violent media content, and will build on historical precedent to direct the path forward regarding criminal and civil responsibility for the harmful effects of violent media.

CHAPTER SIX

From the Ethical Realm of the Real, to the Aesthetic Realm of the Hyperreal, to the Digital Realm of the Unreal: What the Future Holds and What We Can Do About It

There were over 300 mass shootings in the United States in the first six months of 2022 (Ledur et al., 2022), by spring 2023 there were more mass shootings than days (Alfonesca, 2023), and on March 28, 2028, Audrey Hale became the perpetrator of the 130th mass shooting in 2023 killing three children and three staff (a custodian, a teacher, and the head of the school) at a Nashville Tennessee elementary school (Harper, 2023: Levenson, 2023) leaving a detailed map and manifesto (Massie, 2023). Three of the deadliest and most recent of these shootings were the Highland Park, Illinois, July 4, 2022, shooting committed by 21-year-old Robert Crimo III; the Buffalo, New York shooting at a Tops grocery store committed by 18-year-old Payton Gendron on May 14, 2022; and the Uvalde, Texas, shooting at Robb Elementary School committed by 18-year-old Salvador Ramos on May 24, 2022. These three mass shootings occurred within a less than two-month period, the first two within

10 days of each other. In the Uvalde, Texas shooting, 19 children and two adults were murdered and others injured, the youngest nine-year-old student Eliahna Amyah Garcia (Fitz-Gibbon, 2022), who was watching *Lilo and Stich* with her fellow students and teachers in their elementary school classroom in a predominantly Hispanic community (Dey, 2022; Lenthang, 2022; The Texas Tribune, 2022). In the Buffalo, New York shooting, 10 members of a predominantly Black neighborhood who were shopping at their local Tops grocery store were murdered, the oldest 86-year-old Ruth Whitfield, who stopped at the store on her way home after visiting her husband of 68 years at his nursing home Craig, 2022; Ellis, 2022). In the Highland Park shooting, Crimo shot July 4 parade-goers from the rooftop in an affluent, predominantly Jewish Chicago suburban community, murdering 7 people and injuring 39 people ranging in age from 8 to 88. Two of the perpetrators of these mass shootings (Gendron and Crimo) were arrested and one was killed by the police (Ramos).

Two days after the Buffalo shooting, journalist Sarah Manavis (2022) wrote, "How do you begin writing a piece that you've already written so many times before? . . . . Every part of this series of events is familiar—it was deliberately copycat-ed" with elements reminiscent of shootings by Anders Breivik in 2011, Elliot Rodger in 2014, Dylann Roof in 2015, Alek Minassian in 2018, Robert Bowers in 2018, Brenton Tarrant in 2019, Patrick Crusius in 2019, and dozens more. She concluded, "The number of deaths and the increasing frequency of attacks all make this a matter of extreme urgency, while the responses treat each incident like it's an individual, freak accident." In an interview following the Uvalde attack, criminologists Jillian Peterson and James Densley, creators of the mass shooter database and authors of *The Violence Project: How to Stop a Mass Shooting Epidemic*, were asked if the Buffalo and Uvalde incidents were linked. They answered, "We don't know for sure at this point, but our research would say that it's likely" (Warner, 2022).

The key issue this observation of "extreme urgency" highlights is the importance of understanding the individual and cultural impact of rapid technological change and the centrality of mass media and digital communication in everyday life and its influence on criminal behavior and violence. As technology has become more central to everyday life, we have moved from the "ethical realm of the real," to the "aesthetic realm of the hyperreal," to the *digital realm of the unreal*. Whereas John Hinckley and Mark Chapman were young men who committed murder in the 1980s aesthetic realm of the hyperreal (Black, 1991) when mass media and digital culture were rapidly changing at a time when violent themes and images in books and TV and movies were the dominant media

From the Ethical Realm of the Real, to the Aesthetic Realm of the Hyperreal 181

violence concern, Gendron, Ramos, and Crimo are/were young men living in the 2020s at a time when reality and fiction are virtually indistinguishable inside a digital swirl of complex media loops, simultaneously insulated and massively reaching digital subcultures, movies, and video games that merge reality and fantasy.[1] In this new digital realm of the unreal there are endless social media opportunities to make Nobodies into Somebodies that provide a vehicle for a completely unknown, isolated, violent, angry edge-sitter to become a celebrity idolized and emulated by other unknown angry edge-sitters.[2]

The Highland Park, Buffalo, and Uvalde mass shootings had different motivational elements (Crimo methodologically planned his attacks for several weeks; performed as a rapper using the name "Awake"; and posted violent images, music videos, and lyrics on social media prior to the attack, including a YouTube video of him dramatically reenacting the aftermath of a school shooting and another showing a cartoon animation of himself getting shot by police). Gendron was a radicalized white supremacist who wrote a 180-page manifesto who targeted the Black community, and Ramos was himself a member of the Uvalde community with no known criminal or mental health history who bought a gun on his eighteenth birthday and shot his grandmother in the face prior to the shooting at the school. However, Gendron, Ramos, and Crimo all spent time on social media and online multiplayer gaming sites prior to the attacks (Andone & Devine, 2022; Collins & Ali, 2022; Nix & Zakrzewski, 2022; Propper, 2022). Gendron was dubbed in the news media the "copy-paste killer" because he plagiarized large sections of his manifesto from GOP propaganda and the manifestos of mass shooters who came before him (Weill, 2022), and he used a GoPro to livestream during the shooting on Twitch, a platform known for allowing people to watch other people play video games (Chayka, 2022). Ramos threatened to shoot up a school using an AR-15 while playing the online video game *Dead by Daylight* just hours before he attacked the elementary school, and there was also a report that he threatened to shoot up schools when playing the video game *Call of Duty*. Crimo, a former Cub Scout (Chisholm, 2022), was "immersed in fringe internet culture" (Pietsch et al., 2022). In an interview with CNN just after the Tops grocery store mass shooting, sociologist Randy Blazak noted the influence of social media and digital subcultures in the attack and in other right-wing extremist violence:

> There is an increasing utilization not just of social media and the deep web and the dark web and all the kind of the dark corners of the Internet where we would find white supremacy, but gaming platforms. Because gaming

182   *Copycat Crime*

> platforms are where young males occupy space, it's where—it's able to reach them and to kind of pull them into that world and where they're able to communicate and then push out their own activity . . . there is this larger rhetoric that there is a coming apocalypse or coming race war or coming civil war and building up to that there is an effort to sort of raise the stakes. We saw this in 2011 with the shooting and the bombing in Oslo, Norway that killed 77 people. Christchurch, El Paso, they keep trying to kind of outdo each other's body counts as a way of almost playing a video game in the real world itself. . . . to them, they're just these scores . . . these body counts are just sort of scores to compete with each other. . . . (CNN, 2022)

The technology-infused world in which Gendron, Ramos, and Crimo were raised and committed these attacks and the influence of mass media and digital culture in their crimes are important in understanding the nature of their criminal acts in ways that can help prevent future media-mediated acts of violence.

The Buffalo Tops grocery store and the Uvalde elementary school shootings just over a week apart are reminiscent of other media-linked copycat crimes such as the West Nickel Mines Amish schoolhouse shooting on October 2, 2006, that followed just days after the Colorado high school shooting on September 27, 2006, in which both shooters allowed the male students and teachers to leave the classroom and lined the female students up in front of the chalkboard. The eerie similarities in the modus operandi of these two crimes make it difficult to overlook potential copycat elements. Sociology professor Heather Melton noted in the aftermath of the Colorado and West Nickle Mines shootings, "Clearly these people had issues with women. . . . It's girls, they're going after girls. . . . It's not a copycat in the sense that someone saw it last week and decided they would do it. . . . Now the way he did it may be because of what he saw last week" (KLS.com, 2006). Understanding the different ways in which media and digital culture influence these types of crimes, from providing ideas that make their way into modus operandi to being part of the very essence of the violence, is important for criminological understanding, prevention, criminal justice practice, and legal decision-making in the civil and criminal courts.

Moving Beyond the Traditional Media Violence Debate

Central to debate, discourse, and scholarly work on media violence is the recurring comment that arises in discussions on the topic: How is it that millions of people consume violent media every day and a fraction of

From the Ethical Realm of the Real, to the Aesthetic Realm of the Hyperreal 183

those go out and commit violent acts in the real world? This question is generally offered as a cold stop to any suggestion of violent media effects. Joel Silver, who produced *The Matrix* films, said, "I only can comment that 15 million people have seen the movie and I don't know what the links are. . . . It's a wonderful fantasy story that doesn't take place in the real world, so I can't comment on what makes people do what they do" (Fox News, January 13, 2015). The easy fix that media violence activists often suggest are actions that others see as a form of censorship, which leads to the equally oversimplified response, "Should our society be comfortable with an increased censorship of ideas just because some sociopaths read the same books and watch the same movies as we do?" (Campbell, 2000, p. 638).

The notion that the entire phenomenon of copycat crime is debunked because millions of people consume violent media every day and only a fraction go on to mimic violent media is an overly simplistic view of the copycat effect on criminal behavior and violence. The causes of violence are complex, multiple, and interactive (Bushman et al., 2015). The claim that violent media influences only a small group of individuals is a myth (United States Senate Hearing 106-1096, 2000) that ignores hundreds of studies showing a link between violent media and less extreme forms of aggression. This argument also overlooks the "spectatorial investment" in violent media (Young, 2009, p. 17) and the less tangible ways that media violence broadly impacts media consumers.

In his U.S. Senate hearing testimony, Anderson and Dill (2000) explained how media violence plays a role in the development of personality:

> One way to think about this is to realize that the developing personality is like slowly hardening clay. Various life experiences, including exposure to violent media, are like the hands that shape the clay. Changes in shape are relatively easy to make at first, when clay is soft, but later on changes become increasingly difficult as the clay hardens. (United States Senate Hearing 106-1096, 2000)

This view of the role of violent media recognizes violent media effects as one factor, among many others, that play a role in molding personality and ultimately in influencing aggression and criminal behavior and violence.

Spectatorial investment—the impact of the affect and aesthetics of violence on the spectator (Young, 2009)—may hold the answer to the question of why and how violent media content impacts individuals who have risk factors for criminal behavior, those who do not, and those who possess some risk factors teetering on the brink as edge-sitters—thinking and fantasizing about crime and violence but for whom there is time and space between the cognitive script and fantasy driving the motive and engaging in behavior in response to those thoughts and fantasies. While it is true that most who consume violent media will not mimic what they see, the power violent media holds over some individuals is important to explore to better understand the nuances that underlie who will and who will not be affected by what types of media content and when this will occur.

Examining violent media that has been associated with multiple copycat crimes such as films like *The Matrix* and *Natural Born Killers* suggests that the issue of media violence and its effects goes far deeper than simply violent content. It may not be the violence itself, but the way in which violence is presented and how features of media interact with individual, environmental, and cultural risk factors that exacerbates the copycat effect (Helfgott, 2015). Examination of scenes from four films that have been linked to copycat violence—*The Matrix, Natural Born Killers, Elephant,* and *Reservoir Dogs*—help answer the question of how different techniques produce a range of affective responses in the spectator:

> The viewer's affective response . . . can arise in the brief moments immediately preceding violent action, moments that engender for the viewer a pleasurable empathy. These are moments of desire, in which the spectator sees the image on-screen as a kind of reflection of himself or herself. And so, in *The Matrix*, Neo opens his coat to show his guns; in *Reservoir Dogs*, Mr. Blonde starts to dance and sing—at these moments, the spectator smiles, or feels a desire to be or look or dance like that. In *Natural Born Killers*, the spectator is briefly shown the world through Mickey's eyes, in his fantasy of the waitress, and through Mallory's experience, as a stranger attempts to come on to her. Such a world is one of predation and insult; the ensuing violence feels *a little bit* justified, and that little bit is all it takes to generate greater sympathy for Mickey and Mallory than for those they kill. (Young, 2009, p. 18)

The potential for a media source to generate a particular affective response in a viewer is an important element in understanding the nature of the copycat effect and the ways that media violence will differentially impact spectators. Violent media that has been linked to more than one or two copycat crimes is important to examine to answer complex questions regarding why some forms of media impact some people, why most people who consume violent media do not go out and mimic the violence they see, and why some media sources generate a higher number of

From the Ethical Realm of the Real, to the Aesthetic Realm of the Hyperreal   185

copycat crimes committed in some cases by individuals who may not possess risk factors for crime and violence.

Theory and Empirical Research on Copycat Crime

The role that media and digital culture play in influencing crime and violence deserves attention in criminological theory and research. Until very recently, criminology as a discipline has not focused attention on how mass media and digital culture influence criminal behavior and violence beyond a limited focus on cybercrime, surveillance, and digital fraud (Milivojevic, 2021). With the theory and research conducted to date on copycat crime coming from such a small minority of criminologists led by Surette's pioneering work (Surette, 1990, 1998, 2002, 2013a, 2013b, 2014a, 2014b, 2015a, 2015b, 2016a, 2019, 2022; Surette & Chadee, 2020; Surette & Maze, 2015; Surette et al., 2021), this is a scholarly area ripe for theory development and empirical research. Criminologist Sanja Milivojevic (2021) aptly notes:

> . . . criminology of today must engage in emerging technologies as a matter of urgency. As social scientists, we are not well equipped or trained to understand where technologies are heading, and what this means for a range of social issues and relationships. We need a multidisciplinary team of experts in the areas of technology, security, sociology, law, criminology— the list goes on—and we need to broaden our theoretical gaze. (p. 13)

Interdisciplinary perspectives and carefully integrated theories are needed to unravel the complexity of the copycat effect on criminal behavior and violence. Theory and research are needed to respond to the question often posed when there is any discussion of potential copycat crime effects: If millions of people consume violent media every day and only a rare few mimic the violence they see resulting in real-world acts of violence, then how can it be said that media violence has a copycat effect on actual violence?

Research conducted to date suggests that violent media is more likely to have a rudder rather than a trigger effect and gives ideas to individuals who would commit a crime anyway, influencing the modus operandi or the individual's motivation to commit a crime. Thus, violent media is more likely to influence how individual perpetrators carry out their crimes rather than increasing the rate of crime (Rios & Ferguson, 2020; Surette, 2022). In addition, there is a large body of work suggesting that violent media consumption and mass media and digital culture operate as a risk factor for criminal behavior (Anderson & Bushman, 2018; Anderson et al., 2017; Gentile & Bushman, 2012; Helfgott, 2015), acting as a catalyst rather than as a cause of subsequent crime and violence (Markey & Ferguson, 2017; Rios & Ferguson, 2020; Surette, 2013a, 2013b, 2022).

The research conducted to date falls short in explaining how rapid technological change and digital culture influence criminal behavior. The focus on violent media as a trigger or cause versus a rudder or catalyst is important in order to understand the nature and dynamics of the copycat effect. However, this either/or conceptualization oversimplifies the broader influence of mass media and digital culture on criminal behavior. Copycat crime is the product of individual criminogenic and demographic factors, cultural factors, media characteristics, and a person's relationship to a media source and can be viewed along a continuum of influence from minor (influencing modus operandi) to major (playing a primary role in the motivation for and signature elements of the crime) (Helfgott, 2015). Understanding copycat crime from a risk factor perspective along a continuum of influence provides a framework for theory development and empirical research that can help make sense of how rapid technological change in mass media and digital culture influence crime at the individual and aggregate levels to answer questions about the role violent media and digital culture play in crimes committed by individuals and also how the violent media–saturated culture increases crime and violence through contagion (Finkelstein et al., 2020; Gilbert, 2017; Huesmann, 2012; Langman, 2018; Lankford & Tomek, 2017; Nacos, 2009; Towers et al., 2015) or decreases crime through catharsis and/or a routine activity effect (Markey & Ferguson, 2017; Markey et al., 2015).

Rapid global technological change has affected virtually every community and culture.[3] Global society has moved from the *ethical realm of the real* where human interaction and behavior are rooted in physical space and in-person interactions, where people have the opportunity to assess the impact of their decisions and behaviors on others in real time and space in the "ethical norm," to the *aesthetic realm of the hyperreal,* where human interaction is media-mediated and boundaries between reality and fantasy are blurred, providing opportunity for physical and psychological distancing, human objectification, and aesthetic performance to "reveal the 'real'" (Black, 1991, p. 138), to the *digital realm of the unreal* where human behavior and social life are shaped through digital technologies and interactive virtual experiences that have created an entirely unique space in which human beings operate—a "transformed human experience" (Levin & Mamlok, 2021, p. 1) resulting in a "new way of

From the Ethical Realm of the Real, to the Aesthetic Realm of the Hyperreal

being human" where humans and nonhumans interact (Di Nicola, 2022) in a "metaverse" where art shapes reality (Kim, 2022).

A Theoretical Framework for Empirical Investigation of Copycat Crime

Development of a theory of copycat crime requires disciplinary integration and consensus on the definition and measurement of copycat crime. An integrative theory of copycat crime is needed that synthesizes pertinent theory and research from the fields of science and technology, criminology, psychology, sociology, anthropology, media studies, cultural studies, film studies, literature and the arts, gender and feminist studies, artificial intelligence, and other disciplines. Traditional criminological theories do not sufficiently explain crimes that exhibit striking evidence of mimicry that go beyond social learning and modeling of real-world behaviors (the ethical realm of the real), to modeling of media-mediated digital representations (real and fictional) that result in blurred boundaries between fantasy and reality (the aesthetic realm of the hyperreal), to the influence of digital representations that are simultaneously aesthetic and real that provide a vehicle for both mimesis and performance (the digital realm of the unreal).

An integrative theory of copycat crime is needed to inform future empirical research (Helfgott, 2015; Surette, 2022). A theoretical framework for empirical research examining the copycat effect on criminal behavior requires drawing from the theory and research from other lines of research, including copycat crime, the aesthetics of murder, celebrity obsession, social learning, cognitive scripts, cultural criminology, and media effects, from a risk factor approach that understands copycat crime along a theoretical continuum from minor influence to major influence with attention to individual criminogenic and demographic factors, cultural factors, characteristics of a media source, and an individual's relationship to media (Helfgott, 2015). Five theoretical perspectives provide a framework for developing an interdisciplinary theory of copycat crime to take research beyond the overly simplistic notion of causation: 1) imitation (people do as they see); 2) social contagion (people follow the crowd); 3) social diffusion (people like to share good news); 4) social learning (people watch what happens to others and develop expectations of what will happen when they copy others); and 5) media studies (what people believe is real is socially constructed and determined by a mix of personal experience, conversations with others, and media portrayals (Surette, 2022). These five perspectives offer a path forward for continued research to provide answers to the many unanswered questions about the influence of media, technology, and digital culture on criminal behavior and violence:

- Beyond the oversimplified focus on the causal effects of violent media consumption, what do we need to know about the copycat effect on criminal behavior? How does media and digital culture operate as a risk factor in conjunction with other risk factors that trigger an individual edge-sitter from thinking and fantasizing about committing crime and violence to engaging in real-world crime and violence?
- Is there empirical support for the hypothetical continuum of the copycat effect from a minor influence on modus operandi (shaper/rudder) to a major influence on motivation becoming a signature element of a crime (trigger)? Does this continuum encapsulate all forms of the copycat effect? If an individual would have committed a crime anyway, why does it matter what media may have influenced small aspects of the crime?
- What are the characteristics of the typical copycat criminal? Is copycat crime a homogeneous crime type? Or is copycat crime best viewed as a supertype that cuts across all crime categories? How does the conceptualization of copycat crime along the hypothetical continuum inform the development of a typology of copycat crime?
- What is the primary driver of the copycat effect on criminal behavior and violence? Is it violent imagery, a particular idea or value system, the form or technical presentation of violence, and/or the interaction between the viewer and the media source?
- As mass media and digital culture continue to advance, how will the increasingly sophisticated digital world influence criminal behavior and violence? Are children who are born in the digital era increasingly more or less likely to be criminogenically influenced?
- How does the copycat effect change across the life course? Do different forms of media differentially influence different age groups? Is the copycat effect on crime predominantly a phenomenon that impacts youth? If so, what are the age ranges of primary concern?
- How do other demographic characteristics such as gender, education, and socioeconomic status influence copycat crime?
- With the lack of empirical support for the catharsis effect of violent media and studies showing the limited influence of media images of violence on crime rates, why does violent media appear to not significantly change crime rates? Are some forms of media more or less cathartic than others? What exactly is the routine activity effect of different forms of violent media? Would an effect on crime rates be revealed if research isolated specific types of media effects on specific types of crime?
- How can it be determined that a crime is a copycat? How can the copycat effect be empirically measured?

From the Ethical Realm of the Real, to the Aesthetic Realm of the Hyperreal 189

Further development of an integrative interdisciplinary theory of copycat crime and empirical research examining these and other questions are an important next steps in this line of scholarly inquiry.

Measuring Copycat Crime

A starting point for theory development and empirical research is consensus on an operational definition. Among the few scholars who study copycat crime, there is consensus that copycat crime is inspired by some form of media or digital content,[4] where the media or digital image and the crime share a "unique criminogenic connection" (Surette, 2022, p. 3). While there is still some ironing out of aspects of this definition, such as whether the copycat crime needs to be a "copy" of a prior crime and/or simply a particular idea that influences the perpetrator to commit a crime that is tied to a media image,[5] this definition offers a starting point for theory development and empirical research.

The next step beyond building consensus on the definition of copycat crime is the development of a valid and reliable tool to measure copycat crime. Surette's seven-factor procedure for determining the extent to which a crime is a copycat crime (Surette, 2016a, 2022) offers a method to mathematically calculate the extent to which a crime is a copycat crime based on time proximity, theme consistency, scene specificity, repetitive consumption, self-editing, perpetrator statements, and second-party statements. A Bayesian probability can then be calculated to determine the probability of a specific crime being a copycat crime. Utilization of the seven-factor procedure to evaluate the extent to which a crime is a copy-cat crime and the application of Bayes's theorem to calculate the probability estimate of the likelihood that a crime is a copycat crime will bolster researcher confidence when conducting empirical research to ensure that studies involving copycat crime are in fact focused on actual copycat crimes rather than crimes that have been loosely labeled as such in media accounts.

As a pilot example of the application of Surette's seven-factor procedure (2016a, 2022) for evaluating the extent that a crime is a copycat crime is provided in the Appendix including a comprehensive list of 150 copycat crime cases from 1966 to 2022. The case study examples illustrate the nature and scope of the copycat effect on criminal behavior and violence. The scoring of the cases on Surette's seven-factor procedure offers a pilot application of the scoring method to provide a sense of the extent to which each of the copycat crime examples are in fact copycat crimes. New cases will arise every day. One of the most important sources of information about copycat crime lies in the case histories of previous crimes that have involved copycat elements. These copycat crime cases are an important source of information for retrospective analysis to inform development of theories and typologies of copycat crime and empirical research to understand the nature, scope, and extent of copycat crime. The pilot using Surette's seven-factor scoring process offers a guide for future research, and the scores presented in this pilot can be used as a foundation for replication to establish validity and reliability of the scoring method.

Expanding Empirical Research

A deep dive into many remaining questions is needed to better understand the copycat effect on criminal behavior. Several areas that are of particular importance in moving forward with theory and empirical research are discussed in the following sections.

Beyond Catalyst Versus Cause: Mass Media and Digital Culture as a Risk Factor for Criminal Behavior and Violence Along a Continuum of Influence

Further research is needed to examine how mass media and digital culture influence criminal behavior and violence. A body of work has developed that offers a starting point to examine how media violence influences crime and violence to help answer the question of whether media violence operates as a trigger or a shaper/rudder or both. The view of media and digital culture as a technology-related risk factor for criminal behavior and violence needs further exploration. Approaching media and digital culture from a risk factor perspective offers a framework for examining and understanding copycat crime from both perspectives along the continuum of influence from playing a minor role in influencing modus operandi (MO) behavior (as a shaper/rudder) to a major role as a signature element that characterizes the very essence of the crime (as a causal influence) (Helfgott, 2015).

The view of media violence as playing either a causal role as a trigger OR as a catalyst or rudder providing ideas about how to commit a crime is an overly simplistic view of the phenomenon of the copycat crime. Theoretically, it is important to continue to study and to better understand the nature of the copycat effect on criminal behavior. However, this either/ or perspective (violent media as cause or catalyst) in the popular media

From the Ethical Realm of the Real, to the Aesthetic Realm of the Hyperreal

violence debate and empirical research obstructs an understanding of how violent media and digital culture differentially influence different people on both individual and societal-cultural levels. In other words, where is the line between violent media operating as a catalyst influencing the MO and providing ideas to carry out the crime versus influencing the motivation for crime, operating as the ultimate cause of the crime? Can violent media be both catalyst and cause depending upon where the level of the copycat effect lies along the continuum of influence?

From a practical perspective, if a criminal event is inspired by media and digital culture, whether media operated as a minor or proximate cause versus a major or ultimate cause is important for legal purposes in determining culpability and prevention in terms of understanding the exact role media played in a particular individual's criminal behavior. However, whether criminal behavior at the individual level is influenced in a minor or a major way is a matter of degree and does not diminish the importance of understanding how violent media and digital culture operate as a risk factor for crime and violence.

Of critical importance in moving forward with research on copycat crime is utilizing integrative and interdisciplinary theories and creative methodologies to deconstruct cause-and-effect arguments about the links between media violence and real-world violence. A phenomenological understanding of copycat crime[6] that uncovers the meaning the crime holds for the perpetrator, including the role and extent to which media plays a role, is an important next step for future research. Theoretical advances, such as the reformulation of General Strain Theory (GST) within the theoretical context of phenomenology (Polizzi, 2011), and creative methodological approaches, such as Borchard's (2015) autoethnographic method, are needed to consider the ways in which the violent video games *Grand Theft Auto* and *Super Columbine Massacre RPG!* impact the formation of self and offer a promising path forward to move theory and research on copycat crime beyond the traditional examination of cause and effect that may make sense in experimental laboratory but bears little relevance to real life. In addition, narrative analyses of perpetrator narratives and manifestos, videos, and digital trails in the aftermath of copycat crime (Allwinn & Tultschinetski, 2022; Helfgott, 2004, 2014) and attempts to conduct interviews with copycat perpetrators are important next steps (Surette, 2022).

In addition to research on the individual phenomenology of the copycat effect, further study is needed to examine the nature of media elements and how those elements interact with individual and cultural factors and forces to produce the copycat effect. Violent media in general, and different types of violent media in particular, may be more or less criminogenic for different types of people based on their overall risk factors for crime and violence. Media depictions of crime and violence that show the world through the perpetrator's eyes generate sympathy for the perpetrator, justify criminal behavior, and depict lawlessness, as opposed to media depictions that show the world through the victim's eyes, which generate sympathy for the victim, condemn criminal behavior, and depict justice, may have very different impacts individually and culturally. Understanding the differential power of media violence to generate copycat crime and violence on individual, subcultural, and cultural levels is necessary to understand the potential of certain types of violent media to impact more than just a subset of violence-prone individuals. A focus on the heterogeneity of violent imagery "both escapes the polarization which beleaguers the media violence debate, and also acknowledges the power of the cinematic image to get under our skins and keep us enthralled" (Young, 2009, p. 19).

Criminogenic and Cultural Factors That Exacerbate the Copycat Effect

Individual, media, and cultural factors can exacerbate the copycat effect on criminal behavior and violence. Demographic factors such as age, gender, socioeconomic status, and race/ethnicity and individual factors such as personality characteristics and mental health, relationship to media, and the unique elements of the perpetrator's phenomenological experience all interact with violent media and digital culture in ways that decrease or increase the likelihood of the copycat effect. There are several important areas for future research to better understand the role of criminogenic and cultural factors that exacerbate the copycat effect.

The relationship between males and masculinity, consumption and influence of violent media, and copycat crime is important to examine. Recent research suggests that the prevalence of copycat crime is significantly less among females, though this gender gap is narrowing, as it is with the gender gap in crime in general (Estrada et al., 2016; Gunnison et al., 2016; Rennison, 2009). In a study of 575 females and 866 males drawn from four surveys conducted from 2008 to 2015, 11.5 percent of females reported they had considered a copycat crime (compared to 21.6 percent of males) and 6.2 percent of females reported that they had attempted a copycat crime (compared to 17.9 percent of males) (Surette, 2021).

From the Ethical Realm of the Real, to the Aesthetic Realm of the Hyperreal   193

From a risk factor model, there are a range of risk factors that have the potential to exacerbate the copycat effect, including being male, emotional development, personality traits, cognitive schema, history of abuse, and family dysfunction. Socioenvironmental variables interact with these individual-level risk factors to produce a volatile mix. The most aggressive and violence-prone individuals are more likely to be attracted to violent media and digital subcultures that are riddled with images of violence and violent ideology (Courtwright, 1998; Grimes et al., 2008). These aggressive, violence-prone individuals have historically been overwhelmingly male (Gerbner et al., 2014; Katz, 2006; Larson, 2003). The notion that an act of violence can help an individual achieve celebrity status by "going out in a blaze of glory" (Lankford, 2015, p. 370) found in the cognitive scripts of many mass shooters is rooted in and reinforced by violent media and digital subcultures. That most media-mediated perpetrators are male suggests that this idea of violence as an answer to status, recognition, and resolution of personal strain appears to be a predominantly masculine notion. Understanding this mix of risk factors has the potential to interrupt the pathway to media-mediated violence. Future research is needed to explore the relationship between gender and copycat crime, specifically the relationship between males and masculinity and criminogenic media.

Second, examination of the relationship between personality traits, personality disorders, and mental illness and copycat crime is an important next step for theory development and empirical research. Many copycat crimes have involved individuals with a history of mental illness, personality disorders, conduct disorder, and exhibition of callous and unemotional traits in childhood. Theories have been put forth regarding the personality traits that are potentially associated with copycat crime such as antisocial and psychopathic personality traits (Helfgott, 2004, 2015; Webster, 1982). However there has been minimal empirical research on the impact of individual-level risk factors on copycat violence, in particular, the role that psychopathology and personality disorders play in exacerbating a copycat crime effect. Lloyd's (2002) call for future research on the identification of individual and ecological variables along with scholars who have theorized that artistic illiteracy and developmental, identity issues, and personality disorder (e.g., Black, 1991; Meloy, 1998; O'Toole, 2000) contribute to the ways in which individuals interact and internalize media sources suggest that a key variable that needs to be examined in relationship to the copycat effect is psychopathy. Psychopathy is a key piece in untangling the complexities of offender motivation and media criminogenic effects. The psychopath's grandiosity, lack of remorse, lack of empathy, egocentricity, and other personality traits and behaviors provide the perfect mix to fuel antisocial and criminal behavior. Furthermore, Cleckley (1941) suggested that psychopaths have a lowered ability to produce art or humor or to think in the abstract. It is hypothesized that individuals with higher levels of psychopathy will be less able to differentiate reality from fantasy and that specific characteristics of a media source (in interaction with other factors) will exacerbate the copycat effect.

Given the findings of extensive prior research on psychopathy and its relationship to crime, it is a reasonable hypothesis that psychopathy is a significant risk factor for the copycat effect. Striking similarities between motivations articulated in narrative accounts of copycat offenders and features of psychopathy and the primitive defenses generally used by psychopaths have been noted by scholars (e.g., Helfgott, 1997, 2004, 2014, 2019; Meloy, 1988), in particular unconscious defenses such as omnipotence; devaluation; cognitive thinking errors such as entitlement; victim stance (Gacono & Meloy, 1988, 1994; Helfgott, 1997, 2004); and key features of psychopathy such as grandiosity, lack of empathy, superficial charm, lack of remorse (Hare, 1993, 1991, 2003); and contemptuous delight (Meloy, 1988). Furthermore, hypotheses raised by copycat crime scholars regarding the role of lack of identity integration and artistic illiteracy in mimetic crime and violence (Black, 1991; Helfgott, 2015) coupled with reference in the early literature on psychopathy (e.g., Cleckley, 1941) noting the psychopath's inability to have a deep abstract understanding and experience of art raise interesting questions regarding the role of psychopathy level in the tendency toward celebrity obsession, the utilization of media images in MO and motivation, and the commission of copycat crime. If psychopaths lack identity integration, are they more susceptible to the copycat effect because they have an inability to see themselves as distinct from media-mediated images (and celebrity personas they identify with)? If psychopaths are not able to experience art deeply, as Cleckley (1941) suggests, and if they are what Black (1991) referred to as "artistic illiterates," are they more vulnerable to the copycat effect because they are less able to distinguish art and fiction from reality? Research examining the relationship between psychopathic traits and copycat crime would be an interesting line of exploration to determine if the interaction between psychopathic traits and violent media effects exacerbates the copycat effect (Helfgott, 2019).

Many questions remain regarding the nature and extent of copycat crime. Future research is needed that examines the individual and sociocultural factors that influence and exacerbate the copycat effect such as hypermasculinity and copycat crime and the attraction of adolescent males to certain types of violent media and digital subcultures, the differential potential of the influence of different media sources, the role of celebrity culture, and how certain types of digital subcultures exacerbate the copycat effect. Of particular importance in moving forward with research is to better understand how digital culture and digital subcultures enhance the opportunity for subcultural insulation and external validation for distorted thinking and fantasy development of potential edge-sitters and the potential of rapid technological change and digital culture to impact more than just those who have the propensity to commit crime.

Developing a Typology of Copycat Crime

Further research is needed to examine the degree to which copycat crime is a homogeneous crime type or if it is better understood as a super-type that cuts across all crime categories (Helfgott, 2015). Research identifying characteristics of copycat perpetrators, copycat crime pathways (Surette, 2013b, 2022), and a typology of copycat crime will provide information to understand the nature of the copycat effect more fully. A typology of media-mediated crime that includes copycat crime, performance crime, and other forms of media-mediated crime that builds on the theoretical work to date, situating copycat crime along a continuum of influence (Helfgott, 2015) and across multiple pathways (Surette, 2022), is an important next step for research on the copycat effect on criminal behavior and violence.

Surette (2022) offers a copycat crime typology building on earlier work that considers crime type, media role, and crime motivation with attention to crime and perpetrator characteristics, risk factors, perpetrator attitudes and values, and motivators. Empirical research testing this typology in conjunction with further theory development on how Surette's (2013b, 2022) pathways to violence are situated across the copycat crime continuum (Helfgott, 2015) offers an important avenue for future theoretical exploration and empirical research.

Why Copycat Crime Matters: Practical Implications for Legal Decision-making, Threat and Risk Assessment and Management, and Public Safety

It is an irony that the topic of copycat crime has been viewed in criminology as both common and rare (Surette, 2022). Social learning theories of crime are prominent, and it is generally believed that all crime involves some element of imitation. On the other hand, copycat crime is viewed as rare, with a small percentage of crime considered to be an official "copycat." Even in cases where there is evidence that a perpetrator mimicked a scene from a movie or other form of media, investigators sometimes minimize the importance of media, indicating that the crime speaks for itself and it matters little whether the perpetrator got an idea or was immersed in media content (Douglas & Olshaker, 1999; Silverstein, 2022), and in court cases that have raised legal issues regarding the media-crime relationship, judges and juries have historically been hesitant to embrace the notion that a defendant acted under the influence of media or that media creators, producers, and distributors should be held accountable (Cooper, 2007; Firestre & Jones, 2000; O'Neil, 2001; Surette, 2022; Wellstood, 2000).

So why then is it important to study and understand copycat crime and how media and digital culture influence criminal behavior? Two reasons. First, there is evidence to suggest that mass media and digital culture are playing an increasing role in criminal behavior and violence as technology advances (Clarke, 2004). A scholarly focus on copycat crime is long overdue. The growing number of anecdotal accounts of young, mostly male, perpetrators who have histories showing immersion in violent digital subcultures and research results showing that 25 percent of violent juveniles report having committed a copycat crime suggest that the copycat effect on criminal behavior and violence deserves serious attention in academic research. The rapidly changing technology and the questions that arise regarding copycat elements of crimes that appear to occur in clusters, as well as those where perpetrators note celebrity motive and affinity for prior perpetrators both real and fictional in their narratives, manifestos, and digital posts, suggest that systematic study of the copycat effect on criminal behavior is an important and long-neglected area of study. Theoretically, study of copycat crime is important to understand the nature and dynamics of media-mediated crime and broader media effects (Helfgott, 2015) and has relevance for criminological theory, in particular social learning and subcultural theories, cultural criminology, life-course criminology, and the role of media in cognitive processing (Surette, 2022). Ultimately, "copycat crime can provide an untapped reservoir for understanding broader media, crime, and social behavior questions" (Surette, 2022, p. 7).

Answers to these broader media, crime, and social behavior questions are of central importance in both the criminal and civil justice systems. Across the span of the criminal justice system, understanding the nature and dynamics of the copycat effect on criminal behavior and violence is of practical importance. In policing and criminal investigations, if a crime

From the Ethical Realm of the Real, to the Aesthetic Realm of the Hyperreal 197

involves media elements, police can seek investigative leads through media sources used by the perpetrator. Additionally, understanding where a crime sits on the copycat continuum and the influence on MO versus signature behaviors has implications for criminal profiling in terms of case linkage.

In the adjudication process, answers to questions about the copycat effect on criminal behavior have implications for prosecutors in establishing premeditation and aggravating factors and defense attorneys in arguments for not guilty by reason of insanity or diminished capacity defenses and mitigating factors. Long-time violent video game crusader and former attorney Jack Thompson, who believes his lawsuits and crusade against violent video games led to his disbarment, predicts that:

> Someday . . . the defense team in a murder trial is going to argue that their client was revved into a frenzy due to, in part, an inveterate video game habit. The jury will buy it, and the suspect will escape the death penalty. . . . It's going to work, and that's going to get people's attention. . . . People are going to freak out. They're going to say, "Wait a minute, somebody can kill somebody and only be convicted of manslaughter by virtue of a video game defense?" (Jack Thompson in Winkie, 2022)

While Thompson's views may be out of step with research that has failed to establish a causal relationship between violent video games and real-world violence, the World Health Organization's addition of video game addiction to its list of diseases in the International Classification of Diseases (ICD) aligns with Thompson's view and may give some momentum to his prediction for attorneys of the future, who may revisit the *Grand Theft Auto* defense with a foundation to be able to say that their client was operating under the influence of mass media (Winkie, 2022).

Understanding the degree to which a perpetrator is influenced by media and digital culture can also be important in correctional management and treatment. This is particularly important in the juvenile justice system, given that research has found that adolescents and youth are more susceptible to the copycat effect (Surette, 2022). Understanding the role media and digital culture play in the cognitive scripts of perpetrators who have been convicted and are serving their prison sentences can have bearing in correctional management, treatment, and reentry for those who will eventually be released.

In the civil courts, understanding the nature of the copycat effect, the influence of different forms of media, and the relationship between risk factors for copycat crime has a bearing on legal culpability in lawsuits against media companies, as well as in cases involving challenges to the public release of violent video surveillance footage of mass shootings and other violent crimes and has implications for where the lines are drawn between art, obscenity, incitement, and First Amendment protections of free speech. The civil lawsuits that have attempted to hold media artists, producers, and distributors liable for harm resulting from media content have helped draw legal lines that have dictated who can be held responsible. Cases such as *Rice v. Paladin Enterprises, Inc.* (1997) and *Byers v. Edmondson* (1998, 2002) have shown how the nature of media content matters and will inform legal challenges moving forward.

In the arena of risk assessment and public safety, research on the copycat effect on criminal behavior can help to identify red flags in individuals who are potential edge-sitters whose developmental pathway to copycat crime can be interrupted. Understanding copycat crime pathways (Surette, 2013b) and the dynamics of digital subcultures that insulate individuals who are highly susceptible to the copycat effect and the associated red flags can help identify warning signs that can potentially interrupt a crime from occurring. The thing about copycat perpetrators is that they are, by nature, performance artists. They are intimately connected to media and digital culture, and they are highly likely to leave a digital trail prior to committing their acts of violence. Salvador Ramos, the Uvalde, Texas mass shooter, left a warning on TikTok: "Kids be scared" (Katsuyama, 2022). Robert Crimo III, the perpetrator of the Highland Park, Illinois mass shooting, was a loner who kept to himself but who posted violent warnings on social media for three years prior to the attack (Bellware et al., 2022). Buffalo mass shooter Payton Gendron wrote in increasing detail over a five-month period in online posts on Discord prior to his attack at the Tops grocery store (Swaine & Bennett, 2022). A Secret Service study of targeted school violence incidents between 2008 and 2017 involving 41 school shooters (34 of whom were male and 7 of whom were female) found that the shooter motives were multifaceted, with primary and secondary motivation including personal grievances, relationships to peers, desire to kill, suicidal ideation, psychotic symptoms, and fame/ notoriety; that most demonstrated interest in violence through movies, video games, books, or other media; and that two-thirds of the shooters communicated intent to attack and other threatening behaviors to which there was no response prior to the attack. For example, one school shooter planned his attack over summer break and on the morning of the incident posted a message on social media that said, "First day of school, last day of my life" (Alathari et al., 2019, p. 10). With the rapidly increasing role of social media as a way of everyday communication, these warning signs, as

From the Ethical Realm of the Real, to the Aesthetic Realm of the Hyperreal 199

well as answers to the role of media influence as a motivating factor, are likely to be on display in social media. The more the copycat effect on criminal behavior and violence is understood, the more potential there will be to interrupt the pathway to violence for perpetrators who are both inspired by media and use media to announce their intentions and display their crimes as performance.

What Can Be Done in the Here and Now? Minimizing the Harmful Effects of Violent Media and Digital Culture

Based on what is currently known about the copycat effect on criminal behavior and violence, there are ways to minimize the mimetic effect of violent media and digital culture. Telling and retelling stories of crime and violence in ways that do not celebrate or glamorize the perpetrator, that do not make the perpetrator seem appealing, that focus on the victims and community cohesion in the aftermath of crime and violence, and that depict justice over lawlessness have the potential to minimize or mitigate the copycat effect.

Tell Crime Stories in Ways That Deemphasize the Perpetrator, Deglorify Violence, and Celebrate Prosocial Behavior

Social media is increasingly linked with mass shootings (Suciu, 2022). The seemingly endless accounts of copycat perpetrator references to prior perpetrators illustrates the power of violent media to influence the motivations of future attackers. Celebrity culture and the notion that infamy and celebrity can be achieved through acts of violence and the idea that a Nobody can become a Somebody by engaging in a violent act found in literature, the arts, and media (Black, 1991) are rooted in the language, images, and audio used to describe acts of violence in both real and fictional depictions of crime and violence. In other words, how a story is told matters.

One way to minimize or mitigate the copycat effect is to deemphasize the perpetrator and deglorify the violence in real and fictional stories. Fictional stories and news accounts of real-life crimes can be told in ways that deemphasize rather than celebritize the perpetrator. Stories can also be told in ways that carefully pay attention to the ways that certain forms of cinematic violence legitimize, glorify, persuade, and celebrate crime and violence (Young, 2009). This means depicting crime and violence using characters who are not appealing and attractive, showing crime as an unsuccessful rather than successful method to resolve conflict, and showing resolution through justice rather than showing the perpetrators getting away with the crime. While these decisions may be difficult for media producers to implement for economic reasons, altering aspects of media depictions of crime and violence such as the language of violence (Newman, 1998), media looping (Manning, 1998), the affect and aesthetics of violence (Black, 1991; Young, 2009), and elements of media depictions that blur the boundary between fantasy and reality (Helfgott, 2015) may decrease the criminogenic effects of media violence.

Careful attention to the words used to describe perpetrators and thoughtful decisions about when and whether to use perpetrators' names may help diminish the celebritization of perpetrators. For example, campaigns such as "Don't Name Them" and "No Notoriety" contend that a simple and effective way to minimize violence contagion and the copycat effect is to avoid sensationalizing the names of perpetrators and to tell the stories of victims, heroes, and the communities who come together to help each other heal in the aftermath of violence. In addition, using terms in pop culture, news stories, and scholarly writing that glorifies, valorizes, and creates mystery and intrigue such as "lone wolf" terrorist (Berntzen & Bjørgo, 2021) and publishing photos of perpetrators (except when necessary, such as in ongoing searches for escaped suspects) have the potential to glorify violence in ways that contribute to inspiring would-be violent actors (Lankford & Madfis, 2018).

However, telling and retelling stories of crime and violence in ways that do not celebrate the perpetrator is easier said than done for a number of reasons. First, news stories attempt to include details for informational purposes, and these details are important for those who seek to study and understand crime and violence. While digital culture has created a vast opportunity for individual edge-sitters to access images of violence from around the globe in a matter of seconds, it has also created an opportunity to learn about the thought processes of perpetrators through their publicly posted manifestos, social media posts, and video diaries. Additionally, scholarly writing that omits the name of the perpetrator can be confusing for scholars who seek to conduct retrospective analyses that require the name of the perpetrator and as many details as possible. Thus, while not naming the perpetrator is one important way to diminish the glorification of the perpetrator, there are situations and contexts in which naming the perpetrator is necessary and can be beneficial for research and knowledge development. News agencies have begun to develop standards on reporting crime and violence, and scholars have begun to make careful decisions about when and if to use terms

From the Ethical Realm of the Real, to the Aesthetic Realm of the Hyperreal 201

like lone wolf and to name perpetrators in academic writing. For example, National Public Radio (NPR) developed the policy to "Use the name of the killer sparingly and focus on the victims," noting that a shooter is named when it is relevant to the news, when it will help audiences understand possible motives, and to explain what happened in the reporting of the story (McBride & Castillo, 2021). Similarly, scholars have made decisions to omit the name of the perpetrator in published work in academic journals, opting to describe perpetrators by the location of the attack, referring to the subject of study as "the perpetrator." (Allwinn et al., 2022, p. 43).

Media producers, directors, writers, and artists may also make personal decisions about how their work contributes to the glorification of crime and violence. For example, Stephen King, author of the book *Rage* noted by several school shooter perpetrators, said that while he does not believe his novel caused the school shootings, he regards *Rage* as a "possible accelerant" affecting individuals who have mental health problems and troubled backgrounds that have already driven them to the edge. King said he pulled *Rage* from circulation because "in my judgment it might be hurting people" (Adwar, 2014). Similarly, since its publication in 2007, the book *13 Reasons Why* which inspired a subsequent popular Netflix series, has been the target of censorship with multiple school libraries banning the book for its glamorization of suicide and negative portrayals of helping professionals (Strum, 2017; Ruiz, 2019). After more than two years of denying that the graphic suicide in the first season of *13 Reasons Why* could put vulnerable young viewers at increased risk for self-harm, Netflix and the show's creators removed the controversial scene acknowledging research on media contagion and the copycat effect (Gould et al., 2003). The show's creator Brian Yorkey said, "No one scene is more important than the life of the show, and its message that we must take better care of each other. . . . We believe this edit will help the show do the most good for the most people while mitigating any risk for especially vulnerable people" (Marshall, 2019).[7]

Social media companies can also play a role in mitigating the copycat effect through careful monitoring and immediate removal of certain forms of violent imagery such as livestreams of violence. These decisions will be difficult to make. Media companies must carefully balance the protection of individual rights of free speech with public safety, and some argue that they have a moral obligation to make these decisions, "Compromising freedom of speech seems abhorrent until we weigh that compromise against the lives lost in Buffalo or the many other places where radicalized violent extremists found their motivation to kill" (Suciu, 2022).

Deconstruct the Dangerous Cultural Myth That Hypermasculine Violence Equals Power

Many scholars have noted the deep intertwining of hypermasculinity, violent media images, and violent crime (Borchard, 2015; Boyle, 2001; Gerbner et al., 2014; Katz & Earp, 2013; Katz & Jhally, 1999; Kivel & Johnson, 2009; Scaptura & Boyle, 2020; Scharrer, 2009; Silva et al., 2021; Moore, 2002; Tonso, 2009). Cultural narratives depicted in media tell stories of manhood that make their way into the cognitive scripts and identities of predominantly young male perpetrators of violence. These narratives pervade all forms of media and digital culture showing boys and men using violence to get back something they believe has been taken from them in response to the experience of loss and rejection and/or other forms of disappointment. It is jarring to think that the cultural discussion about how to respond to the mass violence problem tends to revolve around mental illness and guns with a glaring lack of attention to the central role of gender (Katz, 2006, 2017; Katz & Earp, 2013; Katz & Jhally, 1999). All it takes to unravel this blind spot is a thought exercise: If 98 percent of perpetrators of mass violence and media-mediated violence were committed by girls and women, would that draw attention to the gendered nature of violence? What laws, policies, and practices would be enacted to address the problem?

A major step toward addressing the issue of copycat violence will involve deconstruction of media images and cultural narratives that depict boys and men who achieve power and control through violence (Naffine, 1998). This means showing media images of boys and men engaged who deal with their problems, insecurities, and rejections through prosocial behaviors. This means telling crime stories in media and digital culture in ways that show boys and men expressing empathy rather than objectification and reducing images of the bodies of mostly sexualized female victims in TV, movies, video games, and social media. And it means reducing opportunities for the economic success of media and digital culture that support this narrative.

Employ a Multipronged Approach to Reduce Media Violence Risk and Increase Resiliency: It will Take a Village

In the aftermath of virtually every act of crime and violence involving media, public reactions can be summarized into two general perspectives: 1) blame whatever media is named in the crime for playing a causal role or 2) go directly to the statement that millions of people watch, play,

From the Ethical Realm of the Real, to the Aesthetic Realm of the Hyperreal

read, and consume the particular media source and have not gone out and committed a crime as a challenge to the claims of media-crime connection. This either/or reaction to media-mediated crime deflects from the reality of the complexity of the media-crime-violence relationship and uses straw man arguments (Bushman et al., 2015) that halt action. Media violence interventions are needed in real time to responsibly respond to media-mediated violence that is increasingly occurring every day on a global level that represents a serious and significant social and public health problem (Huesmann, 2007).

The effects of violent media are more authentically approached from a risk and resilience framework that considers factors that facilitate and inhibit violent media effects (Gentile & Bushman, 2012). Unexplained variance in media effects research offers opportunity to explore individual differences such as personality traits, individual affinities, and selective attention in the media effects process (Oliver, 2002). These individual factors interact with media factors and situational/environmental and cultural influences to produce different types of criminal behavior. Demographic characteristics, criminogenic factors, relationship to media, media characteristics, and cultural-environmental factors all interact to mitigate or exacerbate the copycat effect. It is the unique interaction between these factors and the individual's relationship to media that mitigates and exacerbates the copycat effect (Helfgott, 2015). Identifying what makes the few individual edge-sitters within those millions of people who consume violent media differentially affected will help identify solutions to interrupt the copycat crime pathway.

A risk/resilience approach to understanding the copycat effect on criminal behavior provides the tool to answer the question: What can be done to minimize and/or mitigate the harmful effects of violent media and digital culture? Copycat crimes are ultimately the product of a volatile cluster of risk factors of which media and digital culture are one ingredient. Knowing that individuals high in media consumption exhibit a "reduced happy-face advantage" (Kirsh et al., 2006) and are slower to recognize happy faces and faster to recognize sad, angry faces; are more likely to infer hostile intent in the actions of others (Kirsh, 1998; Kirsh et al., 2006; Kirsh & Olczak, 2002); blur fantasy and reality; absolve feelings of guilt; and have reduced empathy (Ellison, 2012; Helfgott, 2008, 2015) and/or a range of other findings on social information processing (e.g., Anderson & Dill, 2000; Allen et al., 2018; Plante et al., 2020; Riddle et al., 2011) recognizes that social media has the effect of eroding empathy in all of us (Suciu, 2022) and offers information that can guide actions that can be taken to alter the developmental pathway of those at risk for copycat crime and/or to interrupt risk with replacement of resiliency factors to reduce the likelihood of the copycat effect. Knowing that high violent media consumption can negatively impact individuals in ways such as increasing the reduced happy face advantage and lowering empathy, as well as a litany of other negative effects such as an increase in aggressive cognition and aggressive affect, a decrease in proactive executive function, and increased impulsivity, depression, and poor-well-being (Warburton & Anderson, 2022) offers information regarding how spending large amounts of time consuming violent media may impact children, adolescents, and adults over the life course. These risk factors can be mitigated through resiliency factors such as replacing violent media content with other forms of media or reducing the amount of media consumption.

Media and digital culture have arguably more positive influences than negative. Social media companies such as Facebook have attempted to change their algorithms to prioritize "meaningful social interactions" (Jennings, 2021). Recent studies have found that video games can help boost children's intelligence (Sauce et al., 2022) and augmented reality video games such as *Pokémon Go* have been found to be associated with positive responses including friendship formation and intensification, increased positive affect, nostalgic reverie, and walking that predicted enhanced well-being (Bonus et al., 2018). Others suggest that video games are the "ultimate after-school program to reduce crime" from a routine activity perspective by keeping crime-prone adolescent boys inside playing games rather than outside committing crimes (Ferguson, 2010; Markey & Ferguson, 2017). Identifying the positive influences of media can be part of a risk-resiliency response to mitigating the harmful effects of violent media. Media can be used as a tool for education and learning, prosocial socialization, identity development, social development and social networking, satisfaction of curiosity, and management of basic needs (such as using video games and apps for health and fitness) (Warburton & Anderson, 2022). TikTok, for example, has become the most quickly downloaded app in history with over 500 million active users, 90 percent of whom use the app on a daily basis. The very nature of TikTok is imitative, which can be positive as much as it can be negative. TikTok serves as a positive source of entertainment, publicity, education and learning, and access to new opportunities (Simrin, 2020).

Criminal behavior is the product of psychological, sociological, cultural, phenomenological, and situational/ecological/routine activity factors (Helfgott, 2008). Reducing the influence of media and digital culture on criminal behavior and violence requires interrupting its negative

From the Ethical Realm of the Real, to the Aesthetic Realm of the Hyperreal 205

effects using a multipronged approach to reduce risk factors and increase resiliency factors to remove that one ingredient that sends an edge-sitter over the edge. In cases of media-mediated criminal behavior and violence, media and digital culture could be that one factor that divides the edge-sitter from the active shooter. Recognizing this does not mean that attention does not need to be directed to the many other solutions offered in the aftermath of violence such as reduced access to firearms, red flag laws, increased mental health care, and other solutions. Rather, it means recognizing that mass media and digital culture can be a strong influence for some individuals, a minor influence for others, and a risk factor that, if interrupted, can stop a copycat crime from ultimately occurring.

There are some individuals who, in addition to being influenced by media and digital culture, possess a runaway train of risk factors that may be difficult, if not impossible, to interrupt their trajectory for crime and violence. In these cases, it is even more important to understand the copycat elements that are part of the mix of risk factors. In cases where a crime pathway cannot be interrupted at the individual level, knowledge of the role of media and digital culture in the MO and signature elements of a crime can be used for investigative purposes to catch the perpetrator before a crime is committed or in cases of serial or spree crimes, after an initial crime is committed before more harm is done. Knowledge of how an individual interacts with a media (using social media to post threats and information about motives and methods through videos, narratives, manifestos, and memes and/or livestreaming performance crimes) can be of high value in law enforcement investigations and in risk and threat management so that the crime can be disrupted. Highland Park mass shooter Robert Crimo III who online called himself "Awake the Rapper," left a long digital trail of tributes to public murders and mass shootings including graphic depictions of suicide, murder, and death on social media (Collins & Ali, 2022); hate speech with references to Jews, Blacks, and Asians; and sexualized violence including posting an image of a "teenage" sex doll in his closet with a noose around her neck titled "Sophie Killed Herself" (Tacopino & Propper, 2022) dating back years (McBride, 2022).

In Crimo's case (as with Gendron in Buffalo and Ramos in Uvalde), had those around him, including the Illinois State Police who approved his firearms permit prior to the crime, conducted an analysis of his social media posts, perhaps information obtained would have alerted authorities to employ the Illinois red flag law and/or otherwise stopped Crimo from being able to purchase a firearm. Red flag laws are designed to stop individuals who are deemed to be a threat to themselves or others from obtaining firearms (Frattaroli et al., 2015; Phillips, 2022; Swanson et al., 2017). While red flag laws raise constitutional and practical issues (Larosieré & Greelee, 2021; Moran, 2020), utilizing this law in conjunction with identification of risk evident in Crimo's digital history could have interrupted the completion of the crime. However, there are considerable complications involved in the use of social media for background checks for firearms purchases that would require that law enforcement know what to look for, resources to sort through extraordinary amounts of data much of which may contain fabricated untruths, as well as legal and ethical considerations regarding the use of social network analysis and social media algorithms to predict dangerousness and flag future potential criminals (Wagstaff, 2018). This notion of using social media as a part of firearms background checks has gained increasing attention with Democratic leaders in states such as New York advancing new legislation (Associated Press, 2022).

Short of addressing the issue through laws which are far from immediate and dependent upon political processes, in the here and now, it will take a village to identify warning signs in individuals who are prone to the copycat effect. From a threat assessment perspective (Meloy et al., 2012; Meloy et al., 2015; Meloy & Hoffman, 2014; Meloy & O'Toole, 2011), involvement of families, friends, acquaintances, teachers, coworkers, employers, coaches, and community members is critical to identifying potential edge-sitters at the family dinner table, in schools and universities, at the workplace, and in public settings. The mayor of Highland Park, Nancy Rotering, told the media in the aftermath of the shooting that the shooter, Robert Crimo III, was a member of the community. His father had run against her for mayor, and she was Crimo's Cub Scout leader. In an interview with NBC's Today show, she said:

> . . . It's one of those things where you step back and you say, What happened? . . . How did somebody become this angry, this hateful to then take it out on innocent people who literally were just having a family day out. . . . He was just a little boy. . . . We, as a country, have to have a very strong conversation with ourselves. . . . I don't know how many more of these events need to occur. We've been talking about this, literally, for decades at this point. . . . And it's one of those things where you ask yourself if this reflects the values of who we are, then what does that say about us as a nation? (Teh & Snodgrass, 2022)

What happened was that many people were not paying attention to Robert Crimo III as he grew from a Cub Scout to a mass shooter.

From the Ethical Realm of the Real, to the Aesthetic Realm of the Hyperreal   207

Awareness of the copycat effect of violent media and digital culture and how technology-related risk factors interact with other risk factors for crime and violence can provide direction for families, communities, co-workers, gamers, and members of digital communities to help identify those among us who are operating under the influence of mass media and digital culture who may present a threat to themselves or others. The most knowledgeable and detailed information and intelligence about would-be copycat crime perpetrators can be found among friends and family and digital community members. If everyone, in every community, were to be aware of the risk factors and warning signs for the copycat effect on criminal behavior and violence, an opportunity to interrupt that violence may present itself. These opportunities can occur at the individual level by employing interventions for individuals who become unusually immersed in a form of media or a digital subculture; media literacy in schools, universities, and open-source education; and close parental attention to what media children are consuming and interacting with and simply knowing your own child, family members, and friends well enough to notice when something is off; at the societal/environmental/situational level by employing situational controls in environments to minimize risk in the event a person cannot be controlled (such as surveillance and security in schools), or at the cultural level by deconstructing cultural narratives that perpetuate the copycat effect on criminal behavior and violence which can be done by infusing media and digital culture with prosocial messages and narratives that show how power can be achieved and strain relieved through means other than crime and violence.

Intervention strategies need to be employed that combine media literacy with media management strategies. In an era where children are born into digital culture, it is practically difficult and potentially harmful (in terms of reducing the educational and informational advantages) to approach the issue of media violence through media and digital abstinence. In addition, studies have shown that restrictive ratings and advisories on violent media content can backfire, exerting the "forbidden fruit" effect and making the media content even more attractive, increasing the desire to interact with the media content (Arnett, 2007). Thus implementing both media literacy and media management strategies in families, schools, and communities is an important piece in mitigating the harmful effects of media violence. Strategies need to be employed on an everyday family and community level that involve practices such as altering the media-violence viewing experience through active instructive mediation and evaluative guidance (having parents and caregivers engage in conversations with children and adolescents about the violent media they are consuming), promoting media literacy by employing opportunities for critical thinking and discussion about media violence in schools, and using media productions to change violent attitudes and behaviors by showing the serious consequences of violence and/or depicting and exploring alternative ways to solve problems (Cantor & Wilson, 2003).

With the constantly evolving landscape of mass media, digital culture, in particular in the realm of social media (Patton et al., 2014), employing strategies to identify risk, build resiliency, and interrupt the pathway to copycat crime and media-mediated violence will be an ongoing challenge. Focus on singular issues whether it be mental health, firearms, or media as the sole "cause" of the problem will detract from efforts to intervene and interrupt the copycat crime pathway to crime and violence. There is no simple solution. The solution will involve committed and consistent involvement at individual, family, school, public safety, public health, law, and community levels informed by theory and research on the intersection of risk and resiliency factors for media-mediated crime and violence.

From the Ethical Realm of the Real to the Aesthetic Realm of the Hyperreal to the Digital Realm of the Unreal: What Will the Future Hold?

Concerns have been raised about "new media" since well before the advent of social media and video games (Soave, 2021). However, with the extreme pace of technological change over the past 50 years it is impossible to overlook the difference between media in 2022 in comparison with prior eras when concerns were raised about legacy media. In the landmark U.S. Supreme Court case, *Brown v. Merchants Association* (2011), Justice Scalia gave the opinion concluding that video games are protected under the First Amendment. The court noted that all literature is interactive and when it is good, it invites the user to identify with the characters and as a result, video games are protected like books and other forms of media:

> Certainly the *books* we give children to read—or read to them when they are younger—contain no shortage of gore. *Grimm's Fairy Tales*, for example, are grim indeed. As her just [desserts] for trying to poison Snow White, the wicked queen is made to dance in red hot slippers 'till she fell dead on the floor, a sad example of envy and jealousy' . . . . Cinderella's evil stepsisters have their eyes pecked out by doves . . . And Hansel and Gretel (children!) kill their captor by baking her in an oven. (*Brown v. Merchants Association*, 2011)

From the Ethical Realm of the Real, to the Aesthetic Realm of the Hyperreal 209

It is certainly true that since the beginning of time, stories about violence have been told around campfires and in books, the arts, TV, films, comic books, and radio (Black, 1991). However, what this court opinion does not address is how digital culture has expedited the speed at which violent media circulates around the world and the increasingly interactive nature of media violence in the form of video games, social media, and other forms of new media appearing every day.

When Mark Chapman shot John Lennon on December 8, 1980, and John Hinckley attempted to assassinate Ronald Reagan on March 30, 1981, a cultural shift from the "ethical realm of the real" to the "aesthetic realm of the hyperreal" (Black, 1991) contributed to the ways in which Chapman's and Hinckley's crimes were influenced by mass media. Just two years later in 1983, the Internet was born. "The Internet has turned our existence upside down" (Dentzel, 2013, p. 1) and has changed everyday life on a global scale. Ten years after that the first smartphone was invented. And today, almost everyone has a mobile device and are online everywhere, all the time (Dentzel, 2013).

We have moved on a global scale from the ethical realm of the real to the aesthetic realm of the hyperreal, and now, to the digital realm of the unreal. John Hinckley was released to full freedom after 41 years in a mental hospital for his 1981 crime. Hinckley gave his first-ever interview to CBS News saying, "It was a lifetime ago," "It was something I don't want to remember," "it was all just so traumatic" and apologized to the Reagan family and the families of the three other people he shot and to "Jodie Foster for bringing her into this."

> I have true remorse for what I did . . . I'm glad I did not succeed . . . I did not have a good heart. I was doing things a good person doesn't do. It's hard for me to relate to that person back then . . . I was not just a cold, calculating criminal in 1981. I truly believe I had a serious mental illness that was preventing me from knowing right from wrong back then . . . I've been the most scrutinized person in the entire mental health system for 41 years . . . I'm just trying to show people I'm kind of an ordinary guy. . . . I've had remorse for many years for what I did and I would, I swear, I would take it all back. (Evans, 2022)

In a subsequent interview with ABC News when asked about the Brady Law that was enacted after Hinckley's assassination attempt, named after James Brady, who was the most seriously wounded and became permanently disabled in the attack suffering a gunshot wound to the left forehead, Hinckley said, "I certainly don't think the mentally ill should have access to guns. I mean, that's kind of obvious. . . . Background checks are good and waiting periods are good. The climate of the country right now is not good. It's not good to have so many guns. There are too many guns" (Hays, 2022).

It is a bit surreal to hear one of the most historically infamous copycat criminals commenting two generations after his crime on the cultural state of affairs around mental health and gun violence. What, if anything, is helpful from a criminological perspective in hearing from Hinckley so many years after his crime? The most important thing Hinckley said in these interviews was that he was an "ordinary guy." In 1981, Hinckley was an "ordinary guy" who committed a crime "under the influence of mass media," living at a time when legacy media, the new media of the times, had moved society and culture from the "ethical realm of the real" to the "aesthetic realm of the hyperreal" (Black, 1991). Hinckley's clinical mental illness, personality disorders, and identity disturbance; his fascination with the film *Taxi Driver* and celebrity obsession with actress Jodie Foster; his need to turn himself from a Nobody to a Somebody; and his access to guns, among a range of other risk factors, provided the motivation and opportunity to ultimately commit the crime.

What has changed since 1981? Hinckley's observations are enlightening in thinking about the Hinckleys of today and what they might say 40 years in retrospect. In 1981, Hinckley was a mentally disturbed, isolated edge-sitter who was moved and motivated to act out his fantasies, bolstered by his identification with the character Travis Bickle and Bickle's cultural narrative as a male savior who channeled rejection by his political campaign worker and love interest Betsy into a violent mission to rid the world of sleaze and corruption and to protect the teenage prostitute Iris from the filth around her. Hinckley was influenced by *Taxi Driver* even though director Martin Scorsese made the decision to desaturate the blood in the violence scenes to avoid an X rating and to minimize the potential harm to audiences who were still fresh from the rise in crime, terrorist attacks, increased reports of serial killers, and the horrors of the Vietnam War (Madden, 2022). In Hinckley's time, the power of the story's male savior violent masculinity narrative combined with the TV news coverage of the John Lennon murder, and other elements of the pop culture of the times, made its way into Hinckley's cognitive script, fantasies, MO, and signature elements of his crime and ultimately inspired him to go from edge-sitter to attempted assassin.

What is different today is that we no longer live in the 1980s aesthetic realm of the hyperreal. We now live in the digital realm of the unreal. The

From the Ethical Realm of the Real, to the Aesthetic Realm of the Hyperreal

digital realm of the unreal is characterized by the "new" technology of the times—the Internet, social media, video games, and artificial intelligence. This "new" digital culture with the media and technology of the times provides endless opportunities for positive and constructive prosocial imitation and endless opportunities for negative and destructive antisocial imitation. The result is an increasingly alarming potential for violence contagion. The digital realm of the unreal is riddled with powerful cultural forces that have the potential to move "ordinary" everyones from edge-sitters to violent actors, not just a small minority of disturbed individuals. The digital realm of the unreal is composed of distinctive elements—extremely complex media loops and a fast-paced, global, and relentless tangle of real and fantasy images that are virtually impossible to navigate and/or to delineate the real from the unreal. This digital realm of the unreal has the potential, by its very nature, to increase copycat, media-mediated, and performance crime and interact with and exacerbate other violence risk factors to move many more ordinary people from edge-sitters to media-influenced violent actors than was the case in the era of legacy media.

Thus, in 1981 Hinckley was an ordinary 25-year-old with risk factors for violence at a time when the new media of the time had the power to blur the boundary between fantasy and reality in the minds of a small number of media junkies whose crimes were committed under the influence of mass media in the aesthetic realm of the hyperreal. The digital realm of the unreal has the power to affect many more people. In the digital realm of the unreal, practically everyone is a media junkie. The digital realm of the unreal saturates culture with media images of violence in ways the world has never seen before. The influence of violent media in the digital realm of the unreal goes far beyond the Hinckley-Bickle-style blurred boundary between fantasy and reality. The digital realm of the unreal makes everyone forget what's real and what's not real and has the power to make many more "ordinary" people into media violence–prone edge-sitters who ultimately go over that edge to become the copycat, media-mediated, performance criminals of today, with far fewer risk factors than Hinckley had in 1981.

The increase in fame-seeking rampage killers in the aftermath of Columbine is evidence of the stark shift in the role media and digital culture play in influencing criminal behavior and violence. Columbine has been referred to as a cultural turning point because news coverage of the event extended well beyond the local news to worldwide headlines, which brought with it the idea that perpetrating a mass shooting can bring fame and celebrity status (Allwinn et al., 2022; Cordell, 2019; Cullen, 2010).

Studies have shown that 67 percent of U.S. school shooters post-Columbine reference the Columbine killers (Larkin, 2009) and that shooters who were influenced by prior mass shootings have a higher fatality rate (Lankford & Silver, 2020).

The Columbine massacre even inspired the creation of a video game titled *Super Columbine Massacre RPG!* in which players can role-play as computer-generated images of Eric Harris and Dylan Klebold to virtually experience the actions and activities that Harris and Klebold presumably engaged in on the day of the Columbine massacre, including making preparations, getting weapons, leaving final messages, listening to Marilyn Manson music, and playing video games appearing as 16 bit as they would have in 1999, and reenacting the crime itself engaging the player in virtual decision-making about what weapons to use and what classmates to kill, accompanied with flashing and sound effects when a "character" is killed with a screen message, "Another victory for the Trench Coat Mafia!" and a bump up in skill level when more people are killed (Borchard, 2015).

The post-Columbine world in which a video game is created that allows players to identify with and reenact a real-world mass shooting and in which real-life mass shooter after mass shooter references and idolizes prior mass shooters is one of many examples of the cultural shift beyond the aesthetic realm of the hyperreal to the digital realm of the unreal. The digital realm of the unreal goes far beyond the media-mediated aesthetic depiction of violence that characterizes the aesthetic realm of the hyperreal—to the complete digital immersion in violence where it is almost impossible to distinguish where real life ends and digital life begins. In the digital realm of the unreal, digital immersion in violent media cannot be avoided by anyone. While it may be that only a small number of individuals would choose to play a game like *Super Columbine RPG!*, modern-day culture is awash in violent images are almost impossible to avoid. Stories that were once local are now global. Noncelebrities can become celebrities via social media. And crime and violence are not simply aestheticized. Real crime and violence and fictional crime and violence are psycho- and socio-digitally intertwined in a perpetually reflexive state. In this state, it is a matter of perspective as to what is real and what is unreal:

> Virtual reality, which is synonymous with absolute reality, has covered all human communities . . . it is possible to say that today cyber lives have ceased to be a virtual simulation and have turned into reality, and they are

From the Ethical Realm of the Real, to the Aesthetic Realm of the Hyperreal 213

> almost imprisoned in cyber dissociative experiences that make it possible and even normal to experience a social abdication of consciousness or communal dissociation. (Ozturk & Erdogan, 2022, p. 428)

In the digital realm of the unreal, virtual reality is synonymous with actual reality for all but the most psycho- and socio-technologically advanced.

The case of Randy Stair who murdered three co-workers in Weis Market Grocery Store and then committed suicide offers an illustration of a prototype of the media-mediated copycat perpetrator in the digital realm of the unreal. Allwinn et al. (2022) offer a retrospective psychological case study through a content analysis of Stair's preattack communications in her private journal and Twitter profile[8]—referred to as "legacy tokens" such as journals, letters, manifestos, audio files, video posts, plans of attack, and artwork. From a threat assessment perspective, understanding perpetrator motivations through legacy tokens offers deep insight into the perpetrator's identity, thought processes, and fantasy development that can aid in early detection of fame-seeking rampage killers whose crimes tend to have a higher number of casualties. What is striking about this case is the perpetrator's relationship to, and use of, digital materials in the years leading up to the attack and how these digital materials became signature elements of the crime. This case illustrates the intense immersion in digital culture that characterizes how violent media and digital culture influence criminal behavior and violence on an individual level in the current era of the digital realm of the unreal.

Randy Stair was a fame-seeking rampage shooter. Fame-seeking rampage shooters are distinct from other mass shooters because they are motivated by the desire for infamy and meet specific criteria, including 1) making direct statements about becoming famous; 2) seeking media notoriety through legacy tokens; 3) posting on media platforms before and during the crime; and 4) mentioning role models with a history of violence, including both real and fictional characters (Silva & Greene-Colozzi, 2019). Stair founded a fictional group called the "Ember's Ghost Squad" (EGS); posted on social media under the names and alter-egos of fictional characters in the EGS; was preoccupied with death and dying, depression, suicide, and gender identity; was preoccupied with weapons; and had a fascination with rampage shooters, particularly the Columbine killers, and violent fantasies and had a hatred of humanity and specific groups of people, grandiose fantasies, narcissistic traits, and fame seeking. In their analysis of the perpetrator's legacy tokens. Allwinn et al. (2022) identified themes that provide insight into the influence of media and digital culture in the perpetrator's identity and fantasy development and commission of the mass shooting. Dominant themes included:

- **Extensive Online Activity**—This included using multiple social media platforms on a daily basis, including Facebook, Twitter, and YouTube, and producing large amounts of macabre and explicit written, audio, and video content dating back 10 years prior to the crime. The online posts included a YouTube video posted the night before the attack titled "The Westborough High Massacre" that was an animated short about a rampage at a fictional high school committed by her alter-ego who was a character in EGS, and just before the attack, she uploaded a digital manifesto containing multiple files and folders via a link to Twitter with the comment, "All of these recordings and videos are essential for understanding what I did and how I did it." (p. 46)

- **Biographical History/Family Relationship**—She was born in 1992 in Pennsylvania, had a brother two years younger, lived with her family, and characterized herself as shy and said in her journals, "I felt like a nobody." She experienced mild bullying in school and stopped trying to make friends in ninth grade, She had previously worked part-time at the grocery store where she committed the crime and had gotten the job back full-time after completing college and experiencing financial concerns and conflicts with her parents. She expressed hatred for her father, who was a supermarket manager, and contempt for her mother and said she would have killed her father but she wanted them both to suffer alive.

- **Crises, Grievances, and Narcissistic Processing**—She declared herself a narcissist and said in her journal, "I love to hear myself talk on the Internet. . . . I can listen to myself for HOURS."

- **Preattack Communication Themes**—EGS played a crucial role in her thinking, and she became increasingly involved in parasocial relationships with the characters and hoped they would outlive her. She believed her true identity was that of a female ghost, identified as nonhomosexual female, wore her mom's clothes, did not tell anyone about her gender identity, and had a fixation with women saying she had fantasies about killing women, laying their corpses on top of her, and fusing bodies with them because she said "I want to become them." She said "I'm a girl who's been trapped in a man's body . . . I don't belong on this planet, nor have I ever. I need to die, and I'm taking whomever I can down with me." (p. 48)

- **Depression/Suicidal Tendencies/Preoccupation with Death and Dying**—She began to be preoccupied with death and dying between ages 12 and 13, which was the beginning of a downward spiral. She wrote in her journal, "I sit at my computer completely isolated from the world . . ." and

From the Ethical Realm of the Real, to the Aesthetic Realm of the Hyperreal 215

she longed for life after death to live on in a new body as a female ghost and a new family with EGS. She was preoccupied with death, expressed hatred for humans including those in her family and who she worked with, said she was racist, sexist, and prejudiced, and her hate speech was paired with violent fantasies.

- **Fascination with Rampage Shootings/Admiration for Columbine Killers/Violent Fantasies and Weapons**—She had a fascination with rampage killers, said she wanted to meet the Sandy Hook shooter, the Oklahoma City bomber, and the Columbine killers after death. She talked about how the Columbine killers inspired her, was an active member of the Columbine fan forum, wore t-shirts mimicking those worn by the Columbine killer Eric Harris that said "Natural Selection," and created fan art based on a photo of Klebold and Harris. She had violent fantasies, practiced target shooting, was obsessed with firearms, and on Twitter posted that she was going to the beach and was going to cause someone to drown because she always wanted to do that—to "creep below someone underwater and grab 'em."

- **Fame Seeking**—She had a desire for fame, said she was never meant to be famous while alive, said her only alternative was to go down in history for an act of violence, and wanted to inspire other copycats saying, "I hope I inspire more shootings, big and small" and "I know I'll spawn cult followers." (p. 51)

The perpetrator in this case was motivated to commit the shooting to make herself famous posthumously, like her Columbine role models, "trading unattainable fame for attainable infamy" (Allwinn et al., 2022, p. 51). She created the fantasy of the EGS to meet her need for relatedness and belonging and developed dysfunctional coping strategies, including withdrawal, preoccupation with violence, and extensive media consumption, to avoid dealing with negative emotions. The authors describe her as a "modern day narcissist" who communicated with the outside world through her fictional characters creating secondary and tertiary identities. She vacillated between desires for intimacy and distancing, failed to connect to human society, and sought relatedness to fictitious characters that would not reject her.

This case study analysis offers an illustration of a fame-seeking rampage shooter who was a copycat killer whose relationship to media and digital culture show how different media-mediated crime is in the post-Columbine era. This case shares many similarities with other copycat cases in the current era. Reality and fantasy are intertwined in complex ways in the minds of perpetrators, creating an experience of unreality that goes well beyond the aesthetic realm of hyperreality. What occurred in the personality and fantasy development of Stair that ultimately ended in mass murder suicide was in part a product of cyber-dissociation after long use of cyber identities that turned into psychodigital cyber alterpersonalities (Ozturk & Erdogan, 2022). Stair was experiencing a form of trauma-induced psychodigital dissociation that informed her thoughts, fantasy development, and inability to relate to others and to meet her own needs that was an intimately intertwined signature element of her ultimate act of murder-suicide that characterizes and illustrates how mass media and digital culture influence criminal behavior and violence on an individual level in the current era of the digital realm of the unreal. The content analysis of Stairs's online activity shows how digital trails can be used to both understand and identify risk through user-generated online content from a psychological threat assessment perspective (Allwin et al., 2022).

The digital realm of the unreal has the potential to affect spectators in ways that are not currently understood. For example, one of the most bizarre TikTok trends in recent years is the lip-syncing to Angela Simpson's confession of the 2009 murder of 46-year-old disabled man Terry Neely in Arizona (Fowler, 2021). Simpson admitted to stabbing and strangling Neely, torturing him for hours, and pulling his teeth out. After being sentenced to life in prison in 2012, she gave a televised interview in which she matter-of-factly offered a detailed account of her crimes. The interview was inspiration for the television series *Killing Eve* (Waller–Bridge, 2018–2022) (Lindsay, 2019). A video clip of her interview was uploaded to Tik Tok, and the sound of the clip went viral, used by a seemingly endless stream of women who used the sound to mimic Davis's interview using quotes from the interview in their TikTok tag lines "He told me he was a snitch" and "Oops if he wasn't," some garnering hundreds of thousands of views. While some argue that this is a harmless TikTok trend where Tik Tok users can practice and display their acting skills, and at least one actress took part in the trend comparing the experience to her acting takes, other Tik Tok users have commented on the macabre nature of the trend and the harm to victims (Fowler, 2021). Apart from the debate about the appropriateness of the use of the confession in the Tik Tok challenge, the Tik Tok mimicking of the Angela Simpson interview appears so real in so many of the videos that the Tik Tok fictional versions of the confession have the potential to become so realistic, yet so far removed, from the original confession as to create a new untruth that seems as real as, but forgetting, the actual reality.

This real, but unreal, reality is a function of this new era of the digital realm of the unreal. While it is by no means suggested here that the Angela Simpson Tik Tok challengers are potential media-mediated

From the Ethical Realm of the Real, to the Aesthetic Realm of the Hyperreal 217

edge-sitters who will be inspired to mimic Simpson's actual murder, the widespread use of a real confession to a horrific torture-murder of a disabled individual by everyday "ordinary" people who are having a little fun on Tik Tok gives pause for thinking about how media and digital culture affect everyone, not just a small minority of violence-prone individuals. The fact that the Tik Tok challengers in this example are virtually all female is another point of consideration given the association between gender and copycat crime and violence and the narrowing of the gender copycat crime gap. The new digital culture has the potential for broad cultural influence in ways that are far from understood:

> The digital communication networks of today's postmodern societies have created an ambitious, competitive, exhibitionist, discourteous, reversible, insatiable, lying and merciless mass of people focused on the culture of narcissism, and have made possible the existence of psychodigital dissociation. (Ozturk & Erdogan, 2022, p. 427)

This psychodigital dissociation and the impact it has on individuals at risk for crime and violence, and those who do not have these risk factors, have important implications for understanding the copycat effect on criminal behavior and violence.

Concluding Comments

As technology has rapidly advanced, we have moved on a global scale from the ethical realm of the real, to the aesthetic realm of the hyperreal, to the digital realm of the unreal. Mass media technology and digital culture breeds false familiarity, objectification, and disidentification of the other, a psycho- and socio-digital dissociation that intertwines fantasy and reality into a new unreality. Copycat crime exists along a continuum of influence. Mass media technology shapes MO and creates entirely new motivational influences, becoming a signature element of criminal behavior. Celebrity culture and digital culture create opportunities for everyone to become a star and for crime as performance (Lillebuen, 2012; Surette, 2015a). The notion that fame can be achieved through crime, violence, and murder as a problem-solving strategy is part of a pervasive gendered cultural script. Individuals who have risk factors for crime and violence have opportunities to derive their identity through digital communities with minimal human contact in their own physical communities, and these opportunities exacerbate the copycat effect. The digital realm of the unreal has the potential to create new forms of trauma in the form of cyber traumatization and dissociation (Ozturk & Erogan, 2022).

Copycat crime and the influence of media and digital technologies on criminal behavior is an increasingly important focus of study for the future of criminology (Helfgott, 2015; Milivojevic, 2021; Surette, 2022). On the individual level, technology shapes offender motivation and MO and identity and fantasy development. Socially and culturally, technology has changed the nature of social life, which in turn has a profound effect on the nature and dynamics of criminal behavior. Understanding the level of influence of media and digital culture on criminal behavior and violence in general and individual offenses in particular has important implications for the development of criminological theory and criminal justice practice. Future research is needed in many areas, including validation of an instrument to measure copycat crime to build on the work of Surette (2015a, 2022); development and validation of an instrument to quantify media content; continued theory and typology development; ongoing empirical study to identify and better understand individual and ecological variables predictive of media consumption patterns and individual differences in the perception of media images and identity integration; empirical research specifically focused on violent media's influence on criminal and violent behavior; further development of cultural (Ferrell et al., 2015; Hayward & Young, 2004; Ilan, 2019), visual criminology (Hayward, 2009; Young, 2014), and alternative phenomenological perspectives that build on traditional criminological theories (e.g., Polizzi, 2011); and creative methodologies such as analysis of cultural products (e.g., Young, 2009), autoethnographies (e.g., Borchard, 2015), and retrospective case studies from a risk and threat assessment perspective (e.g., Allwin et al., 2022).

How and why people commit crime and violence are constantly evolving. Understanding how technological change influences criminal behavior and violence is critical in developing policy, practice, and strategies to target copycat crime and media-mediated violence and to better understand crime in general and how it may be shaped by media and digital culture as we move into technological futures that haven't yet even been imagined. Simple fixes that focus on single risk factors such as gun violence or mental health that fail to consider the individual and cultural influence of media and digital culture omit critical information necessary to understand the nature and dynamics of criminal behavior as we move into this future. Copycat crime and the criminogenic effects of media and digital culture and approaching technology as both a risk and resiliency factor are of critical importance in the future of criminology and public safety.

APPENDIX

Copycat Crime Cases

The appendix presents a comprehensive list of copycat crimes from 1942 to 2022. Cases are drawn from scholarly literature reviews, court cases that note copycat elements, and open sources. Each case includes the media source that influenced the perpetrator, the location of the crime, the perpetrator, and a brief case description followed by a score based on Surette's scale for measuring copycat crime (Surette, 2016, 2022). The cases are organized generally by date but grouped by the media source that influenced the perpetrator. (The first appearance of a media source is immediately followed by later acts with the same influence.) Using Surette's seven-factor procedure, the crimes were assigned points for each of the following seven indicators:

- Time Order and Proximity: 1 point
- Theme Consistency: 1 point
- Scene Specificity: 2 points
- Repetitive Viewing: 1 point
- Self-Editing: 1 point
- Offender Statements: 2 points plus or minus
- Second-Party Statements: 1 point plus or minus

The total points were then divided by the potential maximum score to get the final copycat crime score ranging from 0 to 1. The case studies show the scope of copycat crime and offer a pilot scoring method to illustrate the degree to which each case is linked to media and digital content (the higher the score, the more evidence that the case is linked to media and digital content).

1942: Gordon Cummins. Influence: Jack the Ripper. London, England. Cummins murdered four women: Evelyn Hamilton (40), Evelyn Oatley (35), Margaret Lowe (43), and Doris Jouannet (32). During his time in the British Royal Air Force, he consorted with prostitutes and stole from them. He would later escalate to killing, which was triggered during World War II. Similarities to Jack the Ripper included mutilation to the bodies. His was driven by the idea that he had sexual needs that needed to be met, and he used air raids as a cover to brutally murder. [Points for theme consistency and scene specificity. Total: 3/9. Score: 0.333.]

1975–1980: Peter William Sutcliffe. Influences: Jack the Ripper. Yorkshire, England. Between 1975 and 1980, Sutcliffe murdered 13 women in England: Wilma McCann (28), Emily Jackson (42), Irene Richardson (28), Patricia Atkinson (32), Jayne MacDonald (16), Jean Jordan (20), Yvonne Pearson (21), Helen Rytka (18), Vera Millward (40), Josephine Whitaker (19), Barbara Leach (20), Marguerite Walls (47), and Jacqueline Hill (20). Sutcliffe's nickname was the Yorkshire Ripper due to his targeting women in the red-light district. Once he had captured his victims, he would strike them with a hammer, then stab them with a knife. His motive was that he was commanded by God to kill prostitutes. [Point for theme consistency. Total: 1/9. Score: 0.111.]

11/12/1966: Robert Benjamin Smith. Influences: Richard Speck and Charles Whitman; fame and television crime news. Mesa, Arizona. In the summer of 1966, stories of Speck murdering 8 women and Whitman shooting and killing 15 people broke news. After seeing the fame the two men were getting, Smith entered the Rose-Mar College of Beauty, ready to gun down someone for his 15 minutes of homicidal fame. He forced five women and two children into a back room and systematically shot them in the head, killing five of them: Joyce Sellers (27), Debbie Sellers (3), Glenda Carter (18), Mary Olsen (18), and Carol Farmer (19). After his arrest, Smith mentioned that he wanted people to know his name and know who he was. [Points for time order and proximity, repetitive viewing, and offender statements. Total: 4/9. Score: 0.444.]

1971: Unknown group of male youths. Influences: *A Clockwork Orange*. United Kingdom. The film is associated with the rape of a 17-year-old girl by a group of male youths singing "Singin' in the Rain" (mimicking a scene from the film) while dressed similarly to the characters attributed to either Stanley Kubrick's 1971 film or the 1962 Anthony Burgess novel of the same name. Kubrick pulled the film in Britain in 1972, and it wasn't re-released there until 2000. [Points for time order and proximity, theme consistency, and scene specificity. Total: 4/7.[1] Score: 0.571.]

12/7/1971–4/29/1984: Robert Hansen. Influences: *The Most Dangerous Game*. Anchorage, Alaska. During the years of 1971 to 1984 Robert Hansen, would abduct, rape, and murder prostitutes and topless dancers. Hansen would let those who submitted to his sexual fantasies live, and those who didn't were raped. They were then stripped naked and released into the wilderness, where he would hunt them. He would then take their jewelry as trophies, bury their bodies, and mark the burial sites on a map. Hansen had many similarities to the main character of the novel, General Zaroff, including being a skilled hunter and having his home loaded with animal mounts. [Points for theme consistency. Total: 1/9. Score: 0.111.]

Appendix

1/15/1974–1/18/1991: Dennis Rader. Influences: H. H. Holmes, Harvey Glatman, and Jack the Ripper. Wichita, Kansas. Rader tortured and murdered 10 people over a 30-year period while watching his own crimes play out in the media. While his motivation for murder was driven by deviant sexual fantasy, sadism, psychopathy, and narcissism, the nature of his crimes and the cat-and-mouse game he played with the media suggest that the cultural lore of the serial killer and his view that becoming a serial killer would make him a somebody greatly influenced him. His "mentors" were H. H. Holmes, Harvey Glatman, and Jack the Ripper, whose "work" he had followed and whom he had been particularly impressed with because these infamous murderers had carried out incredibly heinous acts undiscovered. [Points for time order and proximity, repetitive viewing, self-editing, and offender statements. Total: 5/9. Score: 0.556.]

4/22/1974: William Andrews and Dale Pierre. Influences: *Magnum Force*. Ogden, Utah. In the film starring Clint Eastwood there is a scene where a woman is killed by pouring drain cleaner down her throat. This was modeled by murderers William Andrews and Dale Selby Pierre in what became known as the 1974 Ogden Utah "Hi-Fi murders." The pair robbed a stereo store and during the robbery mimicked the scene in *Magnum Force* by forcing five victims (Carol Naisbitt, Michelle Ansley, Stanley Walker, Cortney Naisbitt, and Orren Walker) to drink Drano before they shot them all in the head. Two of the victims survived, including then 16-year-old Cortney Naisbitt, whose experience was depicted in the book *Victim*. [Points for time order and proximity, theme consistency, scene specificity, self-editing, and offender statements. Total: 7/9. Score: 0.778.]

9/14/1974: Group of minors. Influences: *Born Innocent*. San Francisco, California. Olivia Niemi (9) was attacked by minors at a beach. It is alleged that the group attacked Olivia and then proceeded to forcibly "artificially rape" her with a bottle. It is alleged that the assailants had seen the "artificial rape" scene in *Born Innocent* and that the scene "caused them to decide to do a similar act to a minor girl." [Points for time order and proximity and scene specificity. Total 2/7. Score: 0.285.]

6/4/1977: Ronny Zamora. Influences: *Kojak*. Miami Beach, Florida. Fifteen-year-old Zamora decided to be "Kojak" and investigate a "B&E"—pseudo-police/television parlance for "breaking and entering." Zamora claimed TV shows like *Kojak* led him to shoot his 83-year-old neighbor Elinor Haggart. [Points for time order and proximity, theme consistency, repetitive viewing, offender statements, and second-party statements. Total 6/9. Score: 0.667.]

2/28/1978: Craig Shannon. Influences: *The Mickey Mouse Club*. Georgia. A stunt on *The Mickey Mouse Club* involved rotating a BB pellet in a balloon filled with air to reproduce the sound of a tire coming off an automobile. This led Craig Shannon (11) to put a piece of lead almost twice the size of a BB into a balloon. After causing the balloon to pop, the lead impelled Shannon's eye and partially

222   *Appendix*

blinded him. Shannon tried to sue Walt Disney Productions, Inc., claiming *The Mickey Mouse Club* caused him to pull a stunt that resulted in blindness. [Points for time order and proximity, theme consistency, scene specificity, and offender statements. Total: 6/9. Score: 0.667.]

2/15/1979: Michael Barrett. Influences: *The Warriors.* Boston, Massachusetts. On his way home from work in a Boston-area ski shop, Martin Yakubowicz (16) was confronted by an intoxicated teenager returning from viewing the film *The Warriors.* The teen repeated a line from the movie: "I want you, I'm going to get you." He then fatally stabbed Yakubowicz. [Points for time order and proximity, scene specificity, and second-party statements. Total: 4/9. Score: 0.444.]

3/24/1979: Unknown perpetrator. Influences: *Boulevard Nights.* San Francisco, California. Jocelyn Vargas (15) went to the movies to watch *Boulevard Nights* at the Alhambra Theatre on Polk Street in San Francisco. After leaving the theater, Vargas and her friends were walking down the street to catch a bus when she was shot by someone. The shooter had been attracted to the Alhambra Theatre due to the showing of the violent film. [Points for time order and proximity. Total: 1/7. Score: 0.142.]

5/23/1979: No perpetrator—Suicide. Influences: *Johnny Carson's Tonight Show.* Cranston, Rhode Island. Nicholas and Shirley DeFilippo claim that their son, Nicky (13), regularly watched *The Tonight Show*, and they allege that he viewed a broadcast of the show which featured stuntman Dar Robinson "hanging" Carson as a stunt. Several hours after the broadcast, the DeFilippos found Nicky hanging from a noose in front of the television set, which still on and tuned to WJAR-TV. The DeFilippos claimed *The Tonight Show* was an unreasonably dangerous and defective product because there were inadequate warnings to viewers about imitating the stunt. [Points for time order and proximity, scene specificity, self-editing, and second-party statements. Total: 5/7. Score: 0.714.]

8/20/1979: Albert Fentress. Influences: *Deliverance.* Poughkeepsie, New York. Fentress lured Paul Masters (18) into his basement where he tied Masters up, sexually assaulted him, and mutilated his body before shooting him in the head. Fentress proceeded to cook some of Masters's body parts so he could eat them. After his arrest, Fentress said he had been inspired by the movie *Deliverance* and wrote a script for torturing and killing someone just a few days before. [Points for theme consistency, scene specificity, self-editing, and offender statements. Total: 6/9. Score: 0.667.]

1980: Veronica Lynn Compton. Influences: The Hillside Strangler. Bellingham, Washington. Compton was convicted of trying to strangle Kim Breed (26), a cocktail waitress, in a Bellingham motel so authorities would think the Hillside Strangler who killed 10 women in Los Angeles and 2 in Bellingham was still at large. Compton had said she was in love with Kenneth Bianchi, who pleaded

Appendix   223

guilty to the slayings of two college students in Bellingham and to five of the Los Angeles killings. [Points for time order and proximity, theme consistency, scene specificity, and offender statements. Total: 5/9. Score: 0.556.]

12/8/1980: Mark David Chapman. Influences: *The Catcher in the Rye*. New York City, New York. Mark David Chapman believed himself to be Holden Caulfield, the main character in the book. He murdered John Lennon (40) in 1980 after years of fixation on both Lennon and Caulfield. He is believed to have murdered Lennon because he viewed him as a "phony," a term Caulfield used to refer to people. [Points for scene specificity and offender statements. Total: 3/9. Score: 0.333.]

7/18/1989: Robert Bardo. Influences: *The Catcher in the Rye,* Arthur Richard Johnson. Los Angeles, California. After stalking Rebecca Schaeffer (21) for three years, Bardo traveled to California from his home in Arizona, went to Schaeffer's home with a copy of *The Catcher in the Rye* in his back pocket, shot her point-blank in the chest, and then tossed the book onto the roof of another building as if he believed it was evidence after he fled the scene. Bardo was also said to have been emulating a similar crime in which actress Theresa Saldana was stabbed at her doorstep in 1982 by an obsessed fan named Arthur Richard Johnson who hired a private investigator to find her home address. [Points for time order and proximity, theme consistency, scene specificity, repetitive viewing, self-editing, and offender statements. Total: 8/9. Score: 0.889.]

3/30/1981: John Hinckley Jr. Influences: *Taxi Driver*, Mark David Chapman. Washington, D.C. Hinckley was found not guilty by reason of insanity for the attempted assassination of President Ronald Reagan (70). White House press secretary James Brady (41), Secret Service agent Tim McCarthy (32), and police officer Thomas Delahanty (45) were also injured in the attack. Hinckley's attorneys argued he was fixated on the film, its characters, and actors. Hinckley's obsession with the film was evidence that he had lost the distinction between reality and fiction. Hinckley was said to have used *Taxi Driver* as the primary script and John Lennon's murder by Mark David Chapman as a secondary script in his assassination attempt. The film was played for jurors at his trial. [Points for time order and proximity, theme consistency, scene specificity, and offender statements. Total: 5/9. Score: 0.556.]

3/25/1982: Arthur Jackson. Influences: *I Wanna Hold Your Hand, Defiance*. West Hollywood, California. Jackson became obsessed with actress Theresa Saldana after seeing her in *I Wanna Hold Your Hand* and *Defiance*. Jackson entered the United States illegally and enlisted a private detective to track Saldana down. The subsequent criminal investigation revealed that he wrote in his diary that he was on a "divine mission" to win Ms. Saldana by "sending her into eternity." After he attacked Saldana he spent 10 years in prison and during that time wrote Saldana a letter saying he regretted using a knife in the attack because "a gun

224   *Appendix*

would have given me a better chance of reunion with you in heaven." [Points for time order and proximity and offender statements. Total: 3/9. Score: 0.333.]

10/26/1984: John McCollum. Influences: Ozzy Osbourne, "Suicide Solution." Indio, California. John McCollum (19) shot himself in the head while listening to the Ozzy Osbourne album *Blizzard of Oz*. His parents, blaming the suggestive lyrics of Osbourne's "Suicide Solution" instead of John's emotional problems and alcohol abuse, filed suit against CBS records and Osbourne himself. It was their belief that the record company was negligent in the dissemination of Osbourne's music because the lyrics vividly encouraged suicide, thus aiding and abetting John's tragic end. [Points for time order and proximity, theme consistency, scene specificity, and second-party statements. Total: 4/7. Score: 0.571.]

6/5/1986: Stella Nickell. Influences: Chicago Tylenol Murders. Auburn, Washington. Nickell tampered with five bottles of Excedrin by putting cyanide in the capsules. She then placed them on store shelves in the Seattle area. Six days later, Susan Snow (40) took one of these capsules and died instantly. After her death was reported in the news, Nickell called police to tell them that she thought her husband Bruce Nickell (52) had also been poisoned. Stella did this to claim the life insurance policy she took out on her husband. [Points for time order and proximity, theme consistency, and second-party statements. Total: 3/9. Score: 0.333.]

4/26/1988: Jeffrey Lyne Cox. Influences: *Rage*. San Gabriel, California. Cox entered a classroom with a semiautomatic rifle and held 60 people hostage for half an hour before he was subdued by a heroic classmate named Ruben Ortega. One of Cox's friends told the press that his inspiration for the shooting was a lesser-known Stephen King novel titled *Rage*. [Points for theme consistency, scene specificity, and second-party statements. Total: 4/9. Score: 0.444.]

1989: Dustin Pierce. Influences: *Rage*. McKee, Kentucky. Pierce entered his classroom with a gun but did not harm any teachers. He held 11 of his friends hostages, demanding to speak to his father, whom he hadn't seen since he was four years old. Pierce let the hostages go, unlike in the book. The teenager was apprehended, but the authorities strongly believed the nature of the crime was clearly inspired by the book *Rage*. A copy of the book with detailed notes and pencil underlines was later found in Pierce's room. [Points for time order and proximity, theme consistency, scene specificity, repetitive watching, and self-editing. Total: 5/9. Score: 0.556.]

1/18/1993: Scott Pennington. Influences: *Rage*. Grayson, Kentucky. Pennington brought a gun to school and shot his English teacher, Deanna McDavid (49), during class. She had recently given him a mediocre grade on an essay he wrote about *Rage*. Pennington also killed a school custodian, Marvin Hicks (52). [Points for time order and proximity and theme consistency. Total: 2/9. Score: 0.222.]

Appendix 225

10/24/1988: Mark Branch. Influences: *Friday the 13th*. Greenfield, Massachusetts. Branch actualized the urban legend of a small-town killer inspired by horror movies. Dressed as Jason from the *Friday the 13th* film series, he brutally killed Sharon Gregory (18). Police and the media quickly blamed the tragedy on Branch's obsession with horror movies. [Points for theme consistency and repetitive viewing. Total: 2/9. Score: 0.222.]

September 2004: Daniel Gonzalez. Influences: *Friday the 13th, A Nightmare on Elm Street*. London and Sussex, England. Gonzalez referred to the murders as one of the "best things" he did in his life and bragged about how similar he was to Freddy Kreuger in a series of letters he wrote addressing his alter-ego "Zippy" Gonzalez. Gonzalez often wore a hockey mask, copying Jason in the film *Friday the 13th*. During his killing spree, the 25-year-old murdered Marie Harding (73), Kevin Molloy (46), Derek Robinson (75), and Jean Robinson (60) and injured two others. [Points for theme consistency and offender statements. Total: 3/9. Score: 0.333.]

1/15/1989: Carolyn Warmus. Influences: *Fatal Attraction*. Greenburgh, New York. Similar to the plot of *Fatal Attraction*, Warmus became obsessed with her married colleague, Paul Soloman. The two began an affair, and Soloman told Warmus that he would be divorcing his wife once their teenage daughter Betty graduated high school. Warmus became impatient and wanted Betty to be out of the way. Carolyn pistol-whipped and shot Betty nine times. [Points for time order and proximity. Total: 1/9. Score: 0.111.]

8/20/1989: Lyle and Erik Menendez. Influences: *Billionaire Boys Club*. Beverly Hills, California. Lyle and Erik Menendez shot and killed their parents, Jose (45) and Kitty (48), in their Beverly Hills home. They then drove up to Mulholland Drive, where they dumped their shotguns before going to a local movie theater to buy tickets as an alibi. When the brothers returned home, Lyle called 911 and cried, "Somebody killed my parents!" Just like one of the killers in *Billionaire Boys Club*, Erik Menendez bought a Jeep and wore a Rolex watch. [Points for time order and proximity, theme consistency, and offender statements. Total: 4/9. Score: 0.444.]

March 1990–August 1990: James Cushing. Influences: *The Legend of Lizzie Borden*. Seattle, Washington. Cushing broke into many people's homes to murder them but was unsuccessful. Later, Geneva McDonald (63) was discovered by police brutally chopped by an axe inside of her own home. Cushing took inspiration from watching a movie about Lizzie Borden, who was accused of killing her father and stepmother with an axe. [Points for time order and proximity, theme consistency, scene specificity, and second-party statements. Total: 5/9. Score: 0.556.]

1990–1993: Heriberto Seda. Influences: The Zodiac Killer. Brooklyn, New York. Twenty years after the original Zodiac Killer, Zodiac copycat Seda began his own murder spree in New York City. He murdered victims based on their Zodiac sign using a knife and a homemade pistol. Seda sent cryptic letters to the police in hopes of creating the illusion of the Zodiac Killer having returned, which he admitted in his confession to police. Seda began his copycat spree in November 1989 and over the course of the next three years, Seda murdered three New Yorkers and attempted to kill five more. He was sentenced to 238 years in prison. [Points for theme consistency, scene specificity, self-editing, and offender statements. Total: 6/9. Score: 0.667.]

3/25/1991: Nathaniel White. Influences: *RoboCop 2*. Middletown, New York. The film influenced White, who committed multiple murders in New York. White claimed to have been inspired by the movie *RoboCop 2*, saying: "The first girl I killed was from a 'RoboCop' movie . . . I seen him cut somebody's throat then take the knife and slit down the chest to the stomach and left the body in a certain position. With the first person I killed I did exactly what I saw in the movie." He also claimed that he committed the murders because "voices" told him to. [Points for time order and consistency, scene specificity, self-editing, and offender statements. Total: 6/9. Score: 0.667.]

10/16/1991: George Pierre Hennard. Influences: *The Fisher King*. Killeen, Texas. Hennard drove his 1987 Ford Ranger pickup through the front window of a Luby's Cafeteria in Killeen. Emerging from his truck, Hennard began to open fire on the restaurant's patrons and staff. Over the course of about 15 minutes, Hennard shot and killed 23 people, wounding another 27. Shortly after police arrived and exchanged fire with the gunman, Hennard died by suicide. Police later found a movie ticket stub for *The Fisher King*. [Points for time order and proximity and theme consistency. Total: 2/7. Score: 0.285.]

4/11/1992: Ronald Ray Howard. Influences: Tupac. Port Lavaca, Texas. Listening to a dubbed copy of *2Pacalypse Now*, Howard was pulled over while driving a stolen vehicle. Once Trooper Bill Davidson approached the vehicle, Howard shot him in the neck, killing him. After confessing to the crime, Howard's attorney tried to argue that Tupac's song "Soulja's Story," which describes a traffic stop that ends with a gunshot, got into Howard's head. [Points for time order and proximity and theme consistency. Total: 2/9. Score: 0.222.]

12/19/1992: Jean Powell, Anthony Dudson, Clifford Hayes, Jeffrey Leigh, Bernadette McNeilly, and Glyn Powell. Influences: *Child's Play 3*. Manchester, England. Suzanne Capper (16) died from injuries sustained from being deliberately lit on fire on December 14. Capper had befriended the residents of a home that housed an array of people with criminal backgrounds. Suzanne would often be abused but wanted human contact as well as to be loved. She was lured on the night of December 7 by a group of six friends who tortured her by shaving all her hair and beating her with numerous objects like buckets and wooden spoons. While her torture continued in horrific ways, a soundtrack of Chucky

Appendix 227

played on loop, repeating the words, "I'm Chucky, wanna play?" and rave music. [Points for time order and proximity, theme consistency, and scene specificity. Total: 4/9. Score: 0.444.]

2/12/1993: Robert Thompson and Jon Venables. Influences: *Child's Play 3*. Bootle, United Kingdom. Two-year-old James Bulger was brutally tortured and murdered by two 10-year-olds, Robert Thompson and Jon Venables. Bulger and his mother, Denise Bulger, were at the New Stand Shopping Centre when James Bulger was abducted by the two young boys. The boys took Bulger to nearby railroad tracks where they beat him and shoved paint into his wounds. The two boys then laid the body on the railroad tracks where it was later severed by a train. Prior to this horrific crime, it was reported that the boys may have watched the film *Child's Play 3,* a film that is said to have a scene where the main villain, Chucky, is killed when he is beaten and paint is shoved in his face, very similar to what happened to James Bulger. [Points for time order and proximity, theme consistency, and scene specificity. Total: 4/9. Score: 0.444.]

3/3/1993: James Perry. Influences: *Hit Man: A Technical Manual for Independent Contractors*. Montgomery County, Maryland. After purchasing a how-to manual titled *Hit-Man*, Lawrence Horn hired James Perry to murder his wife Mildred (43), son Trevor (8), and the family's overnight nurse Janice Saunders (38). Horn had been in debt and tried to claim $2 million in life insurance money. Perry followed *Hit Man*'s 130 pages of detailed factual instructions on how to murder and become a professional killer. Perry used the book's instructions on soliciting a client and arranging for a contract murder in his solicitation of and negotiation with Lawrence Horn. [Points for time order and proximity, theme consistency, scene specificity, repetitive viewing, self-editing, and second-party statements. Total: 7/9. Score: 0.778.]

10/6/1993: Austin Messner. Influences: *Beavis and Butt-head*. Moraine, Ohio. Two-year-old Jessica Matthews was killed in a fire by her five-year-old brother Austin Messner, who started the fire. Austin's mother, Jessica Burk, told investigators her son had become fascinated with fire after watching a *Beavis and Butt-head* segment in which the characters set things on fire. Burk told reporters that Austin had become fascinated with fire after watching the show and she had caught him several times before playing with lighters. [Points for time order and proximity, theme consistency, repetitive viewing, and second-party statements. Total: 4/9. Score: 0.444.]

10/4/1994: Florence Rey and Audry Maupin. Influences: *Natural Born Killers*. Paris, France. Four murders were committed by 19-year-old Florence Rey and 22-year-old boyfriend Audry Maupin, who were dubbed "France's Natural Born Killers." The two were involved in a shoot-out followed by a high-speed car chase. The incident involved homicide, hostage taking, and violent robbery. Amadou Diallo (49), Thierry Maymard (30), Laurent Gérard (25), and Guy Jacob

228 *Appendix*

(37) were killed. [Points for time order and proximity and theme consistency. Total: 2/9. Score: 0.222.]

3/7/1995: Benjamin Darras and Sarah Edmondson. Influences: *Natural Born Killers*. Hernando, Mississippi and Ponchatoula, Louisiana. Edmondson, a woman from a prominent family referred to by many as the "Kennedys of Oklahoma," along with her boyfriend Darras, went on a crime spree inspired by the movie, *Natural Born Killers*. Edmondson and Darras, both 18, met in Tahlequah and quickly became inseparable. The two spent the night of March 5, 1995, at Edmondson's family cabin in Welling, where they took LSD and repeatedly watched *Natural Born Killers*. The film is about a couple who go on a multistate killing spree. William Savage (58) and Patsy Byers (35) were killed by the couple. [Points for time order and proximity, theme consistency, repetitive viewing, and offender statements. Total: 5/9. Score: 0.556.]

11/15/1995: Jamie Rouse. Influences: *Natural Born Killers*, death metal. Rouse walked into Richland High School in Tennessee and shot two teachers and a student. Teacher Carolyn Foster and student Diane Collins were killed and Carolyn Yancy was injured. Rouse later said about *NBK* that "it made the killing look easy and fun" (Leung, 2004). [Points for time order and proximity, theme consistency, offender statements, and second-party statements. Total: 4/9. Score: 0.444.]

3/3/1998: Veronique Herbert and Sebastien Paindavoine. Influences: *Natural Born Killers*. Gournay-sur-Marne, Paris. Herbert and Paindavoine were found guilty of murdering 16-year-old Abdeladim Gahbiche. Herbert and Paindavoine were obsessed with *Natural Born Killers*, and it was widely reported that they lured Gahbiche to his death with promises of sex. Unlike the Edmondson-Darras and Rey-Maupin cases, Herbert was said to be the dominant half of this couple and was jailed for 15 years while Paindavoine received 12. [Points for time order and proximity, theme consistency, scene specificity, repetitive viewing, and offender statements. Total: 7/9. Score: 0.778.]

4/23/2006: Jasmine Richardson and Jeremy Allan Steinke. Influences: *Natural Born Killers*. Alberta, Canada. Richardson orchestrated the murder of her parents Debra Richardson (48) and Mark Richardson (42) along with her boyfriend Steinke. Richardson was only 12 years old and Steinke was 23. The night before the assault, Richardson and Steinke ritualistically watched their favorite film, *Natural Born Killers*. Steinke, disguised by a mask and brandishing a large knife, snuck into the family's basement, where he stabbed Debra Richardson 12 times. Marc Richardson rushed to his wife's aid and brawled with Steinke. The younger man ultimately dominated, stabbing Richardson 24 times, including nine deep wounds to the back. Jasmine then joined Steinke as they slipped up to her eight-year-old brother Jacob's bedroom, where he was asleep. Jasmine stabbed her brother four times, and Jeremy slit the boy's throat from ear to ear. [Points for time order and proximity, theme consistency, and repetitive viewing. Total: 3/9. Score: 0.333.]

Appendix 229

11/18/1994: Daniel Sterling. Influences: *Interview with a Vampire*. San Francisco, California. Sterling and his girlfriend, Lisa Stellwagen (23), went to see the film *Interview with a Vampire*. After returning from the movie the couple went to sleep. Stellwagen reports that when she woke up the following morning Sterling was staring at her. When she asked him what was wrong, Sterling told her, "I want to kill you and drink your blood . . . tonight you are going to die." Sterling stabbed Stellwagen multiple times and began drinking her blood. Sterling was found guilty of attempted murder. His defense team tried to argue that Sterling was suffering from a manic episode and was heavily influenced by *Interview with a Vampire*. [Points for time order and proximity, theme consistency, scene specificity, and offender statements. Total: 6/9. Score: 0.667.]

4/19/1995: Timothy McVeigh. Influences: *Red Dawn, The Turner Diaries*. Oklahoma City, Oklahoma. McVeigh planned a strike on the U.S. government and targeted the Alfred Murrah Federal Building in Oklahoma City. At 9:02 a.m., a bomb exploded from a truck which McVeigh had planted, killing 168[2] people and injuring over 800. Although disagreeing with the book's racial and genocidal ideas, the protagonist in *The Turner Diaries* destroys the FBI office in Washington, D.C., with a bomb in a truck. McVeigh's favorite movie, *Red Dawn*, is about the United States being invaded by Soviet and Cuban forces, and civilians begin a guerrilla war against them. McVeigh had rented the film four times prior to the attack and had similar attributes to the main characters in the film. [Points for time order and proximity, theme consistency, and repetitive viewing. Total: 3/9. Score: 0.333.]

11/26/1995: Thomas Malik, Vincent Ellerbe, and James Irons. Influences: *Money Train*. Brooklyn, New York. The film includes a scene where a man douses a subway token booth with a flammable liquid, lights a match, and demands money. When the clerk inside tries to hand him a bag of cash, the man drops the match through the coin slot at the clerk saying that he isn't in it for the money and sets the booth on fire. In the film, the clerk escapes before the booth explodes. Three days after the film opened, two Brooklyn men (19-year-old Malik and 18-year-old Ellerbe) squirted gasoline into a subway booth, setting 50-year-old clerk Harry Kaufman on fire. Kaufman subsequently died two weeks later after succumbing to burns over 80 percent of his body. In the two weeks following the film's opening, a total of eight such subway booth attacks occurred. [Points for time order and proximity, theme consistency, and scene specificity. Total: 4/9. Score: 0.444.]

July 1995: Royce Casey, Joseph Fiorella, and Jacob Delashmutt. Influences: Slayer. Arroyo Grande, California. The night of the murder, Elyse Pahler (15) snuck out of her home to meet the boys after being promised narcotics. The three boys strangled and stabbed Pahler several times before her death. Casey's confession to the authorities mentioned how they wanted to sacrifice Pahler to the devil to help make their band go professional. Pahler's family sued Slayer, a metal band, as they believed the teens were influenced by the band's lyrics. [Points for theme consistency. Total: 1/9. Score: 0.111.]

230   *Appendix*

2/2/1996: Barry Dale Loukaitis. Influences: *Jeremy* music video by Pearl Jam, *Natural Born Killers, Rage*. Moses Lake, Washington. Loukaitis armed himself with a rifle and two handguns, walked into his fifth-period algebra class, and held the class hostage at gunpoint before he was subdued by gym teacher Jonathan Lane. Manual Vela Jr. (14), Arnie Fritz (14), and Leona Caires (49) were killed. According to Terry Loukaitis, one of his son's favorite movies was Oliver Stone's *Natural Born Killers*, a satire in which mass murderers are glorified by the media. Loukaitis had a dubious connection to *Rage*. After he began killing, he told his classmates "This sure beats algebra, doesn't it?" which some believe is similar to something the protagonist in *Rage* says after killing his algebra teacher: "This sure beats panty raids." [Points for time order and proximity, theme consistency, scene specificity, repetitive viewing, self-editing, and second-party statements. Total: 7/9. Score: 0.778.]

4/28/1996: Martin Bryant. Influences: *Child's Play 2*. Port Arthur, Tasmania. Bryant entered the restaurant at the Port Arthur Historic Site, removed a Colt AR-15 rifle from his bag, and began shooting. After killing 22 people in rapid succession, Bryant left the restaurant for the parking lot, where he continued his shooting spree, killing the drivers of two tour buses, some of their passengers, and a mother and her two small children, among others. On his way out of the parking lot, he shot four people in a BMW and drove the car to a nearby gas station, where he shot one woman and took a man hostage, before driving back to the Seascape guesthouse. After an 18-hour stand-off with police, Bryant set the guesthouse on fire, ran outside, and was captured. [Points for theme consistency and second-party statements. Total: 2/9. Score: 0.222.]

5/2/1996: Mechele Linehan and John Carlin. Influences: *The Last Seduction*. Anchorage, Alaska. In May 1996 Kent Leppink, who worked as a fisherman, was shot and killed in the Alaskan wilderness. His fiancé at the time, Linehan, was suspected of the murder along with his former roommate, Carlin. Linehan worked as an exotic dancer in the mid-1990s when she met Leppink. After knowing each other a short while, Leppink proposed and soon Linehan would say yes to three men, having a total of three fiancés. Linehan was believed to be out for money by having a million-dollar insurance policy. Before Leppink died he sent his parents a letter that laid out how to solve his murder. Linehan and Carlin were convicted of murder in 2007, but it was reversed on appeal. [Points for time order and proximity, theme consistency, and scene specificity. Total: 4/9. Score: 0.444.]

7/31/1996: Virginia Kay, Amber Wood, Marica Thomas, Patricia Rosander, and Tiffany Sullivan. Influences: *Set It Off*. Aberdeen, Washington. The film influenced a bank robbery that was committed by two women and three teenagers. The group watched the film prior to the robbery, and witnesses said they counted off exactly like the characters in the film. While one robber held a watch and called out the time in five-second intervals, the others focused on robbing the

Appendix 231

bank. [Points for time order and proximity, theme consistency, scene specificity, and repetitive viewing. Total: 5/9. Score: 0.556.]

2/19/1997: Evan Ramsey. Influences: *Doom*. Bethel, Arkansas. Ramsey killed 15-year-old Josh Palacios, a popular student, as well as the school's principal, Ron Edwards. After wounding several other students, Ramsey then threatened to kill himself, but he ultimately surrendered to the police instead. Ramsey told the authorities that he thought he could shoot, and no one would die, like in the *Doom* video game. [Points for time order and proximity, theme consistency, repetitive viewing, and offender statements. Total: 5/9. Score: 0.556.]

5/6/1997: Marshal Applewhite (cult leader). Influences: Heaven's Gate mass suicide. Rancho Santa Fe, California. Two former members of Heaven's Gate, Wayne Cooke (54) and Charlie Humphreys (54), later died in copycat suicides. The suicide was accomplished by ingestion of phenobarbital mixed with vodka, along with plastic bags secured around their heads to induce asphyxiation. They were found lying in their own bunk beds, with their faces and torsos covered by a square, purple cloth. Cooke's wife, Suzanne Sylvia Cooke, was one of the 39 cult members who swallowed barbiturates and vodka, dying in the belief they would then join a spaceship trailing the Hale-Bopp comet. [Points for time order and proximity, theme consistency, scene specificity, and self-editing. Total: 4/7. Score: 0.571.]

11/22/1997: Yancy Salazar. Influences: *Mortal Kombat*. South Norwalk, Connecticut. Noah Wilson (13) was killed by his friend after being stabbed in the chest with a kitchen knife. While on his way to ask permission to see the *Mortal Kombat* movie, Wilson and his friend Salazar found a knife in the street. They then began to playfully reenact moves from the *Mortal Kombat* game using the knife. Copying Cyrax's finishing move, Salazar stabbed Wilson in the chest. It is believed that the video game influenced Yancy, as he was addicted to it and believed he was the character Cyrax. [Points for time order and proximity, scene specificity, and second-party statements. Total: 4/9. Score: 0.444.]

12/1/1997: Michael Carneal. Influences: *Basketball Diaries, Rage, Quake, Doom*. West Paducah, Kentucky. When he arrived at school, Carneal walked toward a before-school prayer meeting that was just finished, inserted earplugs into his ears, loaded a .22, and then methodically shot eight students from 10 feet. Nicole Hadley (14), Jessica James (17), and Kayce Steger (15) were killed and five other students were wounded. Ben Strong, one of the students, convinced Carneal to drop his weapon and held him down until the school's principal took the gunman away. According to the litigants, Carneal had learned how to shoot accurately from playing the video games *Quake* and *Doom*. Later, he claimed that he was inspired by the movie *The Basketball Diaries* and the book *Rage* by Stephen King. [Points for time order and proximity, theme consistency, offender statements, and second-party statements. Total: 5/9. Score: 0.556.]

232   *Appendix*

1/13/1998: Mario Padilla and Samuel Ramirez. Influences: *Scream*. Lynwood, California. Mario Padilla attacked his mom, Gina Castillo (37), from behind, while Ramirez held her down. They stabbed her 45 times using at least four different knives. The two teenagers admitted being obsessed with the film *Scream*, with one of them saying the slayings in the film were "cool." He reportedly told a friend on the way back from school, "It was the perfect way to kill somebody." The two boys had allegedly discussed real killings as they planned to copy the ones from the 1996 film. They even planned to buy costumes and voice distortion boxes to imitate in detail the killings in the film and spoke about going on a "killing spree." [Points for time order and proximity, theme consistency, scene specificity, repetitive viewing, offender statements, and second-party statements. Total: 8/9. Score: 0.889.]

1/17/1999: Daniel Gill and Robert Fuller. Influences: *Scream*. Harrogate, North Yorkshire. Ashley Murrey (13) was lured to a secluded spot by his then best friend Gill, 14, and fellow student Fuller, 15, where the intention was to sneak into a local birdwatching hut. Instead, the boys attacked him, stabbing him 18 times with a screwdriver and a knife, before wrapping him in a binbag and leaving him for dead. It was two days before he was found, barely alive, by an old man walking his dog. They had watched violent horror films and were dubbed the "Scream" attackers after it emerged that they had been inspired by watching the horror film *Scream*. [Points for time order and proximity and theme consistency. Total: 2/9. Score: 0.222.]

11/9/2001: Thierry Jaradin. Influences: *Scream*. Gerpinnes, Belgium. Alisson Cambier (15) dropped by Jaradin's house, a few doors away from her own, to exchange some videotapes. Jaradin made amorous advances towards her, but when they were rejected, his retribution was brutal. Excusing himself for a few seconds, he stepped into an adjacent room where his Scream costume was waiting, together with two enormous kitchen knives. He stabbed her 30 times, ripping open her left side. He then lowered her blood-soaked corpse onto his bed, slipped a rose into one of her hands and telephoned his father and a colleague to confess. He later told police that his crime had been premeditated and had been motivated by the film series. [Points for theme consistency and offender statements. Total: 3/9. Score: 0.333.]

9/22/2006: Brian Draper and Torey Adamcik. Influences: *Scream*. Pocatello, Idaho. Cassie Stoddart (16) was house-sitting with her boyfriend Matt Beckham for her cousin. The couple had invited their friends, Draper and Adamcik, to hang out. The four teenagers hung out for two hours before Draper and Adamcik left. Beckham had been picked up by his mother shortly after. Re-entering the home through a door they left unlocked, wearing "horror-movie type masks" and armed with knives, both Draper and Adamcik went upstairs. While upstairs, Draper slammed a door, hoping to scare Cassie and draw her towards the noise. When she did not enter the room they were hiding in, they walked into the

Appendix   233

living room. Cassie stated, "Who is that? I'll kick your ass" as she approached them. They stabbed Cassie 30 times and then drove to a rural area with the intention of hiding the evidence. They placed the weapons, clothing, and other evidence in a bag and set it on fire. They documented before and after the crime on a Sony Tape recorder. [Points for theme consistency and offender statements. Total: 3/9. Score: 0.333.]

April 1999: David Copeland. Influences: Centennial Olympic Park Bombing, *The Turner Diaries*. London, England. Copeland bombed three communities of minorities. The first bomb exploded on April 17, 1999, injuring 48 people in an area of South London with many Black residents. On April 24, a second bomb injured 13 people in Brick Lane, home to one of London's largest Bangladeshi communities. The third bomb went off on April 30, at a pub in the heart of London's gay community, killing Andrea Dykes (27), John Light (32), and Nik Moore (31) and injuring 79 people, several of whom later had limbs amputated. Copeland told authorities that he was inspired by the race war novel, *The Turner Diaries*, and wanted to mimic American bomber Eric Rudolph. [Points for time order and proximity, theme consistency, and offender statements. Total: 4/9. Score: 0.444.]

4/20/1999: Eric Harris and Dylan Klebold. Influences: *Doom/Doom II, Basketball Diaries, Natural Born Killers*, Marilyn Manson. Littleton, Colorado. Klebold and Harris went on a shooting spree at Columbine High School, killing 13 people and wounding more than 20 others before committing suicide. Both of the boys dressed in trench coats and moved their way into the school while shooting students. They intended for two duffel bags containing propane bombs to explode in the school cafeteria, but they did not. This was the start of what is known as the Columbine Effect. [Points for time order and proximity, theme consistency, scene specificity, and self-editing. Total: 5/7. Score: 0.714.]

4/28/1999: Todd Cameron Smith. Influences: Columbine High School shooting. Taber, Alberta, Canada. Fourteen-year-old Smith, wearing a blue trench coat, pulled out a sawed-off .22-caliber rifle and fired four shots in the hallway of W. R. Myers High School. The former student fatally shot student Jason Lang (17) at point-blank range. He also shot Shane Christmas (17) and just missed another student. This all happened just eight days after the Columbine massacre, which Smith was obsessed with watching on the news. [Points for time order and proximity, theme consistency, scene specificity, and repetitive viewing. Total: 4/9. Score: 0.444.]

8/30/2006: Alvaro Castillo. Influences: Columbine High School shooting. Orange County, North Carolina. Castillo killed his father, Rafael Castillo, before driving to Orange High School. When he arrived at the school, he set off cherry bombs and fired at students outside before his gun jammed and he was detained by a school deputy sheriff and a retired highway patrol officer. While entering a patrol car, Castillo stated "Columbine, remember Columbine," referring to the attack at Columbine High School in Colorado in 1999. He sent an email to the principal of Columbine High School saying "Dear Principal, in a few hours you will probably hear about a school shooting in North Carolina. I am responsible for it. I remember Columbine. It is time the world remembered it. I am sorry. Goodbye." Castillo made video tapes discussing abuse at the hands of his father and his obsession with Columbine. He bought the same guns that Harris and Klebold used in their shootings, dressed in similar fashion to them, convinced a family member to drive him to Littleton, Colorado, and named his gun (Reb) similar to what Eric Harris named his gun. [Points for theme consistency, scene specificity, offender statements, and second-party statements. Total: 6/9. Score: 0.667.]

4/16/2007: Seung-Hui Cho. Influences: Columbine High School shooting. Blacksburg, Virginia. Cho (23) killed two people in a dorm room, returned to his own dorm room where he rearmed and left a note, then went to a classroom building on the other side of campus. There, he killed 30 more people in four classrooms before shooting himself in the head. A package sent to NBC News headquarters contained a 23-page written statement, 28 video clips, and 43 photos. In the statement he refers to "martyrs like Eric and Dylan"—a reference to the teenage killers in the Columbine High massacre. [Points for offender statements. Total: 2/9. Score: 0.222.]

12/14/2012: Adam Lanza. Influences: Columbine High School shooting. Newtown, Connecticut. Before gunning down 20 children and six adults with a semiautomatic rifle at Sandy Hook Elementary School, Lanza shot dead his own mother at the family home. She had bought him the weapons used in the rampage. The attack began when Lanza forced his way into the locked school by shooting through a window near the front doors. Most of the deceased were killed in two classrooms. Lanza ended the shooting by turning the rifle on himself. Later, police found Lanza's posts on a forum about the video game *Super Columbine Massacre RPG!*, which lets players relive the 1999 Columbine High School massacre from the viewpoint of the killers. Lanza also played a video game called *School Shooter* in which the player guns down students from a first-person view. [Points for time order and proximity and theme consistency. Total: 2/7. Score: 0.285.]

6/5/2014: Aaron Ybarra. Influences: Columbine High School shooting. Seattle, Washington. Ybarra walked onto Seattle Pacific University's campus with a shotgun and a hunting knife. He shot and killed 19-year-old Paul Lee and injured Sarah Williams (22) and Thomas Fowler (24). The shooting ended when a school safety monitor tackled the gunman, doused him with pepper spray, and disarmed him. Ybarra said he heard Satan, God, and Eric Harris, one of two students who took part in a shooting in Columbine High School in 1999. [Points for offender statements. Total: 2/9. Score: 0.222.]

Appendix 235

6/8/2017: Randy Stair. Influences: Columbine High School shooting. Eaton Township, Pennsylvania. Stair trapped and killed three of his co-workers, Victoria Brong (26), Brian Hayes (47), and Terry Sterling (63), at a closed Weis Market. When police arrived, Stair had already killed the three workers and then herself. Police found a paper trail going back to 1999 where Stair referenced and praised the Columbine shooting. A post that was made during the time of the shooting also referenced the shooters from Columbine. Stair made an animated video of a school shooting and wrote "Weis Markets is officially Columbine High School." Using a journal and filming videos, Stair planned out the massacre and stated that he would have gone back to his old high school to commit the shoot, but it had been demolished the year after he graduated. [Points for time order and proximity, theme consistency, scene specificity, and offender statements. Total: 6/9. Score: 0.667.]

2/14/2018: Nikolas Cruz. Influences: School shooters. Parkland, Florida. Cruz made threats and was expelled from school, bragged about killing animals, posed with guns on social media, and went to a mental health clinic seeking treatment before taking the rifle he had legally bought to Stoneman Douglas High School and killing 17 people. Upon entering the school, Cruz opened fire on staff and students before fleeing the scene on foot. Cruz stated he wanted to be the next mass murderer and was inspired by prior school shooters, including Elliot Rodger, Adam Lanza, Seung Hui-Cho, Eric Harris, and Dylan Klebold. [Points for offender statements. Total: 2/9. Score: 0.222.]

5/18/2018: Dimitrios Pagourtzis. Influences: Columbine High School shooting. Santa Fe, Texas. Pagourtzis walked into Santa Fe High School wearing a trench coat and a "Born to Kill" t-shirt and began shooting, killing two teachers and eight classmates and injuring thirteen more students. Taking inspiration from the Columbine shooting, Pagourtzis wore a trench coat during the shooting and brought explosives into the school. He had planned to commit suicide but did not follow through. [Points for theme consistency, scene specificity, and offender statements. Total: 5/9. Score: 0.556.]

11/13/1999: Mark McKeefrey, Allan Bentley, and Graham Neary. Influences: *Reservoir Dogs*. Litherland, England. While watching the film *Reservoir Dogs* and drinking a bottle of vodka, the three boys planned to murder Michael Moss (15). Later, Moss was lured to a playground where he was beaten and stabbed to death. The attack lasted nearly two hours, and Moss was stripped naked then sustained 10 broken ribs, multiple fractures to the bones in his face, two of his vertebrae had been separated due to being kicked, was stabbed 49 times, and received various cuts on his body from a broken vodka bottle. The attack gained notoriety due to the similarity of the attack to a scene from *Reservoir Dogs*. The boys had even sung the song "Stuck in the Middle with You" while attempting to cut Moss's ear off, an exact scene from the film. [Points for time order and proximity, theme consistency, and scene specificity. Total: 4/9. Score: 0.444.]

236   *Appendix*

4/26/1999: Barry George. Influences: Celebrities. London, England. Jill Dando (37) was shot in the head at close range at her doorstep. George, a media obsessed celebrity stalker who had a history of obsession with a number of celebrities (including Princess Diana and Freddie Mercury), was eventually convicted of the murder but later acquitted on appeal and the killer remains unknown. [Points for time order and proximity and repetitive viewing. Total: 2/9. Score: 0.222.]

May 1998, June 1999: Jeremy Dyer. Influences: Barry George. Maidstone, England. Sarah Lockett (32), a news reporter for Meridian Television, was stalked by Jeremy Dyer, a fan who sent her over 80 letters from 1998 to 1999 and was sentenced to prison for two years for harassment. The letters included numerous references to the well-publicized celebrity murder of BBC news reporter Jill Dando. Dyer used the Dando murder to threaten his victim and to validate and reinforce his own stalking behaviors. [Points for time order and proximity, theme consistency, repetitive viewing, offender statements, and second-party statements. Total: 6/9. Score: 0.667.]

3/20/2000: Janice Orndoff. Influences: *Primal Fear.* Catharpin, Virginia. Inspired by the movie *Primal Fear,* Janice Orndorff staged the murder of her husband, Goering Orndorff (47). On the night of their anniversary, Goering told Janice he was planning on filing for divorce. Mid-conversation, Janice went upstairs and grabbed a revolver before returning and shooting Goering four times. Shocked by her actions, Janice began hysterically crying and planted a knife and a base-ball bat on Goering's body. Janice called her lawyer for help then proceeded to call the authorities stating she shot her husband in self-defense. [Points for time order and proximity and theme consistency. Total: 2/9. Score: 0.222.]

3/9/2001: Armin Meiwes. Influences: *Hannibal.* Rotenburg, Germany. Forty-three-year-old Bernd Jürgen Brandes responded to an advertisement posted online by Meiwes looking for a willing victim to be slaughtered and eaten. Mei-wes chopped Brandes up into multiple pieces and kept parts of the body in his freezer to eat over the course of 10 months. Meiwes recorded the entire slaugh-ter. With the release of the 2001 movie *Hannibal,* many chatrooms were created for people to talk about the idea of cannibals. In one of these chatrooms, Meiwes went into detail about his experience and mentioned how he was looking for another victim. [Points for time order and proximity. Total: 1/9. Score: 0.111.]

February 2002–October 2002: John Allen Muhammad and Lee Boyd Malvo. Influences: *The Matrix.* Washington, D.C., Maryland, and Virginia. On Octo-ber 5, 2002, the duo began what became a full-scale spree of random shootings across Virginia, Maryland, and Washington, D.C. Malvo and Muhammad killed multiple people in sniper attacks in the Washington, D.C., area over a three-week period. Malvo, then just a teen, told FBI agents that *The Matrix* holds the key to understanding him. "Free yourself of the matrix," he wrote in his jail cell, *The Washington Post* reported in 2003. "You are a slave to the matrix 'control." His attorneys, too, planned to include the movie's ideas in their insanity defense.

Appendix 237

[Points for time order and proximity, theme consistency, and offender statements. Total: 4/9. Score: 0.444.]

2002: Tonda Lynn Ansley. Influences: *The Matrix*. Hamilton, Ohio. Ansley shot and killed her landlord and employer, Sherry Lee Corbet, and claimed she didn't think she was committing murder because this wasn't reality. After her arrest, she told the police, "They commit a lot of crimes in *The Matrix*." Ansley was found innocent by reason of insanity. [Points for time order and proximity, theme consistency, and offender statements. Total: 4/9. Score: 0.444.]

2/17/2003: Joshua Cooke. Influences: *The Matrix*. Fairfax, Virginia. On Monday, February 17, Cooke went up to his room after eating dinner with his parents. "I just kinda looked over at my *Matrix* poster," he says, "and then I looked over at my gun." The 19-year-old wore combat boots and a black jacket like Neo, the hero of the 1999 movie and its sequels. He filled his pockets with shotgun shells. Then he picked up the 12-gauge he'd bought because it looked like the one in the poster of his favorite movie. Joshua Cooke then marched downstairs to kill both of his adoptive parents, Paul C. Cooke (51) and Margaret Ruffin Cooke (56). [Points for time order and proximity, theme consistency, scene specificity, repetitive viewing, and offender statements. Total: 7/9. Score: 0.778.]

2003: Vadim Mieseges. Influences: *The Matrix*. San Francisco, California. A San Francisco State University student allegedly confessed to killing his landlady, Ella Wong, chopping up her body and leaving the pieces around the city. Mieseges was arrested at a mall after allegedly acting strangely and threatening shoppers. Taken to a police station, Mieseges became lucid and "blurted out" that he had killed his landlady and led authorities to the body parts in Golden Gate Park, San Francisco. Police acted on the advice of the suspect and found a human torso stuffed in a trash bin in Golden Gate Park. Police who had interviewed Mieseges mentioned how he made a reference to being sucked into the matrix. [Points for time order and proximity and offender statements. Total: 3/9. Score: 0.333.]

5/30/2002: Jarrod Dale Majors. Influences: *On Deadly Ground*. Bedford, Iowa. Majors had become obsessed with Hollie Peckham who lived across the street. When no one was home, Majors entered the home wearing a ski mask, gloves, a large knife, and a roll of duct tape on his waist band and held a rifle with a plastic soda bottle taped to the barrel to act as a silencer. Once he entered the home, Majors hid inside the closet of the master bedroom. Once Hollie Peckham (31) and her husband Jamie Peckham (32) returned, Majors emerged from the closet and attacked Hollie. After she ran out of the house to get a neighbor, Jamie restrained Majors until the police arrived. [Points for theme consistency and scene specificity. Total: 2/9. Score: 0.222.]

12/11/2002: Allan Menzies. Influences: *Queen of the Damned, The Vampire Chronicles, Blood and Gold* by Anne Rice. West Lothian, Scotland. Menzies was so obsessed with the film *Queen of the Damned* that he killed his friend Thomas Mckendrick (21), drank his blood, ate part of his head, and buried him in a shallow grave. Menzies thought that just like in the movie, the gruesome act would help him achieve immortality. [Points for time order and proximity, theme consistency, scene specificity, and offender statements. Total: 5/9. Score: 0.556.]

2/10/2003: Leon Wiley, Joe Ralls, Demarcus Ralls, Jhomari Sutton, Deonte Donald, Dorsey Colbert. Influences: *Grand Theft Auto III*. Oakland, California. According to reports, the gang got high and played video games during the day. Their favorite was *Grand Theft Auto III*, in which players win points for committing violent crimes. They called themselves the "Nut Cases" and roamed the city in an old Buick, looking for targets at random, robbing dozens and killing Joseph Mabry (36), Douglas Ware (19), Keith Macki (14), and Jerry Duckworth (24). [Points for time order and proximity, theme consistency, and repetitive viewing. Total: 3/9. Score: 0.333.]

6/7/2003: Devin Moore/Thompson. Influences: *Grand Theft Auto: Vice City*. Fayette, Alabama. Moore/Thompson allegedly played the game for hours before stealing a car and gunning down two police officers, Arnold Strickland (55) and James Crump (40), and 911 dispatcher Leslie Mealer (38). When captured he said "Life is like a video game. Everybody's got to die some time." At trial, it was revealed that he was a compulsive violent video game player who suffered from childhood abuse–related posttraumatic stress disorder. Moore/Thompson's attorneys argued the "*GTA* defense"—that he lost touch with reality and was acting out the virtual violence in *Grand Theft Auto*. Despite his attorney's efforts, the *GTA* defense was unsuccessful, and Moore/Thompson was sentenced to death in 2005. [Points for time order and proximity, theme consistency, scene specificity, repetitive viewing, and offender statements. Total: 7/9. Score: 0.778.]

6/30/2003: Luke Mitchell. Influences: Marilyn Manson, The Black Dahlia case. Easthouses, Scotland. Mitchell had invited Jodi Jones (14) over and when she did not return home later that night, her parents went looking for her. Mitchell had joined Jodi's parents in the search for her. During their search, Mitchell led them to the body of Jones, stating that their dog had found her body. Her injuries were severe and included being bound, beaten, and stabbed before and after her death. Days after the murder, Mitchell had purchased a Marilyn Manson CD and DVD. When police inspected Mitchell's bedroom, they found jars of his own urine and a knife pouch with the satanic numbers 666, the initials J. J., and the dates of Jodi's birth and death. Another similarity found between Marilyn Manson and Jones's murder was the similarities between the state of Jones's body and a painting done by Manson. [Points for time order and proximity, theme consistency, and scene specificity. Total: 4/9. Score: 0.444.]

8/10/2003–8/14/2003: Shawn Lester. Influences: Washington, D.C. sniper attacks. Charleston, West Virginia. Before the one-year anniversary of the

Appendix 239

Washington, D.C. sniper attacks, Lester went on a four-day killing spree using a sniper rifle to shoot three of his victims in the head, killing them. The victims were Jeanne Patton (31), Okey Meadows Jr. (26), and Gary Carrier (44). [Points for time order and proximity and theme consistency. Total: 2/9. Score: 0.222.]

2003–2004: Charles McCoy, Jr. Influences: Washington, D.C. sniper Attacks. Columbus, Ohio. Over the course of five months in 2003 and 2004, McCoy admitted to using a sniper to shoot 23 cars on a busy highway. After shooting at a vehicle on November 25, 2003, McCoy struck and killed Gail Knisley (62). [Points for time order and proximity and theme consistency. Total: 2/9. Score: 0.222.]

2/3/2004: Michael Hernandez. Influences: *American Psycho, Silence of the Lambs.* Miami, Florida. Hernandez was sentenced to life in prison after he killed 14-year-old Jaime Gough at Southwood Middle School. Hernandez stabbed Gough more than 40 times in the school bathroom before hiding the knife in his backpack and going to class. Hernandez identified with the serial killers in movies including *American Psycho* and *The Silence of the Lambs*, adopting some of their behaviors as he pursued a plan to become a serial killer himself. Hernandez believed God agreed with him. After his arrest, Hernandez expected God to give him special powers and help him escape from jail. [Points for time order and proximity, theme consistency, and offender statements. Total: 4/9. Score: 0.444.]

3/2/2004: Matt Baker. Influences: *Casino.* Las Vegas, Nevada. After watching the movie *Casino* multiple times, Baker decided to take a shotgun and shoot Jared Whaley (17) in the chest and in the head. After this, Baker dug a shallow grave and buried Whaley wrapped in green plastic trash bags. Police report that Whaley copied in style a murder plot from the mob film and constantly would quote the film. [Points for time order and proximity, theme consistency, scene specificity, and repetitive viewing. Total: 5/9. Score: 0.556.]

3/21/2005: Jeffrey Weise. Influences: *Elephant*, Columbine High School shooting. Red Lake, Minnesota. Weise shot and killed his grandfather and his grandfather's girlfriend before driving to Red Lake Senior High. Weise entered the school, killing the security guard and four others and wounding three. Weise allegedly asked a student if he believed in God before shooting him. Exiting the classroom, Weise shot four more students before engaging in a shootout with the police. Weise entered an empty classroom and committed suicide. Weise was a huge fan of the film *Elephant* which was believed to have influenced him into committing the crime. Seventeen days prior to the crime, Weise had watched the film and fast-forwarded to the parts of the film where the attacks were being planned and carried out. [Points for time order and proximity, theme consistency, scene specificity, and self-editing. Total: 5/7. Score: 0.714.]

August–September 2006: Derek Brown. Influences: Jack the Ripper. East London, England. Derek Brown, a 47-year-old father of seven, followed in the footsteps of Jack the Ripper before being caught and sentenced to 30 years in prison. Despite neither of the bodies being found, Brown was convicted of murdering two women, Xiao Mei Guo (29) and Bonnie Berrett (24), in 2008. Brown picked his victims from the Whitechapel area of East London, where Jack the Ripper had carried out his five murders 120 years prior. Police believe he chose the Whitechapel area so that he would be compared to Jack the Ripper. Brown read up on local killers in a book containing information about the "Yorkshire Ripper" and other local "greats." Blood evidence was found throughout his home, with the highest concentration of blood stains found in the bathroom where the women were dismembered in the bathtub. Police believe he was on his way to becoming a serial killer, and after he was caught, they linked him to six unsolved sexual assaults. [Points for theme consistency, scene specificity, and repetitive viewing. Total: 4/9. Score: 0.444.]

9/13/2006: Kimveer Gill. Influences: Devin Moore/Thompson, Columbine High School shooting, *Super Columbine Massacre RPG, Postal.* Gill went on a shooting rampage at Dawson College in Montreal, Canada, killing one person (18-year-old Anastasia DeSousa) and injuring 19 others. The day before the shooting he posted photos of himself posing with a rifle, a hunting knife, and a black trench coat and wrote in a post, "Life is like a video game, you gotta die sometime" (which was what Devin Moore/Thompson said after committing his *GTA* copycat crime in 2003). [Points for time/order and proximity, theme consistency, scene specificity (1 point out of 2 possible), repetitive viewing, self-editing, offender statements. Total: 5/9 (2 points subtracted because ended in death). Score: 0.555.]

10/2/2006: Charles Carl Roberts IV. Influences: Duane Morrison. Lancaster, Pennsylvania. On September 27, 2006, Duane Morrison entered a classroom in Colorado, made the boys leave and the girls line up, sexually assaulted two, and killed one before killing himself. Five days later on October 2nd, 2006, Charles Carl Roberts IV, who worked as a milk truck driver, armed himself and entered an Amish schoolhouse, ordering the boys and pregnant women to leave. State police arrived on scene within minutes and began negotiations. However, he would end up shooting 10 girls, killing 5, and then killing himself. The attack was planned, and Roberts armed himself with not only guns with ammunition but also wood and other items to barricade himself in the schoolhouse. He wrote letters and called his wife during the attack and blamed his past actions on why he committed this crime. [Points for time order and proximity, theme consistency, scene specificity, repetitive viewing, and second-party statements. Total: 6/7. Score: 0.857.]

2/18/2008: Wayne Forrester. Influences: Facebook. New Addington, United Kingdom. Emma Forrester (34) had kicked her husband, Wayne Forrester, out of their marital home and had posted on Facebook that she was single and was

Appendix   241

ready to date new men. This infuriated Wayne, making him drive to their home intoxicated on alcohol and cocaine. Wayne broke through a bolted door and stabbed Emma multiple times with a kitchen knife and a meat cleaver. [Points for time order and proximity and offender statements. Total: 3/9. Score: 0.333.]

6/24/2008: Dylan Laird, Stephen Attard, Samuel Philip, Brandon Cruz, Gurnoor Singh, Jaspreet Singh. Influences: *Grand Theft Auto IV.* Long Island, New York. The group of teenagers decided they were going to go out to commit robberies and imitate the lead character, Nico Belic, in the particularly violent video game *Grand Theft Auto IV.* Later, the police found three victims—a supermarket employee who was severely beaten, a woman they tried to carjack, and a man whose car was bashed in. The group also broke into many garages to steal bats and crowbars. [Points for time order and proximity, theme consistency, and offender statements. Total: 4/9. Score: 0.444.]

9/21/2013: Zachary Burgess. Influences: *Grand Theft Auto IV.* Baton Rouge, Louisiana. A college lacrosse player was arrested for allegedly stealing a truck, kidnapping a woman, and smashing into nine cars before telling a police officer he wanted to see "what it was really like to play the video game *Grand Theft Auto.*" [Points for time order and proximity, theme consistency, and offender statements. Total: 4/9. Score: 0.444.]

2008: Olga Louniakova. Influences: *Wedding Crashers.* Seymour, Connecticut. The movie *Wedding Crashers* was the blueprint for Olga Louniakova's poisoning of one of her teachers at the Oxford Academy of Hair Design. Louniakova apparently meant to poison another student and was charged with reckless endangerment and threatening. She was given two years' probation and was killed two years later in a bizarre murder-suicide. [Points for time order and proximity, theme consistency, and scene specificity. Total: 4/9. Score: 0.444.]

October 2011: Luciana Reichel. Influences: *Wedding Crashers.* Madison, Wisconsin. Student Luciana Reichel attempted to prank her roommate Brianna Charapata (20) by dripping Visine solution into her water bottle on several occasions. Charapata's doctor was unable to diagnose her nausea, diarrhea, loss of appetite, and fatigue. When police confronted Reichel about her actions, she confessed and explained that she got the idea from the 2005 comedy *Wedding Crashers.* In the movie, Owen Wilson's character pulls a similar stunt, putting eye drops into a glass of wine belonging to rival Bradley Cooper, causing him to become ill. [Points for theme consistency, scene specificity, and offender statements. Total: 5/9. Score: 0.556.]

3/1/2008: Erin Caffey, Bobbi Johnson, Charlie Wilkinson, and Charles Waid. Influences: *Fear.* Alba, Texas. Due to the family's disapproval of Erin Caffey's boyfriend, Charlie Wilkinson, two young men, Johnson and Waid, burst into the Caffey home and embarked on a killing spree. Penny Caffey (27), Matthew

242 Appendix

Caffey (13), and Tyler Caffey (8) were brutally murdered. Terry Caffey (41) suffered multiple gunshot wounds but was able to drag himself out of the house before it was engulfed in an arson fire. [Points for theme consistency. Total: 1/9. Score: 0.111.]

10/10/2008: Mark Andrew Twitchell. Influences: *Dexter*. Edmonton, Canada. Twitchell lured Johnny Altinger (38) in a garage pretending to be a woman online. The garage was set up like a "kill room" much like a scene from the TV series *Dexter*, which was Twitchell's favorite TV show. Twitchell ambushed him with a butcher knife and a heavy pipe. He bludgeoned Altinger with the pipe and then stabbed him to death. Twitchell then dismembered him and attempted to burn his remains but when this was unsuccessful, he dumped his limbs and organs in a sewer. After the murder, he wrote: "This story is based on true events. The names and events were altered slightly to protect the guilty. This is the story of my progression into becoming a serial killer." [Points for time order and proximity, theme consistency, scene specificity, and offender statements. Total: 7/9. Score: 0.778.]

11/28/2009: Andrew Conley. Influences: *Dexter*. Rising Sun, Indiana. As his mother and adoptive father were working late, Andrew was tasked with watching his brother Connor Conley (10) that night. After multiple attempts to drop his brother off with his grandmother and uncle, the boys returned home. Once at home, the boys began to wrestle. Andrew choked his brother in a headlock, causing Connor to pass out and bleed from the nose and mouth. Andrew then dragged his brother's body into the kitchen and placed a plastic bag over Connor's head, choking him for about 20 minutes. Andrew dragged his brother to the trunk of his car, slammed Connor's head on the concrete multiple times, then drove to his girlfriend's house to watch a movie. Once leaving his girlfriend's house, he drove to a middle school and left his brother's body there covered with sticks and vegetation. During the investigation, Andrew told authorities that he had fantasized about killing people since he was in the eighth grade and that he has told his girlfriend that he wanted to be like Dexter. [Points for time order and proximity, theme consistency, repetitive viewing, offender statements, and second-party statements. Total: 6/9. Score: 0.667.]

7/16/2013: Mark Howe. Influences: *Dexter*. Leicester, England. Howe repeatedly stabbed his mother, Katrina Wardle (48), in the face, mouth, neck, chest, and arms before leaving her to bleed to death on her bedroom floor. He used a photograph of Dexter Morgan with a blood-splattered face as his own Facebook profile picture and had searched "Dexter's kill knife" on the Internet in the run-up to the killing. [Points for time order and proximity and theme consistency. Total: 2/9. Score: 0.222.]

1/24/2014: Steven Miles. Influences: *Dexter*. Surrey, England. Miles stabbed Elizabeth Thomas (17) to death before cutting up her body with saws in his bedroom. Miles had a fascination with horror movies and had wanted to copy the

Appendix 243

actions of Dexter, the main character in an American TV series about a police forensics officer who is also a serial killer. [Points for time order and proximity, theme consistency, and scene specificity. Total: 3/9. Score: 0.333.]

April 2009: Phillip Haynes Markoff. Influences: Craigslist. Boston, Massachusetts. Markoff went on a week-long crime spree. During the spree, Markoff robbed one woman, Trisha Leffler (26), and killed Julissa Brisman (29). Markoff chose Craigslist as his weapon for committing his robberies. This crime is not a copycat crime; however, it can be considered a media-mediated crime on the low end of the continuum because Markoff used an online site to commit robbery and murder. [Points for time order and proximity. Total: 1/9. Score: 0.111.]

5/25/2009: Kyle Shaw. Influences: *Fight Club*. Manhattan, New York. Shaw was arrested and accused of orchestrating an attack on a Starbucks store in New York. Shaw was charged with arson, criminal possession of a weapon, and criminal mischief in the bombing of a Starbucks. The teen created his own fight club in which boys started fights in locations across the city. Shaw then told a friend to "watch the news over Memorial Day" because he was about to launch his own version of Project Mayhem. Police say Shaw picked Starbucks because it was targeted in the movie. Investigators found homemade bomb materials, a copy of *Fight Club,* and a newspaper clipping about the attack at Shaw's home. [Points for theme consistency, scene specificity, and second-party statements. Total: 4/9. Score: 0.444.]

3/8/2009: Christopher Lanum and Patsy Ann Marie Montowski. Influences: *The Dark Knight Rises*. Forst Eustis, Virginia. The morning of the crime, Lanum cleaned his knives and told his girlfriend, Patsy Ann Marie Montowski, that he was "preparing for war." Although he had told her that before, this time he was dressing the part, putting on a Joker costume he previously wore for Halloween. After allegedly slashing Mitchell Stone's throat and shocking him repeatedly with a stun gun, Lanum fled with Montowski in her minivan with a 12-gauge shotgun, several knives, and a bloody razor. Hours later, after a slow-speed police chase through Shenandoah National Park, Lanum was shot dead. Montowski was charged with being an accessory after the fact to Lanum's alleged assault on Stone. [Points for time order and proximity and theme consistency. Total: 2/7. Score: 0.285.]

7/20/2012: James Holmes. Influences: *The Dark Knight Rises*. Aurora, Colorado. Holmes had purchased a ticket to the premiere of *The Dark Knight Rises* before slipping out and propping an emergency exit open. About 30 minutes into the movie, Holmes re-entered the movie auditorium through the emergency exit and detonated multiple smoke bombs before he unloaded four weapons full of ammunition into the unsuspecting crowd of hundreds of attendees. Holmes told arresting officers that he was "The Joker," referring to the villain in the second installment of the Batman movie trilogy, *The Dark Knight*. [Points for time order and proximity and offender statements. Total: 3/9. Score: 0.333.]

3/20/2009: John and Noor, surnames unknown. Influences: *Saw*. Salt Lake City, Utah. John, 15, and Noor, 14, were charged in suburban Salt Lake City, Utah, as juveniles with three counts of conspiracy to commit aggravated kidnapping after telling police they planned to model the killings on the torture scenes in the horror blockbuster *Saw*. The two teenagers had planned to hurt a female student, the school's police officer, and a third intended victim, also female. [Points for time order and proximity, theme consistency, scene specificity, and offender statements. Total: 6/9. Score: 0.667.]

11/20/2010: Matthew Milat and Cohen Klein. Influences: Ivan Milat. New South Wales, Australia. Milat, who is the nephew of the backpack murderer Ivan Milat, idolized his killer uncle and went on to commit murder in the very same Belangalo state forest where Ivan committed his crimes. Celebrating 17-year-old David Auchterlonia's birthday, the group of four boys went to the Belangalo woods to smoke cannabis. After arriving in the woods, they parked the car alongside the trees, with David sitting in the front seat rolling their joints. Matthew got out of the car and walked to the back near the trunk with Cohen. Chase and David remained sitting in the car until Matthew called David to come to the back of the car. When he did, he was immediately struck in the stomach with an ax that Matthew had stashed away in the trunk. While this was happening, Cohen Klein had pulled out a mobile phone and began to record everything instead of intervening. [Points for time order and proximity, theme consistency, scene specificity, and offender statements. Total: 6/9. Score: 0.667.]

2010–2017: Bruce McArthur. Influences: "The Lawnmower Man." Ontario and Toronto, Canada. In Stephen King's macabre short story "The Lawnmower Man," a sex-crazed landscaper murders and dismembers the suburban homeowner who hires him to cut his overgrown lawn. Taking inspiration from this, McArthur dismembered his victims and hid their remains in planters. McArthur may have also buried them in the lawns he tended for his clients. [Points for theme consistency and scene specificity. Total: 2/9. Score: 0.222.]

2/24/2010, 2/14/2012: Akeem Monsalvatge, Edward Byam, and Derrick Dunkley. Influences: *The Town*. Queens, New York. In 2010, the three perpetrators stole over $40,000 from a Pay-O-Matic after gaining entry through the roof. They wore hooded sweatshirts and cloth masks over their faces. In 2012, they robbed another Pay-o-Matic wearing New York City Police Department jackets, badges, and masks that concealed their identities and made them appear to be three white men. [Points for time order and proximity, theme consistency, and scene specificity. Total: 4/9. Score: 0.444.]

5/29/2011: Navahcia Edwards and Lyndon Germel. Influences: *The Town*. Palos Heights, Illinois. Edwards robbed a bank in an attempt to pay back more than $20,000 that she had previously stolen just a few months earlier from a Chase bank where she had worked as a teller. Edwards robbed the bank with her boyfriend, Germel, who testified against her at trial. They forced the two bank

Appendix 245

employees on duty to the vault area, where they were ordered at gunpoint to open the vault. The robbers then placed $120,000 of bank funds into a small gym bag that they had brought with them. The couple then tied up both bank employees with zip ties before fleeing the area in a waiting vehicle. [Points for time order and proximity and theme consistency. Total: 2/9. Score: 0.222.]

4/24/2011: Daniel Bartlam. Influences: *Saw, Coronation Street, Nightmare on Elm Street, Evil Dead.* Nottingham, England. After having an argument with his mother, Jacqueline Bartlam (47), Daniel Bartlam killed his mother in her sleep. Daniel rolled his mother onto the floor and surrounded her with scraps of newspaper. He then poured petrol over the body and set it alight. Daniel told his younger brother about the fire, grabbed the family dog, and ran out of the house. Along with the hammer, police also found violent scenes from popular films, including *Coronation Street,* on his computer. Police also found a document on Daniel's computer where he had written a story featuring a character, named Daniel, who murdered his mother. Daniel was fascinated by fictional violence and gore and enjoyed adult-rated video games and movies, including *Nightmare on Elm Street* and *Evil Dead.* [Points for time order and proximity, theme consistency, scene specificity, and repetitive viewing. Total: 5/9. Score: 0.556.]

5/28/2011: Marcin Kasprzak. Influences: *Kill Bill Volume 2.* Huddersfield, United Kingdom. Kasprzak shot Michelina Lewandowska (27) twice with a 300,000-volt taser-style gun and then bound and gagged her with tape. He later forced her into a cardboard box and drove her into the woods on the outskirts of Huddersfield, where he buried the box in a shallow grave. Michelina escaped using her engagement ring to cut the tape binding her ankles and the box. [Points for theme consistency and scene specificity. Total: 3/9. Score: 0.333.]

7/22/2011: Anders Breivik. Influences: *Call of Duty: Modern Warfare 2.* Oslo and Utoya, Norway. Breivik detonated a fertilizer bomb in downtown Oslo, killing eight people. He then went on a shooting rampage at a summer camp on the island of Utoya, killing 69 people, most of them teenagers. Breivik practiced his aim in the video game *Call of Duty.* [Points for time order and proximity, theme consistency, repetitive viewing, offender statements. Total: 6/9. Score: 0.667.]

3/28/2012: Matthew Tinling. Influences: *Saw 6.* West London, England. Tinling had watched *Saw 6* on DVD while living at a homeless hotel. After watching the film, Tinling proceeded to break into a neighboring room belonging to Richard Hamilton and stabbed him 17 times. Matthew then tried to sever Hamilton's spinal cord in a "savage and prolonged" murder. Tinling wanted to get his PIN number and withdraw £240 to buy crack cocaine. [Points for Time order and proximity, theme consistency, and scene specificity. Total: 4/9. Score: 0.444.]

5/25/2012: Eric Clinton Kirk Newman (aka Luka Mognotta). Influences: Celebrity status, *Basic Instinct.* Quebec, Canada. On May 25, 2012, an 11-minute video titled "1 Lunatic 1 Ice Pick" was uploaded to Bestgore.com, a now-defunct

Canadian shock site that made available highly violent real-life news, photos, and videos. The video depicted a naked male tied to a bedpost who was being stabbed repeatedly with an ice pick and a kitchen knife by someone whose face was not visible. The video showed the dismembering of the man and acts of necrophilia performed on the corpse. Magnotta tied Jun Lin's hands to a bed post with a white string and straddled Jun Lin exactly like the murder scene in *Basic Instinct*. Magnotta claimed a man named "Manny" was the person behind the murder; however, Manny was a figment of Magnotta's imagination and used the name "Manny" after Catherine's former fiancé Manny in *Basic Instinct*. [Points for theme consistency and scene specificity. Total: 3/9. Score: 0.333.]

5/31/2012, 7/22/2021: Tyler Benson. Influences: Ted Bundy. Chattanooga, Tennessee. Benson had told police he had been reading about serial killer Ted Bundy and "wanted to be like him." Tyler Benson tried to rob a prostitute and began beating her on the head with a hammer. About 10 years later, Benson picked up another prostitute and took her to his home, keeping her captive for 18 hours. Benson drugged and violently raped her repeatedly until the victim was able to escape. [Points for theme consistency, scene specificity, and offender statements. Total: 4/9. Score: 0.444.]

7/6/2012: Sheila Eddy and Rachel Shoaf. Influences: *Heathers*. Starcity, West Virginia. Skylar Neese's two best friends, Eddy and Shoaf, lured her out of her bedroom that night, drove to Pennsylvania, and stabbed her to death. Shoaf told police they had stabbed Skylar because they did not like her and did not want to be friends with her anymore. [Points for theme consistency. Total: 1/9. Score: 0.111.]

8/30/2012: Gary George. Influences: *The Loved Ones*. Chester, England. *The Loved Ones* was among George's favorite films, and prosecutors have speculated that it may have been what inspired him to kill one of his best friends, Andrew Nall (53). Mimicking scenes from *The Loved Ones*, George carved symbols into Nall's chest and poured salt into the fresh wounds. A clear substance was found on Nall's face, which was assumed to have been a cleaning product poured directly into Nall's eyes. Finally, George stabbed his best friend a total of 49 times until he left him in a pool of blood in his bedroom. Nall was alive while George performed many of these horrific acts on him. [Points for time order and proximity, theme consistency, and scene specificity. Total: 4/9. Score: 0.444.]

10/3/2012: Jake Evans. Influences: *Halloween*. Annetta, Texas. In a written confession after his arrest, Evans admitted he was inspired by the film's opening scene where Myers kills his family. Evans watched the movie about three times a week before deciding to kill his victims, Mallory Evans (15) and Jamie Evans (48). Originally, Evans wanted to stab his mother and sister using his father's folding knife but did not want to cause them pain. After pausing the movie and throwing the disk away in the trash, Evans shot his sister and mother multiple

Appendix 247

times. [Points for time order and proximity, theme consistency, scene specificity, repetitive viewing, and offender statements. Total: 7/9. Score: 0.778.]

September 2012–July 2013: Michael Madison. Influences: Anthony Sowell. Cuyahoga County, Ohio. On July 19, 2013, police responded to reports of a foul odor coming from a garage leased to Madison and discovered a decomposing body lying inside. Two more bodies were found the following day—one in a backyard and the other in the basement of a vacant house. The bodies of Angela Deskins (38), Shetisha Sheeley (28), and Shirdella Terry (18) were found 100 yards (91 m) to 200 yards (180 m) apart and were each wrapped in plastic bags. After obtaining a search warrant, police entered Madison's apartment and found more evidence of decomposition. After Michael Madison's arrest, he professed an admiration for Anthony Sowell, a Cleveland serial killer convicted in 2011 and sentenced to death for the murders of 11 women. [Points for time order and proximity, theme consistency, scene specificity, and offender statements. Total: 6/9. Score: 0.667.]

2012: Unknown. Influences: *Project X.* Houston, Texas. Hundreds of people were at a Houston "Project X" party, and after locals complained, law enforcement intervened. The party moved to the streets, and at some point, someone pulled out a gun. The shooting that followed claimed the life of 18-year-old Ryan Spikes. Investigator Mark Stephens commented, "When you look at the movie, and you look at what happened here, the parallels are uncanny. It was a copycat. They did everything that I saw in the movie." [Points for time order and proximity, theme consistency, and scene specificity. Total: 4/7. Score: 0.571.]

2/3/2013–2/12/2013: Christopher Dorner. Influences: *Rambo.* Los Angeles, California. Dorner declared war on law enforcement officers and their families in a manifesto posted to the Internet that claims he was racially abused by two fellow officers and complains about his 2008 firing from the Los Angeles Police Department. Styling himself as the main character in the *Rambo* movies, the media quickly began comparing Dorner's actions to a real-life Rambo. For nine days in Southern California, Dorner went on a killing spree, killing four people, injuring many more, and ultimately ending in suicide. [Points for time order and proximity, theme consistency, and scene specificity. Total: 4/7. Score: 0.571.]

August 2013: Derek Medina. Influences: Facebook. Miami, Florida. Medina shot his wife Jennifer Alfonso (27) eight times. He then posted a photo of his deceased wife's body on Facebook with the caption, "RIP Jennifer Alfonso." [Points for time order and proximity and repetitive viewing. Total: 2/9. Score: 0.222.]

May 2013: Jason Hart. Influences: *Breaking Bad.* Spokane, Washington. Hart strangled his girlfriend, Regan Jolley (33), to death and then attempted to dispose of her body by submerging her in a plastic tub filled with acid, copying a scene from *Breaking Bad.* Hart's roommate, Dean Settle, mentioned how *Breaking*

Bad was one of Hart's favorite TV shows. Police found an episode of *Breaking Bad* in Hart's DVD player. [Points for time order and proximity, theme consistency, scene specificity, and second-party statements. Total: 5/9. Score: 0.556.]

8/11/2014: Tony Bagnato and Diego Carbone. Influences: *Fight Club*. Sydney, Australia. Carbone and Bagnato brutally murdered Bradley Dillon (25) after luring him into an underground car park. Dillon was shot three times and stabbed four to five times by the two men who were in a secretive Sydney fight club. [Points for theme consistency. Total: 1/9. Score: 0.111.]

5/31/2014: Anissa Weier and Morgan Geyser. Influences: Slender Man. Waukesha, Wisconsin. Geyser and Weier stabbed Payton Leutner (12) 19 times with a five-inch blade and left Payton in the woods. Payton then crawled to a trail where she was found by a passing bicyclist. Payton survived the stabbing. Geyser and Weier were found hours later by police on the side of the road and told investigators they had to kill Payton or else Slender Man would kill their families. They wanted to prove themselves worthy to Slender Man and this was their way to live with Slender Man. [Points for time order and proximity and offender statements. Total: 3/9. Score: 0.333.]

3/24/2014: Eldon Samuel III. Influences: *Grand Theft Auto V*. Coeur d'Alene, Idaho. Samuel III confessed to the police that he had shot his dad, Eldon Samuel, Jr. (46), with a .45-caliber handgun, before shooting his brother, Jonathan Samuel (13), four times with a shotgun. Samuel III found his brother still alive, picked up a large knife and stabbed him multiple times, and finished him off by striking him 30 times with a machete. Later, Samuel III confessed to authorities about the preplanned murder of his family members after idolizing a violent game character, Trevor, in *Grand Theft Auto V*. [Points for time order and proximity, theme consistency, and offender statements. Total: 4/9. Score: 0.444.]

2014: David Parsons. Influences: The "Yorkshire Ripper" Peter Sutcliffe. North Yorkshire, England. Parsons was obsessed with the Yorkshire Ripper and brutally attacked a prostitute before calling the police to confess what he had done. Later, Parsons told psychiatrists that he wanted to become a serial killer and kill more prostitutes than Sutcliffe. [Points for theme consistency, scene specificity, and offender statements. Total: 5/9. Score: 0.556.]

5/23/2014: Elliot Rodger. Influences: Celebrity culture, *World of Warcraft*. Isla Vista, California. Rodger killed six people and injured thirteen others during a killing spree before committing suicide. Prior to his attacks, Rodger uploaded a video to YouTube titled "Elliot Rodger's Retribution" in which he outlined details of his upcoming attack and the motivations behind the killing spree. Rodger stated his desire to punish women for rejecting him and the desire to punish sexually active men for living a better life than him. Rodger also wrote a 141-page manifesto that he sent out to friends and family, where he expressed his

Appendix 249

frustrations and referred to himself as an addict of the *World of Warcraft* online game. [Points for time order and proximity, repetitive viewing, and offender statements. Total: 4/9. Score: 0.444.]

July 2014–February 2015: Elena Lobacheva, Pavel Voitov, Vladislav Karatayev, Artur Natsissov, and Maxim Pavlov. Influences: *Bride of Chucky*. Moscow, Russia. The gang of neo-Nazis murdered at least 15 unnamed victims. Lobacheva told police that randomly stabbing the victims' bodies brought her pleasure similar to sexual pleasure. Lobacheva was inspired by the murder scenes in the film *Bride of Chucky* and has a tattoo of the doll on her arm. [Points for theme consistency and offender statements. Total: 3/9. Score: 0.333.]

4/4/2015: Amanda Taylor and Sean Ball. Influences: Social media. Ellett, Virginia. Taylor repeatedly stabbed her father-in-law, Charlie Taylor (59), with a bayonet-style knife, and then her accomplice Ball (who had unreciprocated romantic feelings for her) hit Charlie Taylor over the head with a tire iron. After the murder, Amanda Taylor posed with the knife in front of her father-in-law's bloodied deceased body and then posted it on Instagram, calling herself the "Brunette Bomber," and sent it to a crime blogger asking them to post it on their website. In an interview, Taylor said, "I was just really excited, and I was like hey I'm gonna take a picture so I can post it and show everyone. It was just something that I, it made me really happy." [Points for time order and consistency, repetitive viewing, and offender statements. Total: 4/9. Score: 0.444.]

5/23/2015: Jed Allen. Influences: *X-Men*. Oxfordshire, England. After stabbing his family to death using a hunting knife, Allen quickly wrote the words "I'm sorry" on his bedroom wall using the blood of his mother, Janet Jordon (48); her partner, Philip Howard (44); and their six-year-old daughter, Derrin Jordon. Allen was a bodybuilding enthusiast who was obsessed with the X-Men character Wolverine. Many posts on social media include Allen posing with blades between his fingers and showing off large hunting-style knives. After the murders, Jed ended his life by hanging himself in the woods. [Points for time order and proximity and theme consistency. Total: 2/7. Score: 0.285.]

6/14/2015: Gypsy Rose Blanchard and Nicholas Godejohn. Influences: *Tangled*. Springfield, Missouri. For many years, Clauddine Blanchard (48) had lied about her daughter's illness, making many believe she suffered from muscular dystrophy, leukemia, and other ailments. Gypsy set up an online dating profile as a way to escape from her mother. After meeting Godejohn online, Gypsy convinced him to kill Clauddine in order to save Gypsy from a life of abuse. Between hospital visits and charity events, Clauddine had Gypsy watch Disney movies, her favorite being *Tangled*. Kristy Blanchard, Gypsy's stepmother, stated that Gypsy played out a part of the fairytale by getting "rid of the evil [villain]." [Points for time order and proximity, theme consistency, and second-party statements. Total: 3/9. Score: 0.333.]

8/25/2015: Vester Lee Flanagan II. Influences: Performance crime, Dylann Roof, school shootings. Moneta, Virginia. Flanagan approached Alison Parker (23), Adam Ward (27), and Vicki Gardner (61) and began shooting. He fired 15 shots with a handgun he purchased two weeks earlier. Ward and Parker were killed, while Gardner survived with injuries. Social media posts and correspondence to news media that Flanagan made on the day of the event indicated that Flanagan, who was Black and homosexual, believed he was the victim of discrimination, specifically naming Parker and Ward. In a 23-page manifesto, Flanagan blamed Dylann Roof for starting a race war. Flanagan also expressed admiration for the Virginia Tech mass shooter for killing double the amount of people the Columbine school shooters did. [Points for time order and proximity, theme consistency, and offender statements. Total: 4/9. Score: 0.444.]

12/28/2015: Dustin Rittgers. Influences: Facebook. Columbus, Ohio. Rittgers livestreamed himself drinking whisky while driving and one of his friends posted, "Dude Really?" to which he replied, "I'm a good driver. Don't worry." He was arrested after another friend called the police. [Points for time order and proximity, repetitive viewing, and second-party statements. Total: 3/9. Score: 0.333.]

4/14/2016: Kim Edwards and Lucas Markham. Influences: *Twilight*. Spalding, Lincolnshire. Edwards snuck her boyfriend, Markham, into her home and had him kill both her mother, Elizabeth Edwards (49), and her little sister, Katie Edwards (13). After the massacre, Edwards bathed with Markham before heading downstairs to eat, watch *Twilight*, and have sex. [Points for time order and proximity. Total: 1/9. Score: 0.111.]

5/12/2016–5/15/2016: Jonathan Cruz. Influences: *The Purge*. Indianapolis, Indiana. Cruz shot and killed Billy Boyd, Jose Ruiz, and Jay Higginbotham over the course of three days. When arrested, Cruz blamed his criminal actions on the idea that he was "purging," which is a reference to the *Purge* series where citizens are allowed to commit any and all criminal acts with no repercussions for 24 hours. [Points for time order and proximity, theme consistency, scene specificity, and offender statements. Total: 6/9. Score: 0.667.]

6/10/2016: Kevin James Loibl. Influences: Celebrity culture, YouTube. Orlando, Florida. Loibl traveled to a Christina Grimmie (22) concert from St. Petersburg and arrived with two handguns and a hunting knife. Following the performance, Loibl shot Grimmie four times and then shot himself. The investigation revealed that Loibl had an "unrealistic infatuation" with Grimmie. [Points for time order and proximity and offender statements. Total: 3/9. Score: 0.333.]

6/12/2016: Omar Mateen. Influences: Social media. Orlando, Florida. Mateen began shooting in the Pulse Nightclub, a LGBTQ+ club hosting their well-known Latin night. This left 49 victims dead and 50 wounded. The surviving victims sued social media platforms used by ISIS to spread violent and hate messages

Appendix   251

that influenced the perpetrator to commit the mass shooting. [Points for time order and proximity, theme consistency, and second-party statements. Total: 3/7. Score: 0.428.]

8/5/2016: Brittney Dwyer and Bernadette Burns. Influences: *American Horror Story.* Adelaide, Australia. The influence of the horror television series, as well as the greed of a hefty inheritance, made 19-year-old Brittney Dwyer murder her 81-year-old grandfather. Robert Whitwell was brutally stabbed to death in his home. On August 5, 2016, Dwyer and Burns drove down to Adelaide for a second chance at stealing the money. Burns waited in the car while Dwyer went inside and spent some time with her grandfather. When it was time to leave, she suddenly stabbed the elderly man in the throat, leaving him bleeding and gasping for breath. Reports even state that Dwyer helped Robert apply a Band-Aid before doing the dishes as he slowly passed away. Although authorities were unable to get any details on a specific episode Dwyer enjoyed, they believe she was influenced by the show, as many characters do whatever is necessary to get what they want, including murder. [Points for time order and proximity and theme consistency. Total: 2/9. Score: 0.222.]

2/28/2017: Ernest Franklin II and Heather Franklin. Influences: *Manchester by the Sea.* Guilford, New York. In upstate New York, a couple murdered Jeffrey Franklin (16), their adoptive son with special needs, and started a fire in an attempt to cover up their actions. The couple plotted to kill their deaf and mute son after watching the film *Manchester by the Sea,* which tells the story of a man who accidently killed his children in a fire and was not prosecuted. [Points for time order and proximity, theme consistency, and scene specificity. Total: 4/9. Score: 0.444.]

4/16/2017: Steve Stevens. Influences: Facebook. Cleveland, Ohio. Stevens recorded himself driving up to 74-year-old Robert Godwin Sr. and talking to him. Stevens asked the man, "Can you do me a favor?" and "Can you say the name Joy Lane?" Godwin responded, "Joy Lane?" and Stephens replied, "Yeah, she is the reason this is going to happen to you." Stephens then shot and killed Godwin and said to the camera, "This is going to be called the Easter Sunday Joy Lane Massacre. Stephens went on Facebook Live and explained why he had shot Godwin and how he had also killed 13 other people, though no other murders were corroborated by police. [Points for time order and proximity. Total: 1/7. Score: 0.142.]

4/18/2017, July 2018: John Robert Hill. Influences: Instagram. Los Angeles, California. Hill became Instagram-famous for his performance crimes. By July 2018 he had reached over 5 million views on Instagram after posting X-rated graphic content of himself with a woman having sex in various positions until his site was eventually shut down for violating Instagram policies. [Points for time order and proximity. Total: 1/9. Score: 0.111.]

8/12/2017: Jerry Varnell. Influences: Oklahoma City bombing. Oklahoma City, Oklahoma. Parking a van loaded with what was believed to be a working explosive device next to a bank, Varnell dialed a number on a cellphone thinking it would set off the bombs. However, the device was inert and did not explode. The site of this attempt was just a few blocks away from the 1995 bombing that killed 168 people. [Points for theme consistency, scene specificity, and second-party statements. Total: 4/9. Score: 0.444.]

4/24/2018: Alek Minassian. Influences: Incel, Elliot Rodger. Toronto, Canada. Minassian admitted to using a van to kill 10 pedestrians and injure 16 others. Minassian called himself an "incel," referring to an online subculture that promotes the idea of men being entitled to have sex with women. This drew attention to an online world of sexual loneliness, rage, and misogyny. Minassian had never had a girlfriend and was a virgin. He told police that he had been in contact with Elliot Rodger, who was a college student in a similar situation and ended up killing 6 people and wounding 13 in a shooting and stabbing in 2014. [Points for time order and proximity, theme consistency, and offender statements. Total: 4/9. Score: 0.444.]

3/15/2019: Brenton Harrison Tarrant. Influences: Facebook, social media. Christchurch, New Zealand. The Christchurch mosque mass shooting that killed 51 people was livestreamed on Facebook for hours before the horrifying video was taken down. During the livestream, moments before the murders, Tarrant posted a meme endorsing a YouTube star (who unknowingly became entangled in the event), saying "Remember, lads, subscribe to PewDiePie." [Points for time order and proximity. Total: 1/9. Score: 0.111.]

2/9/2020: Sergeant Major Jakrapanth Thomma. Influences: Facebook. Thailand. A conflict culminated in Thomma killing his commanding officer and his mother-in-law at his army base. Thomma then went to a busy shopping mall in the middle of the afternoon, where he shot indiscriminately at mallgoers while posting on Facebook before and during the shooting. [Points for time order and proximity. Total: 1/9. Score: 0.111.]

5/22/2020: Peter Manfredonia. Influences: Adam Lanza. Derby, Connecticut. Two days prior to breaking into 23-year-old Nicholas Eisele's home, Manfredonia had allegedly killed Ted DeMers (62) and attacked an 80-year-old man with a samurai sword. On the May 24, Manfredonia allegedly broke into Eisele's home, shot him, and forced his girlfriend to drive him to New Jersey. At a truck stop in New Jersey, Manfredonia left Eisele's girlfriend there and convinced someone to order him an Uber heading out of the state. Manfredonia grew up on the same street as the Sandy Hook shooter, Adam Lanza, and claimed he "snapped" in a similar way. Prior to his attacks, Manfredonia left a message on the walls of his dorm stating, "We saw what happened when Adam snapped" and another one stating "Now they see what happens when I snap." [Points for time order and proximity, theme consistency, and offender statements. Total: 4/9. Score: 0.444.]

Appendix

253

5/14/2022: Payton Gendron. Influences: Social media. Buffalo, New York. Gendron publicized a racist manifesto on the Internet prior to fatally shooting 10 people in a Black neighborhood. Gendron broadcasted the attack in real time on the social media platform Twitch. Gendron took inspiration from different white supremacists, including Brenton Tarrant, Patrick Crucius, Anders Breivik, Dylann Roof, and John Earnest. [Points for time order and proximity, theme consistency, and offender statements. Total: 4/9. Score: 0.444.]

5/24/2022: Salvador Rolando Ramos. Influences: Social media. Uvalde, Texas. Prior to leaving his home, Ramos messaged a friend on Instagram and posted on Facebook about his plans. After shooting his grandmother in the head, Ramos made his way to Robb Elementary School. Ramos gained access to the school by shooting the glass on the door to a fourth-grade classroom. Entering the classroom, Ramos shot and killed Eva Mireles (44) after stating "Goodnight." Ramos continued to shoot around the classroom before entering another classroom that was connected. He began to play "sad music" and stated, "You are all going to die." An hour later, authorities entered the building and killed Ramos. [Points for time order and proximity and repetitive viewing. Total: 2/7. Score: 0.285.]

5/25/2022: Unnamed male. Influences: Uvalde school shooting. Blaine, Washington. With the media sharing the tragic news about the Robb Elementary School shooting in Uvalde, Texas, threats were made against schools in Blaine, Washington. Authorities in Blaine were notified about threatening messages and were able to confront the boy about the messages. The boy admitted to sending threatening texts as a prank. [Points for time order and proximity, theme consistency, scene specificity, repetitive viewing, and offender statements. Total: 6/9. Score: 0.667.]

5/31/2022: Unnamed 10-year-old boy. Influences: Uvalde school shooting. Cape Coral, Florida. Days after Salvador Rolando Ramos opened fire at Robb Elementary School in Uvalde, Texas, a 10-year-old boy threatened to shoot up his elementary school. The boy was charged with making a written threat to conduct a mass shooting, which occurred through a text. [Points for time order and proximity, theme consistency, scene specificity, and repetitive viewing. Total: 4/9. Score: 0.444.]

7/4/2022: Robert E. Crimo III. Influences: Social media, Lee Harvey Oswald. Highland Park, Chicago. Crimo fired more than 70 shots from a rooftop, killing seven people and wounding several others. Crimo had posted several videos on social media, including some drawings of mass shootings. One video showed Crimo with a newspaper displayed on the wall with the headline about the killing of Lee Harvey Oswald. Paul Crimo, Robert's uncle, told reporters that his nephew spent lots of time on social media and aspired to be an artist and rapper on YouTube. [Points for time order and proximity, theme consistency, repetitive viewing, and second-party statements. Total: 4/9. Score: 0.444.]

Notes

Chapter 1

1. "Chad" and "Stacy" are names used within the Incel movement to refer to the archetypes articulated by Elliot Rodger in his manifesto "My Twisted World" (Rodger, 2014) and his video posts he made prior to the Santa Barbara mass shooting. Incels use the term "Stacy" to refer to women who will not have sex with them and "Chads" to refer to the men who have sex with the Stacys, and to refer to "good-looking people who have no trouble having sex with each other" (Jane, 2018).

2. The video following the event was captured by Pacific Northwest independent media company *Converge Media*: https://www.facebook.com/WWConverge /videos/1202597116759306 was the post-injury hospital interview: https:// www.facebook.com/watch/live/?v=382409882728244&ref=watch_permalink. Diaz Love, the protester who was hit but survived, was filming the Black Femme Nightly March to the West Precinct prior to being hit: https://www.liveleak.com /view?t=9gXWz_1593855261. The news outlet *Pinal Central* put together a compilation of all three of the livestream videos. See: https://www.pinalcentral.com /graphic-seattle-wa-multiple-blm-protesters-struck-by-vehicle-on-freeway-chop /video_97500c4b-f4dc-5f4c-aa61-e555c6b3522d.html

3. There are several variations of the cartoonish meme "All lives splatter" circulating through social media and reproduced on t-shirts, stickers, and bumper stickers that show SUVs, trucks, and cars running into stick figures of people with the running head "All lives splatter," "All lives splatter. Nobody cares. Keep your ass out of the road," "All lives splatter. Nobody cares about your protest," "All lives splatter. Keep your ass off the road," and "All lives splatter. Moral of the Story . . . Stay off the road."

4. You Tube star PewDiePie, whose real name is Felix Kjellberg, quickly distanced himself from the event saying, "I feel absolutely sickened having my name uttered by this person" and sending a message of support to the victims and their families (Chokshi, 2019).

5. The names of individuals who have committed copycat and media-mediated crimes are used throughout this book to understand these individuals

and their crimes. Retrospective analysis of copycat crimes and the individual perpetrators who commit them is critical for theory development and empirical research, and it is difficult to study these individuals without using their names for research and identification purposes. However, some have argued that it is important to not name perpetrators in media accounts (Lankford & Madfis, 2018), and it is important to have ongoing cultural conversations about specific policies and practices that can reduce the incidence of copycat crime.

6. Devin Moore is referred to throughout this text as Moore/Thompson. His name appears as Devin Moore in media accounts. However, his legal name is Devin Darnell Thompson.

7. Neuroscientists have been trying to map the human brain since the early 1900s. The Human Connectome Project has created a multimodal map of the human cortex identifying 180 brain areas (Lewis, 2016). No neuroscientific map is yet able to help us understand the unique meaning media and cultural artifacts of crime hold for perpetrators of crime or the ways in which media elements make their way into their cognitive scripts in ways that would help prevent criminal acts influenced by media, technology, and digital culture.

8. For example, the film *Heathers* inspired a 15-year-old girl to lace a peanut butter sandwich with poison in an attempt to kill her 11-year-old playmate, several teenage girls were inspired by the film *Natural Born Killers* to go on murder sprees with their teenage boyfriends, a trio of female bank robbers were inspired by the film *Set It Off,* and the film *Thelma and Louise* was said to have inspired female duos to commit a variety of crimes including bank robbery (Helfgott, 2015), and a 12-year-old Wisconsin girl, along with her 12-year-old friend, stabbed her classmate 19 times to impress "Slender Man," a fictional online horror character (Moreno, February 2, 2018).

9. Online communities are an aspect of digital culture that exacerbate the copycat effect (Healing & Helfgott, 2019). Well before the exponential growth of internet communities, including many deep within the "dark net" (Bartlett, 2016), Columbine killers Klebold and Harris were part of the *Doom* online gamer community, and Harris is said to have created a "Columbine High School" level of the game, including weapons similar to those used in the real-life mass murder (Simpson & Blevins, 1999). Another example of this sort of online group that serves to insulate and isolate its members is *Gamergate,* which involved a group of male gamers who digitally harassed female gamers (Elise, 2014a) specifically targeting Zoe Quinn, who went on to write *Crash Override* (Quinn, 2017) detailing her experience as a Gamergate victim.

Chapter 2

1. *Mindhunter* ran for two seasons, is among the top five most watched streaming shows, and has been referred to by reviewers as one of the "best shot, best written, best acted shows on Netflix" (Tassi, 2019). Douglas and Olshaker, authors of the books *Journey into Darkness* and *Anatomy of Motive,* wrote 19

Notes 257

episodes of *Mindhunter,* which is directed by David Fincher, who directed the crime dramas *Se7en, Gone Girl,* and *ZØdiac.*

2. When I use the term "safecracker" in my course lectures, I am often met with perplexing looks from students and am asked to explain what a safecracker is. Technology has made the term and the activity obsolete. Before the digital age, safecracking was a highly developed skill. Police and security professionals often used retired safecrackers to gain knowledge in investigating and securing bank robberies that involved breaking into safes and vaults (Blau, 1989; Nicol, 1954). However, there are still modern-day safecrackers who consider the act an art form who "live in a state of magical realism, suspended somewhere between technology and superstition" (Manaugh, 2018).

3. The Ogden, Utah Hi-Fi murders and the story of 16-year-old Courtney Naisbitt, one of the two surviving victims, is depicted in detail in the book *Victim: The Other Side of Murder* (Kinder, 1982). This crime was used in FBI training in the Behavioral Sciences Unit and is used as an example of how media makes its way into MO in the book *Anatomy of Motive* and the *Crime Classification Manual* (Douglas et al., 2006).

4. In 2017, Twitchell posted a dating profile on the dating site for prisoners, *Canadian Inmate Connect.* Twitchell described himself in his dating profile as "insightful, passionate and philosophical with a great sense of humor" and indicated that he was interested in corresponding with an "interesting, intelligent, open-minded, delightfully imperfect woman to relate to and share amusing observations with . . . as well as potentially a long weekend every few months if it gets there naturally." Staff Sergeant Bill Clark, one of the original investigators in the case, referred to Twitchell as a "narcissistic psychopath" who is a "pathological liar" who would be able to "fool some woman into writing him who will fall deeply madly in love with him" (Stevenson, 2017).

5. Psychopaths lack identity integration and use primitive borderline defenses, including splitting, primitive idealization, projective identification, devaluation, omnipotence, and denial. Projective identification is characterized by the tendency to continue to experience an impulse while it is at the same time projected onto another person whereby the individual feels a bond with an object while simultaneously fearing attack from that object (Helfgott, 2004; Meloy, 1988, 1992).

Chapter 3

1. Some accounts of Loukaitis's comments prior to the shooting suggest that the words "This sure beats algebra, doesn't it" are taken verbatim from *Rage.* In his essay *Guns,* Stephen King (2013) himself says that the quote is from *Rage.* Loukaitis's words reference the story in *Rage,* however the closest direct quote to this in the book is when the character Charlie Decker says when questioned by his principal about why he killed his algebra teacher, "I don't know . . . but it sure beats panty raids" (King, 1977, p. 43).

2. *Rage* was first published as a paperback under King's pseudonym Richard Bachman in 1977 and then published in a collection of short novels titled *The Bachman Books* (King, 1986).

3. On Bookfinders.com's top most searched for out-of-print books for 2013, *Rage* is #2. Madonna's *Sex* is #1 (see: https://www.bookfinder.com/books /bookfinder_report/BookFinder_Report_2013.mhtml). In the most recently available report for 2014, *Rage* is ranked #5 (see: https://www.bookfinder.com /books/bookfinder_report/BookFinder_Report_2013.mhtml).

4. Eric Tavulares was said to have watched *NBK* up to 20 times. The night he murdered his girlfriend Lauren Aljubouri the couple had watched both *NBK* and the 1993 film *True Romance* written by Quentin Tarantino and directed by Tony Scott.

5. Noncrime memes have been examined identifying the features of a successful meme, including portrayals of ordinary people rather than celebrities; flawed masculinity in scenes that mock males failing at some basic task; comical depictions linked to flawed masculinity; simplicity/easily copied content; repeated content with instructions on how to copy; and whimsical content, including references to pop culture and portrayals of playful or irrational behavior (Shifman, 2012).

6. For example, Craig Anderson's testimony to the U.S. Senate on the effects of video game violence (U.S. Senate Hearing 106-1096, 2000) and the statement by the American Academy of Pediatrics (Committee on Public Education, 2001).

Chapter 4

1. A comprehensive list of case studies beyond those included in this chapter is provided in the appendix.

2. Lorena Bobbitt chopped off her husband's penis and threw it out her car window and was acquitted for "malicious wounding" after claiming that her husband raped her (Waxman, 2018). Mary Kay Letourneau was a middle school teacher who had a sexual relationship with her 12-year-old student, whom she had two children with and later married after she was released from prison (Hesse, 2020).

3. There have been several films inspired by the Starkweather and Fugate murder spree depicting murderous lovers on a road-trip theme. Some are more closely aligned to the story, while others are only loosely connected. Examples include *The Sadist* (1963), *Murder in the Heartland* (1993), *Badlands* (1974), *Wild at Heart* (1990), *Kalifornia* (1994), and *True Romance* (1994).

4. I saw this film in the theater the day it came out. Every time Mallory Knox killed someone and made a statement like this, the crowd cheered loudly.

5. The victim's name is intentionally omitted out of respect for him and his family. The identity of the victim in this case is widely known after the Netflix documentary. The victim's father has publicly expressed the deep and enduring pain his son's legacy as a victim of this horrific crime has caused him and his family, indicating that his son not only suffered the pain of the murder but now the humiliation of the publicity each time his name is mentioned in the media (Tron, 2019).

Notes 259

6. The blame and stigma placed on the mothers of mass shooters in media and culture are an important issue ripe for examination. Melendez et al. (2016) suggest that the disproportionate blame placed on the mothers of mass shooters is "a worrisome trend." The mothers of mass killers (many of whom were divorced working mothers with primary custody of their children) are stigmatized and blamed, while fathers (many of whom left the family after divorce and did not have primary custody) do not prompt outrage in the media, and the killer's gender (male) passes with little remark.

7. While *The Turner Diaries* is arguably the most notable book said to inspire far-right extremist violence and author William Pierce has been referred to as the "most influential revolutionary theoretician that the American extreme right ever produced," a number of other fantasy novels are popular in extremist milieus that some argue are blueprints for terrorist campaigns and revolutions including *The John Franklin Letters, The Camp of Saints, The Monkey Wrench Gang, Hunter, KD Rebel*, and a series of novels by Howard Covington about the Northwest Volunteer Army (Michael, 2009, p. 153).

Chapter 5

1. The panelists included actor Richard Dreyfus; then ACLU president and author Nadine Strossen; public health leader and professor of medicine, Dr. Prothrow Stith; media producer Rosalyn Weinmann; media activist Terry Rakolta from Americans for Responsible Television; then Illinois Congressman Henry Hyde; then Senator Barney Frank; Houston police officer Mark Clark and executive director of the Houston Police Officers Union; Jeff Ayeroff, president Virgin Records; Grant Tinker, president of CTG Entertainment; Michael Franti, Disposable Heroes of Hiphoprisy; David Harleston; Def Jam Recordings, and Richard Wolf, executive producer at Wolf Films.

2. Though Ogletree does not specifically mention the actual song these lyrics are drawn from, the lyrics are from the 1972 Alice Cooper song "School's Out for Summer."

3. The spelling of Joshua Cooke's name incorrectly appears as "Cook" in this article.

4. The use and success of the insanity defense vary across jurisdictions. Research has found that the use of the insanity defense is extremely rare, used in approximately 1 percent of cases with approximately 15 to 25 percent of those cases ending in a successful NGRI verdict (Adjorlolo et al., 2019; Borum & Fulero, 1999; Buffington-Vollum & Johnson, 2013; Callahan et al., 1991).

5. One of the most outspoken critics against GTA and violent video games who made this reference was Jack Thompson, an attorney and crusader against violent video games, who represented plaintiffs in civil lawsuits involving GTA. Thompson was disbarred in 2007 (Winkie, 2022).

6. The Supreme Court defined "true threat" as "statements where the speaker means to communicate a serious expression of an intent to commit an act of

unlawful violence to a particular individual or group of individuals" (*Virginia v. Black, 2003*).

7. These challenges have examined recent cases, including a lawsuit against Donald Trump for inciting violence at a 2016 political rally where a 21-year-old African American protester, Kashiya Nwabguma, was assaulted by white rally participants after Trump said "get 'em outta here" about the protestors (Calvert, 2019), as well as the case against Donald Trump for inciting the January 6, 2021, insurrection (Reiferson, 2021).

8. For a review of research by Craig Anderson and colleagues and six decades of research on the effects of newspapers, magazines, comics, radio, television, films, and video games, see Bushman et al. (2015), Warburton and Anderson (2022), and Plante et al. (2020). For an overview of research on the absence of a causal link between media violence and real-world violence which has primarily focused on video game violence, see Markey and Ferguson (2017) and Ferguson et al. (2020).

9. Anderson has been an expert in court cases, including *Brown v. Entertainment Merchants Association* (2011); *Video Software Dealers Association v. Schwarzenegger* (2005, 2009); *Entertainment Software Association v. Blagojevich* (2005); *Entertainment Software Association v. Swanson* (2008); *Entertainment Software Association v. Hatch* (2006); and *Entertainment Software Association v. Granholm* (2006), which involved video game company lawsuits against states (California, Minnesota, and Michigan) for imposing restrictions and labeling requirements on the sale and rental of violent video games to minors.

10. The perpetrator in the shooting, Aaron Ybarra, who was convicted and sentenced to 112 years in prison, had researched mass shootings and idolized the Columbine killers (Goins, 2014). On cross-examination at his trial, he told the court, "I was hearing Eric Harris's voice" and the voice of God, telling him to commit the mass shooting specifically at a university "in order to go to hell" (Green, 2017; Green & Coleman, 2016).

11. For example, the Texas social media ban (Pollard, 2021) and Trump's lawsuit against *Twitter, Facebook,* and *YouTube* over censorship and the 230 Communications Decency Act, on one hand (Gerstein, 2022), and the lawsuit against Facebook/Meta for failing to police violent content that contributed to genocidal violence in Rohingya (Chandran & Asher-Schapiro, 2021).

Chapter 6

1. A striking example of this is the use of computer-generated imagery (CGI) to allow completion of the film *Furious 7* after Paul Walker was killed in a car accident before the film was finished. After his death, Paul Walker's brothers, Cody and Caleb Walker, were recruited by Universal Pictures and the film's director, James Wan, to finish his scenes in the Fast & Furious series, and CGI technology was used to digitally re-create Paul Walker to finish playing his character Bryan O'Connor after his death "brought to life by the same company that

Notes 261

made Gollum in *The Lord of the Rings* and Caesar in *Dawn of the Planet of the Apes*" (Hall, 2015). There is speculation that CGI may be used in the future to bring back Paul Walker in the 2023 film (Garbutt, 2022).

2. Columbine killers Dylan Klebold and Eric Harris, Santa Barbara mass shooter Elliot Rodger, and Sandy Hook mass shooter Adam Lanza are among the killers who, while once were unknown edge-sitters themselves, have become idols for like-minded young men who hold them up as their heroes (BBC News, 2018; Follman & Andrews, 2015; Varghese, 2020).

3. There are disparities across cultures in Internet and media consumption (Hermeking, 2017). However, mass media and digital culture have had a global impact (Levin & Mamlok, 2021), and digital globalization has redefined the study of culture, creating opportunities to study cultural patterns from a "one-world view" (Pelzel, 2021).

4. This can be any form of media or digital content, including but not limited to print, visual, audio, social media, memes, video games, or other types of digital content.

5. For example, Holden Caulfield does not commit a murder in the book *The Catcher in the Rye*, yet the ideas in the book influenced Mark Chapman's motivation to murder John Lennon. Young (2009) offers insight into the power of affective connection between a consumer of a media source in this criminogenic and psychological connection between an idea and a subsequent commission of a crime inspired by the source, suggesting that the connection between an individual and media content is less about the violent content and more about the affective encounter between the spectator and "the ways in which the spectator is invited, paradoxically, to see the legitimate as illegitimate through a moment of identification and desire" (p. 19).

6. Phenomenological perspectives on crime and criminal behavior examine the meaning of crime for the perpetrator (Helfgott, 2008). Phenomenological perspectives on crime are rooted in the work of Katz (1988) and other scholars (see Manning & Raphael, 2012) and the cultural criminology concept of criminological *verstehen* (Ferrell & Hamm, 1998; Ferrell & Sanders, 1995).

7. The edits made to the scene involved removing the scene of the protagonist, Hannah Baker, carrying out her suicide in gory detail showing how she harmed herself and replacing it with a scene showing her crying prior to her attempt and then showing her mother standing over her body expressing agony and panic.

8. Allwinn et al. (2022) do not use Stair's name in their study in line with the "No Notoriety" and "Don't Name Them" movements and recommendations by Lankford and Madfis (2018). They also refer to Stair using female pronouns because though Stair was born and socialized as male, she identified as female. Consistent with the authors' use of female pronouns, female pronouns will be used to refer to Stair in this example. However, because perpetrator names are used throughout this book and this case is included in the Appendix, Stair's name is used here for consistency though minimized to respect the authors' decision to omit the perpetrator's name.

Appendix

1. According to Surettes Scale, for crimes where no offender was available—for example, no arrest was made or the offender died—the total possible copycat crime scores ranged from 0 to 7.

2. See the Oklahoma City National Memorial Museum that honors the 168 victims who were killed during the attack: https://memorialmuseum.com/experience/their-stories/those-who-were-killed/

References

ABC News. (2012, December 16). Sandy Hook elementary shooting: Gunman Adam Lanza got guns from mother. *ABC News*. https://www.youtube .com/watch?v=2xaiFLjZn_Y&index=339&list=LLxFxZYlnklH YQK3_M3zEJqA

Abrams v. United States, 250 U.S. 616 (1919). https://supreme.justia.com/cases /federal/us/250/616/

Adams, D. (2005, August 10). Killer tries GTA defense, Jury convicts. *IGN.com*. http://ps2.ign.com/articles/640/640942p1.html

Adjorlolo, S., Chan, H. C., & DeLisi, M. (2019). Mentally disordered offenders and the law: Research update on the insanity defense, 2004–2019. *International Journal of Law and Psychiatry, 67*, 101507. https://doi.org/10.1016/j .ijlp.2019.101507

Adwar, C. (2014, April 1). This Stephen King novel will never be printed again after it was tied to school shootings. *Business Insider*. https://www .businessinsider.com/school-shootings-drove-stephen-king-to-take-rage -off-shelves-2014-3

Ahrens, F. (1995, September 10). Cold blood. *The Washington Post*. https://www .washingtonpost.com/archive/lifestyle/1995/09/10/cold-blood/82d33fa3 -5700-4585-bfc1-858e2dea9d4f/

Alathari, L., et al. (2019). Protecting America's schools: A U.S. Secret Service analysis of targeted school violence. U.S. Department of Homeland Security. United States Secret Service. National Threat Assessment Center.

Alfonseca, K. (2023, March 27). There have been more mass shootings than days in 2023, database shows. *abcNEWS*. https://abcnews.go.com/US/mass -shootings-days-2023-database-shows/story?id=96609874

Algar, S. (2013, July 31). Black robbers used $2,000 white masks to fool victims in $200,000 "Town"-style stickup, prosecutors say. *New York Post*. https://nypost.com/2013/07/31/black-robbers-used-2000-white-masks -to-fool-victims-in-200000-town-style-stickup-prosecutors-say/

Allen, J. J., Anderson, C. A., & Bushman, B. J. (2018). The General Aggression Model. *Current Opinion in Psychology, 19*, 75–80. https://doi.org/10.1016/j.copsyc.2017.03.034

Allwinn, M., Tultschinetski, S., & Görgen, T. (2022). Blazing hate into the world: Psychological case study of a fame-seeking rampage shooter. *Violence and Gender, 9*(1), 42–56. https://doi.org/10.1089/vio.2021.0037

Alter, A. (2021). How "The Turner Diaries" incites white supremacists. *The New York Times.* https://www.nytimes.com/2021/01/12/books/turner-diaries-white-supremacists.html

Altimari, D. (2018, December 9). Sandy Hook shooter Adam Lanza's spreadsheet detailing centuries of mass violence served as a road map to murder. *Hartford Courant.* https://www.courant.com/news/connecticut/hc-news-sandy-hook-lanza-spreadsheet-20181205-story.html

American Academy of Pediatrics, Committee on Public Education. (2001, November). Media Violence. *Pediatrics, 108*(5), 1222–1226. https://doi.org/10.1542/peds.108.5.1222. https://pediatrics.aappublications.org/content/108/5/1222

American Amusement Machine Association v. Kendrick, 115 F. Supp. 2d 943. (S.D. Ind. 2000). https://law.justia.com/cases/federal/district-courts/FSupp2/115/943/2580304/

American Psychological Association (2015). APA task force on violent media. Technical report on the review of the violent video game literature. http://www.apa.org/pi/families/violent-media.aspx

Amman, M., & Meloy, J. R. (2021). Stochastic terrorism: A linguistic and psychological analysis. *Perspectives on Terrorism, 15*(5), 2–13.

Anderson, C. A. (2003, October). Violent video games: Myths, facts, and unanswered questions. *Psychological Science Agenda.* https://www.apa.org/science/about/psa/2003/10/anderson

Anderson, C. A., Berkowitz, L., Donnerstein, E., Huesmann, L. R., Johnson, J. D., Linz, D., Malamuth, N. M., & Wartella, E. (2003a). The influence of media violence on youth. *Psychological Science in the Public Interest, 4*(3), 81–110. https://doi.org/10.1111/j.1529-1006.2003.pspi_1433.x

Anderson, C. A., & Bushman, B. J. (2001). Effects of violent video games on aggressive behavior, aggressive cognition, aggressive affect, physiological arousal, and prosocial behavior: A meta-analytic review of the scientific literature. *Psychological Science, 12*, 353–359. https://doi.org/10.1111/1467-9280.00366

Anderson, C. A., & Bushman, B. J. (2002). The effects of media on society. *Science, 295*(5564), 2377–2379.

Anderson, C. A., & Bushman, B. J. (2018). Media violence and the General Aggression Model. *Journal of Social Issues, 74*(2), 386–413.

Anderson, C. A., Carnagey, N. L., Eubanks, J. (2003b). Exposure to violent media: The effects of songs with violent lyrics on aggressive thoughts and feelings. *Journal of Personality and Social Psychology, 84*, 960–971. https://doi.org/10.1037/0022-3514.84.5.960

References

Anderson, C. A., & Dill, K. E. (2000). Video games and aggressive thoughts, feelings, and behavior in the laboratory and life. *Journal of Personality and Social Psychology, 78,* 772–790. https://doi.org/10.1037/0022-3514.78.4.772

Anderson, C. A., Gentile, D. A., & Bushman, B. J. (Eds.). (2007). *Violent video game effects on children and adolescents.* New York: Oxford University Press.

Anderson, C. A., & Murphy, C. R. (2003). Violent video games and aggressive behavior in young women. *Aggressive Behavior, 29,* 423–429. https://doi.org/10.1002/ab.10042

Anderson, C. A., Suzuki, K., Swing, E. L., Groves, C. L., Gentile, D. A., Prot, S., Lam, C. P., Sakamoto, A., Horiuchi, Y., Krahé, B., Jelic, M., Liuqing, W., Toma, R., Warburton, W. A., Zhang, X., Tajima, S., Qing, F., & Petrescu, P. (2017). Media violence and other aggression risk factors in seven nations. *Personality and Social Psychology Bulletin, 43*(7), 986–999.

Andone, D., & Devine, C. (2022, July 5). What we know about the Highland Park shooting suspect. *CNN.com.* https://www.cnn.com/2022/07/05/us/robert-e-crimo-highland-park-suspect/index.html

Andone, D., Spells, A., & Royal, D. (2022, November 9). Parkland school shooter avoids the death penalty after jury recommends life in prison. *CNN.com.* https://www.cnn.com/2022/10/13/us/nikolas-cruz-jury-deliberation-thursday/index.html

Andrea, H. (2022). All 15 Grand Theft Auto (GTA) games in order of chronological release. *Tech 21 Century.* https://www.tech21century.com/gta-video-games-in-order/

Andrews, D. A., & Bonta, J. (2016). *The psychology of criminal conduct* (6th Ed.). Cincinnati: Elsevier.

Appelbaum, R. (2017). *The aesthetics of violence: Art, fiction, drama, and film.* New York: Rowman & Littlefield.

Arnett, J. J. (Ed.). (2007). Forbidden fruit hypothesis. *Encyclopedia of Children, Adolescents, and the Media, 1,* 359–359. https://dx.doi.org/10.4135/9781412952606.n183

Ascher, R. (Writer & Director). (2021). *A Glitch Inside the Matrix* [Film]. Campfire/Valparaiso Pictures.

Associated Press. (1998, August 13). National news briefs: Women held in robbery inspired by gang thriller. *The New York Times.* https://www.nytimes.com/1998/08/13/us/national-news-briefs-women-held-in-robbery-inspired-by-gang-thriller.html

Associated Press. (2003, December 8). Malvo defense to air "The Matrix." *CBS News.* https://www.cbsnews.com/news/malvo-defense-to-air-the-matrix/

Associated Press. (2005, August 9). Blaming video game fails for murder defense. *NBC News.* https://www.nbcnews.com/id/wbna8889445

Associated Press. (2006, September 28). Attack on Colorado school hostages sexual in nature, sheriff says. *The Blade.* https://www.toledoblade.com/local/police-fire/2006/09/28/Attack-on-Colorado-school-hostages-sexual-in-nature-sheriff-says/stories/200609280020

Associated Press. (2015, January 13). Ex-Stripper who murdered fiancé in "Last Seduction" plot gets 99 years. *Fox News*. https://www.foxnews.com/story/ex-stripper-who-murdered-fiance-in-last-seduction-plot-gets-99-years

Associated Press. (2022, July 1). New York's proposed gun laws include "character and conduct" social media check. *Spectrum News NY1*. https://www.ny1.com/nyc/all-boroughs/politics/2022/07/01/new-york-s-proposed-gun-laws-include—character-and-conduct—social-media-check

Atkinson, M. (1999). The movies made me do it. How much are "Natural Born" Killers affected by film violence? *The Village Voice*. http://www.villagevoice.com/news/9918,atkinson,5325,1.html

Atkinson, R., & Rodgers, T. (2016). Pleasure zones and murder boxes: Online pornography and violent video games as cultural zones of exception. *British Journal of Criminology, 56*(6), 1291–1307. https://doi.org/10.1093/bjc/azv113

Bacon, J. (2015). Suspect in on-air murder of journalists kills himself. *USA Today*. https://www.usatoday.com/story/news/nation/2015/08/26/reports-two-dead-virginia-shooting-live-tv/32391633/

Bailey, E. (2014, June 12). Paul Lee, Seattle Pacific University shooting victim, was "a brother to everybody," family says. *Oregon Live*. http://www.oregonlive.com/north-of-26/index.ssf/2014/06/paul_lee_seattle_pacific_unive.html

Bal, H. M., & Baruh, L. (2015). Citizen involvement in emergency reporting: A study on witnessing and citizen journalism. *Studies in Communication & Culture, 6*(2), 213–231.

Baldwin, D. (2010, May 20). Sarah Edmondson to serve parole in Oklahoma. *The Oklahoman*. https://oklahoman.com/article/3462570/sarah-edmondson-to-serve-parole-in-oklahoma

Bandura, A. (1977). *Social learning theory*. Englewood Cliffs, NJ: Prentice Hall.

Barlett, C. P., Anderson, C. A., & Swing, E. L. (2009). Video game effects—Confirmed, suspected, and speculative: A review of the evidence. *Simulation & Gaming, 40*(3), 377–403. https://doi.org/10.1177/1046878108327539

Bartlett, J. (2016). *The dark net: Inside the digital underworld*. New York: Melville House.

Bazzaz, D., Fields, A., & Lacitis, E. (2020, July 4). 1 protester dead, 1 injured after man drives into protesters on I-5 in Seattle. *The Seattle Times*. https://www.seattletimes.com/seattle-news/2-people-hit-by-car-on-i-5-in-downtown-seattle-during-protest/

BBC News. (2018, April 26). Elliot Rodger: How misogynist killer became "incel hero." *BBC News*. https://www.bbc.com/news/world-us-canada-43892189

Bean, M. (2003, May 21). "Matrix" makes its way into courtrooms as defense strategy. *CNN*. https://www.cnn.com/2003/LAW/05/21/ctv.matrix.insanity/

Bellisle, M. (2020, July 4). Protester killed on Seattle freeway was dedicated to cause. *WMC5*. https://www.wmcactionnews5.com/2020/07/04/police-women-hit-by-car-seattle-highway-amid-protests/

References

Bellware, K., Berman, M., Pietsch, B., & De Vynck, G. (2022, July 5). Threats from Highland Park suspect drew police attention in 2019. *The Washington Post*. https://www.washingtonpost.com/nation/2022/07/05/robert-crimo-highland-park-parade-shooting/

Bengtsson, S., & Johansson, B. (2018). "Media micro-generations": How new technologies change our media morality. *Nordicom Review, 39*(2), 95–110.

Benitz, S. (2018, July 2). Rapper Boonk Gang's instagram gets deleted after he posts his own X-rated videos to his stories. *InTouch*. https://www.intouchweekly.com/posts/boonk-gang-instagram-shut-down-162697/

Berger, J. M. (2016). The Turner legacy: The storied origins and enduring impact of White Nationalism's deadly bible. *International Centre for Counter-Terrorism—The Hague, 7*(8). https://doi.org/10.19165/2016.1.11

Berkowitz, B., Blanco, A., Mayes, B. R., Auerbach, K., & Rindler, D. (2019). More and deadlier: Mass shooting trends in America. *The Washington Post*. https://www.washingtonpost.com/nation/2019/08/05/more-deadlier-mass-shooting-trends-america/?arc404=true

Berntzen, L. E., & Bjørgo, T. (2021). The term "lone wolf" and its alternatives: Patterns of public and academic use from 2000 to 2020. *Perspectives on Terrorism, 15*(3), 132–141.

Bilefsky, D., & Austen, I. (2018, April 24). Toronto van attack suspect expressed anger at women. *The New York Times*. https://www.nytimes.com/2018/04/24/world/canada/toronto-van-rampage.html?module=inline

Black, J. (1991). *The aesthetics of murder*. Baltimore: Johns Hopkins University Press.

Black, J. (1998). Grisham's demons. *College Literature, 25*(1), 35–40.

Black, J. (2002). *The reality effect: Film, culture, and the graphic imperative*. New York: Routledge.

Blain, L. (2015, April 17). And now GTA 5's an actual murder simulator. *Gamesradar.com*. https://www.gamesradar.com/gta-5-mods-murder-simulator/

Blau, R. (1989). The last safecracker. *Chicago Tribune*. https://www.chicagotribune.com/news/ct-xpm-1989-03-30-8903300970-story.html positive medis

Boduszek, D., Dhingra, K., & Debowska, A. (2016). The integrated psychosocial model of criminal social identity (IPM-CSI). *Deviant Behavior, 37*(9), 1023–1031.

Body Count. (1992). "Cop Killer" [Song]. On Body Count. Warner Brothers Records.

Bonus, J. A., Peebles, A., Mares, M., & Sarmiento, I. G. (2018). Look on the bright side (of media effects): Pokémon Go as a catalyst for positive life experiences. *Media Psychology, 21*(2), 263–287. https://doi.org/10.1080/15213269.2017.1305280

Borchard, K. (2015). Super columbine massacre RPG! and grand theft autoethnography. *Cultural Studies—Critical Methodologies, 15*(6), 446–454. https://doi.org/ 10.1177/1532708615614018

Borum, R., & Fulero, S. M. (1999). Empirical research on the insanity defense and attempted reforms: Evidence toward informed policy. *Law and Human Behavior, 23*(3), 375–395.

Bosman, J., Taylor, K., & Arango, T. (2019, August 10). A common trait among mass killers: Hatred toward women. *The New York Times.* https://www.nytimes.com/2019/08/10/us/mass-shootings-misogyny-dayton.html

Boxer, P., Huesman, L. R., Bushman, B. J., O'Brien, M., & Moceri, D. (2009). The role of violent media preference in cumulative developmental risk for violence and general aggression. *Journal of Youth and Adolescence, 38,* 417–428.

Boyle, K. (2001). What's natural about killing? Gender, copycat violence and Natural Born Killers. *Journal of Gender Studies, 10*(3), 311–321. https://doi.org/10.1080/09589230120086511

Boyle, K. (2005). *Media and violence.* Thousand Oaks, CA: Sage Publications.

Bracetti, A. (2011). World wide dead: 25 real life social networking Murders Wayne forrester. *Complex.* https://www.complex.com/pop-culture/2011/01/world-wide-dead-25-real-life-social-networking-murders/wayne-forrester

Bramesco, C. (2019, August 26). Natural Born Killers at 25: The problem with Oliver Stone's hit film. *The Guardian.* https://www.theguardian.com/film/2019/aug/26/natural-born-killers-problem-oliver-stone-hit-film-25-year-anniversary

Brandenburg v. Ohio, 395 U.S. 444 (1969). https://supreme.justia.com/cases/federal/us/395/444/

Branson-Potts, H., & Winton, R. (2018, April 26). How Elliot Rodger went from misfit mass murderer to "saint" for group of misogynists—and suspected Toronto killer. *Los Angeles Times.* https://www.latimes.com/local/lanow/la-me-ln-elliot-rodger-incel-20180426-story.html

Brooks, X. (2002). Natural born copycats. *The Guardian.* https://www.theguardian.com/culture/2002/dec/20/artsfeatures1

Brown, G. R. (2016). The blue line on thin ice: Police use of force modifications in the era of camera phones and YouTube. *British Journal of Criminology, 56*(2), 293–312.

Brown v. Entertainment Merchants Association, 131 S.Ct. 2729 (2011). https://www.leagle.com/decision/insco20110627000t

Browne, K. D., & Hamilton-Giachritis, C. (2005). The influence of violent media on children and adolescents: A public-health approach. *The Lancet, 365*(9460), 702–710. https://doi.org/10.1016/S0140-6736(05)17952-5

Brownfield, T. (2019, July 18). The Hollywood murder that made states take stalking seriously. *The Saturday Evening Post.* https://www.saturdayeveningpost.com/2019/07/the-hollywood-murder-that-made-states-take-stalking-seriously/

Bryant, J., & Zillman, D. (Eds.). (2002). *Media effects: Advances in theory and research.* Mahwah, NJ: Lawrence Erlbaum Associates.

Buffington-Vollum, J. K., & Johnson, W. W. (2013). *The criminalization of mental illness.* Carolina Academic Press.

References

Bushman, B. J. (1995). Moderating role of trait aggressiveness in the effects of violent media on aggression. *Journal of Personality and Social Psychology, 69*(5), 950–960. https://doi.org/10.1037/0022-3514.69.5.950

Bushman, B. J. (1998). Priming effects of media violence on the accessibility of aggressive constructs in memory. *Personality and Social Psychology Bulletin, 24*(5), 1552–7433. https://doi.org/10.1177/01461672982450091

Bushman, B. J. (2016). Violent media and hostile appraisals: A meta-analytic review. *Aggressive Behavior, 42*(6), 605–613. http://doi.org/10.1002/ab.21655

Bushman, B. J., Gollwitzer, M., & Cruz, C. (2015a). There is broad consensus: Media researchers agree that violent media increase aggression in children, and pediatricians and parents concur. *Psychology of Popular Media Culture, 4*(3), 200–214. http://dx.doi.org/10.1037/ppm0000046

Bushman, B. J., Gollwitzer, M., & Cruz, C. (2015b). Agreement across stakeholders is consensus: Response to Ivory et al. (2015). *Psychology of Popular Media Culture, 4*(3), 230–235. http://dx.doi.org/10.1037/ppm0000061

Bushman, B. J., & Huesmann, L. R. (2006). Short-term and long-term effects of violent media on aggression in children and adults. *Archives of Pediatric Adolescent Medicine, 160*(4), 345–352. https://doi:10.1001/archpedi.160.4.348

Bushman, B. J., & Huesmann, L. R. (2012). Effects of violent media on aggression. In Singer, D. G. & Singer, J. L. (Eds.), *Handbook of children and the media* (pp. 231–248). Thousand Oaks, CA: Sage.

Butler, S. L. (2018, October 5). On prosthetic legs, man challenges marathon's 3-hour barrier. *Runner's World.* https://www.runnersworld.com/runners-stories/a23597848/man-tries-to-break-3-hours-on-two-prosthetic-legs/

Byers v. Edmondson, 712 So.2d 681 (1998). https://www.leagle.com/decision/19981393712so2d68111301

Byers v. Edmondson, 826 So.2d 551 (2002). https://www.leagle.com/decision/20021377826so2d55111367

Calabasas rapper Boonk gang out on bail after assault weapon and narcotics charges. (2018). https://www.dailynews.com/2018/03/09/calabasas-rapper-boonk-gang-due-in-court-on-assault-weapon-and-narcotics-charges/

Caldwell, D. (2018). Boonk gang. https://knowyourmeme.com/memes/people/boonk-gang

Callahan, L. A., Steadman, H. J., McGreevy, M. A., & Robbins, P. C. (1991). The volume and characteristics of insanity defense pleas: An eight-state study. *Bulletin of the American Academy of Psychiatry and Law, 19*(4), 331–338.

Calvert, C. (2019). First Amendment envelope pushers: Revisiting the incitement-to-violence test with Messrs, Brandenburg, Trump, & Spencer. *Connecticut Law Review, 51*(1), 117–154. https://opencommons.uconn.edu/law_review/411

Campbell, C. E. (2000). Murder media—Does media incite violence and lose First Amendment protection? *Chicago-Kent Law Review, 76*(1), 637–669.

Campbell, D. (2003, May 19). Matrix films blamed for series of murders by obsessed fans. *The Guardian.* https://www.theguardian.com/world/2003/may/19/usa.filmnews

Campbell, J. C. (2015, May 31). Bob Dole, Hollywood, and "mainstreaming of deviancy," 1995. *The 1995 Blog: The Year the Future Began.* https://1995blog.com/2015/05/31/bob-dole-hollywood-and-the-mainstreaming-of-deviancy-1995/

Campbell, K. (2002, October 10). As sniper hunt grows role of media blurs. *Christian Science Monitor.* http://www.csmonitor.com/2002/1010/p01s03-usju.htm)

Campbell-Kelly, M., & Garcia-Swartz, D. D. (2015). *From mainframes to smartphones: A history of the international computer industry.* Cambridge, MA: Harvard University Press.

Can a video game lead to murder? (2005, March 6). *CBS News.* http://www.cbsnews.com/stories/2005/03/04/60minutes/main678261.shtml.

Canadian Press. (2012, December 23). "Canadian psycho" Luka Magnotta named Canadian Press newsmaker of the year. *National Post.* https://nationalpost.com/news/canada/canadian-psycho-luka-magnotta-named-canadian-press-newsmaker-of-the-year

Canadian Press. (2017, June 20). Convicted killer Luka Rocco Magnotta getting married: Report. *CTV News.* https://www.ctvnews.ca/canada/convicted-killer-luka-rocco-magnotta-getting-married-report-1.3468515

Cantor, J., & Wilson, B. J. (2003). Media and violence: Intervention strategies for reducing aggression. *Media Psychology, 3,* 363–403. https://doi.org/10.1207/S1532785XMEP0504_03

Capps, D. (2013). John W. Hinckley, Jr.: A case of Narcissistic Personality Disorder. *Pastoral Psychology, 62*(1), 247–269. https://doi.org/10.1007/s11089-012-0443-2

Chadee, D., Surette, R., Chadee, M., & Brewster, D. (2017). Copycat crime dynamics: The interplay of empathy, narrative persuasion and risk with likelihood to commit future criminality. *Psychology of Popular Media Culture, 6*(2), 142–158.

Chandran, R., & Asher-Shapiro, A. (2021, December 10). Analysis: Rohingya lawsuit against Facebook a "wake-up call" for social media. *Reuters.* https://www.reuters.com/technology/rohingya-lawsuit-against-facebook-wake-up-call-social-media-2021-12-10/

Chapman, F., & Tarasuk, L. (2016). Slender man on trial: Has media taken the minds of the young? *Criminal Law Bulletin, 52*(3), 715–735.

Chayka, K. (2022, May 19). The online spaces that enable mass shooters. *The New Yorker.* https://www.newyorker.com/culture/infinite-scroll/the-online-spaces-that-enable-mass-shooters

Cheston, P. (2008). Wife hacked to death by husband for saying she was "single" on Facebook. *Evening Standard.* http://www.standard.co.uk/news/wife-hacked-to-death-by-husband-for-saying-she-was-single-on-facebook-6916665.html

References 271

Childress, S. (2013, February 19). Richard Novia: Adam had episodes. He would completely withdraw. *Frontline*. https://www.pbs.org/wgbh/frontline/article/richard-novia-adam-had-episodes-he-would-completely-withdraw/

Chisholm, J. (2022, July 5). Highland Park mayor reveals she was Robert Crimo's Cub Scout leader: "How did somebody become this angry?" *The Independent*. https://www.independent.co.uk/news/world/americas/crime/highland-park-mayor-cub-scout-crimo-b2116212.html

Chiu, A. (2018, August 21). She "looked like a fireball": Internet "fire challenge" leaves 12-year-old Detroit girl severely burned. *The Washington Post*. https://www.washingtonpost.com/news/morning-mix/wp/2018/08/21/she-looked-like-a-fireball-internet-fire-challenge-leaves-12-year-old-detroit-girl-severely-burned/

Chokshi, N. (2019, March 15). PewDiePie put in spotlight after New Zealand shooting. *The New York Times*. https://www.nytimes.com/2019/03/15/technology/pewdiepie-new-zealand-shooting.html

Chong, P. H. S. (2012). "Asian really don't do this": On-scene offense characteristics of Asian American school shooters, 91–07. *Asian Criminology, 7*(3), 251–272.

Clarke, R. V. (2004). Technology, criminology, and crime science. *European Journal on Criminal Policy and Research, 10*(1), 55–63. https://doi.org/10.1023/B:CRIM.0000037557.42894.f7

Claroni, P., Dodson, B., Oblaender, C., & Afferbach, J. (Executive Producers) (2016). *Copycat Killers* [TV Series]. Story House Productions, Reelz, USA.

Cleary, T. (2017, October 16). Vester Lee Flanagan: 5 fast facts you need to know. *Heavy.com*. https://heavy.com/news/2015/08/lester-lee-flanagan-flanighan-flanigan-wdbj-tv-disgruntled-employee-virginia-shooting-suspect-cameraman-photos-video-chase-gun-gunman-arrested/

Cleckley, H. (1941). *The mask of sanity*. Augusta, GA: Emily S. Cleckley.

Clement, J. (2020, June 4). Worldwide digital population as of April 2020. *Statistica*. https://www.statista.com/statistics/617136/digital-population-worldwide/

Clements, C. (2012). Protecting protected speech: Violent video game legislation post- Brown v. Entertainment Merchants Ass'n. *Boston College Review, 53*(2), 661–692.

CNN. (2003, May 20). Obsessed with "The Matrix." *CNN.com*. http://www.cnn.com/TRANSCRIPTS/0305/20/ltm.06.html

CNN. (2013, August 24). Piers Morgan has man who kills parents to say if I had assault weapon, things much worse. https://www.youtube.com/watch?v=TO0QQEp-1p4

CNN. (2022, May 16). 10 people killed in racially motivated shooting in Buffalo. https://transcripts.cnn.com/show/cnr/date/2022-05-16/segment/18

Cochran, L. (2008, June 27). Teens say: Video game made them do it. *ABC News*. https://abcnews.go.com/TheLaw/story?id=5262689&page=1

Cockerell, I. (2021, February 17). Capitol insurrection captured, and then erased on social media. *Coda*. https://www.codastory.com/disinformation/social-media-platforms-rewriting-history/

Cohen, F. (2016). John Hinckley, Jr.: Once again. *Correctional Mental Health Report, 18*(3), 42–42.

Cole, D. (2019, September 10). John Hinckley Jr. to seek unconditional release by end of year. *CNN.* https://www.cnn.com/2019/09/10/politics/john-hinckley-unconditional-release-motion/index.html

Coleman, L. (2004). *The copycat effect: How the media and popular culture trigger mayhem in tomorrow's headlines.* New York: Paraview Pocket Books.

Collins, B., & Ali, S. S. (2022, July 4). Highland Park shooting person of interest left online trail of violent imagery. *NBC News.* https://www.nbcnews.com/news/us-news/chicago-shooting-person-interest-left-online-trail-violent-imagery-rcna36628

Commonwealth v. Knox, 190 A.3d 1146 (Pa. 2018). https://casetext.com/case/commonwealth-v-knox-30

Commonwealth v. O'Brien, 432 Mass.578 (2000). https://www.leagle.com/decision/20001010432mass5781970

Connor, J. (2018, April 9). Grand Theft Auto V—the highest grossing media title ever. *TweakTown.* https://www.tweaktown.com/news/61482/grand-theft-auto-highest-grossing-media-title/index.html

Cooper, C. A. (2007). *Violence in the media and its influence on criminal defense.* Jefferson, North Carolina: McFarland & Co.

Corcoran, K. (2018, February 19). A 15-year-old boy was arrested over a threat of copycat killings posted to Instagram after the Florida high school shooting. *Business Insider.* https://www.businessinsider.com/boy-15-arrested-for-threatening-copycat-florida-attack-on-instagram-2018-2

Cordell, K. (2019). The news coverage of Columbine helped turn the tragedy into an international phenomenon. Columbine: 20 years later. *5280.* https://columbine.5280.com/the-news-coverage-of-columbine-helped-turn-the-tragedy-into-an-international-phenomenon/

Cornwell, R. (2009, June 20). Sex, death and cyberspace: Who is the craigslist killer? *Independent.* http://www.independent.co.uk/news/world/americas/sex-death-and-cyberspace-who-is-the-]\craigslist-killer-1707653.html

Cotter, J. (2016, January 1). Website owner gets conditional sentence for posting Magnotta video. *CTV News Canada.* https://www.ctvnews.ca/canada/website-owner-gets-conditional-sentence-for-posting-magnotta-video-1.2750483

Courtwright, D. T. (1998). Way cooler than Manson: Natural born killers (1994). *Film & History: An Interdisciplinary Journal, 28*(3), 28–36. muse.jhu.edu/article/395866

Craig, D. (2022, May 17). Buffalo victim Ruth Whitfield visited husband at nursing home and went to Tops. He doesn't know she died. *USA Today.* https://www.usatoday.com/story/news/nation/2022/05/17/buffalo-shooting-victim-husband-nursing-home/9807556002/

Crime Beat TV. (2008, November 30). 16x9-Mark Twitchell: The copycat killer? https://www.youtube.com/watch?v=ozTotjIHkEM

References 273

Cross, B. W., & Pruitt, S. W. (2013). Dark Knights rising: The Aurora theatre and Newtown massacres and shareholder wealth. *Journal of Criminal Justice, 41*(6), 452–457. https://doi: 10.1016/j.jcrimjus.2013.09.002

Crowely, K. (2008, June 26). Video villains come to life. *New York Post.* https://nypost.com/2008/06/26/video-villains-come-to-life/

Crump, D. (1994). Camouflaged incitement: Freedom of speech, communicative torts, and the borderland of the Brandenburg Test. *Georgia Law Review, 29*(1), 1–80.

Cruz, C. (2014, August 13). SPU shooter: Despite troubling history, law let him have guns. *The Seattle Times.* https://www.seattletimes.com/seattle-news/spu-shooter-despite-troubling-history-law-let-him-have-guns/

Cullen, D. (2004, April 20). The depressive and the psychopath: At last we know why the Columbine killers did it. *Slate.* https://slate.com/news-and-politics/2004/04/at-last-we-know-why-the-columbine-killers-did-it.html

Cullen, D. (2007, April 20). Psychopath? Depressive? Schizophrenic?: Was Cho Seung-Hui really like the Columbine killers? *Slate.* http://www.slate.com/id/2164757/).

Cullen, D. (2010). *Columbine.* New York: Riverrun.

Curiel, J. (2000, June 6). Suspect in dismemberment slaying ruled unfit to stand trial / S.F. man will go to psychiatric institution. *SFGate.* https://www.sfgate.com/news/article/Suspect-in-Dismemberment-Slaying-Ruled-Unfit-to-2756388.php

Curry, C. (2013, November 25). Sandy Hook report offers grim details of Adam Lanza's bedroom. *ABC News.* https://abcnews.go.com/US/sandy-hook-report-inside-gunman-adam-lanzas-bedroom/story?id=21009111

Davidson v. Time Warner, Inc., WL 405907 (S.D. Tex. March 31, 1997). https://www.pdf-archive.com/2017/08/09/sc19950-taupier-appx-msb/sc19950-taupier-appx-msb.pdf

Davies, K., & Woodhams, J. (2019). The practice of crime linkage: A review of the literature. *Journal of Investigative Psychology & Offender Profiling, 16*(3), 169–200. https://doi.org/10.1002/jip.1531

Davies, L., & Razlogova, E. (2013). Framing the contested history of digital culture. *Radical History Review, 117,* 5–31. https://doi.org/10.1215/01636545-2210446

de Bie, J. L., de Poot, C. J., & van der Leun, J. P. (2015). Shifting modus operandi of Jihadist foreign fighters from the Netherlands between 2000 and 2013: A crime script analysis. *Terrorism and Political Violence, 27,* 416–440. https://doi.org/10.1080/09546553.2015.1021038

de Graaf, B. (2021). How contagious were the capitol riots in Europe—In praxis and in perception? *Terrorism and Political Violence, 33*(5), 922–925. https://doi.org/10.1080/09546553.2021.1932346

DeCook, J. R. (2018). Memes and symbolic violence: #proudboys and the use of memes for propaganda and the construction of collective identity. *Learning, Media, and Technology, 43*(4), 485–504. https://doi.org/10.1080/17439884.2018.1544149

Denham, J., & Spokes, M. (2019). Thinking outside the "murder box": Virtual violence and pro-social action in video games. *British Journal of Criminology, 59*(3), 737–755. https://doi:10.1093/bjc/azy067

Dentzel, Zaryn. (2013). "How the Internet Has Changed Everyday Life." In Ch@nge: 19 Key Essays on How the Internet Is Changing Our Lives. Madrid: BBVA. https://www.bbvaopenmind.com/en/articles/internet-changed-everyday-life/

Desjardins, J. (2016, October 10). The slow death of legacy media. *Business Insider.* https://www.businessinsider.com/the-slow-death-of-legacy-media-2016-10

Dey, S. (2022, May 24). 21 killed at Uvalde elementary in Texas' deadliest school shooting ever. *Texas Tribune.* https://www.ksat.com/news/texas/2022/05/24/two-killed-others-injured-in-school-shooting-in-uvalde-hospital-officials-say/

Di Nicola, A. (2022). Towards digital organized crime and digital sociology. *Trends in Organized Crime.* https://doi.org/10.1007/s12117-022-09457-y

Diener, E., Oishi, S., & Park, J. (2014). An incomplete list of eminent psychologists of the modern era. *Archives of Scientific Psychology, 2,* 20–32. http://dx.doi.org/10.1037/arc0000006

DocuCloud.org. (2014). *My twisted world: The story of Elliot Rodger.* https://www.documentcloud.org/documents/1173619-rodger-manifesto

Doley, R., Ferguson, C., & Surette, R. (2013). Copycat firesetting: Bridging two research areas. *Criminal Justice and Behavior, 40*(12), 1472 –1491. https://doi.org/10.1177/0093854813496997

Donnerstein, E. (2011). Media and aggression: From TV to the Internet. In Forgas, J.P., Kruglanski, A.W., & Williams, K.D. (Eds.), *The psychology of social conflict and aggression* (pp. 267–284). Psychology Press.

Does 15 15 2014 v. King County LLC KCPQ TV Q13 TV TV LLC TV 100 (2014). https://caselaw.findlaw.com/wa-court-of-appeals/1721824.html

D'Oro, R. (2010, February 6). "Last Seduction" appeal granted. *The Spokesman-Review.* https://www.spokesman.com/stories/2010/feb/06/last-seduction-appeal-granted/

Douglas, J. E., Burgess, A. W., Burgess, A. G., & Ressler, R. K. (2006). *Crime classification manual.* San Francisco: Josey-Bass Publishers.

Douglas, J. E., & Olshaker, M. (1997). *Journey into darkness: The FBI's premier investigator penetrates the minds and motives of the most terrifying serial killers.* New York: Pocket Books.

Douglas, J. E., & Olshaker, M. (1997). *Mind hunter: Inside the FBI's elite serial crime unit.* Pocket Books.

Douglas, J. E., & Olshaker, M. (1999). *The anatomy of motive.* New York: Pocket Books.

Douglas, J. E., Ressler, R. K., Burgess, A. W., & Hartman, C. R. (2004). Criminal profiling from crime scene analysis. In Keppel, R. (Ed.), *Offender profiling* (pp. 23–34). Belmont, CA: Wadsworth.

References

Draper, K. (2019, August 5). Video games aren't why shootings happen. politicians still blame them. *The New York Times.* https://www.nytimes.com/2019/08/05/sports/trump-violent-video-games-studies.html

Dwoskin, E. (2021, January 13). Facebook's Sandberg deflected blame for Capitol riot, but new evidence shows how platform played role. *The Washington Post.* https://www.washingtonpost.com/technology/2021/01/13/facebook-role-in-capitol-protest/

Earle, R. (2021). Exploring narrative, convictions and autoethnography as a convict criminologist. Tijdschrift over Cultuur & Criminaliteit. *Journal of Culture and Crime, 2020*(3), 80–96. http://oro.open.ac.uk/75897/1/TCC%20Dutch%20journal%20CC%20published%20copy.pdf

Ehrenberg, R. (2012). Bionic women (and men) get closer to reality. *Science News, 182*(13), 20–21.

Elise, A. (2014a, October 22). After gamergate: Connection between video game violence and real-world behavior is complicated. *International Business Times.* https://www.ibtimes.com/after-gamergate-connection-between-video-game-violence-real-world-behavior-complicated-1710360

Elise, A. (2014b, November 19). Experts: "GTA V's" sex scenes could trigger violence against women. *International Business Times.* https://www.ibtimes.com/experts-gta-vs-sex-scenes-could-trigger-violence-against-women-1725799

Ellis, N. T. (2022, May 22). "Traumatizing" Buffalo massacre strikes a chord with families who have lost loved ones to racist mass shootings. *CNN.* https://www.cnn.com/2022/05/22/us/buffalo-shooting-reaction-other-racist-shootings/index.html

Ellis, N. T. (2022, May 28). Oldest Buffalo massacre victim Ruth Whitfield honored at funeral service. *CNN.* https://www.cnn.com/2022/05/28/us/buffalo-victim-ruth-whitfield-funeral/index.html

Ellison, G. C. (2012). Fantasy as addition to reality? An exploration of fantasy aggression and fantasy aggression in violent media. *Pastoral Psychology, 61*, 513–530. https://doi.org/10.1007/s11089-011-0426-8

Elson, M., Ferguson, C. J., Gregerson, M., Hogg, J. L., Ivory, J., Klisanin, D., Markey, P. M., Nichols, D., & Siddiqui, S. (2019). Do policy statements on media effects faithfully represent the science? *Advances in Methods and Practices in Psychological Science, 2*(1), 12–25. https://doi.org/10.1177/2515245918811301

Enos, L. (1999). Copycat crimes [Documentary]. *Investigative Reports.* Chicago, IL: Kurtis Productions.

Entertainment Software Association v. Blagojevich, 404 F.Supp.2d 1051 (2005). https://www.leagle.com/decision/20051455404fsupp2d105111364

Entertainment Software Association v. Granholm, 426 F.Supp.2d 646 (2006). https://www.leagle.com/decision/20061072426fsupp2d64611027

Entertainment Software Association v. Hatch, 443 F.Supp.2d 1065 (2006). https://www.leagle.com/decision/20061508443fsupp2d106511425

Entertainment Software Association v. Swanson, 519 F.3d 768 (2008). https://www.leagle.com/decision/20081287519f3d76811279

Epstein, S. C. (1995). The new mythic monster. In Ferrell, J., & Sanders, C. R. (Eds.), *Cultural criminology* (pp. 66–70). Northeastern University Press.

Eschner, K. (2017, August 28). The farmboy who invented television. *Smithsonian Magazine.* https://www.smithsonianmag.com/smart-news/farmboy-who -invented-television-while-plowing-180964607/

Estrada, F., Bäckman, O., & Nilsson, A. (2016). The darker side of equality? The declining gender gap in crime: Historical trends and an enhanced analysis of staggered birth cohorts. *British Journal of Criminology, 56,* 1272– 1290. https://doi.org/10.1093/bjc/azv114

Eustachewich, L. (2020, July 2). Seattle sees 525 percent spike in crime thanks to CHOP: Mayor Durkan. *New York Post.* https://nypost.com/2020/07 /02/seattle-sees-525-percent-spike-in-crime-thanks-to-chop-mayor -durkan/

Evans, G. (2022, June 28). John Hinckley Jr. tells "CBS Mornings" no concerts planned; apologizes to Jodie Foster, shooting victims' families. *Deadline.* https://deadline.com/2022/06/john-hinckley-jr-cbs-morning-major -garrett-interview-jodie-foster-ronald-reagan-apology-1235053258/

Ewen, N. (2020). "Talk to each other like it's 1995": Mapping nostalgia for the 1990s in contemporary media culture. *Television & New Media, 21*(6), 574–580.

Exclusive Prison Interview: Amanda Taylor Talks. (2019, April 25). *True Crime Daily.* https://www.youtube.com/watch?v=6kE4tPfOoZo

Extremera, N., Quintana-Orts, C., Sánchez-Álvarez, N., & Rey, L. (2019). The role of cognitive emotion regulation strategies on problematic smartphone use: Comparison between problematic and non-problematic adolescent users. *International Journal of Environmental Research and Public Health.*

Fagan, J., Wilkinson, D.J., Davies, G. (2007). Social contagion of violence. In Flannery, D. J., Vazsonyi, A. T., & Waldman, I. D. (Eds.), *The Cambridge handbook of violent behavior and aggression* (pp. 688–723). Cambridge University Press. https://doi.org/10.1017/CBO9780511816840 .037

Fahey, R. A. Matsubayashi, T., & Ueda, M. (2018). Tracking the Werther Effect on social media: Emotional responses to prominent suicide deaths on twitter and subsequent increases in suicide. *Social Science and Medicine, 219,* 19–29. https://doi.org/10.1016/j.socscimed.2018.10.004

Farmer, A. K., & Sun, I. Y. (2016). In Deflem, M. (Ed.), Citizen journalism and police legitimacy: Does recording the police make a difference? *The Politics of Policing: Between Force and Legitimacy (Sociology of Crime, Law and Deviance), 21,* 239–256). Bingley: Emerald Group Publishing Limited.

Farrell, N. (2005, August 12). Grand Theft Auto player gets death penalty. *The Inquirer.* https://www.theinquirer.net/inquirer/news/1014067/grand-theft -auto-player-death-penalty

Farrell, P. (2018, April 24). What is the Incel movement? 5 fast facts you need to know. https://heavy.com/news/2018/04/incel-movement-alek-minassian -elliot-rodger/

References

Fawcett, A. (1980). *John Lennon: One day at a time*. New York: Grove Press.

Feaver, D. B. (1981, March 31). Three men shot at the side of their president. *The Washington Post*. http://www.washingtonpost.com/wp-dyn/articles/A38802 -2004Jul9.html

Feiner, L. (2022, May 31). Supreme Court blocks Texas social media law that tech companies warned would allow hateful content to run rampant. *CNBC*. https://www.cnbc.com/2022/05/31/supreme-court-blocks-texas -social-media-law-tech-companies-warned-would-allow-hateful-content -to-run-rampant.html

Felson, R. B. (1996). Mass media effects on violent behavior. *Annual Review of Sociology, 22*, 103–128.

Feral, R. (1985). *Hit man: A technical manual for independent contractors*. Paladin Press.

Ferguson, C. J. (2010). Video games and youth violence: A prospective analysis in adolescents. *Journal of Youth and Adolescence, 40*(4), 377–391. https:// doi.org/10.1007/s10964-010-9610-x

Ferguson, C. J. (2013, September 17). Stop tearing ourselves up about mass killings. *Time*. https://ideas.time.com/2013/09/17/viewpoint-navy-yard-shooters -motive-is-irrelevant/

Ferguson, C. J. (2013, September 20). Don't link video games with mass shootings. *CNN*. https://www.cnn.com/2013/09/20/opinion/ferguson-video -games/index.html?iref=allsearch

Ferguson, C. J. (2013, November 12). Parents, relax: Movie violence up, real violence down. *Time*. https://ideas.time.com/2013/11/12/parents-relax -movie-violence-up-real-violence-down/

Ferguson, C. J. (2013, November 27). Adam Lanza's motive a mystery in Sandy Hook killings. *CNN*. https://www.cnn.com/2013/11/27/opinion/ferguson -sandy-hook/index.html?iref=allsearch

Ferguson, C. J. (2014, May 25). Misogyny didn't turn Elliot Rodger into a killer. *Time*. https://time.com/114354/elliot-rodger-ucsb-misogyny/

Ferguson, C. J. (2015). Do Angry Birds make for angry children? A meta-analysis of video game influences on children's and adolescents' aggression, mental health, prosocial behavior, and academic performance. *Perspectives on Psychological Science, 10*(5), 646–666. https://www.jstor.org/stable /44281927

Ferguson, C. J. (2018, September 19). Strawberry sabotage: What are copycat crimes and who commits them? *The Conversation*. https://theconversation .com/strawberry-sabotage-what-are-copycat-crimes-and-who-commits -them-103423

Ferguson, C. J., Copenhaver, A., & Markey, P. (2020). Reexamining the findings of the American Psychological Association's 2015 Task Force on Violent Media: A meta-analysis. *Perspectives on Psychological Science, 15*(6), 1423– 1443. https://doi.org/10.1177/1745691620927666

Ferguson, C. J., Coulson, M., & Barnett, J. (2011). Psychological profiles of school shooters: Positive directions and one big wrong turn. *Journal of*

Police Crisis Negotiations, 11, 141–158. https://doi.org/10.1080/15332586
.2011.581523

Ferguson, C., Klisinan, D., Hogg, J. L., Wilson, J., Markey, P., Przybylski, A., Elson, M., Ivory, J., Linebarger, D., Gregerson, M., Farley, F., & Siddiqui, S. (2017). News media, public education and Public Policy Committee. *The Amplifier Magazine.* Society for Media, Psychology, & Technology, Division 46 of the American Psychological Association. https://div46amplifier.com/2017/06/12/news-media-public-education-and-public-policy-committee/

Ferguson, C. J., Smith, S., Miller-Stratton, H., Fritz, S., & Heinrich, E. (2008). Aggression in the laboratory: Problems with the validity of the modified Taylor Competitive Reaction Time Test. *Journal of Aggression, Maltreatment & Trauma, 17*(1), 118–132.

Ferrara, J. (May 11, 2016). The psychology of copycat crime. *JSTOR Daily.* https://daily.jstor.org/psychology-copycat-crime/

Ferrell, J. (1995). Culture, crime, and cultural criminology. *Journal of Criminal Justice and Popular Culture, 3*(2), 25–42.

Ferrell, J. (1999). Cultural criminology. *Annual Review of Sociology, 25,* 395–418.

Ferrell, J., & Hamm, M. S. (1998). *Ethnography at the edge: Crime, deviance, and field research.* Belmont, CA: Wadsworth.

Ferrell, J., Hayward, K., & Young, J. (2006). *Cultural criminology: An invitation.* Thousand Oaks, CA: Sage Publications.

Ferrell, J., Hayward, K., & Young, J. (2015). *Cultural criminology: An invitation, 2nd edition.* Thousand Oaks, CA: Sage Publications.

Ferrell, J., & Sanders, C. R. (1995). *Cultural criminology.* Boston: Northeastern University Press.

Finkel, N. J. (1989). The Insanity Defense Reform Act of 1984: Much ado about mothing. *Behavioral Sciences & the Law, 7*(3), 403–419.

Finkelstein, J., Goldenberg, A., Stevens, S., Jussin, L., Donohue, J. K., & Paresky, P. (2020). Network-enabled anarchy: How militant anarcho socialist networks use social media to instigate widespread violence against political opponents and law enforcement. Network Contagion Research Institute. https://networkcontagion.us/reports/network-enabled-anarchy/

Firestre, R., & Jones, K. Y. (2000). Catchin' the heat of the beat: First amendment analysis of music claimed to incite violent behavior. *Loyola of Los Angeles Entertainment Law Review, 20*(1), 1–31. https://digitalcommons.lmu.edu/elr/vol20/iss1/1

Fister, B. (2005). Copycat crimes: Crime fiction and the marketplace of anxieties. *Clues, 23*(3), 43–56.

Fitz-Gibbon, J. (2022, June 6). Youngest victim of Uvalde school massacre laid to rest as heartbreaking funerals continue. *New York Post.* https://nypost.com/2022/06/06/youngest-victim-of-uvalde-school-massacre-laid-to-rest/

Follman, M. (2019). Armed and misogynist: How toxic masculinity fuels mass shootings. *Mother Jones.* https://www.motherjones.com/crime-justice/2019/06/domestic-violence-misogyny-incels-mass-shootings/

References

Follman, M., & Andrews, B. (2015, October 5). How columbine spawned dozens of copycats. *Mother Jones*. https://www.motherjones.com/politics/2015/10/columbine-effect-mass-shootings-copycat-data/

Ford, D. (2015, November 26). Facebook murder photo: Husband found guilty in death. *CNN*. https://www.cnn.com/2015/11/25/us/florida-facebook-murder-guilty/index.html

Forsyth, M., & Gibbs, P. (2020). Contagion of violence: The role of narratives, worldviews, mechanisms of transmission and contagion entrepreneurs. *International Journal for Crime, Justice, and Social Democracy, 9*(2), 37–59. https://doi.org/10.5204/ijcjsd.v9i2.1217

Fowler, K. (2021, May 21). TikTokers are lip-syncing to Angela Simpson's murder confession in bizarre trend. *Newsweek*. https://www.newsweek.com/angela-simpson-viral-tiktok-trend-audio-acting-challenge-1593629

Fox News. (2015, January 13). The Matrix made me do it. *Fox News*. https://www.foxnews.com/story/the-matrix-made-me-do-it

Franklin, D. (2019). Mental resilience in dealing with traumatic events. *Australian Journal of Forensic Sciences, 51*(4), 369–370. https://doi.org/10.1080/00450618.2019.1608700

Frattaroli, S., McGinty, E. E., Barnhorst, A., & Greenberg, S. (2015). Gun violence restraining orders: Alternative or adjunct to mental health-based restrictions on firearms? *Behavioral Sciences and the Law, 33* (2/3), 290–307.

Frazin, R. (2019, April 17). Investigation shows more than 100 copycat shooters inspired by Columbine since 1999. *The Hill*. https://thehill.com/blogs/blog-briefing-room/news/439263-investigation-shows-more-than-100-copycat-shooters-inspired-by

Frontline (2000). The lawsuits: A summary of the civil lawsuits being filed in school shootings, as of January 2000. *PBS.org*. https://www.pbs.org/wgbh/pages/frontline/shows/kinkel/blame/summary.html

Frye v. United States, 293 F. 1013 (D.C. Cir. 1923). https://casetext.com/case/frye-v-united-states-7

Fuqua, L. M. (2020, April 10). The Catcher in the Rye's connection to murder. *Medium.com*. https://medium.com/true-crime-addiction/the-catcher-in-the-ryes-connection-to-murder-true-crime-5c920e88d6d8

Gacono, C. B., & Meloy, J. R. (1988). The relationship between conscious cognitive style and unconscious defensive process in the psychopath. *Criminal Justice and Behavior, 15*, 472–483. https://doi.org/10.1177/0093854888015004004

Gacono, C. B. & Meloy, J. R. (1994). *The Rorschach assessment of aggressive and psychopathic personalities*. Lawrence Erlbaum Associates, Publishers.

Gaines, J. R. (1987). Mark Chapman: The man who shot Lennon. *People*. https://people.com/archive/cover-story-mark-chapman-the-man-who-shot-lennon-vol-27-no-8/

Gambino, L., & Swaine, J. (2015, August 26). Virginia TV shooter Vester Lee Flanagan was a "disturbed" and "unhappy man". *The Guardian*. https://www.theguardian.com/us-news/2015/aug/26/vester-lee-flanagan-virginia-tv-news-shooter

Ganguzza (Director) (1992). *Rage, Rights, Responsibilities* [Film]. Warner Music Group Incorporated—A Time Warner Company/Films for the Humanities & Sciences.

Garbutt, E. (2022, March 24). Vin Diesel heavily hints that CGI Paul Walker will be in Fast 10. *GamesRadar+*. https://www.gamesradar.com/vin-diesel-fast-10-cgi-paul-walker/

Garcia, S. E. (2018, September 25). Ex-content moderator sues Facebook, saying violent images caused her PTSD. *The New York Times*. https://www.nytimes.com/2018/09/25/technology/facebook-moderator-job-ptsd-lawsuit.html

Garland, D. (2001). *The culture of control: Crime and social order in contemporary society*. Chicago: University of Chicago Press.

Gaziano, C. (2001). Toward a broader conceptual framework for research on social stratification, childrearing patterns, and media effect. *Mass Communication & Society, 4*(2), 219–244. https://doi.org/:10.1207/S15327825MCS0402_06

Gentile, D. A., & Bushman, B. J. (2012). Reassessing media violence effects using a risk and resilience approach to understanding aggression. *Psychology of Media Culture, 1*(3), 138–151. https://doi.org/10.1037/a0028481

Gerbner, G. (1994). Reclaiming our cultural mythology: Television's global marketing strategy creates a damaging and alienated window on the world. *The Ecology of Justice, 38*. Retrieved February 28, 2004: http://www.context.org/ICLIB/IC38/Gerbner.htm.

Gerbner, G., Jhally, S., & Kilbourne, J. (2014). *The killing screens: Media and the culture of violence*. San Francisco: Kanopy Streaming. https://www.youtube.com/watch?v=2PHxTr-59hE

Gerler, E. R. (2007). What the Amish taught us. *Journal of School Violence, 6*(3), 1–2. https://doi.org/10.1300/J202v06n03_01

Germaine, A. (2021). "You're Too Taboo": Rapper Ice-T reveals controversial "Cop Killer" record nearly ruined his career. *Atlanta Black Star*. https://atlantablackstar.com/2021/07/06/youre-too-taboorapper-ice-t-reveals-controversial-cop-killer-record-nearly-ruined-his-career/

Germaine, D. (2001). Regulating rap music: It doesn't melt in your mouth. *DePaul Journal of Art, Technology & Intellectual Property Law, 11*(1), 83–131. https://via.library.depaul.edu/jatip/vol11/iss1/4

Gerstein, J. (2022, May 6). Judge tosses Trump suit against Twitter. *Politico*. https://www.politico.com/news/2022/05/06/judge-tosses-trump-suit-against-twitter-00030825

Gibbs, N., & Roche, T. (1990, December 20). The columbine tapes. *Time*. http://content.time.com/time/magazine/article/0,9171,992873,00.html

Gilbert, S. (2017, August 1). Did 13 reasons why spark a suicide contagion effect? A new study reveals that internet searches for suicide skyrocketed in the wake of the show's release. *The Atlantic*. https://www.theatlantic.com/entertainment/archive/2017/08/13-reasons-why-demonstrates-cultures-power/535518/

References

Gilbert, F., & Daffern, M. (2017). Aggressive scripts, violent fantasy and violent behavior: A conceptual clarification and review. *Aggression and Violent Behavior, 36,* 98–107. https://doi.org/10.1016/j.avb.2017.05.001

Global News. "Mark Twitchell: The copycat killer?" *16x19 on Global.* https://www.youtube.com/watch?v=ozTotjIHkEM

Goins, D. (2014, June 8). "Please Hurry": Seattle Pacific University shooting 911 calls released. *NBC News.* https://www.nbcnews.com/news/us-news/please-hurry -seattle-pacific-university-shooting-911-calls-released-n125636

Goodman, W. (1992). Review/Television; High Road is crowded as seminar discusses inflammatory lyrics. *The New York Times.* https://www.nytimes .com/1992/12/15/news/review-television-high-road-is-crowded-as -seminar-discusses-inflammatory-lyrics.html

Gould, M., Jamieson, P., & Romer, D. (2003). Media contagion and suicide among the young. *American Behavioral Scientist, 46*(9), 1269–1284. https://doi.org/10.1177/0002764202250670

Graphic Seattle, WA. Multiple #BLM protesters struck by vehicle on Freeway #CHOP. *Pinal Central.* https://www.pinalcentral.com/graphic -seattle-wa-multiple-blm-protesters-struck-by-vehicle-on-freeway-chop /video_97500c4b-f4dc-5f4c-aa61-e555c6b3522d.html

Grayson, N. (2022, May 20). How Twitch took down Buffalo shooter's stream in under two minutes. *The Washington Post.* https://www.washingtonpost .com/video-games/2022/05/20/twitch-buffalo-shooter-facebook-nypd -interview/

Green, S. J. (2016, November 11). Aaron Ybarra found guilty of first-degree murder in Seattle Pacific University shooting. *The Seattle Times.* https://www .seattletimes.com/seattle-news/crime/ybarra-found-guilty-of-seattle -pacific-university-shootings/

Green, S. J. (2016, October 31). Ybarra tells jury voices of God, Columbine shooter compelled him to go on SPU rampage. *The Seattle Times.* https://www.seattletimes.com/seattle-news/law-justice/ybarra-said-voices-of -god-columbine-shooter-compelled-him-to-go-on-spu-rampage/

Green, S. J. (2017, February 17). Aaron Ybarra sentenced to 112 years for deadly shooting at Seattle Pacific University. *The Seattle Times.* https://www .seattletimes.com/seattle-news/crime/aaron-ybarra-sentenced-to-112 -years-for-deadly-shooting-at-seattle-pacific-university/

Green, S. J., & Coleman, S. (2016, October 16). Ybarra tells jury voices of God, Columbine shooter compelled him to go on SPU rampage. *The Seattle Times.* https://www.seattletimes.com/seattle-news/law-justice/ybarra-said -voices-of-god-columbine-shooter-compelled-him-to-go-on-spu-rampage/

Greer, C., & McLaughlin, E. (2010). We predict a riot? Public order policing, new media environments and the rise of the citizen journalist. *British Journal of Criminology, 50*(6), 1041–1059.

Grimes, T., Anderson, J. A., & Bergen, L. (2008). *Media violence and aggression: Science and ideology.* Thousand Oaks, CA: Sage.

Grimes, W. (2016, June 8). Theresa Saldana, actress and attack survivor, dies at 61. *The New York Times.* https://www.nytimes.com/2016/06/09/arts/television /theresa-saldana-actress-and-attack-survivor-dies-at-61.html#:~:text =Theresa%20Saldana%2C%20who%20played%20Joe,Ms

Grisham, J. (1996). Unnatural killers. *The Oxford American, 9*(2), 343–350.

Grossman, D., & Paulsen, K. (2018). On media violence and aggression. *Journal of the American Academy of Physician Assistants, 31*(8), 11–12.

Grygiel, J. (2019, March 21). Livestreamed massacre means it's time to shut down Facebook Live. *The Conversation.* https://theconversation.com/livestreamed -massacre-means-its-time-to-shut-down-facebook-live-113830

Guillen, T. (2002). Serial killer communiqués: Helpful or hurtful? *Journal of Criminal Justice and Popular Culture, 9*(2), 55–68.

Gunnison, E., Bernat, F. P., & Goodstein, L. (2016). *Women, crime, and justice: Balancing the scales.* Hoboken, NJ: Wiley-Blackwell.

Gutierrez, L. (2017, September 21). Sharing an "All Lives Splatter" meme is not a good idea, these public officials learn. *The Kansas City Star.* https://www .kansascity.com/news/nation-world/article174568231.html#storylink=cpy

Guynn, J. (2021, January 6). "Burn down DC": Violence that erupted at Capitol was incited by pro-Trump mob on social media. *USA Today.* https://www .usatoday.com/story/tech/2021/01/06/trump-riot-twitter-parler-proud -boys-boogaloos-antifa-qanon/6570794002/

Hall, J. (2015, March 25). How "Furious 7" created a digital Paul Walker for his unfinished scenes. *Screen Crush.* https://screencrush.com/furious-7 -digital-paul-walker/

Hamm, M., & Spaaij, R. (2015). Lone wolf terrorism in America: Using knowledge of radicalization pathways to forge prevention strategies. National Criminal Justice Reference Service. https://www.ojp.gov/pdffiles1/nij /grants/248691.pdf

Hanley, C. (2000, May 7). San Francisco slaying hits home. *Los Angeles Times.* https://www.latimes.com/archives/la-xpm-2000-may-07-me-27353 -story.html

Hansen, M. (2006). How the cops caught BTK. *ABA Journal, 92* (4), 44–48.

Harbers, E., Deslauriers-Varin, N., Beaugrgard, E., & Van der Kemp, J. J. (2012). Testing the behavioural and environmental consistency of serial sex offenders: A signature approach. *Journal of Investigative Psychology and Offender Profiling, 9*(3), 259–273. https://doi.org/10.1002/jip.1368

Hare, R. D. (1991, 2003). *Manual for the psychopathy checklist-revised.* Toronto, Ontario: Multi-Health Systems.

Hare, R. D. (1993). *Without conscience: The disturbing world of psychopaths among us.* New York: Pocket Books.

Harper, N. (2023, April 3). Tracking gun violence in America: Nashville marks the 130th mass shooting this year. *Tr!llMag.* https://www.trillmag.com /news/politics/tracking-gun-violence-in-america-nashville-marks-the -130th-mass-shooting-this-year/

References

Hartocollis, A., & Eligon, J. (2008, May 7). Thurman's pursuer is found guilty. *The New York Times.* https://www.nytimes.com/2008/05/07/nyregion/07uma.html

Harvey, D. (2002). *Obsession: Celebrities and their stalkers.* Dublin, Ireland: Merlin Publishing.

Haselton, T., & Graham, M. (2019, October 9). The German synagogue shooting was streamed on Amazon's Twitch. *CNBC.* https://www.cnbc.com/2019/10/09/the-german-synagogue-shooting-was-streamed-on-twitch.html

Hays, G. (2022). ABC lets Reagan shooter John Hinckley advocate gun control, Twitter slams "off the rails" interview. *Fox News.* https://www.foxnews.com/media/abc-reagan-shooter-john-hinckley-advocate-gun-control-twitter-slams-off-rails-interview

Hayward, K. (2009). Visual criminology: Cultural criminology-style: Keith Hayward makes the case for "visual criminology." *Criminal Justice Matters, 78*(1), 12–14.

Hayward, K. J., & Young, J. (2004). Cultural criminology: Some notes on the script. *Theoretical Criminology, 8*(3), 259–273. https://doi:10.1177/1362480604044608

Hazelwood, R., & Warren, J. (2003). Linkage analysis: Modus operandi, ritual, and signature in serial sexual crime. *Aggression and Violent Behavior, 8*(6), 587–599.

Healing, C., & Helfgott, J. B. (2019). Victims of virtual violence. In Parkin, W. S. & Collins, P. A. (Eds.), *Victims of violence: For the record.* San Diego, CA: Cognella Publishing Company, 269–296.

Heartfelt Thanks from Letterman. (2005, March 22). *CBS News.* http://www.cbsnews.com/stories/2005/03/22/entertainment/main682106.shtml).

Hegedus, E. (2019, December 20). Netflix documentary about twisted killer disturbs fans on social media. *News.com.au.* https://www.news.com.au/entertainment/tv/netflix-documentary-about-twisted-killer-disturbs-fans-on-social-media/news-story/f3e7284da4b67b6fdb610d10454e30a7

Helfgott, J. B. (1997b). The unconscious defensive process/conscious cognitive style relationship in psychopaths. *Criminal Justice and Behavior, 24,* 278–293. https://doi.org/10.1177/0093854897024002008

Helfgott, J. B. (2004). Primitive defenses in the language of the psychopath: Considerations for forensic practice. *Journal of Forensic Psychology Practice, 4*(3), 1–29. https://doi.org/10.1300/J158v04n03_01

Helfgott, J. B. (2008). *Criminal behavior: Theories, typologies, and criminal justice.* Thousand Oaks, CA: Sage Publications.

Helfgott, J. B. (2014). Fame, media, and mass shootings: Culture plays a role in creating these tragedies. *Crosscut.* http://crosscut.com/2014/06/08/crime-safety/120459/fame-media-and-mass-shootings-culture-playing-role/?page=2.

Helfgott, J. B. (2015). Criminal behavior and the copycat effect: Review of the literature and theoretical framework for empirical investigation. *Aggression and Violent Behavior, 22,* 46–64. https://doi.org/10.1016/j.avb.2015.02.002

Helfgott, J. B. (2018). Searching for glimmers of ethnography in jailhouse criminology. In Rice, S. K & Maltz, M. (Eds.), *Using ethnography in criminology: Discovery through fieldwork*. Springer.

Helfgott, J. B. (2019). *No remorse: Psychopathy and criminal justice*. Santa Barbara, CA: Praeger.

Hemraj, F. (2021, January 10). The selfie killer: Caught by a true crime blogger. *Medium.com*. https://medium.com/chameleon/the-selfie-killer-caught-by-a-true-crime-blogger-eb1bd8cea9f6

Hermann, P., Duggan, P., & Alexander, K. (2015). Vester Lee Flanagan was "a man with a lot of anger," station manager says. *The Washington Post*. https://www.washingtonpost.com/local/crime/suspect-identified-in-shootings-of-va-reporter-camerman/2015/08/26/f1724618-4c05-11e5-84df-923b3ef1a64b_story.html

Henderson, J. (2018, November 22). Reporters look back on Dexter-inspired killer. *St. Albert Today*. https://www.stalberttoday.ca/local-news/reporters-look-back-on-dexter-inspired-wannabe-serial-killer-1300232

Hermeking, M. (2017). Culture and Internet consumption: Contributions from cross-cultural marketing and advertising research. *Journal of Computer-Mediated Communication, 11*(1), 192–216. https://doi.org/10.1111/j.1083-6101.2006.tb00310.x

Hern, A. (2017, January 5). Facebook Live is changing the world—but not in the way it hoped. *The Guardian*. https://www.theguardian.com/technology/2017/jan/05/facebook-live-social-media-live-streaming

Herz, A. (2016, June 15). Did we learn anything from seeing footage of the SPU shooting? *The Stranger*. https://www.thestranger.com/slog/2016/06/15/24218201/did-we-learn-anything-from-seeing-footage-of-the-spu-shooting

Hess, T. H., Hess, K. D., & Hess, A. K. (1999). The effects of violent media on adolescent inkblot responses: Implications for clinical and forensic assessments. *Journal of Clinical Psychology, 55*(4), 439–445. https://doi:10.1002/(sici)1097–4679(199904)55:4<439::aid-jclp8>3.0.co;2–3

Hesse, M. (2020). America's confused obsession with Mary Kay Letourneau. *The Washington Post*. https://www.washingtonpost.com/lifestyle/style/americas-confused-obsession-with-mary-kay-letourneau/2020/07/08/a7c6e842-c136-11ea-b178-bb7b05b94af1_story.html

Hill, G. (1992). *Illuminating shadows: The mythic power of film*. Boston: Shambhala Publications.

Hill, K. (2014, May 27). Elliot Rodger's videos were removed from YouTube, but only temporarily. *Forbes*. https://www.forbes.com/sites/kashmirhill/2014/05/27/youtube-finally-takes-down-all-of-elliot-rodgers-videos/#49b2ba70779a

Hines, A. (2019, May 28). How many bones would you break to get laid? *The Cut*. https://www.thecut.com/2019/05/incel-plastic-surgery.html

Hodge, M. (2019, July 12). Documentary explores the twisted world of women-hating "incels." *New York Post*. https://nypost.com/2019/07/12/documentary-explores-the-twisted-world-of-women-hating-incels/

References

Hoffner, C. A., Fujioka, Y., Cohen, E. L., & Seate, A. A. (2017). Perceived media influence, mental illness, and responses to news coverage of a mass shooting. *Psychology of Popular Media Culture, 6*(2), 159–173. http://dx.doi .org/10.1037/ppm0000093

Hopper, T. (2012, June 1). Luka Rocco Magnotta hunted by online sleuths over kitten videos long before murder accusations. *National Post.* https:// nationalpost.com/news/canada/luka-rocco-magnotta-kitten-video

Horne, D., & Simms, R. (2020, July 4). Protester dies, another fights for life after car drives into crowd on I-5. *KIRO 7 News.* https://www.kiro7.com/news /local/2-protesters-critically-injured-after-car-drives-into-crowd-i-5 /UQCNROPHTRB2DPPEEYJY5YQZAA/

Hough, Q. V. (2020, April 4). Taxi Driver ending explained: What's real and what's in Travis's head? *Screen Rant.* https://screenrant.com/taxi-driver -ending-travis-bickle-explained/

Hudson, D. L., Jr. (2009). Obscenity and pornography. *The first amendment encyclopedia.* https://www.mtsu.edu/first-amendment/article/1004/obscenity -and-pornography

Huesmann, L. R. (1998). The role of information processing and cognitive schema in the acquisition and maintenance of habitual aggressive behavior. In Geen, R. B., & Donnerstein, E. (Eds.), *Human aggression: Theories, research, and implications for social policy.* San Diego: Academic Press, 73–109.

Huesmann L. R. (2007). The impact of electronic media violence: scientific theory and research. *Journal of Adolescent Health, 41*(6). 1–12. https://doi.org /10.1016/

Huesmann, L. R. (2012). The contagion of violence: The extent, the processes, and the outcomes. In Patel, D. M., & Taylor, R. M. (Eds.), *Social and economic costs of violence: Workshop summary* (pp. 63–69). Washington, DC: The National Academies Press.

Huffman, Z. (2017, March 9). Robbers convicted off clips of "The town" lose appeal. *Courthouse News Service.* https://www.courthousenews.com/robbers -convicted-off-clips-town-lose-appeal/

Hummer, T. A., Wang, Y., Kronenberger, W. G., Mosier, K. M., Kalnin, A. J., Dunn, D. W., et al. (2010). Short-term violent video game play by adolescents alters prefrontal activity during cognitive inhibition. *Media Psychology, 13*, 136–154.

Hughes, S. S. (2012). US domestic surveillance after 9/11: An analysis of the chilling effect on first amendment rights in cases filed against the Terrorist Surveillance Program. *Canadian Journal of Law & Society, 27*(3), 399–425.

Ilan, J. (2019). Cultural criminology: The time is now. *Critical Criminology, 27*, 5–20. https://doi.org/10.1007/s10612-019-09430-2

Interactive Digital Software Association v. St. Louis County, Missouri 200 F. Supp. 2d 1126 (E.D. Mo. 2002). https://law.justia.com/cases/federal/district -courts/FSupp2/200/1126/2422093/

Iqbal, M. (2020, July 30). Facebook revenue and usage statistics. Business of Apps. https://www.businessofapps.com/data/facebook-statistics/

Islam, N., & Want, R. (2014). Smartphones: Past, present, and future. *IEEE Pervasive Computing, 13*(4), 89–92. https:\\10.1109/MPRV.2014.74

Ismail, A., Torosyan, G., & Tully, M. (2019). Social media, legacy media and gatekeeping: the protest paradigm in news of Ferguson and Charlottesville. *The Communication Review, 22*(3), 169–195. https://doi.org/10.1080/10714421.2019.1651153

Issa, Y. (2019). "A profoundly masculine act": Mass shootings, violence against women, and the amendment that could forge a path forward. *California Law Review, 107*(2), 673–706. https://www.californialawreview.org/print/a-profoundly-masculine-act-mass-shootings-violence-against-women-and-the-amendment-that-could-forge-a-path-forward/#clr-toc-heading-4

Jackman, T. (2003, May 17). Escape "The Matrix," go directly to jail. *The Washington Post.* https://www.washingtonpost.com/archive/politics/2003/05/17/escape-the-matrix-go-directly-to-jail/9cbda793-6af5-47a1-85ea-b1aa37afaac2/

Jackman, T. (2003, June 25). Virginia teenager pleads guilty to murdering parents. *The Washington Post.* https://www.washingtonpost.com/archive/local/2003/06/25/virginia-teenager-pleads-guilty-to-murdering-parents/b7d9ac19-56e7-49e0-a448-ea9f8b58fae7/

Jackman, T. (2003, October 2). Oakton son sentenced in slayings. *The Washington Post.* https://www.washingtonpost.com/archive/local/2003/10/02/oakton-son-sentenced-in-slayings/0104f11d-7388-41c6-be77-be0e696d3f77/

Jackson, C. (2020, November 27). Mass shootings in the US have risen sharply in 2020—why? *The Conversation.* https://theconversation.com/mass-shootings-in-the-us-have-risen-sharply-in-2020-why-150981

Jacobson, S. H. (2017). Random acts of violence? Examining probabilistic independence of the temporal distribution of mass killing events in the United States. *Violence and Victims, 32*(6), 1014–1023. https://doi:10.1891/0886-6708.VV-D-16-00039

James, M. (2018). Parkland's Nikolas Cruz made chilling videos before shooting: "You're all going to die." *USA Today.* https://www.usatoday.com/story/news/2018/05/30/parkland-killer-video-im-going-next-school-shooter/657774002/

James v. Meow Media, Inc., 90 F. Supp. 2d 798 (W.D. Ky 2000). https://law.justia.com/cases/federal/district-courts/FSupp2/90/798/2478891/

Jane, E. (2018). Stacys, Brads and 'reverse rape': inside the terrifying world of 'incels.' *Australian Broadcasting Corporation.* https://www.abc.net.au/news/2018-04-27/incels-inside-their-terrifying-online-world/9700932

Jenkins, P. (1994). *Using murder: The social construction of serial homicide.* Aldine de Gruyter.

Jennings, R. (2021, September 21). What would a healthy social media platform even look like? *Vox.* https://www.vox.com/the-goods/22684293/facebook-antitrust-lawsuit-wall-street-journal-report

References

Jobes, D. A., Berman, A. L., O'Carroll, P. W., Eastgard, S., & Knickmeyer, S. (1996). The Kurt Cobain suicide crisis: Perspectives from research, public health, and the news media. *Suicide & Life—Threatening Behavior, 26*(3), 260–264.

Jones, A. (2014, August 13). The girls who tried to kill for slender man. *Newsweek.* https://www.newsweek.com/2014/08/22/girls-who-tried-kill-slender -man-264218.html

Jones, J. (1992). *Let me take you down: Inside the mind of mark David Chapman, the man who killed John Lennon.* New York: Villard Books.

Kain, E. (2018, February 22). Trump blames violent video games for school shootings—Here's why he's wrong. *Forbes.* https://www.forbes.com/sites /erikkain/2018/02/22/trump-blames-violent-video-games-for-school -shootings-heres-why-hes-wrong/?sh=3476297c67f3

Kalvert, S. (1995). *The basketball diaries.* New Line Cinema.

Kardaras, N. (2016). *Glow kids: How screen addiction is hijacking our kids and how to break the trance.* New York: St. Martin's Griffin.

Karimi, F. (2021, January 19). Fearing more violence, online platforms are cracking down on livestreams from Washington. *CNN.* https://www.cnn .com/2021/01/19/us/capitol-attack-livestream-companies-trnd/index .html

Katsiyannis, A., Whitford, D. K., & Ennis, R. P. (2018). Historical examination of United States intentional mass school shootings in the 20th and 21st centuries: Implications for students, schools, and society. *Journal of Child and Family Studies, 27*(8), 2562–2573.

Katsuyama, J. (2022, May 31). There were warning signs on social media before the Texas mass shooting. *KTVU.com.* https://www.ktvu.com/news/mass -shooter-warning-signs-call-for-more-awareness

Katz, J. (1988). *Seductions of crime: Moral and sensual attractions in doing evil.* New York: Basic Books.

Katz, J. (2006). *The Macho Paradox: Why some men hurt women and how all men can help.* Napperville, IL: Sourcebooks.

Katz, J. (2017, October 9). The role of gender in mass shootings: Violence— Jackson Katz. *RT.com.* https://www.youtube.com/watch?v=FYUOpUqUSLE

Katz, J. (Writer) & Jhally, S. (Director) (1999). *Tough guise* [film]. Producer: Media Education Foundation.

Katz, J. (Writer) & Earp, J. (Director) (2013). *Tough guise 2* [film]. Producer: Media Education Foundation.

Kennedy-Kolar, D., & Charles, C. A. D. (2013). Hegemonic masculinity and mass murderers in the United States. *The Southwest Journal of Criminal Justice, 8*(2), 62–74.

Kepes, S., Bushman, B. J., & Anderson, C. A. (2017). Violent video game effects remain a societal concern: Reply to Hilgard. Engelhardt, and Rouder. *Psychological Bulletin, 143*(7), 775–782. https://doi.org/10.1037 /bul0000112

Keppel, R. D., & Birnes, W. (1997). *Signature killers.* New York: Pocket Books.

Keppel, R. D., Weis, J. G., Brown, K. M., & Welch, K. (2005). The Jack the Ripper murders: A modus operandi and signature analysis of the 1888–1891 whitechapel murders. *Journal of Investigative Psychology and Offender Profiling, 2*(1), 1–21. https://doi.org/10.1002/jip.22

Khavin, D., Willis, H., Hill, E., Reneau, N., Jordan, D., Engelbrecht, C., Triebert, C., Cooper, S., Browne, M., & Botti, D. (2021). Day of rage: How Trump supporters took the U.S. Capitol. *The New York Times.* https://www.nytimes.com/spotlight/us-capitol-riots-investigations

Kiehl, S. (December 5, 2003). Malvo art indicates "Matrix" obsession. *The Baltimore Sun.* https://www.baltimoresun.com/maryland/bal-te.md.drawings05dec05-story.html

Kirkpatrick, D. D. (2019, March 15). Massacre suspect traveled the world but lived on the internet. *The New York Times.* https://www.nytimes.com/2019/03/15/world/asia/new-zealand-shooting-brenton-tarrant.html

Kim, K. (2022, June 16). In the metaverse, life imitates art. *The New York Times.* https://www.nytimes.com/2022/06/16/special-series/krista-kim-metaverse-nft-art-reality.html

Kindelan, K., & Ghebremedhin, S. (2017, June 28). 2 California families claim "13 reasons why" triggered teens' suicides. *ABC News.* https://abcnews.go.com/US/california-families-claim-13-reasons-triggered-teens-suicides/story?id=48323640

Kinder, G. (1999). *Victim: The other side of murder.* Atlantic Monthly Press.

King, D. M., & Jacobson, S. H. (2017). Random acts of violence? Examining probabilistic independence of the temporal distribution of mass killing events in the United States. *Violence & Victims, 32*(6), 1014–1023.

King, S. (1986). *The Bachman books.* New York: Penguin.

King, S. (2013). *Guns.* Amazon (Kindle Single).

Kirby, T. (1993, November 26). Video link to Bulger murder disputed. *Independent.* https://www.independent.co.uk/news/video-link-to-bulger-murder-disputed-1506766.html

Kirsh, S. J. (1998). Seeing the world through "Mortal Kombat" colored glasses: Violent video games and the development of a short-term hostile attribution bias. *Childhood, 5*(2), 177–184.

Kirsh, S. J., Mounts, J. R. W., & Olczak, P. V. (2006). Violent media consumption and the recognition of dynamic facial expressions. *Journal of Interpersonal Violence, 21*(5), 571–584. https://doi.org/10.1177/0886260506286840

Kirsh, S. J., & Olczak, P. V. (2002). The effects of extremely violent comic books on social information processing. *Journal of Interpersonal Violence, 17*(11), 1830–1848.

Kirsta, A. (1994). *Deadlier than the male: Violence and aggression in women.* Hammersmith, London: HarperCollins.

Kiselyak, C. (Producer, Director) (1996). *Natural born killers—Director's cut* [Film]. Warner Brothers Productions.

Kivel, B. D., & Johnson, C. W. (2009). Consuming media, making men: Using collective memory work to understand leisure and the construction of masculinity. *Journal of Leisure Research, 41*(1), 110–134. https://doi.org/10.1080/00222216.2009.11950162

Klebold, S. (2016). *A mother's reckoning: Living in the aftermath of tragedy.* New York: Crown Publishers.

Klein, E. (2014, May 25). Mass murderers want glory and fame. Somehow, we need to stop giving it to them. *Vox.* https://www.vox.com/2014/5/25/5749416/don-t-give-elliot-rodger-in-death-the-fame-he-wanted-in-life

KLS.com. (2006, October 2). Experts say school shooting isn't necessarily a copycat crime. *KLS.com.* https://www.ksl.com/article/536081/experts-say-school-shooting-isnt-necessarily-a-copycat-crime

Kondrasuk, J. N. (2004). The effects of 9/11 and terrorism on human resource management: Recovery, reconsideration, and renewal. *Employee Responsibilities and Rights Journal, 16*(1), 25–35.

Kovner, J., & Altimari, D. (2018, December 9). More than 1,000 pages of documents reveal Sandy Hook shooter Adam Lanza's dark descent. *Los Angeles Times.* https://www.latimes.com/nation/la-na-adam-lanza-sandy-hook-20181209-story.html

Kraybill, D. B., Nolt, S. M., & Weaver-Zercher, D. L. (2010). *Amish Grace: How forgiveness transcended tragedy.* Jossey-Bass.

Krishnamurthy, S. (2018, August 23). Why Dennis Rader's court confession was compared to an "Academy Awards Acceptance Speech.". *Oxygen.* https://www.oxygen.com/snapped/crime-time/btk-killer-dennis-rader-court-confession-academy-awards-speech

Kunich, J. C. (2000). Natural born Copycat killers and the law of shock torts. *Washington University Law Review, 78*(4), 1157–1270.

Lane, J., & Ramirez, F. A. (2021). Social media as criminal evidence: New possibilities, problems. *Footnotes: A Magazine of the American Sociological Association, 49*(4). https://www.asanet.org/social-media-criminal-evidence-new-possibilities-problems.

Lang, C., & Schull, G. (Directors) & Tucker, K. M. (2017). John Muhammad and Lee Malvo—Copycat killers (Season 2, Episode 1) [TV Series Episode]. *Copycat Murders.* Story House Productions. https://www.youtube.com/watch?v=9RezM07g000

Langley, T., O'Neal. E. C., Craig, K. M., & Yost, E. A. (1992). Aggression-consistent, -inconsistent, and -irrelevant priming effects on selective exposure to media violence. *Aggressive Behavior, 18*(5), 349–356.

Langman, P. (2014, July 14). Aaron Ybarra: An analysis. *SchoolShooters.info* https://schoolshooters.info/sites/default/files/ybarra_analysis_1.1_0.pdf

Langman, P. (2017). Role models, contagions, and copycats: An exploration of the influence of prior killers on subsequent attacks. *SchoolShooters.info.* https://schoolshooters.info/sites/default/files/role_models_2.1.pdf

Langman, P. (2018). Different types of role model influence and fame seeking among mass killers and copycat offenders. *American Behavioral Scientist, 62*(2) 210–228.

Lankford, A. (2015). Mass shooters in the USA, 1966–2010: Differences between attackers who live and die. *Justice Quarterly, 32*(2), 360–379. http://dx.doi.org/10.1080/07418825.2013.806675

Lankford, A., & Madfis, E. (2018). Don't name them, don't show them, but report everything else: A pragmatic proposal for denying mass killers the attention they seek and deterring future offenders. *American Behavioral Scientist, 62*(2), 260–279. https://doi.org/10.1177/0002764217730854

Lankford, A., & Silver, J. (2020). Why have public mass shootings become more deadly? *Criminology & Public Policy, 19*, 37–60. https://doi.org/:10.1111/1745-9133.12472

Lankford, A., & Tomek, S. (2017). Mass killings in the United States from 2006 to 2013: Social contagion or random clusters? *Suicide and Life-Threatening Behavior, 48*(4), 459–467.

Larkin, R. W. (2009). The Columbine Legacy: Rampage shootings as political acts. *American Behavioral Scientist, 52*(9), 1309–1326. https://doi.org/10.1177/0002764209332548

Larson, M. S. (2003). Gender, race, and aggression in television commercials that feature children. *Sex Roles, 48*(1/2), 67–75.

Larosiere, M., & Greenlee, J. G. S. (2021). Red Flag laws raise red flags of their own. *Law and Psychology Review, 45,* 155–168.

Lasky, S. (2012). Natural born Copycat killers. *Security Technology Executive.* https://www.securityinfowatch.com/home/article/10754400/copycat-crimes-are-a-serious-problem

Lattanzio, R. (2019, October 8). Oliver Stone: "Joker" reminds me of "Natural Born Killers' backlash"—"The future is murder." *Indie Wire.* https://www.indiewire.com/2019/10/oliver-stone-interview-natural-born-killers-1202176848/

Leblanc, A. (2016). "Confession of a serial killer" takes readers inside the mind of BTK. *KMUW Witchita/NPR.* https://www.kmuw.org/post/confession-serial-killer-takes-readers-inside-mind-btk

Ledur, J., Rabinowitz, K., & Galocha, A. (2022, July 5). There have been over 300 mass shootings so far in 2022. *The Washington Post.* https://www.washingtonpost.com/nation/2022/06/02/mass-shootings-in-2022/

Lee, C. D., & Daiute, C. (2019). Introduction to developmental digital technologies in human history, culture, and well-being. *Human Development, 62,* 5–13. https://doi.org/10.1159/000496072

Lenthang, M. (2022, June 1). Uvalde shooting's evolving narrative: Here are the details police have walked back. *NBC News.* https://www.nbcnews.com/news/us-news/uvalde-shootings-evolving-narrative-are-details-police-walked-back-rcna31391

Leonard, T. (2008, June 27). "Grand theft auto gang" arrested. *The Telegraph.* https://www.telegraph.co.uk/news/worldnews/northamerica/usa/2207044/Grand-Theft-Auto gang-arrested.html

Leukfeld, R., & Jansen, J. (2015). Cyber criminal networks and money mules: An analysis of low-tech and high-tech fraud attacks in the Netherlands.

References

International Journal of Cyber Criminology, 9(2), 173–184. https://doi: 10
.5281/zenodo.56210

Leung, R. (2004). The mind of a school shooter. *CBS News.* https://www
.cbsnews.com/news/the-mind-of-a-school-shooter/

Leung, R. (2005). Can a video game lead to murder? Did "Grand Theft Auto"
cause one teenager to kill? *60 Minutes.* https://www.cbsnews.com/news
/can-a-video-game-lead-to-murder-04-03-2005/

Levin, I., & Mamlok, D. (2021). Culture and society in the digital age. *Information, 12*(2), 2–13. https://doi.org/10.3390/info12020068

Lewis, T. (2016, July 20). Mapping the human connectome. *The Scientist.* https://
www.the-scientist.com/daily-news/mapping-the-human-connectome
-33161

Lichfield, J. (1998, October 12). Sex-trap teenage killers may serve half jail term.
Independent. https://www.independent.co.uk/news/sex-trap-teenage-killers
-may-serve-half-jail-term-1177815.html

Lillebuen, S. (2012). Murderers have become online broadcasters. And their
audience is us. *The Globe and Mail Canada.* https://www.theglobeandmail
.com/news/national/murderers-have-become-online-broadcasters-and
-their-audience-is-us/article4226048/

Lindsay, K. (2019). Killing Eve's Villanelle was inspired by this real-life female
killer. *Refinery29.* https://www.refinery29.com/en-us/2019/04/228970
/killing-eve-villanelle-inspired-by-angela-simpson

Lloyd, B. T. (2002). A conceptual framework for examining adolescent identity,
media influence, and social development. *Review of General Psychology,
6*(1), 73–91. https://doi.org/10.1037/1089-2680.6.1.73

Long, A. (2015, December 29). Facebook video showing man drinking while driving leads to drunk driving arrest. Retrieved from https://www.nbc4i.com
/news/man-arrested-for-drunk-driving-after-facebook-post/1114275203

Loofbourow, L. (2020, July 27). The cancel culture trap: Can Black Lives Matter
accomplish what Me Too couldn't? *Slate.* https://slate.com/news-and
-politics/2020/07/black-lives-matter-me-too-cancel-culture-blacklash.html

Lösel, F., & Farrington, D. P. (2012). Direct protective and buffering protective
factors in the development of youth violence. *American Journal of Preventive Medicine, 43*(2SI), S8–S23.

Low, P. W., Jeffries, J. C., & Bonnie, R. J. (1986). *The trial of John W. Hinckley, JR:
A case study in the insanity defense.* Mineola, NY: The Foundation Press.

Lupica, M. (2013, March 25). Lupica: Morbid find suggests murder-obsessed
gunman Adam Lanza plotted Newtown, Conn.'s Sandy Hook massacre
for years. *New York Daily News.* https://www.nydailynews.com/news
/national/lupica-lanza-plotted-massacre-years-article-1.1291408

Lusher, A. (2019, April 26). Who killed Jill Dando? The main theories behind
murder of British TV's golden girl. *Independent.* https://www.independent
.co.uk/news/uk/crime/jill-dando-murder-theories-what-happened-who
-barry-george-bbc-documentary-a8851491.html

Lyon, D., & Haggerty, K. D. (2012). The surveillance legacies of 9/11: Recalling, reflecting on, and rethinking surveillance in the security era. *Canadian Journal of Law & Society, 27*(3), 319–339.

MacDonald, A. (1978). *The Turner diaries.* The National Alliance.

MacFarquhar, N. (2020, July 7). Drivers are hitting protesters as memes of car attacks spread. *The New York Times.* https://www.nytimes.com/2020/07/07/us/bloomington-car-attack-protesters.html

Madden, C. (2022, February 3). The taxi driver controversy explained: How Martin Scorsese's ultra-violent ending shocked audiences. *Film.* https://www.slashfilm.com/756410/the-taxi-driver-controversy-explained-how-martin-scorseses-ultra-violent-ending-shocked-audiences/

Madrigal, A. C. (2018, May 30). When did TV watching peak? *The Atlantic.* https://www.theatlantic.com/technology/archive/2018/05/when-did-tv-watching-peak/561464/

Malesky, L. A., Jr. (2007). Predatory online behavior: Modus operandi of convicted sex offenders in identifying potential victims and contacting minors over the Internet. *Journal of Child Sexual Abuse, 16*(2), 23–32. https://doi.org/10.1300/J070v16n02_02

Mallahan, K. (2016, June 14). Timeline: Seattle pacific university shooting. *King 5 News.* https://www.king5.com/article/news/local/timeline-seattle-pacific-university-shooting/281-244056933

Mallonee, M. K. (2014, August 9). James Brady's death ruled a homicide, police say. *CNN.com.* https://www.cnn.com/2014/08/08/politics/brady-death-homicide

"Man murdered wife over Facebook posting." (2008, October 17). *Independent.* https://www.independent.co.uk/news/uk/crime/man-murdered-wife-over-facebook-posting-965056.html

Manaugh, G. (2018, December 13). Meet the safecracker of last resort. *The Atlantic.* https://www.theatlantic.com/technology/archive/2018/12/professional-safecracker-reveals-his-craft/577897/

Manavis, S. (2022, May 17). Attacks like the Buffalo shooting have become numbingly inevitable. *The New Statesman.* https://www.newstatesman.com/world/americas/north-america/us/2022/05/attacks-like-the-buffalo-shooting-have-become-numbingly-inevitable

Manning, P. (1998). Media loops. In Bailey, F., & Hale, D. (Eds.), *Popular culture, crime, and justice* (pp. 25–39). Belmont, CA: Wadsworth.

Manning, P. K., & Raphael, M. W. (2012). Phenomenological theories of crime. CUNY Academic Works. https://academicworks.cuny.edu/cgi/viewcontent.cgi?article=1027&context=gc_studentpubs

Markey, P., & Ferguson, C. J. (2017). *Moral combat: Why the war on violent video games is wrong.* BenBella Books.

Markey, P., & Ferguson, C. J. (2017, May 4). Don't fall for the "Grand Theft Fallacy." *US News & World Report.* https://www.usnews.com/opinion/civil-wars/articles/2017-05-04/dont-buy-the-grand-theft-fallacy-that-video-games-cause-violent-crime

References 293

Markey, P., Markey, C. N., & French, J. E. (2015). Violent video games and real-world violence: Rhetoric versus data. *Psychology of Popular Media Culture, 4*(4), 277.

Marlowe, L. (1998, September 30). Verdict on surviving French rebel without a cause today. *The Irish Times.* https://www.irishtimes.com/news/verdict-on-surviving-french-rebel-without-a-cause-today-1.198589

Marshall, A. (2019, July 16). Netflix deletes "13 reasons why" suicide scene. *The New York Times.* https://www.nytimes.com/2019/07/16/arts/television/netflix-deleted-13-reasons-why-suicide-scene.html

Marx, G. T. (1995). Electric eye in the sky: Some reflections on the new surveillance and popular culture. In Ferrell, J., & Sanders, C. R. (Eds.), *Cultural criminology* (pp. 106–141). Northeastern University Press.

Massie, G. (2023, March 28). Audrey Hale: Former student left map and manifesto after shooting six at Nashville Christian school. *Independent.* https://www.independent.co.uk/news/world/americas/crime/audrey-hale-nashville-shooter-identified-b2309144.html

Masters, T. (2022, May 17). Texan law could see Twitch sued for removing Buffalo shooter's stream. *INVENGlobal.* https://www.invenglobal.com/articles/17202/texan-law-could-see-twitch-sued-for-removing-buffalo-shooters-stream

Matlin, M. W. (2005). *Cognition.* New York: John Wiley & Sons, Inc.

McAdams, D. D. (2009). TV sets outnumber people in U.S. homes. *TV Technology.* https://www.tvtechnology.com/news/tv-sets-outnumber-people-in-us-homes

McBride, J. (2022, July 5). Awake the rapper: Robert Crimo's videos & social media. *Heavy.* https://heavy.com/news/awake-the-rapper-robert-crimo-videos-social-media/

McBride, K., & Castillo, A. (2021, March 25). NPR standards need more clarity around when to name a mass shooter. *NPR.* https://www.npr.org/sections/publiceditor/2021/03/25/981170871/npr-standards-need-more-clarity-around-when-to-name-a-mass-shooter

McCollum v. CBS, INC., 202 Cal. App. 3d 989—Cal: Court of Appeal, 2nd Appellate Dist., 3rd Div. (1988). https://law.justia.com/cases/california/court-of-appeal/3d/202/989.html

McLaughlin, E. C. (2018). Social media paints picture of racist "professional school shooter." *CNN.* https://www.cnn.com/2018/02/14/us/nikolas-cruz-florida-shooting-suspect/index.html

Meindl, J. N., & Ivy, J. W. (2018). Mass shootings: The role of the media in promoting generalized imitation. *American Journal of Public Health, 107*(3), 368–370. https://doi: 10.2105/AJPH.2016.303611

Melendez, M. S., Lichtenstein, B., & Dolliver, M. J. (2016). Mothers of mass murderers: Exploring public blame for the mothers of school shooters through an application of courtesy stigma to the Columbine and Newtown tragedies. *Deviant Behavior, 37*(5), 525–536.

Meloy, J. R. (1992). *Violent attachments.* Northvale, NJ: Jason Aronson.

Meloy, J. R. (Ed.). (1998). *The psychology of stalking: Clinical and forensic perspectives*. San Diego, CA: Academic Press.

Meloy, J. R. (1988). *The psychopathic mind: Origins, dynamics, and treatment*. Northvale, NJ: Jason Aronson.

Meloy, J. R., & Hoffman, J. (2014). *International handbook of threat assessment*. Oxford: Oxford University Press.

Meloy, J. R., Hoffman, J., Guldimann, A., & James, D. (2012). The role of warning behaviors in threat assessment: An exploration and suggested typology. *Behavioral Sciences and the Law, 30*, 256–279. https://doi.org/ 10.1002/bsl.999

Meloy, J. R., Mohandie, K., Knoll, J. L., & Hoffman, J. (2015). The concept of identification in threat assessment. *Behavioral Sciences and the Law, 33*, 213–237. https://doi.org/ 10.1002/bsl.2166

Meloy, J. R., & O'Toole, M. E. (2011). The concept of leakage in threat assessment. *Behavioral Sciences and the Law, 29*, 513–527. https://doi.org /10.1002/bsl.986

Messerschmidt, J. W. (2018). *Masculinities and crime: A quarter century of theory and research*. Rowman & Littlefield Publishers.

Michallon, C. (2021). What happens when books inspire real-life violence? *Independent*. https://www.independent.co.uk/arts-entertainment/books /features/the-turner-diaries-capitol-insurrection-books-b1800572.html

Micheal, G. (2009). Blueprints and fantasies: A review and analysis of extremist fiction. *Studies in Conflict & Terrorism, 33*(2), 149–170. https://doi.org /10.1080/10576100903488451

Milivojevic, S. (2021). *Crime and punishment in the future Internet: Digital frontier technologies and criminology in the Twenty-First Century*. Routledge.

Miller, L. (2015, August 25). If these girls knew that slender man was a fantasy, why did they want to kill their friend for him? *New York Magazine*. http:// nymag.com/intelligencer/2015/08/slender-man-stabbing.html

Miller v. State of California, 413 U.S. 15. 93 S.Ct. 2607. 37 L.Ed.2d 419 (1973). https://www.law.cornell.edu/supremecourt/text/413/15

Milian, J. (2018, May 31). Nikolas Cruz's chilling videos: Students who see something are saying something. *The Palm Beach Post*. https://www .palmbeachpost.com/news/parkland-wake-students-who-see-something -are-saying-something/9SgfD9s3N0buvuhBfntsuN/

Miller, J., Serafin, B., & Schabner, D. (2006, January 6). Tarot card may give sniper clues. *ABC News*. https://abcnews.go.com/US/story?id=91149&page=1

Mirea, M., Wang, V., & Jung, J. (2019). The not so dark side of the darknet: A qualitative study. *Security Journal, 32*, 102–118. https://link.springer.com /article/10.1057/s41284-018-0150-5

Mohseni, R. A., Latifinia, A., & Afjeh, S. S. (2016). The effect of media on crime: With emphasis on pathological aspects of TV and internet. *Mediterranean Journal of Social Sciences, 7*(4), 154–162. https://doi.10.5901/mjss.2016 .v7n4S2p154

Moise J. F., & Huesmann L. R. (1996). *Television violence viewing and aggression in females*. Annals of the New York Academy of Sciences, 794, 380–383.

References

Moltenbrey, K., & Donelan, J. (2002). Gaming retrospective. *Computer Graphics World, 25*(3), 20–23.

Montgomery, D. B. (2012). Conviction upheld in "03 Fayette slayings: Video game defense used in officers" slayings spurred national debate. *Tuscaloosa News.* https://www.tuscaloosanews.com/story/news/2012/02/18/conviction-upheld-in-03-fayette-slayings/29889742007/

Moore, M. (2002). *Bowling for Columbine* [Film]. United Artists.

Moran, B. M. (2020). Note—Red Flag Laws: The constitutionality of mental health provisions for gun regulation in modern-day America. *Journal of Health & Biomedical Law, 17*(1), 92–118. https://bpb-us-e1.wpmucdn.com/sites.suffolk.edu/dist/e/1232/files/2016/12/Moran_.pdf

Moreno, I. (2018, February 1). Girl in Slender Man stabbing gets 40 years in mental hospital. *Chicago Sun Times.* https://chicago.suntimes.com/2018/2/1/18372031/girl-in-slender-man-stabbing-gets-40-years-in-mental-hospital

Mosley, T., & Hagan, A. (2021, January 7). How social media fueled the insurrection at the U.S. Capitol. *WBUR.* https://www.wbur.org/hereandnow/2021/01/07/social-media-capitol-mob

Nacos, B. L. (2009). Revisiting the contagion hypothesis: Terrorism, news coverage, and Copycat attacks. *Perspectives on Terrorism, 3*(3), 3–13. https://www.jstor.org/stable/26298412

Naffine, N. (1997). *Feminism and criminology.* Polity.

Naranjo, C. (2015, February 20). Elliot Rodger rehearsed killing roommates before UCSB rampage. *KRON4.* https://www.kron4.com/news/elliot-rodger-rehearsed-killing-roommates-before-ucsb-rampage/

Natanson, E. (2017, July 22). Artificial Intelligence smart assistants: The next big thing in computing? *Forbes.* https://www.forbes.com/sites/nvidia/2018/09/10/qa-with-nvidias-chintan-patel-simplifying-access-to-hpc-and-ai-with-containers/#140fdf035591

Natural Born Killers lawsuit finally thrown out. (2001, March 13). *The Guardian.* https://www.theguardian.com/film/2001/mar/13/news

Neklason, A. (2019, April 19). The columbine blueprint. *The Atlantic.* https://www.theatlantic.com/education/archive/2019/04/columbines-20th-anniversary-mass-media-shooting/587359/

Newcomb, A. (2013, August 8). Facebook post claims Miami man killed wife, shows apparent photo of body. *ABC News.* https://abcnews.go.com/US/facebook-post-claims-miami-man-killed-wife-shows/story?id=19910020

Newman, G. (1998). Popular culture and violence: Decoding the violence of popular movies. In Bailey, F. Y., & Hale, D. C. (Eds.), *Popular culture, crime, and justice* (pp. 40–56). Belmont, CA: Wadsworth.

Newman, K. S., Fox, C., Harding, D., Mehta, J., & Roth, W. (2004). *Rampage: The social roots of school shootings.* New York: Basic Books.

Nicol, W. (2019, December 27). The decade in dystopia: Technological trends inching us closer to collapse. *Digital Trends.* https://www.digitaltrends.com/news/decade-of-dystopia/?itm_medium=topic&itm_source=7&itm_content=2x6&itm_term=2430354

Nicole, J. D. (1954). Police science technical abstracts and notes. *Police Science Foreign Periodicals*, 110–111.

Niederkrotenthaler, T., Till, B., Herberth, A., Kapusta, N. D., Voracek, M., Dervic, K., Etzerdorfer, E., & Sonneck, G. (2009). Can media effects counteract legislation reforms?: The case of adolescent firearm suicides in the wake of the Austrian firearm legislation. *Journal of Adolescent Health, 44*, 90–93. https://doi: 10.1016/j.jadohealth.2008.05.010

Nikkelen, S. W. C., Valkenburg, P. M., Huizinga, M., & Bushman, B. J. (2014). Media use and ADHD-related behaviors in children and adolescents: A meta-analysis. *Developmental Psychology, 50*(9), 2228–2241. httpsL//doi.org/10.1037/a0037318

Nix, N., & Zakrzewski, C. (2022, May 26). As young gunmen turn toward new social networks, old safeguards fail. *The Washington Post.* https://www.washingtonpost.com/technology/2022/05/26/shooters-social-media/

Noack, R., Beck, L., & Morris, L. (2019). Gunman live-streamed attack outside German synagogue that left two dead. *The Washington Post.* https://www.washingtonpost.com/world/shooting-near-synagogue-in-germany-leaves-at-least-two-people-dead-police-say/2019/10/09/08214514-ea89-11e9-9306-47cb0324fd44_story.html

Nowicka, H. (1993, December 19). Chucky films defended. *Independent.* Retrieved from https://www.independent.co.uk/news/uk/chucky-films-defended-1468498.html

O'Dea, S. (2019). Smartphone users worldwide 2016–2021. *Statistica.* https://www.statista.com/statistics/330695/number-of-smartphone-users-worldwide/

Olito, F. (2020, August 20). The rise and fall of Blockbuster. *Business Insider.* https://www.businessinsider.com/rise-and-fall-of-blockbuster

Oliver, M. B. (2002). Individual differences in media effects. In Bryant, J. & Zillman, D. (Eds.), *Media effects: Advances in theory and research* (pp. 507–524). Mahwah, NJ: Lawrence Erlbaum.

Olivia N. v. National Broadcasting Co., 126 Cal. App. 3d 488—Cal: Court of Appeal, 1st Appellate Dist., 4th Div. (1981). https://law.justia.com/cases/california/court-of-appeal/3d/74/383.html

O'Neil, R. M. (2001). *The first amendment and civil liability.* Bloomington, IN: Indiana University Press.

O'Neill, J. P, Miller, J. J., & Waters, J. R. (2016). Active shooter: Recommendations and analysis for risk mitigation. New York City Police Department. https://www1.nyc.gov/assets/nypd/downloads/pdf/counterterrorism/active-shooter-analysis2016.pdf

Omand, D. (2015). The dark net: Policing the Internet's underworld. *World Policy Journal,* 75–82. https://doi-org.proxy.seattleu.edu/10.1177/0740277515623750

Orion, D. (1997). *I know you really love me: A psychiatrist's journal of erotomania, stalking, and obsessional love.* New York: Macmillan.

O'Toole, M. E. (2000). The school shooter: A threat assessment perspective. Federal Bureau of Investigation. https://files.eric.ed.gov/fulltext/ED446352.pdf

O'Toole, M. E. (2014). Celebrities through violence: The copycat effect and the influence of violence in social media on mass killers. *Violence and Gender, 1*(3), 107–116. https://doi.org/10.1089/vio.2014.1512

Ozturk, E., & Erdogan, B. (2022). On the psychodigital components of cyber traumatization and dissociation: A psychosocial depiction of cyber societies as dissociogenic. *Medicine Science, 11*(1), 422–428. https://doi.org/10.5455/medscience.2021.12.411

Paddock, R. C., Suhartono, M., & Jirenuwat, R. (2020, February 10). Thai soldier in mass shooting had business clash with his commander. *The New York Times.* https://www.nytimes.com/2020/02/10/world/asia/thai-shooting-gunman.html

Pahler v. Slayer, 2001 WL 1736476, at *6-7 (Cal. Super. Oct. 29, 2001).

Pankratz, H., & Ingold, J. (2003). Columbine killers left paper trail. Violent writings by killers released along with horrific details of massacre. *The Denver Post,* A-1.

Paperny, A. M., & Saminather, N. (2018, April 24). Toronto police eye deadly van attack suspect's "cryptic message." *Reuters.* https://www.reuters.com/article/canada-us-canada-van-court-idCAKBN1HV1V2-OCADN

Patten, D. (1997). Rising body count. *Salon.com.* Retrieved: August 25, 2005.

Patton, D. U., Hong, J. S., Ranney, M., Patel, S., Kelley, C., Eschmann, R., & Washington, T. (2014). Social media as a vector for youth violence: A review of the literature. *Computers in Human Behavior, 35,* 548–553.

Park, M., & Howard, J. (2019, May 8). Why female shooters are rare. *CNN.* https://www.cnn.com/2019/05/08/health/female-shooters-rare/index.html

Parker, R. (2019, September 24). Aurora shooting victims voice fears over 'Joker' in letter to Warner Bros. *The Hollywood Reporter.* https://www.hollywoodreporter.com/news/aurora-shooting-victims-voice-concerns-joker-emotional-letter-warner-bros-1241599

Pearce, M. (2013, November 27). Adam Lanza's files show him as another shooter caught up in Columbine. *Los Angeles Times.* https://www.latimes.com/nation/nationnow/la-na-nn-lanza-columbine-20131127-story.html

Pelzel, K. (2021, September 13). Global digital culture involves billions of objects and hundreds of millions of contributors. *Medium.com/Global Perspectives.* https://medium.com/global-perspectives-with-kristi-pelzel/global-digital-culture-involve-billions-of-objects-and-hundreds-of-millions-of-contributors-9fe9cb595809

Penfold, R. (2004). The star's image, victimization and celebrity culture. *Punishment & Society, 6*(3), 289–302.

Penn, C. (2016, October 7). What's the difference between social media and new media? *Medium.* Retrieved by https://medium.com/@cspenn/whats-the-difference-between-social-media-and-new-media-71f7f5ae1eea

People v. Miesegaes. (2014). Court of Appeal of the State of California First Appelate District Division One. https://www.casemine.com/judgement/us/5914f01dadd7b049349720c8

Perl, P. (2003, November 30). "I don't think they deserved it." *The Washington Post*. https://www.washingtonpost.com/archive/lifestyle/magazine/2003/11/30/i-dont-think-they-deserved-it/359622bb-90d2-43f8-97ec-be37f03e2ee7/

Perry, N. (2019, August 14). A letter from the alleged Christchurch Mosque attacker has been posted online. *Time*. https://time.com/5651671/christchurch-mosque-attack-gunman-letter/a

Perse, E. M. (2001). *Media effects and society*. Lawrence Erlbaum.

Peterson-Manz, J. (2002). Copycats: Homicide and the press. Dissertation Abstracts International. Unpublished Doctoral Dissertation, Claremont Graduate University.

Phillips, A. (2022, June 14). What are red flag laws? *The Washington Post*. https://www.washingtonpost.com/politics/2022/06/14/what-is-a-red-flag-law/

Phillips, C. (1992, September 20). Music to kill cops by? Rap song blamed in Texas trooper's death. *The Washington Post*. https://www.washingtonpost.com/archive/lifestyle/style/1992/09/20/music-to-kill-cops-by-rap-song-blamed-in-texas-troopers-death/20b49755-7835-4cb0-a53a-d78ccf65f9a7/

Pietsch, B., De Vynck, G., & Berman, M. (2022, July 5). Highland Park shooting suspect plotted "for several weeks," police say. *The Washington Post*. https://www.washingtonpost.com/nation/2022/07/05/robert-crimo-highland-park-parade-shooting/

Pilkington, E. (2013, November 25). Sandy Hook report – shooter Adam Lanza was obsessed with mass murder. *The Guardian*. https://www.theguardian.com/world/2013/nov/25/sandy-hook-shooter-adam-lanza-report

Pizarro, J. M., Chermak, S., & Gruenwald, J. A. (2007). Juvenile "Super-Predators" in the news: A comparison of adult and juvenile homicides. *Journal of Criminal Justice and Popular Culture, 14*(1), 84–111.

Plante, C., Anderson, C. A., Allen, J. J., Groves, C., & Gentile, D. A. (2020). *Game on: Sensible answers about video games and media violence*. ZenGen, LLC.

Plywaczewski, E. W., & Cebulak, W. (2017). Inspiring copycat violent crime—A question of social responsibility. *Internal Security, 9*(2), 137–147. https://doi:10.5604/01.3001.0012.1708

Polizzi, D. (2011). Agnew's General Strain Theory reconsidered: A phenomenological perspective. *International Journal of Offender Therapy and Comparative Criminology, 55*(7), 1051–1071. https://doi.org/10.1 177/0306624X 10380846

Pollard, J. (2021, September 22). Texas sued over bill stopping social media companies from banning users for political views. *The Texas Tribune*. https://www.texastribune.org/2021/09/21/texas-social-media-law/

Portland (ME) Police. (2019, January 11). Let's talk bird box challenge [Tweet]. https://twitter.com/PolicePortland/status/1083836127042326532

Proman, J. M. (2004). Liability of media companies for the violent content of their products marketed to children. *St. John's Law Review, 2*(78), 427–448.

References

Propper, D. (2022, May 26). Texas shooter may have revealed sick massacre plan in video game rant: Report. *New York Post.* https://nypost.com /2022/05/26/salvador-ramos-mightve-revealed-shooting-plan -reporttexas-shooter-may-have-revealed-sick-massacre-plan-in-video -game-rant-report/

Quinn, Z. (2017). *Crash override: How Gamergate (nearly) destroyed my life, and how we can win the fight against online hate.* New York: Public Affairs/ Hachette Book Group.

Ramsland, K. (2013, July 23). Murder mentors for copycat killers. *Psychology Today.* https://www.psychologytoday.com/us/blog/shadow-boxing/201307 /murder-mentors-copycat-killers

Rafter, N. (2006). *Shots in the mirror: Crime films and society.* Oxford: Oxford University Press.

Rahman, K. (2020, February 9). Facebook removes profile of soldier who posted on social media while committing Thailand/s worst mass shooting. *Newsweek.* https://www.newsweek.com/facebook-takes-down-page-soldier -rampage-thailand-1486413

Rash, W. (2021, January 19). Disinformation propelled by social media and conspiracy theories led to insurrection. *Forbes.* https://www.forbes.com /sites/waynerash/2021/01/19/disinformation-propelled-by-social-media -and-conspiracy-theories-led-to-insurrection/?sh=35612e4e34e0

Reiber, R. W., & Green, M. (1989). The psychopathy of everyday life: Antisocial behavior and social distress. In Rieber, R. W. (Ed.), *The individual, communication, and society* (pp. 48–89). Cambridge University Press.

Reiferson, B. (2021, April 19). Making the case for Trump's January 6th speech as incitement. *Princeton Legal Journal.* https://legaljournal.princeton.edu /making-the-case-for-trumps-january-6th-speech-as-incitement/

Reising, K., Farrington, D. P., Ttofi, M. M., Piquero, A. R., & Coid, J. W. (2019). Childhood risk factors for personality disorder symptoms related to violence. *Aggression and Violent Behavior, 49,* 1–13. https://doi.org/10.1016/j.avb .2019.07.010

Reilly, T. (2009). The "spiritual temperature" of contemporary popular music: An alternative to the legal regulation of death-metal and gangsta-rap lyrics. *Vanderbelt Journal of Entertainment and Technology Law, 11*(2), 335–396. https://udayton.edu/directory/law/documents/the-spiritual-temperature -of-contemporary-popular-music.pdf

Rennison, C. M. (2009). A new look at the gender gap in offending. *Women & Criminal Justice, 19*(3), 171–190. https://doi.org/10.1080/08974450903001461

Ressler, R. K. (1993). *Whoever fights monsters: My twenty years tracking serial killers for the FBI.* New York: St. Martin's Paperbacks.

Ressler, R. K., Burgess, A. W., & Douglas, J. E. (1992). *Sexual homicide: Patterns and motives.* New York: Simon & Schuster.

Reynolds, E. (2015, August 26). Deadly obsessions: People who kill for a character. *News.com.au.* https://www.news.com.au/lifestyle/real-life/true-stories

300 References

/deadly-obsessions-people-who-kill-for-a-character/news-story/372203e
82cfbaa95ab18377566e6c806

Rice, S. K., & Maltz, M. (Eds.). (2018). *Using ethnography in criminology: Discovery through fieldwork*. Springer. *Rice v. Paladin Enterprises, Inc.*, 128 F.3d 233 (4th Cir. 1997). https://casetext.com/case/rice-v-paladin-enterprises-inc

Richter, G., & Richter, A. (2019, March 12). The Incel killer and the threat to the campus community. *Security Magazine*. https://www.securitymagazine .com/articles/89962-the-incel-killer-and-the-threat-to-the-campus -community

Riddle, K., Potter, W. J., Metzger, M. J., Nabi, R. L., & Linz, D. G. (2011). Beyond cultivation: Exploring the effects of frequency, recency, and vivid auto-biographical memories for violent media. *Media Psychology, 14*, 168–191. https://doi.org/10.1080/15213269.2011.573464

Rios, V., & Ferguson, C. J. (2020). News media coverage of crime and violent drug crime: A case for cause or catalyst? *Justice Quarterly, 37*(6), 1012–1039.

Roberts, M. (2018, February 27). Why Keanu Reeves has been blamed for both Parkland and Columbine. *Westword*. https://www.westword.com/news /keanu-reeves-blamed-for-parkland-and-columbine-10010081

Robertson, A. (2022). A court just blew up internet law because it thinks You-Tube isn't a website. *The Verge*. https://www.theverge.com/2022/5/13 /23068423/fifth-circuit-texas-social-media-law-ruling-first-amendment -section-230

Rodger, E. (n.d). My twisted world: The story of Elliot Rodger. https://www .documentcloud.org/documents/1173808-elliot-rodger-manifesto

Rogers, J. (2019, August 6). Horrific footage of Christchurch mosque shooting surfaces on YouTube and Instagram. *Fox News*. https://www.foxnews .com/tech/footage-christchurch-mosque-shooting-youtube-instagram

Rojas, R., & Hussey, K. (2018, December 10). Newly released documents detail Sandy Hook shooter's troubled state of mind. *The New York Times*. https:// www.nytimes.com/2018/12/10/nyregion/documents-sandy-hook -shooter.html

Roose, K. (2019, March 15). A mass murder of, and for, the internet. *The New York Times*. https://www.nytimes.com/2019/03/15/technology/facebook -youtube-christchurch-shooting.html

Roppel, J. (2010, March 25). MU prof's killer barred from Hamilton, will get more freedom. *Journal-News*. https://www.journal-news.com/news /crime—law/prof-killer-barred-from-hamilton-will-get-more-freedom /GGy4LIzb0xJUT1jvGPk8JN/

Rosenfeld, R., & Lopez, E. (2021, May). Pandemic, social unrest, and crime in U.S. cities. March 2021 Update. Washington, D.C.: Council on Criminal Justice. file:///C:/Users/jhelfgot/Downloads/Pandemic,_Social_Unrest,_and _Crime_in_US_Cities_-_March_2021_Update.pdf

Rosenwald, M. S. (2021, February 12). The landmark Klan free-speech case behind Trump's impeachment defense. *The Washington Post*. https://www

References

.washingtonpost.com/history/2021/02/10/brandenburg-trump-supreme
-court-klan-free-speech/

Ross, C. J. (2021, January 19). What the first amendment really says about whether trump incited the capitol riot. *Slate.* https://slate.com/technology /2021/01/trump-incitement-violence-brandenburg-first-amendment.html

Roth v. United States, 354 U.S. 476 (1957). https://www.leagle.com/decision /1957830354us4761808

Rozgonjuk, D., & Elhai, J. (2018). Problematic smartphone usage, emotion regulation, and social and non-social smartphone use. *TechMindSociety, 35,* https://doi-org.proxy.seattleu.edu/10.1145/3183654.3183664

Rubenstein, D. (1999). Plaintiff attorney targets Warner Bros., Oliver Stone after deadly rampage. *Corporate Legal Times, 54.*

Ruiz, R. (2019, July 18). Netflix finally removed the graphic suicide scene from "13 Reasons Why." It was the right thing to do. *Mashable.* https://mashable .com/article/13-reasons-why-netflix-removes-suicide-scene

Rutter, M. (2003). Commentary: Causal processes leading to antisocial behavior. *Developmental Psychology, 39*(2), 372–378.

Salinger, J. D. (1945, 1946, 1951). *Catcher in the Rye.* New York: Little, Brown, & Company.

Samaha, A. (2014). Men convicted of Hollywood-style $200k Pay-O-Matic robbery receive 32-year sentence. *The Village Voice.* https://www.villagevoice .com/2014/04/04/men-convicted-of-hollywood-style-200k-pay-o-matic -robbery-receive-32-year-sentence/

Sauce, B., Liebherr, Judd, N., & Klingberg, T. (2022). The impact of digital media on children's intelligence while controlling for genetic differences in cognition and socioeconomic background. *Scientific Reports, 12*(7720). https://www.nature.com/articles/s41598-022-11341-2

Savage, J. (2004). Does viewing violent media really cause criminal violence? A methodological review. *Aggression and Violent Behavior, 10,* 99–128. https://doi:10.1016/j.avb.2003.10.001

Savage, J., & Yancy, C. (2008). The effects of media violence exposure on criminal aggression: A meta-analysis. *Criminal Justice and Behavior, 35*(6), 772–791.

Scaptura, M. N., & Boyle, K. M. (2020). Masculinity threat, "incel" traits, and violent fantasies among heterosexual men in the United States. *Feminist Criminology, 15*(3), 278–298.

Scharrer, E. (2009). Hypermasculinity, aggression, and television violence: An experiment. *Media Psychology, 7*(4), 353–376. https://doi.org/10.1207 /S1532785XMEP0704_3

Schildkraut, J., Elsass, H. J., & Meredith, K. (2018). Mass shootings and the media: Why all events are not created equal. *Journal of Crime and Justice, 41*(3), 223–243.

Schone, M. (2003, December 9). The Matrix defense. *Boston.com.* http://archive .boston.com/news/globe/ideas/articles/2003/11/09/the_matrix_defense/

Schweizer, P. (1998, December 31). Bad imitation: An Oliver Stone movie finds murderous admirers. *National Review.*

Scorsese, M. (1976). *Taxi driver* [Film]. Columbia Pictures

Secret Confessions of BTK. (2005). Dateline NBC. *NBC News.* https://www.nbcnews.com/id/wbna8917644

Sedesky, S. J., III. (2013, November 25). Report of the state's attorney for the judicial district of Danbury on the shootings at Sandy Hook Elementary School and 36 Yogananda Street, Newtown, Connecticut on December 14, 2012. Danbury, CT: Office of the State's Attorney General Judicial District of Danbury. https://cspsandyhookreport.ct.gov/

Selk, A., Bever, L., Holley, P., & Lowery, W. (2017, April 18). "Facebook killer" dies after three-day police pursuit in Pennsylvania. *The Washington Post.* https://www.washingtonpost.com/news/post-nation/wp/2017/04/18/facebook-murder-suspect-steve-stephens-is-dead-police-say/

Sergeant, J. (1996). *Born bad: The story of Charles Starkweather & Caril Ann Fugate.* London, England: Creation Books.

Shafer, D. M. (2009). The role of moral disengagement in the judgment of characters and the enjoyment of violent film. *Electronic Theses, Treatises and Dissertations.* Florida State University Libraries: https://diginole.lib.fsu.edu/islandora/object/fsu:253999/datastream/PDF/view

Shapiro, D. M. (2007). Natural born killers. *Crime Library.* Retrieved May 13, 2007: http://www.crimelibrary.com/notorious_murders/celebrity/natural_born_killers/1.html

Shear, M. D., Pérez-Peña, R., & Blinder, A. (2015, August 26). Ex-broadcaster kills 2 on air in Virginia shooting; Takes own life. *The New York Times.* https://www.nytimes.com/2015/08/27/us/wdbj7-virginia-journalists-shot-during-live-broadcast.html

Shifman, L. (2012). An anatomy of a YouTube meme. *New Media & Society, 14*(2), 187–203.

Shim, M. P. (2004). Predictors of children's violent media use. *Dissertation Abstracts International: Section B: The Sciences and Engineering, 65*(10-B), p. 5440.

Shipley, S. L., & Arrigo, B. A. (2004). *The female homicide offender: Serial murder & the case of Aileen Wuornos.* Upper Saddle River, NJ: Prentice-Hall

Sickles, J. (2014, June 9). Social media accounts paint chilling portrait of Las Vegas cop killers. *Yahoo News.* http://news.yahoo.com/social-media-accounts-paint-chilling-portrait-of-alleged-las-vegas-cop-killers-194220082.html

Sikes, G. (1996). *8 Ball chicks: A year in the violent world of girl gangsters.* New York: Doubleday.

Silva, J. R., & Capellan, J. A. (2018). The media's coverage of mass public shootings in America: Fifty years of newsworthiness. *International Journal of Comparative and Applied Criminal Justice.* 43(1), 1–21. https://doi.org/10.1080/01924036.2018.1437458

References

Silva, J. R., & Capellan, J. A. (2019). A comparative analysis of media coverage of mass public shootings: Examining rampage, disgruntled employee, school, and lone-wolf terrorist shootings in the United States. *Criminal Justice Policy Review, 30*(9), 1312–1341.

Silva, J. R., Capellan, J. A., Schmuhl, M. A., Mills, C. E. (2021). Gender-based mass shootings: An examination of attacks motivated by grievances against women. *Violence against Women, 27*(12–13), 1–24. https://doi.org /10.1177/1077801220981154

Silva, J. R., & Greene-Colozzi, E. A. (2019). Fame-seeking mass shooters in America: Severity, characteristics, and media coverage. *Aggression and Violent Behavior, 48*, 24–35.

Silverstein, E. (2022, October 10). Law Vegas murders on mass shootings' anniversary is coincidence, experts say. *Casino.org.* https://www.casino.org/news /vegas-murders-occurring-on-mass-shootings-anniversary-is-coincidence -experts-say/

Silverstein, J. (2017, April 17). Steve Stephen's murder video is the latest atrocity watched widely on Facebook. *NY Daily News.* http://www.nydailynews .com/news/national/stevestephens-murder-video-latest-horror-facebook -article-1.3064857

Simon, R. J., & Aaronson, D. E. (1988). *The insanity defense: A critical assessment of law and policy in the post-Hinckley era.* Praeger.

Simpson, K., & Blevins, J. (1999, May 4). Did Harris preview massacre on "Doom?" *The Denver Post.* https://extras.denverpost.com/news/shot0504f .htm

Simrin, S. (2020, August 5). How TikTok is affecting youth: Positive and negative effects. *Medium.com.* https://medium.com/linens-n-love/how-tik-tok-is -affecting-youth-the-positive-and-negative-effects-7381b17ac43a

Sitzer, P. (2013). The role of media content in the genesis of school shootings: The contemporary discussion. In Böckler, N., Seeger, T., Sitzer, P., & Heitmeyer, W. (Eds.), *School shootings: International research, case studies, and concepts for prevention* (pp. 283–307). New York: Springer.

Slater, M. D., Henry, K. L, Swaim, R. C., & Anderson, L. L. (2003). Violent media content and aggressiveness in adolescents: A downward spiral model. *Communication Research, 30*(6), 713–736. http://dx.doi.org/10.1177 /0093650203258281

Slater, M. D., Henry, K. L, Swaim, R. C., & Cardador, J. M. (2004). Vulnerable teens, vulnerable times: How sensation seeking, alienation, and victimization moderate the violent media content—aggressiveness relation. *Communication Research, 31*(6), 642–668. https://doi.org/10.1177 /0093650204269265

Sloane, D. (2015, December 8). Inside the mind of John Lennon's killer. *CNN.* https://www.cnn.com/2015/12/08/us/mark-david-chapman-lennon -interviews/index.html

Smith, A. (2022, May 16). Twitch could be sued for removing Buffalo shooter's gruesome livestream under Texas "censorship" law. *Independent*. https://www.independent.co.uk/tech/twitch-buffalo-shooter-livestream-texas-hb-20-b2080167.html

Smith, B. (2019). *Tools and weapons: The promise and the peril of the digital age*. New York: Penguin Press.

Smith, J. (2017). Selfie murderer, 26, says she took photo next to body of her father-in-law because it "made her really happy" as she reveals she tried to contact ISIS before her arrest but got no response. *DailyMail.com*. https://www.dailymail.co.uk/news/article-4517230/Selfie-killer-reveals-took-photo-body.html

Smith, T. (2005). "Grand Theft Auto" cop killer found guilty. *The Register*. https://www.theregister.co.uk/2005/08/11/gta_not_guilty/

Soave, R. (2021, November). People have been panicking about new media since before the printing press. *Reason*. https://reason.com/2021/09/29/people-have-been-panicking-about-new-media-since-before-the-printing-press/

Sparks, G. G. (2016). *Media effects research, 5th edition*. Boston, MA: Cengage.

Sparks, G. G., & Sparks, C. W. (2002). Effects of media violence. In Bryant, J., & Zillman, D. (Eds.), *Media effects: Advances in theory and research* (pp. 269–285). Mahwah, NJ: Lawrence Erlbaum.

Sparks, R. (1992). *Television and the drama of crime: Moral tales and the place of crime in public life*. Philadelphia: Open University Press.

Spyrou, C. (2017). Viral instagram food thief finally gets arrested for stealing dunkin' donuts. *Foodbeast*. https://www.foodbeast.com/news/instagram-food-thief-arrested/

State v. Johnson, 343 So.2d 705 (La. 1977). https://casetext.com/case/state-v-johnson-731

State v. Majors, 940 N.W.2d 372 (2020). https://www.leagle.com/decision/iniaco20200306271

State v. Ridgway, 57 Wn. App. 915, 57 Wash. App. 915, 790 P.2d 1263 (Wash. Ct. App. 1990)

State of Washington v. Ridgway (2004): 01-1-10270-9SEA: released by King County of Washington State pursuant to RCW 42.17.260. King County (Wash.). Prosecutor's Office; King County (Wash.). Sheriff's Office.; Chameleon Data Corporation.

State v. Taylor, 838 So.2d 729 (2003). https://www.leagle.com/decision/20031567838so2d72911527

Statistica. (2020a, April 24). Number of movie tickets sold in the U.S. and Canada from 1980 to 2019. *Statistica*. https://www.statista.com/statistics/187073/tickets-sold-at-the-north-american-box-office-since-1980/

Statistica. (2020b, July). Number of social network users worldwide from 2017 to 2025. *Statistica*. https://www.statista.com/statistics/278414/number-of-worldwide-social-network-users/

Steinkoler, M. (2017). Lone wolf terrorists: Howling in the eye of the wind—The case of Adam Lanza. *International Forum of Psychoanalysis, 26*(4), 217–225.

Steinlage, M. (2020, February 7). Liability for mass shootings: Are we at a turning point? *American Bar Association.* https://www.americanbar.org/groups/tort_trial_insurance_practice/publications/the_brief/2019-20/winter/liability-mass-shootings-are-we-a-turning-point/

Stelter, B., & Paget, S. (2022, May 15). Twitch says livestream of Buffalo mass shooting was removed in less than 2 minutes. *CNN.* https://www.cnn.com/2022/05/15/business/twitch-livestream-buffalo-massacre/index.html

Stern, S. (2003, June 12). "The Matrix" made me do it. *The Christian Science Monitor.* https://www.csmonitor.com/2003/0612/p13s02-lire.html

Stevenson, S. (2017, January 9). "Dexter killer" Mark Twitchell among members of dating site for inmates. *CBC.* https://www.cbc.ca/news/canada/edmonton/dexter-killer-mark-twitchell-among-members-of-dating-site-for-inmates-1.3925555

Stickle, B., & Felson, M. (2020). Crime rates in a pandemic: The largest criminological experiment in history. *American Journal of Criminal Justice, 45,* 525–536. https://doi.org/10.1007/s12103-020-09546-0

Stockton, R., & Kuroski, J. (2021, June 10). How Aileen Wuornos became history's most terrifying female serial killer. *ati.* https://allthatsinteresting.com/aileen-wuornos

Stokel-Walker, C. (2019, May 3). What the murder of Christina Grimmie by a fan tells us about YouTube influencer culture. *Time.* https://time.com/5581981/youtube-christina-grimmie-influencer/

Stone, O. (1994). *Natural Born Killers* [Film]. Warner Brothers.

Storer, H. L., & Strohl, K. R. (2017). A primer for preventing teen dating violence? The representation of teen dating violence in young adult literature and its implications for prevention. *Violence Against Women, 23*(14), 1730–1751.

Strasburger, V., Donnerstein, E., & Bushman, B. (2014). Why is it so hard to believe that media influence children and adolescents? *Pediatrics, 133*(4), 1–3. 10.1542/peds.2013-2334

Strickland v. Sony Corporation of America, et al. (2005). https://www.govinfo.gov/content/pkg/USCOURTS-alnd-6_05-cv-00479/pdf/USCOURTS-alnd-6_05-cv-00479-0.pdf

Strum, L. (2017, September 28). Banning books like "13 Reasons Why" makes it harder for teens to open up to adults, author says. *PBS.org.* https://www.pbs.org/newshour/arts/banning-books-like-13-reasons-makes-harder-teens-open-adults-author-says

Suciu, P. (2022, May 25). Social media increasingly linked with mass shootings. *Forbes.* https://www.forbes.com/sites/petersuciu/2022/05/25/social-media-increasingly-linked-with-mass-shootings/?sh=75e17f3b3c73

Sukosd, C. (2015). Man arrested after reportedly posting video of himself drinking and driving. *Fox 11 News.* http://fox11online.com/news/offbeat/man-arrested-for-ovi-after-posting-video-of-him-drinking-and-driving

Sullivan, J. (2004, April 8). Police arrest man accused of stalking singer Avril Lavigne. *The Seattle Times.* https://archive.seattletimes.com/archive/?date=20040408&slug=webstalker09m

Surette, R. (1990). Estimating the magnitude and mechanisms of copycat crime. In Surette, R. (Ed.), *The media and criminal justice policy: Recent research and social effects.* Springfield, IL: CC Thomas Publishers.

Surette, R. (1998). *Media, crime, & justice: Images and realities.* Belmont, CA: Wadsworth.

Surette, R. (2002). Self-reported copycat crime among a population of serious and violent adult offenders. *Crime & Delinquency, 48*(1), 46–69. https://doi.org/10.1177/0011128702048001002

Surette, R. (2013a). Cause or catalyst: The interaction of real world and media crime models. *American Journal of Criminal Justice, 38*(3), 392–409.

Surette, R. (2013b). Pathways to copycat crime. In Helfgott, J. B. (Ed.), *Criminal psychology, vol. 2* (pp. 251–273). Santa Barbara, CA: Sage.

Surette, R. (2014a). *Media, crime, & justice: Images and realities.* Boston, MA: Cengage.

Surette, R. (2014b). Estimating the prevalence of copycat crime: A research note. *Criminal Justice Policy Review, 25*(6), 703–718. https://doi.org/10.1177/0887403413499579

Surette, R. (2015a). Performance crime and justice. *Current Issues in Criminal Justice, 27*(2), 195–216. https://doi.org/10.1080/10345329.2015.12036041

Surette, R. (2015b). Thought bit: A case study of the social construction of a crime and justice concept. *Crime, Media, Culture: An International Journal, 11*(2), 105–132. https://doi.org/10.1177/1741659015601172

Surette, R. (2016a). Measuring copycat crime. *Crime, Media, Culture: An International Journal, 12*(1), 37–64. https://doi.org/10.1177/1741659015601172

Surette, R. (2016b, January 28). How social media is changing the way people commit crimes and police fight them. *LSE USCentre.* http://blogs.lse.ac.uk/usappblog/2016/01/28/how-social-media-is-changing-the-way-people-commit-crimes-and-police-fight-them/

Surette, R. (2019). A copycat crime meme: Ghost riding the whip. *Crime Media Culture, 1*–26. https://doi.org/10.1177/1741659019865305

Surette, R. (2021). Female copycat crime: An exploratory analysis. *Violence and Gender, 1*(8), 1–7.

Surette, R. (2022). *Copycat crime and copycat criminals.* Lynne Rienner.

Surette, R., & Chadee, D. (2020). Copycat crime among non-incarcerated adults. *Current Issues in Criminal Justice, 32*(1), 59–75. https://doi.org/10.1080/10345329.2019.1640058

Surette, R., Helfgott, J. B., Parkin, W., & O'Toole, M. E. (2021). The social construction of copycat crime in open access media. *Journal of Criminal Justice and Popular Culture, 21*(1), 104–127. https://jcjpc.org/s/Social-Construction-of-Copycat-Crime-Surette-Revised.pdf

Surette, R., & Maze, A. (2015). Video game play and copycat crime: An exploratory analysis of an inmate population. *Psychology of Popular Media Culture, 4*(4), 360–374. https://doi.org/10.1037/ppm0000050

References

Swaine, J., & Bennett, D. (2022, May 16). Buffalo shooting suspect wrote of plans 5 months ago, messages show. *The Washington Post.* https://www.washingtonpost.com/investigations/2022/05/16/buffalo-shooting-previous-supermarket-confrontation/

Swanson, J. W., Norko, M. A., Hsiu-Ju, L., Alanis-Hirsch, K., Frisman, L. K., Baranoski, M. V., Easter, M. M., Robertson, A. G., Swartz, M. S., & Bonnie, R. J. (2017). Implementation and effectiveness of Connecticut's risk-based gun removal law: Does it prevent suicides? *Law & Contemporary Problems, 80*(2), 179–208. http://scholarship.law.duke.edu/lcp/vol80/iss2/8

Swing. E. L., & Anderson, C. A. (2014). The role of attention problems and impulsiveness in media violence effects on aggression. *Aggressive Behavior, 40*(3), 197–203. https://doi:10.1002/ab.21519

Tacopino, J., & Propper, D. (2022, July 6). Highland Park parade shooting suspect Robert Crimo posted pics of his "teen sex doll" online. *New York Post.* https://nypost.com/2022/07/06/highland-park-parade-shooting-suspect-robert-crimo-posted-pics-of-his-teen-sex-doll/

Tassi, P. (2019, August 19). "Mindhunter" season 2 cements it as a top five Netflix show. *Forbes.* https://www.forbes.com/sites/paultassi/2019/08/19/mindhunter-season-2-cements-it-as-a-top-five-netflix-show/#19c3ac54c1bb

Taub, A. (2018, May 9). On social media's fringes, growing extremism targets women. *The New York Times.* https://www.nytimes.com/2018/05/09/world/americas/incels-toronto-attack.html

Teh, C., & Snodgrass, E. (2022, July 6). Highland Park mayor says she was the shooting suspect's Cub Scout leader, questions how he became "this angry" and "hateful." *Insider.* https://www.insider.com/highland-park-mayor-was-shooting-suspect-cub-scout-leader-2022-7

Terhune, D. B., Cardena, E., & Magnus, L. (2011). Dissociative tendencies and individual differences in high hypnotic suggestibility. *Cognitive Neuropsychiatry, 16*(2), 113–135.

The Texas Tribune. (n.d.). Uvalde school shooting. https://www.texastribune.org/series/uvalde-texas-school-shooting/

"Thailand shooting: Soldier kills 21 in gun rampage." (February 9, 2020). *BBC.* https://www.bbc.com/news/world-asia-51427301

Thomas, J. (2001). Behind a book that inspired McVeigh. *The New York Times.* https://www.nytimes.com/2001/06/09/us/behind-a-book-that-inspired-mcveigh.html

Thompson, D. (2021). Why America's great crime decline is over. *The Atlantic.* https://www.theatlantic.com/ideas/archive/2021/03/is-americas-great-crime-decline-over/618381/

Thompson v. State, No. CR-05-0073 (Ala. Crim. App. Feb. 17, 2012). https://caselaw.findlaw.com/al-court-of-criminal-appeals/1594962.html

Thompson v. State, No. CR-16-1311 (Ala. Crim. App. Feb. 7, 2020). https://casetext.com/case/thompson-v-state-112113

Tietchen, T. E. (1998). Samples and copycats: The cultural implications of the postmodern slasher in contemporary American film. *Journal of Popular Film and Television, 26*, 98–101.

Timberg, C., Dwoskin, E., & Albergotti, E. (2021, October 22). Inside Facebook, Jan. 6 violence fueled anger, regret over missed warning signs. *The Washington Post.* https://www.washingtonpost.com/technology/2021/10/22/jan-6-capitol-riot-facebook/

Timberg, C., & Stanley-Becker, I. (2020, September 17). Violent memes and messages surging on far-left social media, a new report finds. *The Washington Post.* https://www.washingtonpost.com/technology/2020/09/14/violent-antipolice-memes-surge/

Tomkinson, S., Attwell, K., & Harper, T. (2020, May 26). "Incel" violence is a form of extremism. It's time we treated it as a security threat. *The Conversation.* https://theconversation.com/incel-violence-is-a-form-of-extremism-its-time-we-treated-it-as-a-security-threat-138536

Tonso, K. L. (2009). Violent masculinities as tropes for school shooters: The Montréal massacre, the Columbine attack, and rethinking schools. *American Behavioral Scientist, 52*(9), 1266–1285. https://doi.org/10.1177/0002764209332545

Towers, S., Gomez-Lievano, A., Khan, M., Mubayi, A., & Castillo-Chavez, C. (2015). Contagion in mass killings and school shootings. *PLoS ONE 10*(7). https://doi.org/10.1371/journal.pone.0117259

Tremblay, P. F., & Dozois, D. J. A. (2009). Another perspective on trait aggressiveness: Overlap with early maladaptive schemas. *Personality and Individual Differences, 46*(5–6), 569–574.

Tron, G. (2019, December 23). Who was Jun Lin, the man whose brutal murder went viral in "Don't F**k With Cats?" *Oxygen.* https://www.oxygen.com/true-crime-buzz/jun-lin-luka-magnotta-victim-dont-f-with-cats-netflix-who-was-he

Ttofi, M. M., Farrington, D. P., Piquero, A. R., & DeLisi, M. (2016). Protective factors against offending and violence: Results from prospective longitudinal studies. *Journal of Criminal Justice, 45*, 1–3.

Tufekci, Z. (2015, August 27). The Virginia shooter wanted fame. Let's not give it to him. *The New York Times.* https://www.nytimes.com/2015/08/27/opinion/the-virginia-shooter-wanted-fame-lets-not-give-it-to-him.html

Turkle, S. (1995). *Life on the screen: Identity in the age of the Internet.* New York: Touchstone.

Turkle, S. (2011). *Alone together: Why we expect more from technology and less from each other.* New York: Basic Books.

Turkle, S. (2015). *Reclaiming conversation: The power of talk in a digital age.* New York: Penguin Books.

Ueda, M., Mori, K., Matsubayashi, T., & Sawada, Y. (2017). Tweeting celebrity suicides: Users' reaction to prominent suicide deaths on Twitter and subsequent increases in actual suicides. *Social Sciences and Medicine, 189*, 158–166. http://dx.doi.org/10.1016/j.socscimed.2017.06.032

References

309

Uenuma, F. (2019, December 30). 20 years later, the Y2K bug seems like a joke—Because those behind the scenes took it seriously. *Time.* https://time.com/5752129/y2k-bug-history/

U.S. Const. amend. I. https://constitution.congress.gov/constitution/amendment-1/

United States Office of the Surgeon General. (2001). Youth violence: A report of the surgeon general. National Center for Injury Prevention and Control; National Institute of Mental Health; Center for Mental Health Services. Rockville (MD): Office of the Surgeon General. https://www.ncbi.nlm.nih.gov/books/NBK44293/#A12873

United States Senate Hearing 106-1096. (2000, March 21). The impact of Interactive violence on children. Washington, D.C.: U.S. Government Printing Office. https://www.govinfo.gov/content/pkg/CHRG-106shrg78656/html/CHRG-106shrg78656.htm

United States v. Monsalvatge, 850 F.3d 483 (2017). https://www.leagle.com/decision/infco20170308090

Valentis, M., & Devane, A. (1994). *Female rage: Unlocking its secrets, claiming its power.* New York: Carol Southern Books.

Van Derbeken, J. (2000, May 4). Man says he killed, chopped woman / police say confession came out of the blue. *SFGate.* https://www.sfgate.com/news/article/Man-Says-He-Killed-Chopped-Woman-Police-say-2761437.php

VanDerWerff, E. (2021, January 8). Is the country falling apart? Depends on where you get your news. *Vox.* https://www.vox.com/culture/22217782/capitol-insurrection-cable-news-twitch-mob-siege

Varghese, J. (2020, May 26). Peter Manfredonia idolized his "neighbor" Sandy Hook shooter Adam Lanza. *International Business Times.* https://www.ibtimes.sg/peter-manfredonia-idolized-his-neighbor-sandy-hook-shooter-adam-lazna-45738

Vice Staff. (2022, May 31). Killer incels: How misogynistic men sparked a new terror threat. *Vice World News.* https://www.vice.com/en/article/bvnw3d/incels-elliot-rodger-misogyny-far-right

Vidal, Z. A., Ehrnborg, G., & Vyas, N. (2021, April 6). How has the pandemic's impact influenced our digital habits? *Ericsson.com.* https://www.ericsson.com/en/blog/2021/4/pandemic-influence-digital-habits

Video Software Dealers Association v. Schwarzenegger, 401 F.Supp.2d 1034 (2005). https://www.leagle.com/decision/20051435401fsupp2d103411353

Video Software Dealers Association v. Schwarzenegger, 556 F.3d 950 (2009). https://www.leagle.com/decision/infco20090220097

Virginia v. Black, 538 U.S. 343 (2003). https://supreme.justia.com/cases/federal/us/538/343/

Virtanen, M. (2012, August 23). Mark David Chapman, John Lennon's killer, denied parole again. *The Christian Science Monitor.* https://www.csmonitor.com/USA/Latest-News-Wires/2012/0823/Mark-David-Chapman-John-Lennon-s-killer-denied-parole-again

310 References

Voytko, L. (2020, July 9). "All Lives Splatter" meme gets Seattle cop suspended after protester killed by driver. *Forbes.* https://www.forbes.com/sites /lisettevoytko/2020/07/09/all-lives-splatter-meme-gets-seattle-cop -suspended-after-protester-killed-by-driver/#6b471afc3842

Wachowski, L. (2021). *The Matrix Resurrections* [Film]. Warner Brothers.

Wachowski, L., & Wachowski, L. (1999). *The Matrix* [Film]. Warner Brothers.

Wachowski, L., & Wachowski, L. (2003a). *The Matrix Reloaded* [Film]. Warner Brothers.

Wachowski, L., & Wachowski, L. (2003b). *The Matrix Revolutions* [Film]. Warner Brothers.

Wagstaff, K. (2018, March 2). Why social media surveillance isn't the answer to our gun crisis. *Mashable.* https://mashable.com/article/gun-control -social-media-background-checks

Walker, R., & Mallahan, K. (2016, June 14). Court releases video from SPU shooting showing student's heroic actions. *King 5 News.* https://www .king5.com/article/news/local/court-releases-video-from-spu-shooting -showing-students-heroic-actions/281-244202869

Walker, T. (2020, April 15). Social-emotional learning should be priority during COVID-19 crisis. *neaToday.* https://www.nea.org/advocating-for-change /new-from-nea/social-emotional-learning-should-be-priority-during -covid-19

Walker v. Peters, 863 F. Supp. 671 (N.D., Illinois, 1994). https://www.leagle .com/decision/19941534863fsupp67111411

Waller-Bridge, P. (Writer/Producer) (2018–2022). *Killing Eve* [Television Series]. Sid Gentle Films/BBC America.

Walsh, M., & Gentile, D. A. (Directors). (2003). *Sex, murder, and video games* [Film]. National Institute on Media and the Family.

Warburton, W. A., & Anderson, C. A. (2022). Children, impact of media on. *Encyclopedia of Violence, Peace, & Conflict, 4,* 195–208. https://doi.org /10.1016/B978-0-12-820195-4.00026-1

Warner, M. (2022, May 27). Two professors found what creates a mass shooter. Will politicians pay attention? *Politico.* https://www.politico.com/news /magazine/2022/05/27/stopping-mass-shooters-q-a-00035762

Watters v. TSR, Inc., 715 F. Supp. 819 (W. D. Ky. 1989). https://law.justia.com /cases/federal/district-courts/FSupp/715/819/1763244/

Watson, H. (2012). Dependent citizen journalism and the publicity of terror. *Terrorism and Political Violence, 24*(3), 465–482. https://doi.org/10.1080 /09546553.2011.636464

Waxman, O. B. (2018). "He could have killed me." Lorena Bobbitt on domestic abuse and what she wants you to know about her case 25 years later. *Time.* https://time.com/5317979/lorena-bobbitt-today-anniversary-interview/

Waxman, S. (2001). Did "Death Metal" music incite murder? *The Washington Post.* https://www.washingtonpost.com/archive/business/2001/01/23 /did-death-metal-music-incite-murder/63cf6de7-fdd1-4067-a49f -9946f111e6a2/

Webster, B. (1982, October 30). Experts theorize about "copycat syndrome." *The New York Times*. https://www.nytimes.com/1982/10/30/us/experts-theorize-about-copycat-syndrome.html

Webster, E. S. (2018, April 3). Meet the double amputee athlete set to kick serious ass at the para athletics world cup. *Men's Health*. https://www.menshealth.com/fitness/a19671889/brian-reynolds-double-amputee-athlete/

Weill, K. (2022, May 17). Buffalo killer ripped off past manifestos—and mainstream GOP talking points. *Daily Beast*. https://www.thedailybeast.com/buffalo-killer-ripped-off-past-manifestos-and-mainstream-gop-talking-points

Weirum v. RKO Gen., Inc. - 15 Cal. 3d 40, 123 Cal. Rptr. 468, 539 P.2d 36 (1975). https://law.justia.com/cases/california/supreme-court/3d/15/40.html

Weisholtz, D., & Caulfield, P. (2019, July 8). Why actress Rebecca Schaeffer's 1989 murder was Hollywood's wake-up call. *Today*. https://www.today.com/news/why-actress-rebecca-schaeffer-s-1989-murder-was-hollywood-s-t157444

Wellstood, J. (2000). Tort liability of the media. *Journal of Civil Rights and Economic Development, 15*(2), 187–221. https://scholarship.law.stjohns.edu/cgi/viewcontent.cgi?article=1241&context=jcred

West, A., & Wells, T. (2012). Cannibal on run after warning the sun: I can't stop killing. *The Sun*. https://www.thesun.co.uk/archives/news/659030/cannibal-on-run-after-warning-the-sun-i-cant-stop-killing/

Whitfield, S. J. (1997). Cherished and cursed: Toward a social history of *The Catcher in the Rye*. *The New England Quarterly, 70*(4), 567–600. https://doi.org/10.2307/366646

Wiedeman, A. M., Black, J. A., Dolle, A. L., Finney, E. J., & Coker, K. L. (2015). Factors influencing the impact of aggressive and violent media on children and adolescents. *Aggression and Violent Behavior, 25*(Part A), 191–198. https://doi.org/10.1016/j.avb.2015.04.008

Wilber, D. Q. (2011). *Rawhide Down: The near assassination of Ronald Reagan*. New York: Henry Holt & Company.

Wilkinson, A. (2021, January 7). This is not Hollywood, and the heroes are not coming. *Vox*. https://www.vox.com/culture/22218583/trump-movie-hollywood-capitol-insurrection-biden-hawley

Williams, C. (1981, April 1). The obsession of John Hinckley Jr. *The Washington Post*. https://www.washingtonpost.com/archive/lifestyle/1981/04/01/the-obsession-of-john-hinckley-jr/d66acb0a-24d6-40e3-a1bf-8b08d33ae577/

Williams, J. (2015, December 3). Court shines a light on mass-shooting footage. *Courthouse News Service*. https://www.courthousenews.com/court-shines-a-light-on-mass-shooting-footage/

Wilson, S., Dempsey, C., Farnham, F., Manze, T., & Taylor, A. (2018). Stalking risks to celebrities and public figures. *BJPsych Advances, 24*(3), 152–160.

Winkie, L. (2022, March 10). Jack Thompson still has a grudge. *The Verge*. https://www.theverge.com/2022/3/10/22956300/jack-thompson-interview-violent-games-gta-doom-attorney

Wongcha-Um, P. (2020, February 9). Thai soldier kills 26 in shooting rampage. *Guardian News*. https://www.nambuccaguardian.com.au/story/6620874/thai-soldier-kills-26-in-shooting-rampage/?cs=10970

Wolf, B. (March 18, 2005). Stalkers, controversy thwart late-night host's yearning for privacy. *ABC News*. Retrieved from http://abcnews.go.com/Entertainment/story?id=593753@page=1

Wooden, W. S., & Blazak, R. (2001). *Renegade kids, suburban outlaws: From youth culture to delinquency*. Belmont, CA: Wadsworth.

Woods, J. (2015, December 30). Man arrested after posting video of himself swigging whiskey while driving. *The Columbus Dispatch*. https://www.dispatch.com/article/20151230/NEWS/312309860

Wright, M. (2018, April 14). Haunting images show the aftermath of the slender man stabbing scene. *Daily Mail*. http://www.dailymail.co.uk/news/article-5616815/Haunting-images-aftermath-Slender-Man-stabbing-scene.html

Wynne, R. (2017, September 25). What's new about the "new" new media. *Forbes*. https://www.forbes.com/sites/robertwynne/2017/09/25/whats-new-about-the-new-new-media/#3a6af9c65ea9

Xiaoming, H. (1994). Television viewing among American adults in the 1990s. *Journal of Broadcasting & Electronic Media, 38*(3), 353–360. https://doi.org/10.1080/08838159409364270

Yager, J., & Smith, M. (Producers). (2015). Love and death in Alaska. *CBS News*. https://www.cbsnews.com/news/48-hours-presents-love-and-death-in-alaska-leppink-murder/

Yakubowicz v. Paramount Pictures Corp. (404 Mass. 624, 1989). https://www.leagle.com/decision/19891028404mass6241955

Yan, H., & Simon, D. (2017). Cleveland murder suspect Steve Stephens kills himself after pursuit. *CNN*. https://www.cnn.com/2017/04/18/us/cleveland-facebook-killing-video/index.html

Yar, M. (2012). Crime, media and the will-to-representation: Reconsidering relationships in the new media age. *Crime, Media, and Culture, 8*(3), 245–260. https://doi.org/10.1177/1741659012443227

Young, A. (2009). The screen of the crime: Judging the affect of cinematic violence. *Social & Legal Studies, 18*(1), 5–22. https://doi.org/10.1177/0964663908100331

Young, A. (2014). From object to encounter: Aesthetic politics and visual criminology. *Theoretical Criminology, 18*(2), 159–175. https://doi.org/10.1177/1362480613518228

Zamora v. Columbia Broadcasting System, 480 F. Supp. 199—Dist. Court, SD Florida (1979). https://law.justia.com/cases/federal/district-courts/FSupp/480/199/1531301/

Zona, M. A., Palarea, R. E., & Lane, J. C. (1998). Psychiatric diagnosis of the offender-victim typology of stalking. In Meloy, J. R. (Ed.), *The psychology of stalking: Clinical and forensic perspectives* (pp. 69–84). San Diego, CA: Academic Press. https://doi.org/10.1016/B978-012490560-3/50023-2

Zoppo, A. (2021, September 27). 11th Circuit upholds dismissal of Pulse Night-club shooting lawsuit against Twitter, Facebook and Google. *Law.com.* https://www.law.com/dailybusinessreview/2021/09/27/11th-circuit-upholds-dismissal-of-pulse-nightclub-shooting-lawsuit-against-twitter-facebook-and-google/

Index

Abdul, Paula, 70
Abe, Gloria, 89–90
Active shooters, 19. *See also* Mass shooters
Adamcik, Torey, 232–33
Adelman, Roger, 143
Aggression: in cognitive scripts and schemas, 51; criminal, 59; mimicry of, 53; research on, 49; and violent media, 51, 59, 62–63, 78; and violent video games, 170–72
Alfonso, Jennifer, 114–15, 247
Alhadeff, Alyssa, 122
Aljubouri, Lauren, 258n4 (chapter 3)
Allen, Jed, 249
Altinger, John Brian "Johnny," 37
Altinger, Johnny, 242
American Horror Story (television series), 251
American Psycho (film), 239
American Psychological Association (APA), 171–72
Amish schoolhouse shootings, 8, 20, 75, 182, 240
Anderson, Craig, 169, 170–71, 173, 174, 258n6 (chapter 3), 260n8, 260n9

Andrews, William, 33, 221
Aniston, Jennifer, 70
Ansley, Michelle, 221
Ansley, Tonda Lynn, 108, 109, 145–46, 149, 178, 237
Antifa, 127
Antisocial personality disorder, 122
Applewhite, Marshal, 231
Arousal, 58
Artificial intelligence, 187, 211
Asperger syndrome, 118
Atkinson, Patricia, 220
Attachment failure, 107
Attard, Stephen, 13, 241
Attention deficit/hyperactivity disorder (ADHD), 84, 144
Attribution bias, hostile, 60
Auchterlonia, David, 244
Aurora Cinemark theater (Colorado) shooting, 66, 243
Autoethnography, 61, 218
Ayeroff, Jeff, 136, 259n1

Badlands (film), 258n3 (chapter 4)
Bagnato, Tony, 248
Baker, Matt, 239
Ball, Sean, 115–16, 249
Bandura, Albert, 12

316   *Index*

Bank robbery, 28, 31, 32, 34, 166, 230, 244–45, 256n8, 257n2
Bardo, Robert, 46, 70, 223
Barrett, Michael, 158–59, 222
Bartlam, Daniel, 245
Bartlam, Jacqueline, 245
"Basement Tapes" (Harris and Klebold), 56
Basic Instinct (film), 245–46
Basketball Diaries, The (film), 2, 46, 49, 56, 103, 163, 164, 231, 233
Bateman, Justine, 70
Baudet, Thierry, 131
Bayes's theorem, 189
Beavis and Butt-head (television show), 227
Beckham, Matt, 232–33
Belew, Kathleen, 127
Belic, Nico (character), 13, 109, 241
Benson, Tyler, 246
Bentley, Allan, 235
BeReal, 67. *See also* Social media
Berkowitz, David, 25–26, 26
Berrett, Bonnie, 240
Bestgore.com, 112
Bianchi, Kenneth, 222
Bickel, Travis (character), 31, 38, 92, 141, 142. *See also Taxi Driver* (film)
Biegel, Scott, 122
Billionaire Boys Club (film), 225
"Bird Box Challenge," 1–4
Bird Box (film), 1, 3
Black Dahlia case, 238
Black Lives Matter, 127
Blanchard, Clauddine, 249
Blanchard, Gypsy Rose, 249
Blanchard, Kristy, 249
Blazak, Randy, 181
Blood and Gold (film), 237
BloodRayne (video game), 105
Bobbitt, Lorena, 95, 100, 124, 258n2 (chapter 4)
"Bobo Doll" experiments, 12
"Bodies" (Drowning Pool), 105

Boogaloo movement, 130–31
"Boonk Gang," 116
Born Innocent (film), 158, 221
Boulevard Nights (film), 222
Bowers, Robert, 180
Boyd, Billy, 250
Brady, James, 8, 91–92, 209, 223
Brady Bill/Law, 92, 209
Branch, Mark, 225
Brandenburg, Clarence, 156
Brandenburg test, 156–57, 163
Brandenburg v. Ohio, 163
Brandes, Bernd Jürgen, 236
Breaking Bad (television series), 247–48
Breed, Kim, 222
Breivik, Anders, 180, 245, 253
Bride of Chucky (film), 249
Brisman, Julissa, 35, 243
Brong, Victoria, 235
Brooking, Emerson, 126
Brown, Derek, 239–40
Bryant, Martin, 230
BTK Killer, 26, 66, 77, 88
Bulger, Denise, 227
Bulger, James, 56, 227
Bullock, Sandra, 71
Bundy, Ted, 26, 88, 246
Bunkley, Derrick, 34
Burgess, Ann, 25
Burgess, Zachary, 241
Burk, Jessica, 227
Burnett, Johnny, 164
Burns, Bernadette, 251
Bush, George H. W., 135
Bushman, Brad, 107, 147, 151, 169
Byam, Edward, 34, 153, 244
Byers, Patsy, 96, 97, 165, 169, 228

Caffey, Erin, 241–42
Caffey, Matthey, 241–42
Caffey, Penny, 241–42
Caffey, Terry, 241–42
Caffey, Tyler, 241–42

Index 317

Caires, Leona, 230
Call of Duty (video game), 75, 85, 181, 245
Cambier, Alisson, 232
Camp of Saints, The (novel), 259n7
Capitol Hill Autonomous Zone/Capitol Hill Occupation Protest (CHAZ/CHOP), 124–25
Capitol Insurrection, 122, 125–31, 260n7
Capper, Suzanne, 226–27
Carbone, Diego, 248
Carlin, John, III, 152, 230
Carneal, Michael, 19, 49, 99, 163, 231
Carpenter, William, Jr., 141–42
Carrier, Gary, 239
Carter, Glenda, 220
Casey, Royce, 159, 229
Casino (film), 239
Castillo, Alvaro, 233–34
Castillo, Gina, 232
Castillo, Rafael, 233
Castle Wolfstein (video game), 164
Catcher in the Rye (novel): as inspiration for Bardo, 223; as inspiration for Chapman, 2, 8, 29, 30–31, 38, 46–47, 70, 89–91, 133, 138, 139, 140, 223, 261n5; as inspiration for Hinckley, 93, 141. *See also* Caulfield, Holden (character)
Catharsis, 58
Catharsis effect, 188
Catharsis theory, 62
Caulfield, Holden (character), 2, 8, 30–31, 38, 46, 89–91, 138, 139, 223, 261n3. *See also Catcher in the Rye* (novel)
Celebrity culture, 63, 199
Celebrity obsession, 50, 67–72, 187
Censorship, 137, 176–77, 183, 260n11
Centennial Olympic Park Bombing, 233

Chapman, Mark David: as celebrity stalker, 71; as edge-sitter, 8; and Holden Caulfield, 2, 8, 30–31, 38, 46, 89–91, 138, 139, 223, 261n5; in the realm of hyperreality, 3, 16–17, 93–94, 131, 180, 209; influence of *Catcher in the Rye* on, 29, 70, 133, 139, 140; as inspiration for other criminals, 37, 141; media influence on, 7, 23, 32; shooting Lennon, 7, 89–91; trial and conviction of, 137–138
Charapata, Brianna, 241
Charleston, South Carolina, church shooting, 36, 113–14, 180, 238, 250, 253
Cher, 70
Chicago Tylenol Murders, 224
Child Online Protection Act (COPA), 173
Child's Play 2 (film), 230
Child's Play 3 (film), 56, 226
Cho, Seung-Hui, 9, 36, 77, 119. 234, 235
Choi, Sophia, 148
Christchurch, New Zealand, Mosque shooting, 6, 17, 47, 128, 131, 177, 182, 252
Christmas, Shane, 233
Citizen journalism, 4, 5
Clark, Bill, 257n4
Clark, Mark, 137, 259n1
Clockwork Orange (film and novel), 220
Code, Raymond, 13
Cognitive dissonance, 62
Cognitive schema, 51, 193
Cognitive scripts, 18–19, 38, 51, 81, 187, 197, 210
Colbert, Dorsey, 238
Columbine High School killings: copycat influence of, 2, 20, 71, 77–78, 114, 118–19, 121, 130, 143, 211–13, 215, 233–35, 239, 260n10;

as desire for fame, 77, 106–7; lawsuits resulting from, 164–65; *NBK* linked to, 48, 56, 99–100, 163, 233; outline of crime, 233; research inspired by, 72; video games inspired by, 175; video games linked to, 56, 163, 233

Communications Decency Act, 260n11

Compton, Veronica Lynn, 222–23

Computer-generated imagery (CGI), 260–61n1

Conduct disorders, 193

Conley, Andrew, 242

Conley, Connor, 242

Contagion effect, 1, 3, 9, 41, 200. *See also* Copycat effect; Social contagion

Cooke, Joshua, 105, 146–49, 237

Cooke, Margaret Ruffin, 105, 237

Cooke, Paul C., 105, 237

Cooke, Suzanne Sylvia, 231

Cooke, Wayne, 231

Cooper, Alice, 259n2

"Cop Killer" (Ice T), 94, 135, 156

Copeland, David, 233

Copycat crime: defined and examples, 7–12; demographic influences on, 188, 203; evaluation of, 189–90; factors that exacerbate, 186; gender gap, 192–93, 202; interdisciplinary theory of, 187–89; in legal defenses, 178; measurement of, 188–90, 218, 219; nature and mechanisms of, 76–79; phenomenology of, 191, 218; research on, 49–50, 54–58, 185–95; theoretical model of, 49–54, 63, 79, 187–89, 218; typology of, 195, 218. *See also* Copycat effect; Criminal behavior; "GTA defense"; *Matrix, The* (film), "*Matrix* defense"

Copycat criminals: avoiding using names of, 200–201, 255–56n5; characteristics of, 188; seeking

fame, 94, 196, 215, 217, 220. *See also* Mass shooters

Copycat effect: and celebrity obsession, 71–72; changes across life course, 188; copycat crime continuum, 32–37, 39–40, 43, 188; and criminal behavior, 44–45, 199; factors that exacerbate, 79, 94–96, 184, 192–96; factors that influence, 78–81, 82, 83–86; long-term/short-term, 47; offender characteristics, 83–86; research on, 11–12, 50; risk factors for, 83–84; risk/resilience approach to, 203–4; technology and culture and, 3–4. *See also* Contagion effect; Copycat crime

Corbett, Sherry Lee, 108, 145–46, 237

Coronation Street (film), 245

Court cases, 137–38; civil courts, 138, 155–57, 197–98; favoring the media, 160, 161; implications for future legal decision-making, 177–78; John Hinckley, Jr./*Taxi Driver*, 140–43; Mark Chapman/*Catcher in the Rye*, 138–40; mass school shooting lawsuits, 163–77; *Matrix* Defense, 143–50; Mechele Linehan/*The Last Seduction*, 152

Court cases (by name): *Abrams et al. v. United States*, 160; *American Amusement Machine Association v. Kendrick*, 173; *Brandenburg v. Ohio*, 156, 162; *Brown v. Entertainment Merchants Association*, 172, 173–75, 178, 208, 260n9; *Byers v. Edmondson*, 166–67, 198; *Commonwealth v. Knox*, 156; *Commonwealth v. Obrien*, 165, 166; *Davidson v. Time Warner*, 155, 156, 164; *Devin Darnell Thomson v. State of Alabama*, 150–51; *Does 15 15 2014 v. King County LLC KCPQ TV Q13*

Index   319

TV LLC TV 100, 176; *Entertainment Software Association v. Blagojevich*, 260n9; *Entertainment Software Association v. Granholm*, 260n9; *Entertainment Software Association v. Hatch*, 260n9; *Entertainment Software Association v. Swanson*, 260n9; *Frye v. United States*, 151; *Grand Theft Auto*, 150–52; *Interactive Digital Software Association v. St. Louis County, Missouri*, 173; *James v. Meow Media, Inc.*, 155, 164; *Jane Does 1 through 15, Appellant v. King County*, 155; *McCollum et al. v. CBS, Inc., et al.*, 155, 157–58, 164; *Miller v. California*, 168; *Olivia N. v. National Broadcasting Company*, 155, 158; *Pahler v. Slayer*, 159–60; *People v. Mieseges* 144; *Rice v. Paladin Enterprises, Inc.*, 155, 161–63, 167, 198; *Roth v. United States*, 167, 173; *State v. Johnson*, 168; *State v. Majors*, 154–55; *State v. Taylor*, 165, 166; *Strickland v. Sony Corporation of America, et al.*, 172–73; *U.S. v. Monsalvatge/The Town*, 153–54; *Video Software Dealers Association v. Schwarzenegger*, 260n9; *Walker v. Peters*, 166; *Watters v. TSR, Inc.*, 164; *Yakubowicz v. Paramount Pictures Corp.*, 155, 158–59; *Zamora v. Columbia Broadcasting System*, 158, 164

COVID-19 pandemic, 122–24, 125

Covington, Howard, 259n7

Cox, Jeffrey Lyne, 224

Craigslist, 243

"Craigslist Killer," 34–35

Creepypasta, 3

Crime: aesthetics of, 63; aesthetization of, 65; as art, 65–67; media-mediated, 2–3, 7, 43, 49–54, 196, 243; mimetic, 194; performance, 6, 7, 50, 56–57, 110–12, 114–15, 250,

251; phenomenology of, 50, 73–76, 261n5; self-representation of, 67; standards for reporting, 200–201; telling stories of, 199–201. *See also* Copycat crime; Criminal activity; Criminal behavior

Criminal activity: modus operandi (MO), 27–28, 32–41, 57, 85, 111–12, 130, 153, 188, 194, 197, 205, 218; offender characteristics, 80–81; risk factors for, 78; signature, 28–33, 113, 197

Criminal behavior: and copycat crime, 190–91; and the copycat effect, 195–96; factors that influence, 185, 186, 188; influence of, 196; influence of digital culture on, 204–5, 213; influence of media on, 218; media-mediated, 205; protective factors for, 60–61; risk factors for, 59–61, 85–86, 183–84, 191–93, 204–5, 217

Criminal justice, 196–97, 218

Criminology: cultural, 61, 63, 187, 196, 261n6; life-course, 196; narrative, 61; theory and research, 185, 187

Crimo, Paul, 253

Crimo, Robert, III, 179–80, 181, 182, 198, 205, 206, 253

Croft, Lara (character), 95

Crucius, Patrick, 253

Crump, James, 108, 173, 238

Crusius, Patrick, 6, 180

Cruz, Brandon, 13, 241

Cruz, Jonathan, 250

Cruz, Nikolas, 9, 121–22, 235

Cultivation and fear, 59

Cultivation theory, 54

Cultural Indicators Project, 49, 59

Cultural scripts, 51

Cultural studies, 61

Cummins, Gordon, 219–20

Cunanan, Andrew, 71

Cushing, James, 225
Cyber traumatization, 218
Cybercrime, 185
Cybersocializing, 67
Cyberswarming, 125

Dando, Jill, 72, 236
Danskin, Ian, 69
Dark Knight Rises, The (film), 66, 243
Darras, Benjamin, 96–98, 103, 165,
    166–67, 168, 228
D.C. Sniper shootings, 77, 144–45,
    236–37, 238, 239
De Filippo, Nicholas, 222
De Filippo, Shirley, 222
Dead by Daylight (video game), 181
Def Jam Recordings, 259n1
Defiance (film), 69, 223
DeFiliippo, Nicky, 222
Delahanty, Thomas, 7, 91, 223
Delashmutt, Jacob, 159, 229
Deliverance (film), 222
DeMers, Ted, 252
Densley, James, 180
Depression, 75, 158, 204, 213,
    214–15
Desensitization, 58
Deskins, Angela, 247
Dexter (television series), 37–38, 242,
    243
Dexter Copycat crime, 37–38
Diallo, Amadou, 227
Diana (Princess of Wales), 72, 94, 236
Dietz, Park, 143
Digital culture: and the 2020 surge
    in violence, 122–24; and copycat
    crime, 3–4, 10, 182, 217–18; and
    criminal behavior, 21–23, 133, 186,
    197, 213, 218; cultural disparities,
    261n3; and far-right propaganda,
    127; and hyperreality, 15–17;
    and the incel movement, 52; and
    masculinity, 202; and mass media,
    18–19; and mass shootings, 117;

and memes, 57–58, 125, 127,
258n5 (chapter 3); minimizing
the harmful effects of, 199–208;
negative influence of, 21–23,
40–41; online communities,
256n9; and performance crime 7;
positive influences of, 204; as risk
factor, 54–55, 134, 188, 190, 191;
and social learning, 12–15, 49; and
unreality, 210–13, 216–17, 217; and
violence, 44–48, 191; and violent
crime, 124–25. *See also* Technology
Digital fraud, 185
Digital subcultures, 180, 181, 193,
    195, 196, 198
Dillon, Bradley, 248
Dirty Harry (film), 33
Dissociation, 213, 216, 217, 218
DLive, 128
Donald, Deonte, 238
Doom (video game), 2, 56, 103, 105,
    149, 163, 164, 231, 233
Doom II (video game), 233
Dorner, Christopher, 247
Douglas, John, 25, 33–34
Draper, Brian, 232–33
Dreyfus, Richard, 136, 259n1
Drivers Policy Protection Act
    (California), 70
Duckworth, Jerry, 238
Dudson, Anthony, 226
Dungeons & Dragons (board game),
    164
Dunkley, Derrick, 153, 244
Duque, Martin, 122
Dworet, Nicholas, 122
Dwyer, Brittney, 251
Dyer, Jeremy, 72, 236
Dykes, Andrea, 233

Earnest, John, 253
Eddy, Sheila, 246
Edge-sitters: examples of, 8, 19–20,
    37, 118, 120, 121, 210, 261n2;

Index 321

media exposure for, 2, 14, 46, 69, 78, 120, 181, 200, 217; movement to criminal activity, 21, 51, 63, 66, 69, 71, 73, 74, 99, 94, 95, 101, 181, 184, 188, 195, 198, 203, 205, 206, 211; role models for, 19, 20, 78, 261n2
Edmondson, Sarah, 96–98, 103, 165, 166–67, 168, 169, 228
Edwards, Elizabeth, 250
Edwards, Katie, 250
Edwards, Kim, 250
Edwards, Navahcia, 244–45
Edwards, Ron, 231
Eisele, Nicholas, 252
Elephant (film), 184, 239
Ellerbe, Vincent, 229
Emotional development, 193
Entertainment education theory, 79
Evans, Jake, 246–47
Evans, Jamie, 246
Evans, Mallory, 246
Evil Dead (film), 245

Facebook: and celebrity obsession, 67; influence of, 250, 251, 252; lawsuits and censorship, 165, 178, 260n11; and performance crime, 110–11, 113–17; positive influence of, 204; QAnon-related sites, 127, 131; Trump banned from, 128; use by criminals, 35–37, 110–11, 113–17, 214, 247, 252; use by victims of crimes, 111, 240. *See also* Social media
Fame seeking, 196, 215, 217, 220
Family dysfunction, 193
Fantasy: and crime, 21, 29, 38, 73, 141, 167, 215; development of, 32, 40, 50, 119, 195, 213–14, 216, 218; pathological, 83; vs. reality, 3, 8, 10, 14, 15, 16, 17, 21, 23, 38–39, 65, 77, 78, 81, 85, 87, 100, 105, 118, 178, 181, 186, 187, 194, 200,

203, 211, 215–16, 217; sexual, 66, 221; violent, 28, 58, 86, 101, 109, 118; virtual, 20
Farmer, Carol, 220
Farnsworth, Philo Taylor, 4
Fatal Attraction (film), 225
Faulty reasoning, 62
Fear (film), 241
Feis, Aaron, 122
Fentress, Albert, 222
Feral, Rex, 161
Ferguson, Christopher, 169–70, 171–72
Fetal alcohol spectrum disorder, 122
Fierro, Rachel, 148–49
Fight Club (film), 243, 248
Fiorella, Joseph, 159, 229
Firearm sales, 92, 205–6, 210
First Amendment protections: and civil liability, 155; freedom of expression, 2; freedom of speech, 2, 6, 156, 177, 198, 201; freedom of the press, 2; incitement exclusion, 156, 157, 160, 167; vs. negligence, responsibility, and harm, 134–37; for surveillance videos, 176; for video games and movies, 165, 167, 169, 172, 173; for violent media, 177, 178
Fisher King, The (film), 226
Flanagan, Vester Lee, II, 36–37, 113–114, 250
Floyd, George, 5, 122–24, 124–25
Forrester, Emma, 111–12, 240–41
Forrester, Wayne, 111–12, 240–41
Foster, Jodie, 8, 31, 70, 92–93, 141–42, 143, 209
Fowler, Thomas, 121, 234
Frank, Barney, 259n1
Franklin, Ernest, II, 251
Franklin, Heather, 251
Franklin, Jeffrey, 251
Franti, Michael, 136–37, 259n1
Friday the 13th (film), 225

Friendly, Fred W., 135
Fritz, Arnie, 230
Fugate, Caril Ann, 95, 258n3
  (chapter 4)
Fuller, Robert, 232
Fuller, Vincent, 142
Furious 7 (film), 260–61n1

Gahbiche, Abdeladim, 98, 165, 228
Garcia, Eliahna Amyah, 180
Gardner, Vicki, 113, 250
Gender gap, 192–93
Gendron, Payton, 177, 180, 181, 182,
  198, 205, 253
General Aggression Model (GAM),
  53–54, 80, 134, 170
General Learning Model (GLM),
  53–54, 170
Generalized imitation, 50, 52–54
George, Barry, 72, 236
George, Gary, 246
Gérard, Laurent, 227
Germel, Lyndon, 244–45
Geyser, Morgan, 3, 248
Gifford, Kathie Lee, 70
Gill, Daniel, 232
Glatman, Harvey, 66, 221
Gless, Sharon, 70
Glitch Inside the Matrix, A
  (documentary), 148
Godejohn, Nicholas, 249
Godwin, Robert, Sr., 114, 251
Goethe, Johann Wolfgang von, 10–11
Golden, Andrew, 19
Golden State Killer, 88
Gomez, Selena, 71
Gonzalez, Daniel, 225
Google, 165
Gough, Jaime, 239
Grand Theft Auto (GTA) (video game):
  and copycat crime, 14, 76, 80, 109–
  10, 131, 191; degree of violence
  in, 85; *Grand Theft Auto III*, 105,
  108, 172, 238; *Grand Theft Auto*
IV, 241; *Grand Theft Auto V*, 248;
  influence on Burgess, 241; influence
  on Cooke, 105, 149; influence on
  Lanza, 75; influence on Long Island
  murders, 14, 109, 241; influence
  on Moore/Thompson, 14, 108–10,
  172–73, 238; influence on Oakland
  murders, 238; influence on Samuel,
  248; lawsuits involving, 138,
  150–52, 172, 197, 259n5; *Liberty
  City Stories*, 13; popularity of, 104;
  Vice City, 13, 108, 172, 238. *See also*
  "*GTA* defense"
Green River Killer, 26, 77, 88
Gregory, Bridget (character), 152
Gregory, Sharon, 225
Grimmie, Christina, 68–69, 250
Grisham, John, 96–97, 103, 168
"*GTA* defense," 13, 108, 134, 150–52,
  178, 197, 238
Gun sales. *See* Firearm sales
Guo, Xiao Mei, 240
Guttenberg, Jaime, 122

Hadley, Nicole, 231
Haggart, Elinor, 158, 221
Halloween (film), 246
Hamilton, Evelyn, 219
Hamilton, Richard, 245
Hannibal (film), 236
Hansen, Robert, 220
Harding, Marie, 225
Harleston, David, 136–37, 259n1
Harling, Anna-Sophie, 130
Harris, Eric: "Basement Tapes," 56;
  as edge-sitter, 19, 261n2; and
  hyperreality, 3; image in video
  game, 212; as inspiration for later
  crimes, 9, 36, 77–78, 103, 118, 121,
  235, 260n10; media influences, 2,
  99–100, 103, 163, 165, 233. *See also*
  Columbine High School killings
Hart, Jason, 247–48
Hate speech, 137, 177, 205, 215

Index 323

Hayes, Brian, 235
Hayes, Clifford, 226
Haymarket Square bombing
    (Chicago), 11
Heathers (film), 246, 256n8
Heath High School (Paducah)
    shooting, 48, 99, 163, 231
Heaven's Gate mass suicide, 231
Hennard, George Pierre, 226
Herbert, Veronique, 98–99, 165,
    228
Hernandez, Michael, 239
Hicks, Marvin, 224
"Hi-Fi Murders," 33, 221, 257n3
Higginbotham, Jay, 250
Highland Park, IL, shooting, 179, 180,
    181, 198, 205, 206, 253
Hill, Jacqueline, 220
Hill, John Robert, 116, 251
Hillside Strangler, 222
Hinckley, John, Jr.: CBS news
    interview, 209; and copycat crime,
    7, 16–17, 31–32; as edge-sitter, 8,
    210; and hyperreality, 3, 131, 180,
    211; media influences, 2, 23, 37,
    38, 46, 92, 133, 136, 140–43, 223;
    shooting Reagan, 29, 91–94, 223; as
    stalker, 70, 93; trial, 92, 140–43
*Hit Man: A Technical Manual for
    Independent Contractors* (Feral),
    161–63, 227
Hitler, Adolf, 2
Hixon, Chris, 122
Hollywood denials, 62
Holmes, H. H., 66, 221
Holmes, James, 66, 67, 243
Holmes, Oliver W., 160
Homicide, 8, 27, 54, 92, 123–24, 157,
    227; double, 36; motivations for, 75.
    See also Mass shootings; Murder
Hopper, John, 143
Horan, Robert, 147
Horn, Lawrence, 161, 227
Horn, Mildred, 161–62, 227

Horn, Trevor, 161–62, 227
Hostage-taking, 45, 224, 227, 230
Houston, Whitney, 70
Howard, Philip, 249
Howard, Ronald Ray, 156, 226
Howe, Mark, 242
Hoyer, Luke, 122
Human Connectome Project, 256n7
Humphreys, Charlie, 231
Hunter (novel), 259n7
Hypermasculinity, 20, 50, 63, 194, 202
Hyperreality, 15–17, 60, 85, 91, 180,
    186, 187, 208–17; aesthetic, 93–94

I Wanna Hold Your Hand (film), 69,
    223
Identity disturbance, 7, 30, 51, 60,
    210
Imitation, 187
Incel movement, 2, 7, 20–21, 27–28,
    52, 130, 252
Insanity defense. *See* Not guilty by
    reason of insanity (NGRI)
Instagram, 67, 110, 116, 125, 251. *See
    also* Social media
Internet, 3, 45, 120, 209, 211; self-
    representation of crime on, 67; used
    to facilitate crime, 35
Intervention strategies, 207–8
Interview with a Vampire (film), 229
Irons, James, 229

Jack, Russell, 3
Jack the Ripper, 28, 66, 219, 219–21,
    239–40
Jackson, Arthur, 69–70, 223–24
Jackson, Emily, 220
Jackson, Janet, 70
Jacob, Guy, 227
James, Jessica, 231
Jaradin, Thierry, 232
Jason (character), 225
Jeremy (music video), 46, 103, 163,
    230

Index

John (Salt Lake City), 244
John Franklin Letters, The (novel), 259n7
Johnny Carson's Tonight Show (television show), 222
Johnson, Arthur Richard, 47, 223
Johnson, Bobbi, 241–42
Johnson, Mitchell, 19
Joker (film), 66
Jolley, Regan, 247
Jones, Jodi, 238
Jordan, Jean, 220
Jordon, Derrin, 249
Jordon, Janet, 249
Jouannet, Doris, 219
Juvenile justice system, 197

Kalifornia (film), 258n3 (chapter 4)
Karatayev, Vladislav, 249
Kardaras, Nicholas, 17
Kasprzak, Marcin, 245
Kaufman, Harry, 229
Kay, Virginia, 230–31
KD Rebel (novel), 259n7
Kennedy, John (Dr.), 146
Keyes, Emily, 8
Kidnapping, 244
Kill Bill Volume 2 (film), 245
Killing Eve (television series), 216
King, Rodney, 100, 124
King, Stephen, 201, 224, 231, 244. *See also Rage* (King)
Kjellberg, Felix, 255n4
Klebold, Dylan: "Basement Tapes," 56; as edge-sitter, 19, 261n2; and hyperreality, 3; image in video game, 212; as inspiration for later crimes, 9, 36, 103, 106, 118, 235; media influences on, 2, 99–100, 103, 163, 165, 233 *See also* Columbine High School killings
Klein, Cohen, 244
Knisley, Gail, 239
Knox, Mallory (character), 95–96, 101–3, 165, 167, 184, 258n4

(chapter 4). *See also Natural Born Killers* (film)
Knox, Mickey (character), 95–96, 99, 101–3, 165, 167, 184. *See also Natural Born Killers* (film)
Kojak (television series), 221

Laird, Dylan, 13, 241
Lane, Jonathan, 230
Lane, Joy, 114, 251
Lang, Jason, 233
Lanum, Christopher, 243
Lanza, Adam, 9, 75–76, 117, 234, 235, 252; as edge-sitter, 19–20, 118, 261n2
Lanza, Nancy, 117–18
Last Seduction, The, 138, 152, 230
Lavigne, Avril, 71
"Lawnmower Man, The" (King), 244
Leach, Barbara, 220
Lee, Paul, 120–21, 234
Leffler, Trisha, 34–35, 243
Legacy media, 4
Legend of Lizzie Borden (film), 225
Leigh, Jeffrey, 226
Lennon, John, 2, 7, 29–30, 38, 46, 70, 89–91, 93, 133, 137, 138–39, 141, 143, 209, 210, 223, 261n5
Leppink, Kent, 152, 230
Lester, Shawn, 238–39
Let Me Take You Down (Jones), 90
Letourneau, Mary Kay, 95, 258n2 (chapter 4)
Letterman, David, 70
Leutner, Payton "Bella," 3, 248
Lewandowska, Michelina, 245
Light, John, 233
Lin, Jun, 246
Linehan, Mechele, 138, 152, 230
LinkedIn, 67. *See also* Social media
Lobacheva, Elena, 249
Lockett, Sarah, 71–72, 236
Loibl, Kevin James, 68, 250

Index

Long Island shootings, 13–14, 109, 110, 241
Loughran, Cara, 122
Loukaitis, Barry, 45–46, 49, 99, 103, 163, 230
Loukaitis, Terry, 230
Louniakova, Olga, 241
Love, Diaz, 255n2
Loved Ones, The (film), 246
Lowe, Margaret, 219

Mabry, Joseph, 238
Macdonald, Andrew, 126–27
MacDonald, Jayne, 220
Macki, Keith, 238
Madison, Michael, 247
Madonna, 70
Magnotta, Luka Rocco, 112–13, 131
Magnum Force (film), 33, 221
Majors, Jarrod Dale, 154, 237
Malik, Thomas, 229
Malvo, Lee Boyd, 77, 107, 109, 143, 144–45, 236–237
Manavis, Sarah, 180
Manchester by the Sea (film), 251
Manfredonia, Peter, 252
Manson, Marilyn, 2, 56, 103, 212, 238
Manson murders, 100
Marjory Stoneman Douglas High School shooting, 9, 121–22, 143, 235
Markey, Patrick, 170
Markham, Lucas, 250
Markoff, Phillip Haynes, 34–35, 243
Martinez, Nathan, 99
Mass shooters: characteristics of, 47, 214–15; as edge-sitters, 19; fame-seeking rampage shooters, 213–16; as heroes, 3, 261n2; manifestos, 2, 6, 9–10, 20–21, 67, 181, 200; media influence on, 2; mothers of, 117–18, 259n6 (chapter 4); suicide by, 9, 20, 45, 75–76, 163, 213, 216, 226, 233,
239, 241, 248; using names of in news reports, 200–201, 255–56n5; and violent masculinity, 19–20. *See also* Active shooters; Edge-sitters
Mass shootings: Amish schoolhouse shootings, 8, 20, 75, 182, 240; Aurora Cinemark theater (Colorado), 66, 243; Charleston, South Carolina, church, 36, 113–14, 180, 238, 250, 253; Christchurch, New Zealand, mosque, 6, 17, 47, 128, 131, 177, 182, 252; and the copycat effect, 8, 117–22; D.C. Sniper shootings, 77, 144–45, 236–37, 238, 239; El Paso, 182; Heath High School (Paducah), 48, 99, 163, 231; Highland Park, IL, 179, 180, 181, 198, 205, 206, 253; Marjorie Stoneman Douglas high school, 9, 121, 143, 235; Oslo, Norway, 182, 245; as performance crime, 6, 7, 50, 56–57, 110–12, 114–15, 250, 251; Platte Canyon High School, 8; Pulse Nightclub, 165, 250–51; Robb Elementary School (Uvalde, TX), 179–82, 198, 205, 253; Sandy Hook Elementary School, 19–20, 117, 215, 234, 252, 261n2; at schools, 47, 49, 72–73, 94–95, 98, 99–100, 117–22, 131, 235; Seattle Pacific University (SPU), 77, 120–21, 176, 234; surveillance videos of, 198; in Thailand, 35–36, 38; threatened, 253; as ticket to celebrity and fame, 181, 211; Tops grocery store (Buffalo, NY), 176–77, 179–80, 181, 182, 198, 201, 205, 253; University of Santa Barbara, 6, 20, 119–20, 121, 248, 255n1, 261n2; University of Texas, 100; Virginia Tech, 36, 77, 114, 119, 121, 175, 234, 250. *See also* Columbine High School killings

Masters, Paul, 222
Mateen, Omar, 250–51
Matrix, The (film): and copycat crime, 80, 104–5, 131, 149–50, 182–83; influence on Ansley, 105, 108, 109, 145–46, 149, 237; influence on Cooke, 105–7, 146–49, 237; influence on Malvo, 77, 107, 109, 143, 144–45, 236–37; influence on Mieseges, 105, 107–8, 109, 143–44, 237; influence on school shootings, 143; "*Matrix* Defense," 105–6, 134, 138, 143–50, 178; Neo (character), 105, 106–7, 143, 145, 148, 184
Maupin, Audry, 98, 165, 227–28
Max Payne (video game), 149
Maymard, Thierry, 227
McArthur, Bruce, 244
McCann, Wilma, 220
McCarthy, Tim, 7, 91, 223
McCollum, John, 157–58, 161, 224
McCoy, Charles, Jr., 239
McDavid, Deanna, 224
McDonald, Geneva, 225
McKeefrey, Mark, 235
Mckendrick, Thomas, 238
McNeilly, Bernadette, 226
McVeigh, Timothy, 2, 77, 126–27, 229
Meadows, Oakey, Jr., 239
Mealer, Leslie "Ace," 108, 173, 238
"Mean world syndrome," 81, 87
Media: and copycat crime, 7; criminogenic, 193; effects of, 49, 58–63, 187; electronic, 22; influence of, 218; legacy, 4–5, 46, 56, 57–58, 69, 128, 208, 210, 211; legal role of, 133; microgenerations of, 5; new media forms, 4–5, 15, 44, 56, 57, 67, 178, 208–9; propaganda in, 127; as risk factor for criminal behavior, 61. *See also* Media effects; Media violence; Social media

Media literacy, 207–8
Media looping/loops, 81, 100–101, 180, 211
Media studies, 61, 187
Media violence: and the catharsis effect, 188; creators and distributors of, 137, 196; images of, 202; imitation of 52–54; influence of digital culture on, 69, 190; influence on criminal behavior and violence, 78, 80, 83–84, 170–71, 183, 186, 191–92, 207, 211, 218; and masculinity, 192–95, 202; minimizing the harmful effects of, 199–208; negative effects of, 12, 23, 47–48, 58–63, 203–4; reducing risk of, 202–8; public access to, 176–78; scripts and schemas, 50–51; as shaper/rudder, 54–56, 78, 103, 130, 185, 186, 188, 190; as trigger, 32, 39, 54–56, 78, 80, 103, 130–31, 185, 186, 188, 190. *See also* Violence
Medina, Derek, 114–15, 247
Meis, Jon, 121
Meiwes, Armin, 236
Melton, Heather, 182
Memes, 57–58, 125, 258n5 (chapter 3)
Menendez, Erik, 100, 124, 225
Menendez, Jose, 225
Menendez, Kitty, 225
Menendez, Lyle, 100, 124, 225
Mental illness, 16, 20, 72, 75, 109–10, 147, 149, 151, 171, 193, 202, 209–10. *See also* Personality disorders; Psychopathy
Menzies, Allan, 237–38
Meoli, Anthony, 145
Mercury, Freddie, 72, 236
Messner, Austin, 227
Metal Gear Solid (video game), 149
Metaverse, 187
Michael Stormer Story, The (film), 135

Index

Mickey Mouse Club (television show), 221
Mieseges, Vadim, 105, 107–8, 109, 143–44, 237
Milat, Ivan, 244
Milat, Matthew, 244
Miles, Steven, 242–43
Militias, 125
Milivojevic, Sanja, 185
Millward, Vera, 220
Minassian, Alek, 2, 27–28, 180, 252
Mindhunter (Netflix series), 25–26, 256–57n1
Mireles, Eva, 253
Mitchell, Luke, 238
Modus operandi (MO), 27–28, 32–41, 57, 85, 111–12, 130, 153, 188, 194, 197, 205, 218
Mognotta, Luka, 245–46
Molloy, Kevin, 225
Monalto, Gina, 122
Money Train (film), 229
Monkey Wrench Gang, The (novel), 259n7
Monroe, Marilyn, 11
Monsalvatge, Akeem, 34, 153, 244
Montowski, Patsy Ann Marie, 243
Moore, Nik, 233
Moore/Thompson, Devin, 12–13, 14, 108, 109–10, 150–51, 172–73, 256n6, 238
Morgan, Dexter (character), 37–38
Morrison, Duane, 8, 240
Mortal Kombat (video game), 163, 231
Moss, Michael, 235
Most, Johann, 11
Most Dangerous Game, The (film and short story), 220
Muhammad, John Allen, 77, 107, 144–45, 236–37
Murder: aesthetics of, 50, 187; Facebook-related, 111; and suicide, 216; and torture, 217, 221, 222,

226–27. *See also* Homicide; Mass shootings
Murder duos, 49
Murder in the Heartland (film), 258n3 (chapter 4)
Murray, John, 151
Murrey, Ashley, 232
My Sister Sam (television series), 46, 70
"My Twisted Life" manifesto (Rodger), 20–21, 67, 119, 120, 248, 255n1

Naisbitt, Carol, 221
Naisbitt, Cortney, 221, 257n3
Narcissism, 66, 118, 130, 214–15, 221, 257n4
Narcissistic personality disorder, 141, 143
National Association of School Psychologists, 11
National Center for the Analysis of Violent Crime, 72
Natsissov, Artur, 249
Natural Born Killers (*NBK*) (film): appeal of, 100–104; and copycat crime, 80, 94–100; influence on Columbine killers, 2, 56; influence on Darras and Edmondson, 96–98, 228; influence on Loukaitis, 46, 48, 163, 230; influence on other criminals, 227–29, 256n8, 258n4 (chapter 3); lawsuits, 134, 138, 165–69; story, 95–96; violent images in, 124, 184. *See also* Knox, Mallory; Knox, Mickey
Neary, Graham, 235
Neely, Terry, 216
Neese, Skylar, 246
Netflix, 1, 11, 25, 113, 201, 256n1, 258n5 (chapter 4)
Neo (character), 105, 106–7, 143, 145, 148, 184. *See also* Matrix, *The* (film)
Newman, Eric Clinton Kirk, 112–13, 245–46

Index

Newton-John, Olivia, 70
Nickell, Bruce, 224
Nickell, Stella, 224
Niemi, Olivia, 221
Nightmare on Elm Street (film), 225, 245
Noor (Salt Lake City), 244
Northweast/1999 Seattle World Trade Organization (WTO), 125
Not guilty by reason of insanity (NGRI), 92, 105, 134, 143, 149–50, 178, 197, 259n4
Nwabguma, Kashiya, 260n7

Oath Keepers, 130
Oatley, Evelyn, 219
Obscenity, 167, 168
Ogletree, Charles, 135–37
Oklahoma City bombing, 77, 126–27, 215, 229, 252, 262n2
Oliver, Joaquin, 122
Olsen, Mary, 220
On Deadly Ground (film), 237
Orange High School, 233
Orndorff, Goering, 236
Orndorff, Janice, 236
Ornsteiner, J. Buzz Von, 145
Ortega, Ruben, 224
Osbourne, Ozzie, 157–58, 164, 224
Oswald, Lee Harvey, 253

Padilla, Mario, 232
Pagourtzis, Dimitrios, 235
Pahler, Elyse, 159, 229
Paindavoine, Sebastian, 98–99, 165, 228
Palacios, Josh, 231
Paladin Enterprises, 161–63
Paparazzi, 67–68
Paramount Pictures, 158–59
Parker, Alison, 36, 113, 250
Parler, 127. *See also* Social media
Parsons, David, 248

Patton, Jeanne, 239
Pavlov, Maxim, 249
Paxton, Ken, 177
Pay-O-Matic robbery, 34, 244
Pearson, Yvonne, 220
Peckham, Hollie, 154, 237
Peckham, Jamie, 154, 237
Pennington, Scott, 224
Performance artists, 198
Performance crime, 6, 7, 50, 56–57, 110–12, 114–15, 250, 251
Perry, James, 161–62, 227
Personality disorders, 59–60, 193, 210. *See also* Mental illness
Personality theory, 49
Personality traits, psychopathic, 193–94
Peterson, Jillian, 180
Petric, Dan, 17
Petty, Alaina, 122
PewDiePie, 6, 252, 255n4
Phenomenology, 73–76, 191, 218, 261n5
Philip, Samuel, 13, 241
Phillips, David, 11
Phillips, Jessica, 66
Phillips, Sandy, 66
Pierce, Dustin, 224
Pierce, William Luther, 126–27, 259n7
Pierre, Dale, 33, 221
Pitt, Brad, 70
Platte Canyon High School, 8
Poisoning, 224, 241, 256n8
Pokemon Go (video game), 204
Pollack, Meadow, 122
Portland Youth Liberation Front (YLF), 125
Posttraumatic stress disorder (PTSD), 13, 108, 150, 151, 152
Powell, Glyn, 226
Powell, Jean, 226
Primal Fear (film), 236
Priming, 58, 59
Project X (film), 247

Index 329

Prosocial behavior and messages, 199–201, 207, 211
Prothrow-Stith, Dr., 136
Psychological reactance, 62
Psychopathology, 78, 193–94
Psychopathy, 66, 221, 257n5. *See also* Mental illness
Public safety, 195–99, 198, 218
Pulse Night Club shooting, 165, 250–51
Purge, The (television series), 250

QAnon, 127, 131
Quake (video game), 149, 164, 231
Queen of the Damned (film), 237–38
Queens robberies, 34

Racial justice, 5
Rader, Dennis, 26, 66, 67, 77, 221
Rage (King), 45–46, 49, 103, 163, 201, 224, 230, 231, 258n2 (chapter 3), 258n3 (chapter 3)
Rage, Rights, Responsibilities (documentary), 135–37
Raging Bull (film), 69
Rakolta, Terry, 259n1
Ralls, Demarcus, 238
Ralls, Joe, 238
Rambo (film), 247
Ramirez, Richard, 100
Ramirez, Samuel, 232
Ramos, Salvador, 179, 180, 182, 205, 253
Ramsay, Helena, 122
Ramsey, Evan, 231
RapeLay (Internet game), 85
Reagan, Ronald, 2, 7, 29, 31, 38, 88, 91, 93, 134, 141, 209, 223
Red Dawn (film), 229
Red Lake Senior High, 239
Reddit, 124, 125
Redneck Revolt, 124
Reichel, Luciana, 241
Reservoir Dogs (film), 184, 235
Resiliency, 202–8

Ressler, Robert, 25
"Retribution" video (Rodger), 20–21, 67, 119, 120, 248
Revolutionary War Science (Most), 11
Rey, Florence, 98, 165, 227–28
Richardson, Debra, 228
Richardson, Irene, 220
Richardson, Jacob, 228
Richardson, Jasmine, 99, 228
Richardson, Mark/Marc, 228
Ridgeway, Gary, 26, 77
Risk assessment, 195–99, 198
Rittgers, Dustin, 116–17, 250
Robb Elementary School (Uvalde, TX) shooting, 179–82, 198, 205, 253
Roberts, Charles Carl, IV, 8, 240
Robinson, Dar, 222
Robinson, Derek, 225
Robinson, Jean, 225
RoboCop 2 (film), 226
Rodger, Elliot: as edge-sitter, 20–21, 120, 261n2; and the incel movement, 2, 6–7, 27, 52, 130, 252; influences on, 252; as influence on others, 2, 6–7, 9, 27, 52, 71, 121, 130, 180, 235; "My Twisted Life" manifesto, 20–21, 67, 119, 120, 248, 255n1; as performance criminal, 131; "Retribution" video, 20–21, 67, 119–20, 248
Rohingya, 260n11
Roof, Dylann, 36, 114, 180, 250, 253
Rosander, Patricia, 230–31
Rotering, Nancy, 206
Rudolph, Eric, 233
Ruiz, Jose, 250
Rytka, Helen, 220

Sadism, 66, 221
Sadist, The (film), 258n3 (chapter 4)
Safecrackers, 257n2
Salazar, Yancy, 231

Index

Saldana, Theresa, 47, 69–70, 223
Samuel, Eldon, III, 248
Samuel, Eldon, Jr., 248
Samuel, Jonathan, 248
Sandy Hook Elementary School
  shootings, 19–20, 117, 215, 234,
  252, 261n2
Santa Fe High School, 235
Saunders, Janice, 161–62, 227
Savage, William "Bill," 96, 97, 98, 103,
  165, 168, 228
Saw (film), 244, 245
Saxon Theatre Corporation, 158–59
Schachter, Alex, 122
Schaeffer, Rebecca, 46, 70, 223
Schentrup, Carmen, 122
Schizophrenia, 90, 141, 142, 147
"School Shooter, The: A Threat
  Assessment Perspective," 72–73
School Shooter (video game), 75, 118,
  234
Scott, Zach, 117
Scream (film), 231, 232
Seattle Pacific University (SPU)
  shooting, 77, 120–21, 176, 234
Seda, Heriberto, 225–26
Sellers, Debbie, 220
Sellers, Joyce, 220
Sensory processing disorder, 118
Serial killers, 26, 28, 66, 77, 94–95,
  221, 239, 246, 248
Set It Off (film), 28, 31, 32, 230, 256n8
Settle, Dean, 247–48
Sexual abuse, 96
Sexual fantasy, 66
Shakur, Tupac, 156, 226
Shannon, Craig, 221–22
Shaw, Kyle, 243
Sheeley, Shetisha, 247
Sherwin, Robert, 145–46
Shoaf, Rachel, 246
Shostak, David, 109, 147
Silence of the Lambs (film), 239
Silver, Joel, 183

Simpson, Angela, 216
Simpson, O. J., 100, 124
Singh, Gurnoor, 13, 241
Singh, Jaspreet, 13, 241
Slayer (band), 159, 229
"Slender Man" (character), 3, 248,
  256n8
Smartphones, 4, 45, 209
Smith, Robert Benjamin, 220
Smith, Todd Cameron, 233
Snapchat, 110. *See also* Social media
Snow, Susan, 224
Social contagion, 49, 187
Social development, 204
Social diffusion, 187
Social identity: antisocial, 60; criminal,
  44, 60; formation of, 16, 91
Social learning: and copycat crime,
  49, 81, 187, 195, 196; in digital
  space, 7, 12, 43, 48, 49, 55, 109;
  mechanisms of, 14; and violent
  media, 54–55, 58
Social learning theory (SLT), 12–15,
  52–53, 76, 195, 196
Social media: and the Capitol
  Insurrection, 125–31; and celebrity
  obsession, 67; censorship of,
  176–77, 260n11; cultural saturation
  of, 85; and the digital realm of the
  unreal, 211; DUI on, 116–17; and
  empathy, 203–4; extensive use of,
  214; influence of, 122–24, 181, 249,
  250, 252, 253; legal challenges to,
  178; and mass shootings, 9–10, 12;
  mitigation of copycat effect by, 201;
  opportunity for fame created by 5,
  15, 36, 181, 211; and performance
  crime, 56; prosocial uses of, 85; self-
  representation of crime on, 5–6, 15,
  67; as site for social learning, 7; use
  by criminals, 6, 36, 198, 205; used
  as legal evidence, 133; used by ISIS,
  165; and violent extremism, 128. *See
  also* Facebook; YouTube

Index 331

Social scripts, 51–52
Socialist Rifle Association, 124
Sodders, William, 99
Soloman, Paul, 225
Sommers, Suzanne, 70
"Son of Sam," 25–26
Sorrows of Young Werther, The (Goethe),
  10–11
"Soulja's Story" (Tupac Shakur), 226
Sowell, Anthony, 247
Speck, Richard, 220
Spielberg, Steven, 70
Spikes, Ryan, 247
Spronsen, Willem Van, 125
Stair, Randy, 213–16, 234, 261n7
Stalkerazzi, 67–68
Stalking: of celebrities, 68, 69–71,
  83, 92, 236; laws against, 70;
  psychology of, 50
Starkweather, Charles, 95, 258n3
  (chapter 4)
Stebbins, Danny, 75
Steger, Kayce, 231
Steinke, Jeremy Allen, 99, 228
Stellwagen, Lisa, 229
Stephens, Mark, 247
Sterling, Daniel, 229
Sterling, Terry, 235
Stevens, Steve, 114, 251
Stith, Prothrow, 259n1
Stoddart, Cassie, 232–33
Stone, Mitchell, 243
Stone, Oliver, 48, 95, 100, 102–3,
  230; *NBK* case against, 97, 134,
  138, 165–69, 178
Strickland, Arnold, 108, 173, 238
Strong, Ben, 231
Strossen, Nadine, 259n1
Styles, Harry, 71
Subcultural theories, 196
Suicidal ideation, 198
Suicidal tendencies, 214–15
Suicide: clusters, 45; copycat, 11,
  231; deflected, 107, 147; firearm,

14; glamorization of, 201; graphic
depictions of, 11, 201, 205, 261n7;
mass, 231; media depictions
of, 261n7; media-mediated, 1,
157–58, 164, 222, 224; and
murder, 75, 216, 241, 249; and
Osborne's "Suicide Solution,"
157–58, 164, 224; by shooters,
9, 20, 75–76, 163, 213, 216, 226,
233, 239, 241, 248
Suicide clusters, 45
Suicide copycats, 11
Sullivan, Tiffany, 230–31
Super Columbine Massacre RPG (video
  game), 191, 212, 234
Superpredators, 94
Surette, Ray, 49, 54–58, 77, 79, 154,
  155, 185, 195, 218
Surette's Scale, 189–90, 219, 262n1
Surveillance videos, 176–77, 185, 198
Sutcliffe, Peter William, 220, 248
Sutton, Jhomari, 238

Tangled (film), 249
Tarde, Gabriel, 11
Tarrant, Brenton Harrison, 6, 17, 180,
  252
Tavulares, Eric, 258n4 (chapter 3)
Taxi Driver (film), 2, 8, 29, 31, 38,
  92, 93, 133, 136, 137, 140–43,
  210, 223. *See also* Bickel, Travis
  (character)
Taylor, Amanda, 115–16, 249
Taylor, Charlie, 115, 249
Taylor, Rex, 115
Technology: addiction to, 16;
  and copycat crime, 3–4, 10,
  12, 71, 131–32, 217–18; and
  criminal behavior, 186, 218; and
  hyperreality, 15–17; and media,
  4–7, 67, 217; related risk factors,
  21–23; as risk factor for criminal
  behavior, 44; and social learning,
  76. *See also* Digital culture

332 Index

Television, 4
Terrorism, 56–57, 156; stochastic, 129–30
Terry, Shirdella, 247
Tetreault, Gilles, 38
The Town (film), 34, 153–54, 244
TheDonald (message board), 127
Thelma and Louise (film), 95, 256n8
"Third-Person Effect," 61
13 Reasons Why (Netflix drama), 11, 201
Thomas, Clarence, 174–75, 178
Thomas, Elizabeth, 242
Thomas, Marica, 230–31
Thomma, Jakrapanth, 35–36, 38, 252
Thompson, Jack, 13, 163–64, 197, 259n5
Thompson, Robert, 56, 227
Threat assessment, 206, 216, 218
Thurman, Uma, 71
Tik Tok, 67, 110, 198, 204, 216–17. *See also* Social media
Tinker, Grant, 259n1
Tinling, Matthew, 245
Tops grocery store (Buffalo, NY) shooting, 176–77, 179–80, 181, 182, 198, 201, 205, 253
Torture, 217, 221, 222, 226–27, 244
True Romance (film), 258n4 (chapter 3), 258n3 (chapter 4)
Trump, Donald, 126, 127, 128, 130, 170, 260n7
Turkle, Sherry, 17
Turner Diaries, The (novel/film), 126–27, 128, 229, 233, 259n7
Twilight (film), 250
Twitch, 110, 128, 177, 178, 181, 253. *See also* Social media
Twitchell, Mark Andrew, 37–38, 242, 257n4
Twitter, 113, 124, 126, 165, 178, 214, 260n11. *See also* Social media
Tylenol Murders, 224

University of Santa Barbara shooting, 6, 20, 119–20, 121, 248, 255n1, 261n2
Unreality, 210–13, 216–17

Vampire Chronicles, The (film), 237
Vargas, Jocelyn, 222
Varnell, Jerry, 252
Vela, Manual, Jr., 230
Venables, Jon, 56, 227
Versace, Gianni, 70
Victims for Victims, 69
Video games: addiction to, 197; and the digital realm of the unreal, 211; encouraging positive interaction, 204; First Amendment protections, 208; violent, 23, 50, 85, 104, 105, 108–10, 145, 149, 151–52, 173, 174–75, 197, 259n5, 260n9. *See also Doom* (video game); *Grand Theft Auto (GTA)* (video game)
Violence: aesthetics of, 63, 66–67; aesthetization of, 17, 65; affective response to, 184; cinematic, 199–200; and digital culture, 44–48; etiology of, 59–60; female empowerment through, 95–96, 101; in films, 50; gendered nature of, 202; genocidal, 260n11; glorification of, 77, 78, 81, hyperaestheticized, 17; hypermasculine, 202; incel-related, 52; instrumental, 135; involving police and protestors, 124–25; legitimation of, 81; livestreamed, 6, 110–11, 126–29, 176–77, 178, 181, 201, 205, 252, 255n2; masculinization of, 102, 202; media-mediated, 80, 102–3, 193, 218; mimetic, 67, 100; normalization of, 21; relationship to media and crime, 203; research on, 49; right-wing extremist, 181–82; risk factors for, 59–60, 64, 72–73;

Index 333

stories about, 209; television, 14, 59, 158; 2020 surge in, 122–24; video game, 23, 50, 85, 104, 105, 108–10, 145, 149, 151–52, 173, 174–75, 197, 259n5, 260n9; virtual, 13; against women, 73. *See also* Media violence

Violence contagion, 50

Violent masculinity, 19–20, 47, 72–73, 81

Violent media. *See* Media violence

Virginia Tech shootings, 36, 77, 114, 119, 121, 175, 234, 250

Virtual reality, 212–13

Voitov, Pavel, 249

Volland, Philip, 152

W. R. Myers High School, 233

Waid, Charles, 241–42

Walker, Caleb, 260–61n1

Walker, Cody, 260–61n1

Walker, Orren, 221

Walker, Paul, 260–61n1

Walker, Stanley, 221

Walls, Marguerite, 220

Wang, Peter, 122

Ward, Adam, 36, 113, 250

Wardle, Katrina, 242

Ware, Douglas, 238

Warmus, Carolyn, 225

Warner Brothers, 165–69

Warriors, The (film), 158–59, 222

Wedding Crashers (film), 241

Weier, Anissa, 248

Weinmann, Rosalyn, 259n1

Weir, Anissa, 3

Weis Market Grocery Store, 213

Weise, Jeffrey, 239

"Werther Effect," 11

Whaley, Jared, 239

Whitaker, Josephine, 220

White, Nathaniel, 226

White, Vanna, 70

White supremacists, 6, 126, 181, 253

Whitfield, Ruth, 180

Whitman, Charles, 100, 220

Whitwell, Robert, 251

Wild at Heart (film), 258n3 (chapter 4)

Wiley, Leon, 238

Wilkinson, Charlie, 241–42

Williams, Bryce, 113–14

Williams, Sarah, 121, 234

Wilson, Noah, 231

Wolf, Richard, 259n1

Wong, Ella, 143–44, 237

Wood, Amber, 230–31

World of Warcraft (video game), 248–49

X-Men (film), 249

Yakubowicz, Martin, 158–59, 222

Ybarra, Aaron, 77, 120, 121, 176, 234, 260n10

Yorkey, Brian, 201

Yorkshire Ripper, 220, 240, 248

YouTube, 68–69, 110, 112, 122, 128, 181, 214, 250, 252, 260n11; Elliot Rodgers's videos, 20–21, 67, 119–20, 248. *See also* Social media

Zamora, Ronny, 158, 161, 221

Zodiac Killer, 225

Zuckerberg, Mark, 111

About the Author

Jacqueline B. Helfgott, PhD, is Professor and Director of the Crime and Justice Research Center in the Seattle University Department of Criminal Justice, Criminology, and Forensics. She is the author of *No Remorse: Psychopathy and Criminal Justice* and *Criminal Behavior: Theories, Typologies, and Criminal Justice,* editor of *Criminal Psychology,* four volumes; and coauthor of *Women Leading Justice: Experiences and Insights* and *Offender Reentry: Beyond Crime and Punishment.*